Photo by H. C. Mann

"And at sunset, after a day of hard but honest toil, the Confederate soldier, home from Appomattox, looked up again to the friendly stars and prayed that here he might live to labor and to love, to claim his promised bride, to rear his little children and at the close of his day to leave Virginia for his Home Eternal." —Page 115.

Unleashed at Long Last

Reconstruction in Virginia

APRIL 9, 1865—JANUARY 26, 1870

BY

W. H. T. Squires

W. H. T. SQUIRES, M.A., D.D., LITT.D.

Author of

THE LAND OF DECISION, *the Splendor of Virginia's Story*
THROUGH CENTURIES THREE, *a Short History of the People of
Virginia*
THE DAYS OF YESTER-YEAR, *in Colony and Commonwealth*
WHO AM I, *a Genealogical Record Book*
PEREGRINE PAPERS, *a Tale of Travel in the Orient*
ACADIE DAYS, *Sketches of New Scotland*
THROUGH THE YEARS IN NORFOLK, *&c.*

THIS BOOK IS NUMBER

429

OF THE FIRST EDITION

FULLY ILLUSTRATED

PRINTCRAFT PRESS, INC.
PORTSMOUTH, VA.
MCMXXXIX

D. O. M.

Deo Optimo Maximo

EMILY ELIZABETH TAPPEY-SQUIRES
September 21, 1844—May 21, 1926

AND

EMILY ELIZABETH SQUIRES-HANNING
March 9, 1910—December 26, 1936

D. O. M.

Dominus Omnium Magister

Table of Contents

Illustrations

Foreword

In time the sword will always be beaten.
                                                     —*Napoleon*.

Two generations have passed, and a third is growing into strong and stalwart manhood, the kind of men Virginians ought to be, since the events here related took place upon the war-blistered soil of this Commonwealth.

Those who love the land would fain forget the strife and the storms which swept a defenseless State and scourged a proud and potent people; but that cannot be. Too permanent and too insistent are the political and economic reactions which still affect both State and Nation—reactions only explained by the political persecution endured through those trying years.

Every adversity has a compensation. The blacker the night, the brighter the stars. And the stars are emblems of hope lit by the Hand of God, harbingers of a better day. He who stands amidst the wreck and ruin of all he holds dear and lifts his eyes to the stars, self-contained and self-controlled—he who bends his back to the burden and who lays again the foundations destroyed—he is no less a hero than one who braves the blasts of shot and shell upon the bloody battle-field. And such were the heroes who laid again substantial foundations amidst dust and

ashes in the stricken South.   Milton's familiar line,
"Peace hath her victories no less renowned than war"
is trite, but true.   And nowhere on earth more clearly
shown than in Virginia through the Reconstruction
era.   Moral heroism is less frequent, and less ac-
claimed, than physical courage.

The Virginians have no reason to blush for the
record made in those bitter, blasted years (1865-'70);
years infinitely more trying than the dreadful quadrennium that preceded.   The blue banner of Virginia
was proscribed, a rag, not a flag, and the proud Commonwealth became a "military district"; but when
the blue banner was Unleashed At Long Last to the
breeze, no blot, no disgrace and no dishonor stained
its folds.

It is our conviction and our contention that Virginia lost—to win.   From the exhaustion of utter
failure, the Virginians plucked the crown of brilliant
success, and have acquired abiding power and prosperity.   *Virginia in vinculis* became by sheer moral
courage *Virginia invicta.*

Unleashed at Long Last

BOOK ONE

APRIL 9, 1865—DECEMBER 4, 1865

CHAPTER I

GENERAL LEE'S FAREWELL

**Always before the eyes of their souls moved that
beautiful, heroic, silent figure, riding away into some
realm of glory—the figure of the patriot Lee.**
—W. Gordon McCabe.

The green shadows of an April day fell like a pall of
sorrow over the fields and forests of Virginia. Wearied
and disconsolate Confederates, officers and men, wrapped their frayed blankets about them and, lulled by the
gentle whisper of the wind in the pines, they slept[1]
. . . soldiers for the last time! Too tired to think,
too hopeless to plan, they dreamed, upon their beds
of moss and leaves, of their wives, their homes, their
little ones, their parents, their promised brides, and
—peace. Nowhere in the wide world does twilight
fall so softly green, and night descend "so velvet-
footed through the air,"[2] as on the gently swelling
hills and pleasant valleys of piedmont Virginia.

Thank God, the war was over at last, and they
were still alive! Thousands of their comrades rotted
in nameless graves. Theirs was the bitterness of defeat, but with no taint of cowardice or dishonor.

[1]"We made soft berths of forest leaves and spread our tattered blankets
over them, and so spent the night of April 9, undisturbed in our pleasant
dreams."—*The diary of a Confederate Soldier.*
[2]NANCY BYRD TURNER, a poem, "Return."

Palm Sunday, April 9, 1865, Virginia's day of doom, closed a week plethoric of disaster.[3]   At three in the morning the half-starved and wholly ragged remnants of the once powerful Army of Northern Virginia moved under Fitzhugh Lee and John Brown Gordon to their last battle.   So fiercely fell they upon the well-drilled, well-fed, well-equipped Federal cavalry under Philip Henry Sheridan, that he re-treated a mile and a half before the assault.   But as the sun lifted over the forested hills of Appomattox and flooded the land with light, Sheridan drew his horsemen aside, as a man draws a curtain, and the victorious Confederates halted!   The Army of the James, 40,000 strong, under Edward Otho Cresap Ord, stood ready at a word to turn loose a hurricane of lead and hurl the last man of them into eternity.[4]

From six in the morning until two in the afternoon both armies stood at attention, like silent statues, waiting . . . waiting . . . waiting the decision of their chiefs.   At eleven o'clock Generals Lee and Grant and their aides entered the residence of Wilbur McLean.   Their arrival was described in detail by an eye witness.[5]   Lee was "superbly mounted."   His noble countenance, commanding form and dignified

---

[3] *The Land of Decision*, Squires, pp. 17-40, gives an accurate and detailed description of Lee's retreat and surrender.

[4] *Appleton's Cyclop. Amer. Biog.*, Vol. IV: General Sherman said he under-stood that Ord's skilful and difficult march the night of April 8 was one of the chief reasons for Lee's surrender.

HELEN D. LONGSTREET, "Lee and Longstreet at High Tide," p. 212.

[5] JOSHUA LAWRENCE CHAMBERLAIN, *The Passing of the Armies*, p. 247.

Land of Decision, SQUIRES, Chap. II.

ALEXANDER HAMILTON STEPHENS, *War Between the States*, pp. 803-6, gives the correspondence between Lee and Grant in full.

bearing, did not disguise an expression of "deep sadness," despite his splendid self-control. General Grant arrived with his aide, Colonel Newhall. He wore the uniform of an ordinary soldier, unbuttoned at the throat, a slouch hat without a cord, high boots, generously splashed with the sticky, red mud of Appomattox County. The General's trousers were tucked within his boots, and he wore no sword. But he sat in his saddle with ease, a born commander and master of men. Four stars upon his collar indicated his rank. He, too, was in profound thought, for he took little or no notice of those about him. His brow, deeply furrowed, was stern but calm.

There were, of course, a number of other officers present. When at last they came casually from the McLean residence, Lee had surrendered.[6]

The text of General Lee's parole[7] interests posterity:

"We, the undersigned, prisoners of war, belonging to the Army of Northern Virginia, having been this day surrendered by General Robert E. Lee, commanding said army, to Lieut.-General Grant, commanding the armies of the United States, do hereby give our solemn parole of honor that we will not hereafter serve the armies of the Confederate States, or in any military capacity whatever against the United States of America, or render aid to the

---

[6]PHILIP H. SHERIDAN, *Last Days of the Rebellion*, Amer. Review, July, 1883, p. 17: "Those who entered with Gen. Grant, as nearly as I can recollect, were Ord, Rawlings, Seth Williams, Ingalls, Babcock, Parker and myself."

[7]ALEX H. STEPHENS, *War Between the States*, p. 627: "On the ninth of April at Appomattox the sword of Lee was surrendered."

The sword of Lee was *not* surrendered.

enemies of the latter until properly exchanged in such manner as shall be mutually approved by the relative authorities.

(Signed)   "R. E. LEE, General.

"W. H. TAYLOR, Lieut.-Col. and Adj.-General.

"CHARLES S. VENABLE, Lieut.-Col. and Acting Adj.-General.

"H. E. PEYTON, Lieut.-Col. and Inspector-General.

"GILES BROOKE, Major and A. A. Surgeon-General.

"H. S. YOUNG, Acting Adj.-General.

"Done at Appomattox
C. H. Va. the Ninth
(9th) day of April
1865."

"Countersigned:

"The above named officers will not be disturbed by the U. S. authorities as long as they observe their parole and the laws in force where they may reside.

(Signed)   "GEO. H. SHARPE, Gen'l and Asst. Provost Marshal."[8]

When General Lee passed the Federal sentinels they involuntarily saluted, as in the presence of a conqueror, not a captive.   When the Confederate soldiers recognized their beloved chief on "Traveler," they could not be restrained.   No victor returning

---

[8]FITZHUGH LEE, *Life of Lee*, p. 399.

CHARLES FRANCIS ADAMS, *Military Studies*, p. 326.   In his judgment no other incident reflects more credit on our leaders.

HARVEST TIME IN PATRICK COUNTY

"As the long summer days grew shorter, and the autumn winds took keener edge the harvests ripened in the countryside and it was evident, once again, that Nature is a generous Mother."—Page 79.

"Over and over again General Lee advised his friends to go home and go to work; not to desert Virginia, but to rebuild the foundations deep and strong."—Page 10.

The River Roanoke near Salem, Virginia. This river takes its name from Roanoke Island, the site of the Lost Colony, 1585. In its middle course it takes the name Staunton, but in the Valley of Virginia it recaptures its original name, Roanoke, and gave its name to Roanoke County (1838), which in turn gave its name to Roanoke City (1884).

Roanoke, one of America's youngest cities, has one of the country's most ancient names.

triumphantly from field of conquest ever received such homage, such a tribute of affection. The devotion of the fathers is the heritage of the sons. The passing years have not tarnished the lustre of his name. His fame has grown, even amongst those once his foes; and his genius is now the pride of all America.

General Sheridan promptly distributed rations, and for the first time in long weeks the hunger of the Confederate soldiers was appeased.

Their erstwhile foes sauntered into the Confederate lines and were cordially received. Around a thousand camp fires tobacco, spirits, coffee and food were passed. In the green twilight of declining day they fought their battles over again. Why should they not be friends? The war was none of theirs. It is notorious that those who make wars do not fight them.[9]

The courtesy and kindliness of General George Gordon Meade was as the balm of Gilead. He came at once[10] to Lee's tent in the woodlands, to clasp the hand of the "paroled prisoner of war." On the blazing heights of Gettysburg, General Meade stood between Lee and conclusive victory. These intimate friends[11] of old army days were separated four years before by their conscientious convictions.

[9]ARMISTEAD LINDSAY LONG, *Memoirs of General Robert E. Lee*, Chap. 21. Also FITZHUGH LEE, *General Lee*, Chap. 15.

[10]Some authorities, notably WALTER HERRON TAYLOR, place Meade's visit on Monday. A. L. LONG, *Lee*, p 426, says explicitly "the afternoon of the day of the surrender."

[11]For an account of their conversations, see *The Land of Decision*, SQUIRES, p. 39.

Mrs. Meade and Mrs. Henry Alexander Wise were sisters, the daughters of John Sergeant, of Philadelphia, candidate on the Whig ticket, with Henry Clay, for Vice-President in 1832.

Generals Henry Jackson Hunt of Detroit and Henry Alexander Wise also called. General Hunt said of his visit:

"At Appomattox[12] I spent half-an-hour with General Lee in his tent. He looked weary and care-worn, but in this supreme hour was the same self-possessed, dignified gentleman I had always known him. After a time General Wise came in and I took my leave. This was the last time I saw General Lee, a truly great man, as great in adversity as in prosperity."

General Lee called his officers to headquarters for their last meeting. He was cheerful, but the deep lines in his face were eloquent of mental anguish. His officers, too, made brave efforts, but the frugal meal was the saddest ever spread in Virginia. Each officer knew that his comrades carried hearts too heavy for tears. A proud people, after four years of prodigious effort, were sunk into the abyss of hopeless defeat.

And so this day of Virginia's most poignant grief closed in at last.

---

[12]PHILIP H. SHERIDAN, "Last Days of the Rebellion," *N. Amer. Review*, July, 1883, pp. 8-18, gives an interesting personal account of the surrender. Not all the details agree with other authorities, but the variations are slight and of no material importance.

HORACE GREELEY, *The Amer. Conflict*, Vol. II, p. 745: "They crowded around their chief, who, with streaming eyes, grasped and pressed their hands, at length finding words to say, 'Men, we have fought through the war together. I have done for you the best that I could.' As fast as paroled the Confederates returned to their several homes."

II

When the rising sun flung soft and healing rays across the war-blasted fields of Virginia, the officers of both armies were busily preparing for the parole.[13] General Lee issued his Farewell Address. Its dignity, simplicity and self-control do not conceal the grief of a great heart broken.

"After four years of arduous service, marked by unsurpassed courage and fortitude, the Army of Northern Virginia has been compelled to yield to overwhelming numbers and resources. I need not tell the survivors of so many hard-fought battles, who have remained steadfast to the last, that I consented to this result from no distrust of them; but feeling that valor and devotion could accomplish nothing that could compensate for the loss that must have attended the continuance of the contest, I determined to avoid the useless sacrifice of those whose past service has endeared them to their countrymen."

During this busy Monday General Grant[14] requested General Lee to use his influence and to secure, if possible, the surrender of those Southern armies

---

[13]WALTER HERRON TAYLOR, *Four Years With Lee*, p. 153. "The work of paroling the army was completed the 10th day of April." This is surely a mistake.

JOHN ESTEN COOKE, *Lee*, p. 464: "On the following day (Monday) the painful arrangements connected with the capitulation were concluded."

CAPT. R. E. LEE, JR., *Lee:* "The day after the surrender, Lee started for Richmond." This is surely a mistake.

JAMES D. MC CABE, *Lee*, p. 636, also seems erroneous. "On April 12 the Confederate Army was formed into divisions for the last time."

[14]J. WILLIAM JONES, *Lee*, p. 378: "The day after the surrender Grant and Lee met on horseback in a field north of Appomattox C. H. and conversed for an hour."

still in the field. The continuation of the struggle
was manifestly useless, and the shedding of blood
should be avoided. General Joseph Eggleston Johnston with approximately 35,000 men lay between
General Sherman and Raleigh. The Confederacy
had shrunk to a few counties in North Carolina.

General Grant left at once for Washington,[15] but
he tactfully avoided going by way of Richmond.

During Monday and Tuesday there was much
visiting and fraternizing by the soldiers of both
armies. At noon, Tuesday, April 11, the Army of
the James moved westward from Appomattox Station,[16] following the Southside Railway toward
Lynchburg, which had been General Lee's objective.

Wednesday brought cold winds, and the clouds
were heavy and gray. This was the day for the
Confederate soldiers to lay down their arms, surrender their tattered battle-flags, receive their paroles
and, in many cases, start on the long journey homeward.

They broke camp for the last time, fell into line
and marched under General John B. Gordon to the
rendezvous, with the long, swinging stride for which
the Southern infantry was famous. The Union
soldiers—their friends now, and foes no more—
were interested and sympathetic spectators. It was
noted that they made no demonstration, but watched
in silence.

The Confederates fixed their bayonets, stacked

[15]HORACE PORTER, *Grant:* "General Grant left Appomattox Monday,
April 10, for Washington."

[16]J. L. CHAMBERLAIN, *The Passing of the Armies*, p. 247: "Lee and Grant
had both left."   He is mistaken in saying that Lee had left.

their arms and cartridge-boxes and laid them on the ground side by side. All went well until the command was given to furl the tattered and blood-stained battle-flags. They, too, must be laid by the arms and the cannon, low upon the earth.

As the flags were lowered, the Confederate soldiers could not control their emotions; they broke ranks, rushed to the flags, knelt beside them, took them in their arms, as if the banners were living things, pressed them to their lips, and wept over them . . . manly tears, not of weakness born, but of blood and fire and strength.

At last the ordeal was over, and they turned to give their word of honor never again to take arms against the Stars and Stripes.

That word was kept, inviolate, and is sacred to their children and their children's children. In not one instance has a Confederate soldier proven false to his parole.

Less than 8,000 men had arms to surrender, although the whole army, including the wounded, stragglers, teamsters, extra-duty men and camp-followers numbered 26,000.[17]

---

[17]JAMES D. MC CABE, *Lee*, p. 636: "On April 12 the Confederate Army was formed into divisions for the last time. They parked their artillery, rifles, accoutrements and flags, 7,500 men and 18,000 stragglers. 2,000 Cavalry under Fitz Lee and Rosser escaped, but were surrendered with the rest. General Grant was not present."

EDWARD CHANNING, *Hist. of U. S.*, p. 635, quotes J. L. Chamberlain and the above. He says the Union soldiers saluted, and that General Gordon "honored their salute."

A. L. LONG declared that "during Wednesday" Lee made his final report to "His Excellency Jefferson Davis," dated "near Appomattox C. H." He quotes the report verbatim—*Lee*, p. 693.

The report must have been written previously and dated Wednesday, the day General Lee left Appomattox.

III

Anxious as he must have been to leave these scenes of recent humiliation and disaster, General Lee would not, as a matter of principle, leave Appomattox so long as his soldiers might need his help. His army rapidly disappeared. As each man received his parole, he turned eager steps homeward.[18]

Wednesday morning[19] General Lee took the road to Richmond (April 12) with a few members of his staff, a wagon and an ambulance. They discussed the future with its opportunities and difficulties. War and defeat were taboo. Over and over again the General advised his friends to go home and go to work; not to desert Virginia, but to rebuild foundations deep and strong. It was worse than useless to repine.

He was deeply concerned over the poverty of the countryside and the disastrous effects of the war. The farmers, especially the women, along the road offered him many courtesies, which touched him. "These good people are kind—too kind," he said over and over again. "They do too much for us,

---

[18]A. L. LONG: "Three days after the surrender the army had dispersed in every direction," and with no hint of disorder, but in perfect quietness.

[19]WALTER HERRON TAYLOR, *Lee*, p. 296: "On April 12, I think it was, General Lee started on his journey to Richmond, accompanied by Colonels Venable, Marshall and myself."

S. M. WILLIAMS, Quartermaster, Surry Light Artillery, wrote: "We remained until Wednesday morning, when we got our paroles, and started for home."

PHILIP ALEX. BRUCE, *Lee*, p. 310: "The next day (Wednesday) he set out for Richmond."

J. D. MC CABE, p. 636: "He reached Richmond on the afternoon of April 12." This is certainly a mistake.

more than they are able." Their hearts seemed as full as when the war began four years before.

If they traveled thirty miles (and that would be a good day's journey over such roads and with such baggage), they would reach the vicinity of Cumberland Court House by nightfall.

The General declined the offer of a comfortable home, and remarked to Colonel Walter Herron Taylor that he would submit to the privations of a soldier until he reached Richmond.[20]

IV

Thursday morning Colonel Charles Scott Venable took an affecting leave and turned southward to his home near Farmville. The travelers covered another thirty miles, and reached the home of General Lee's brother, Charles Carter Lee, in Powhatan County, near the James. The General spent a quiet evening with the family at the fireside, but declined the hospitality of his brother's home for the night, although it was raining. He spent the night in a little, black carriage he used when not on "Traveler." Progress was slow, and not until Saturday morning, April 15,[21] was Richmond reached. Two aides, Colonels Charles

---

[20] EDWARD LEE CHILDE, *Campaigns of Lee*, pp. 323-4. Mr. Childe states that an escort of cavalry and twenty-five Confederate officers accompanied him. Walter Herron Taylor alludes to neither. Colonel Taylor was probably Lee's most intimate friend.

[21] WALTER H. TAYLOR, *Lee*, p. 297: "We reached Richmond April 15."

WILLIAM A. CHRISTIAN, *Richmond*: "General Lee rode into Richmond with five members of his staff, Saturday, April 15."

JAMES C. YOUNG, *Marse Robert*: "Lee reached his home, Franklin Street, Friday, April 14."

EDWARD A. POLLARD, *The Lost Cause*, p. 712: "The afternoon of April 12."

Marshall, of Baltimore,[22] and Walter H. Taylor, of Norfolk, were still with General Lee. The once fair and familiar city was a smoking ruin. Falling walls and debris blocked the streets. The very atmosphere was fevered and poisoned. Death, dread and desolation hung like horrid clouds over the stricken inhabitants.

Federal sentinels, everywhere on duty, recognized General Lee, saluted him and cheered. He acknowledged their greeting by raising his hat time and time again. He crossed the river by a pontoon bridge below Mayo's Bridge, which had been burned, and rode along Main Street through the burnt district to his home in Franklin street, near Capitol Square.

One who saw him wrote that his uniform showed the effect of hard travel. He looked fatigued. Even "Traveler" was dispirited. His aides were gaunt and pallid; they, too, were travel-stained, soiled and wearied.

General Lee mounted the steps to the front door of his home, backward, as he acknowledged the "vociferous greetings of the soldiers in blue." As he entered, the military career of Robert E. Lee came to an end—a career which compels the admiration of the world.

He had only received the welcome of his wife and daughters when a hurried message was delivered (at 11 a. m.).

"Lincoln was assassinated last night and died this morning at 7 o'clock."

The General was struck dumb. At last, finding

---

[22]CHARLES MARSHALL, strange to say, closes his valuable book at Appomattox, and does not mention the return to Richmond.

RECONSTRUCTION BEGAN FOR RICHMOND APRIL 2, 1865, WHEN THE CONFEDERATE ARMY WITHDREW

"The once fair and familiar city was a smoking ruin. Falling walls and debris blocked the streets. The very atmosphere was fevered and poisoned."—Page 12.

his voice he declared, "It is a crime previously unknown to history; one that must be deprecated by
every American."[23]

He could not know that the sensational crime of a
degenerate madman would be laid at his door! That
men would cry out against him, declaring that both he
and President Davis should be hanged! He could not
guess that eight million people in eleven great States
would be cruelly punished through ten, terrible years,
largely because of President Lincoln's tragic fall.[24]

As the curtain falls thus upon the public and the
military career of Robert E. Lee, we know of no
better word than that of General Viscount Wolseley,
whose prophecy has been verified:

"When all the anger aroused by secession is buried,
when Americans can view the history of their last,
great rebellion with calm impartiality, I believe that
General Lee will tower above all men on either side
in that struggle; I believe he will be regarded not
only as the most prominent figure of the Confederacy
but as the great American of the Nineteenth Century,
whose statue is well worthy to stand on an equal
pedestal with that of Washington, and whose memory
is equally worthy to be enshrined in the hearts of all
his countrymen."

[23]CHAS. FRANCIS ADAMS, *Lee's Centennial*, p. 55: "A small group of horsemen appeared in the morning hours on the further side of the Richmond pon-
toons across the James. By some strange intuition it became known that
General Lee was of the party."

MARY NEWTON STANARD, *Richmond*, p. 213, quotes verbatim a neighbor
who saw General Lee arrive—Saturday a. m., April 15.

[24]HENRY ALEX. WHITE, *Lee*, p. 427: "He denounced the assassination of
Lincoln as a grievous crime, and deplored the intensified animosity toward the
South on the part of the dominant political faction at Washington."

ALEX H. H. STUART, *Narrative*: "There is good reason to believe that, but
for the atrocious murder of President Lincoln, satisfactory peace could have
been adjusted."

CHAPTER II

LINCOLN IN VIRGINIA

> With malice toward none, with charity for all;
> with firmness in the right, as God gives us to see
> the right, let us strive on to finish the work we are
> in; to bind up the Nation's wounds; to care for him
> who shall have borne the battle, and for his widow
> and his orphan—to do all which may achieve and
> cherish a just and lasting peace among ourselves
> and with all nations.
>
> —*Abraham Lincoln.*

As the Confederate States tottered to their fall, President Lincoln watched Grant's strategy with intense interest and obvious concern.[1]   The General's tactics of gradual but certain attrition were slowly bleeding the South to death.   Twice as many men fell before the ramparts of Petersburg and Richmond as Lee commanded, yet the Federal hosts advanced in increasing numbers and undiminished vigor.

President Lincoln made his home upon a man-of-war lying in the James off City Point (Hopewell), March 24, 1865.   As in 1862, during McClellan's campaign, the placid river became an avenue of war

---

[1] G. F. MILTON, *Age of Hate*, makes the suggestion that he went to City Point to escape greedy politicians as much as to observe the army's movements.

NATHANIEL WRIGHT STEPHENSON, *Lincoln*, p. 407.

U. S. GRANT, *Memoirs*, Vol. II, p. 459.

IDA M. TARBELL, *Lincoln*, Vol. II, p. 229.

leading into the very heart of Virginia. Innumerable ships and transports filled to the gunwales with men, arms, food, ammunition and all the appurtenances of war, steamed up the James from the Chesapeake and down again when their cargoes were delivered.

Mrs. Lincoln was with the President for a while. One beautiful afternoon (for spring came to Virginia early in 1865) they drove through the countryside.

There are, and have always been, quiet rural cemeteries in the valley of James River where the dead of a neighborhood, a family or a congregation, be asleep side by side. As they passed one such graveyard the President and Mrs. Lincoln alighted from their carriage, and walked among the graves. Tender leaves cast a cool and tranquil shade, great limbs of trees seemed to protect and bless the dead who lay so peacefully asleep.

"Mary," said the President, "you are younger than I, and will survive me. When I am gone lay my remains in some quiet place like this."[2]

II

Sherman's army, 80,000 strong, was breaking in the "backdoor" of the Confederacy. They had marched up from Georgia, and were resting at Goldsboro, N. C. Joseph E. Johnston faced them, and protected Raleigh with 35,000 men.

[2]NATH. WRIGHT STEPHENSON, *Lincoln*, page 415: It is strange that the only place President Lincoln expressed a wish to be buried was beneath the soil of Virginia.

Sherman came to City Point for a long conference with Lincoln and Grant[3] (Monday, March 27). He wrote Mrs. Sherman that President Lincoln looked haggard and careworn. "There is no doubt we have got the rebels in a tight place," he told her.

Next day, Tuesday, March 28, the two generals and Admiral Porter talked to the President. The generals thought there would have to be one more decisive battle; but it would be the last.

President Lincoln was in "an exceedingly pleasant mood," but hoped that another great battle could be avoided. He said that too much blood had already been shed. The conversation lasted fully an hour and a half. The President wanted to get the Confederate soldiers "back on the farms" as soon as possible.

General Sherman asked Lincoln whether he wanted Jefferson Davis captured, or would prefer for him to escape. Lincoln replied with one of his inimitable stories: A friend of his "back in Illinois" took the temperance pledge. When invited to have a drink with some of the "good fellows," he called for lemonade. They protested, and suggested that "a finger or two" of brandy would help the mild beverage, to which the abstainer replied "rather wistfully" that if someone would put the brandy in "unbeknownst to him" he would not object.

Obviously Lincoln could not suggest that Davis escape, but if he got to Cuba "unbeknownst" to him

---

[3]The house in which he made his headquarters has been destroyed, but the foundation may be seen on the grounds of Appomattox Manor, the home of Miss Mary Epes.

the administration would be saved considerable embarrassment.[4]

III

At nine o'clock Saturday night, April 1, General Sheridan notified General Grant that Lee's lines had been pierced at Five Forks, eighteen miles southwest of Petersburg.

Grant brought the news to Lincoln that Sheridan "carried everything before him." It was indeed the beginning of the end, the prelude to the final drama of victory and defeat; of blood, assassination and of final peace.

Five Forks is, as the name implies, a crossroad. It is not even a village, nor a post office. The forks of the road were a mile and a half south of the Southside Railway (Norfolk & Western).

If Lee's lines were pierced at Five Forks, the railway would be cut. If so, Petersburg must be surrendered. If so, Richmond would fall. If so, the Confederate cause was lost. In the gigantic chessboard of war strategic issues hung upon the roads that crossed through the corn and tobacco fields of Five Forks.

It happened with startling rapidity[5] and completeness. Before sunrise Sunday morning General Am-

---

[4]G. F. MILTON, *Age of Hate*, p. 152.

Lincoln authorized Sherman to inform Governor Vance of North Carolina that, when the armies surrendered, the people "would at once be guaranteed all their rights as citizens of a common country." Lincoln wished to avoid anarchy. State governments then in existence with their civil functionaries would be recognized as government *de facto* "until Congress could provide others."

[5]HORACE GREELEY, *American Conflict*, Vol. 2, p. 731.

U. S. GRANT, *Personal Memoirs*, Chap. 63: "Pursuit continued until about nine o'clock that night."

HORACE PORTER, *Five Forks and the Pursuit of Lee*.

brose Powell Hill fell (6:40 a. m.). General Grant
notified President Lincoln that Lee could not hold
his lines. At 10:30 a. m., General Lee notified President Jefferson Davis that Petersburg and Richmond
must be evacuated that night.[6]

Monday morning at sunrise the last Confederate
soldier was gone, and the Army of the Potomac
entered Petersburg, the Ninth Corps leading. The
President came with the army and telegraphed Secretary Stanton that he "stayed with General Grant
an hour and a half." At 8:30 Monday morning
General Weitzel entered Richmond with Wisconsin
troops, quieted the panic-stricken people, and set
his soldiers stamping out the frightful conflagration
which burned the heart of the city.

President Lincoln, accompanied by Admiral Porter
and "ten soldiers armed with carbines," sailed up
the James in a barge to Richmond. He walked
about the streets and was everywhere recognized.
The citizens were dignified and courteous, and no
suggestion of rudeness nor of animosity was offered.

The colored people cheered him as their Emancipator. The President called on General Weitzel[7]
in the "Confederate White House," for the General
had moved in Monday, twenty hours after President
Davis moved out.[8]

---

[6] *The Land of Decision*, squires, Chap. II; also Chap. X.

The message was delivered to President Davis in his pew at St. Paul's
Church.

[7] julian hawthorne, *History of U. S.*, Vol. III, p. 1031: "He held a reception in what had been the Confederate Executive mansion."

Lincoln did just the reverse. He paid a quiet and unostentatious call on
General Weitzel.

w. e. carson, *Historic Shrines*, p. 34: "On April 4 the House was visited
by Lincoln, who remained some time."

[8] william e. carson, *Historic Shrines of Virginia*, p. 34.

The President was greatly interested in the former tobacco warehouse of Libby & Co., famous ever since as "Libby Prison." As he looked at the sombre building with its unpleasant associations, one of the party suggested that "Jefferson Davis ought to be hanged." To which the President made the significant reply, "Judge not that ye be not judged."[9]

Wednesday brought more news of victory from Grant. "The retreat of the enemy is rapidly become a rout. I see no escape for Lee."

The Vice-President, Andrew Johnson, with Preston King, Colonel William B. Browning and Henry C. Warmouth,[10] reached Richmond Wednesday (April 5) aboard the U. S. S. "Dictator," a dispatch boat. Andrew Johnson came at Lincoln's request. He was entertained at the Spotswood Hotel, the famous inn of ante-bellum Richmond. Charles A. Dana was also stopping there.

News came that General Sheridan had cut the railway to Danville and North Carolina, and when Lee reached Amelia Court House that day there was not an ounce of food, owing to a "misapprehension of orders." Grant was right; there was no hope for the starving, retreating and helpless remnants of the once invincible Army of Northern Virginia. President Lincoln[11] had two long talks with Judge John Archibald Campbell, of Alabama. They had been great friends in the old Whig party long years be-

[9]THEODORE TILTON, in his "Independent," wrote: "The welfare of society and all the interests of humanity demand that Davis, Lee & Company shall be tried, found guilty and hanged by the neck until they are dead."

[10]HENRY CLAY WARMOUTH, *War, Politics and Reconstruction*, pp. 25-7.

[11]President Lincoln called upon Mrs. Pickett, the wife of George Edward Pickett, whom he had known well in early life.

fore.   As a judge of the Supreme Court and a pronounced Union man, Judge Campbell did his utmost
to prevent secession.

President Lincoln met the Judge at General
Weitzel's office.   He said he had three points to
maintain in dealing with the States recently in the
Confederacy.

    1.   The paramount authority of the Federal
Government.

    2.   The abolition of slavery.

    3.   The surrender of all forces still in arms
against the Federal Government.

This reasonable and just program was readily
agreed upon, and when President Lincoln returned
to City Point Thursday (April 6) he ordered General
Weitzel to permit "the gentlemen who have acted
as the Legislature of Virginia," to meet at Richmond
and make this program effective.

A call, signed by influential citizens, men of pru-
dence and distinction, asking the General Assembly
to convene in the Capitol April 25, was sent out
April 12, but General E. O. C. Ord, who had just
taken command, rescinded the call the day following
(April 13).   Reconstruction was not to begin so
promptly nor to be carried out so simply.

Posterity is impressed with the sympathy, gentle-
ness and consideration of Abraham Lincoln for the
war-worn and now vanquished people of the South.
The frightful ordeal of war, the colossal burden of
responsibility and the long-drawn uncertainty of the
issues at stake softened, broadened and mollified the

BLACK BEARD'S HILL.

Rises 50 feet above a desert of shifting sand.

* * * *

In every corner of Virginia there are romantic spots where memory loves to linger, where battles were fought, where heroes were born, or mighty deeds were done.

These are possessions, priceless, in a land long settled.

Photo by H. C. Mann

man, bringing out the true gold of his rugged character.

Abraham Lincoln was Southern, born to a father whose father, Abraham Lincoln, had lived in the Valley of Virginia near Harrisonburg. As he neared the end of life, the call of the blood responded. It may be said truthfully of Abraham Lincoln that the more he saw of Virginia, the more he loved, understood and appreciated the Virginians. Had he remained in Richmond, he would not have been assassinated!

He left Richmond Friday, April 7, and returned from City Point to Washington, Saturday and Sunday (April 8 and 9), while Lee and Grant were arranging the terms of surrender at Appomattox.

When news of the surrender reached Washington,[12] great crowds of rejoicing people called at the White House to offer their congratulations. All day Monday, a milling multitude besieged the President. He twice acknowledged the ovation, and promised to speak Tuesday night.

The Secretary of the Navy, Gideon Welles, wrote: "Guns are firing, bells ringing, flags flying; men are laughing, children cheering—all are happy and jubilant."

As it proved, this (Tuesday night) was Lincoln's last public appearance and his final pronouncement.[13] In it he outlined briefly the principles that he intended to follow in the reconstruction of the South. There would be no bloodshed, no vindictiveness, no

[12]When news of Lee's surrender reached Richmond, a salute of two hundred guns was fired in the Capitol Square.

[13]President Lincoln raised the blockade of Virginia ports Tuesday, April 11.

punishment for a whole people who had fought so
bravely for their constitutional rights. "We all
agree," he said, "that the seceded States are out of
their proper, practical relation to the Union, and
that the sole object of the Government, civil and
military, in regard to these States is to get them
again into their proper, practical relation" (Tuesday,
April 11). As he concluded, he said that he wanted
the band to play a piece of Confederate music,
"Dixie," which the armies had fairly captured. It
was received with immense enthusiasm.

On Thursday (April 13) enlisting ceased, and steps
were taken to muster out the men and reduce the
army as rapidly as might be.

Friday, known in the church calendar as Good
Friday, the day of the Crucifixion of the Lord Jesus
Christ (two days before Easter), was the day of
America's greatest tragedy, albeit a happy day for
President Lincoln. His son, Robert, who served on
General Grant's staff and who was present at the
surrender of General Lee, brought home first hand
reports from the army and gave full information of
all that happened the preceding Sunday at Appo-
mattox.

The Cabinet met. General Grant was present,
and all were very happy over the prospect of peace.

Lincoln told the Cabinet[14] that there had been
enough bloodshed and sorrow. He did not propose

[14]Secretary Stanton was much displeased that Lincoln permitted the
assembling of the Legislature of Virginia.

Secretary Welles declared that Stanton had already prepared a "Plan of
subjugation, tending, and I think, designed, to increase alienation and hatred
between the different sections of the Union."

Ah! Gideon Welles was a true prophet.

to treat the late "rebels" as if he were a "master," but rather as a brother. They have rights and these rights are to be respected.

He then told the Cabinet of a dream he had the night before. He had the same dream, queerly enough, before each important event in the war. In the vision he saw a mysterious and indescribable vessel moving through dark and troubled waters. He was aboard, and the destination was an hazy, dim and distant shore. Before Sumter he had seen the same strange vessel, and before Bull Run, Antietam, Gettysburg, Stone River, Vicksburg and Wilmington. "I think," he concluded, "we will have good news from Sherman."

At 2 o'clock General Grant bade him farewell, although Lincoln urged him to remain and attend the theatre that evening. Laura Keene was playing at Ford's Theatre, "Our American Cousin." But the General declined. He was to meet his family in New Jersey.

In the afternoon the President took a long drive with Mrs. Lincoln, and talked for an hour with Robert about his war experiences.

At 7:30 Schuyler Colfax, Speaker of the House of Representatives, called, and somewhat after eight o'clock a party of four, President and Mrs. Lincoln, Major H. R. Rathbone, and his fiancee, the daughter of Senator Ira Harris of New York, drove to the theatre and entered the box.

The President[15] seemed to enjoy the evening, and

---

[15] J. J. JUSSERAND, *Americans of Past and Present Days*, pp. 294-5, gives a detailed description of Lincoln as seen by a French visitor just before his assassination.

especially the humor of the play.   At 10:30 a shot
rang through the theatre, and he sank from his
chair, an unconscious heap, beside his wife.   They
carried him across the street, and though he lived
until 7:22 Saturday morning, he never regained
consciousness.

As his pulse ceased to beat Secretary Stanton, who
stood beside his bed, broke the silence of the death
chamber:

"And now he belongs to the ages."[16]

---

[16]IDA MINERVA TARBELL, *Life of Lincoln.*
  NICHOLAY AND HAY, *Lincoln.*

CHAPTER III

AMERICA'S CHIEF CRIMINAL

Out—out are the lights—out all!
    And, over each quivering form,
The curtain, a funeral pall,
    Comes down with the rush of a storm;
And the angels, all pallid and wan,
    Uprising, unveiling, affirm
That the play is the tragedy, "Man,"
    And its hero the Conquering Worm.

—*Edgar Allan Poe.*

Junius Brutus Booth (1796-1852), the father of
the madman who perpetrated the most sensational
crime in American history, came of an English-
Hebrew family. The brilliant but erratic actor
married Mary Anne Holmes (January 13, 1821), and
sailed to America aboard the good ship "Two
Brothers." He landed at Norfolk, but remained
only long enough to secure passage to New York,
by way of Richmond.

Booth soon became the most popular actor in this
country. His renditions of Richard III, Shylock
and Iago were especially brilliant. Such were his
talents and his character that he was naturally
effective in erratic and grotesque roles. From time
to time he was subject to attacks of insanity; was
always intense, irresponsible and intemperate. So
fine an artist was he that the public forgave him,
even when he attempted suicide.

He bought a farm near Bel Air, Maryland, in a beautiful secluded vale, and made his home in a log cabin, amidst flowers, gardens, trees, fish-ponds and pastures. Four children were born to him there, of whom Edwin was the second and John Wilkes the fourth.

Edwin Booth (1833-1893) was perhaps the most popular and gifted of all American actors. The spur which John Wilkes Booth wore when he shot Lincoln, and which caught in the flag when he jumped to the stage, was given to Edwin Booth by their father, who said at the time, "Edwin, I hope you will wear it with credit."

From infancy[1] John Wilkes Booth exhibited the traits of his erratic father, his genius and his madness. He was a lad of extraordinary beauty, with a face that suggested Lord Byron or Edgar Allan Poe. He had coal-black hair and flashing eyes. Though small in stature he was the embodiment of masculine grace. He had the masculine power and abandon of Aaron Burr. Before he was seventeen he began a career in Baltimore, and had played in Richmond, Philadelphia and practically all the cities of the country.

---

[1] John Wilkes Booth, born (1839) forty-two years after the death of the erratic and dissipated John Wilkes, received his name, as we surmise, from that unfortunate English politician. It was a bad selection. Wilkes was born in London (1727), and made such libelous attacks upon King George III and the Bute ministry that he was thrown into prison. He was expelled from Parliament (1764) as punishment for a scandalous "Essay on Woman." Again elected to Parliament (1768) he was again imprisoned and expelled (1769). In 1774 he became Lord Mayor of London. Again returned to Parliament, he was allowed to take his seat, and remained a member until 1790. His hectic career ended in 1797. The author has no authority for the statement that Junius Brutus Booth named the unfortunate child for the unfortunate agitator, but he deems it likely.

During the War Between the States he played
Mark Anthony so magnificently that he took Boston
by storm. The critics declared that he surpassed
his late father and his famous brother, Edwin.

His last appearance was at Ford's Theatre, Washington, March 18, 1865,[2] less than a month before
he enacted the most desperate tragedy of American
history in the same theatre. The Booth family was
not Southern in any respect,[3] and their sympathy
was wholly with the Union cause. But John Wilkes
Booth, perhaps from a natural, intense perversity,
espoused the cause of slavery and of secession with
great vehemence. He was the kind of man that is
born on the "other side" of any question. Had all
his people and friends been secessionists, John
Wilkes Booth would no doubt have been as violently
Unionist as he now appeared a Secessionist.

He journeyed as a volunteer to Charles Town in
Virginia (1859) and was present at the arrest and
execution of John Brown. Booth was as madly
anti-abolitionist as Brown was madly anti-slavery.
The opposites met!

In 1864 Booth devolved a wild scheme to kidnap
President Lincoln, take him to Richmond, and so
end the war. Just how such an absurd and fantastic
attempt upon the person of the President would have

[2]w. j. FERGUSON, in *I Saw Booth Shoot Lincoln*, tells how Booth, in playing
Romeo, cast himself on the platform, exclaiming "Take the measure of an
unmade grave." He acted the part so realistically that he wounded himself
on the very spot where he fell, after leaping to the stage, from Lincoln's box.

[3]ARTHUR MEIER SCHLESINGER, *Political Hist. of U. S.*, Vol. II, p. 235:
'Lincoln's death at the hands of a drink-crazed Southern zealot put the North
in an ugly humor."

Booth was not a "Southern zealot"; all his affiliations were anti-Southern.

any effect upon the war, except to stir up more
strife and sectional hatred, especially against the
South, does not appear.

About Christmas-time (1864) he met the Surratts,
mother and son. John had been educated for the
priesthood, but served as a spy during the war. The
mother kept a cheap boarding-house in Washington.
David Herold, a feeble-minded nineteen-year-old
boy, and George Atzerodt, another spy, and Lewis
Payne, a half-mad, half-starved prisoner, captured
at Gettysburg, and the son of a Baptist preacher in
Florida, made an erratic company of conspirators.
It will be noted that only Payne could be called
"Southern."

Not until noon of Friday, April 14, did Booth
learn that President Lincoln would attend Ford's
Theatre that night. He planned his sensational
crime with dramatic effect and great rapidity. Atzerodt was to murder Andrew Johnson at his hotel;
Payne was to assassinate Seward at his home; but
Booth reserved the stellar role for himself.

Having free access to the theatre, at all hours,
known to all the force, coming and going at will and
without arousing any suspicion, it was easy for
Booth to arrange the details of the ghastly murder.
In the partition behind the President's box he cut
away two inches of plaster and bored a hole through
the door by which he could watch those in the box.
This was probably done after the rehearsal and before
the light in the narrow passage failed, as evening
waned.

At ten o'clock, long after the play began, Booth,
dressed in a dark sack-coat, took a stiff drink of

Photo by W. H. T. S.

IN THE BLUE RIDGE

Photo by W. H. T. S.

IN SHENANDOAH VALLEY

"The soldier, who faced the setting sun as he returned from Appomattox, trudged through magnificent forests, thousands of acres of which had never been cleared. The far dim summits of the Blue Ridge lifted against the sky. In cool shadows crystal fountains spring from moss-covered rocks and rollicking little rivulets race down umbrageous valleys."—Page 41.

brandy, entered the theatre and passed along the passage to the rear of the boxes without being noticed.[4] He loitered in the shadows and took his time. He was about five feet behind President Lincoln, who was seated in a rocking-chair, well screened from the audience by heavy curtains. In front of the box a large American flag was draped about a picture[5] of George Washington.

The assassin took steady aim and fired. The shot lodged behind the President's left ear. As he thrust forward to the front of the box, smoking pistol in hand, Major Henry Reed Rathbone of Albany, New York, an officer of the U. S. Volunteers, seated in the box with the President and Mrs. Lincoln, and Miss Harris, seized Booth's coat. The assassin, as quick and as agile as he was desperate, slashed the Major severely, hissing at him the familiar Latin quotation,[6] "Sic semper tyrannis." He jumped from box to stage, and fell, breaking his leg, when his spur caught in the folds of the flag. Booth was observed to fall on his left knee. But he sprang to his feet, limped directly across the stage in plain view of the entire audience and disappeared behind the wings, reaching the lane in the rear of the theatre unmolested. He kicked the lad who patiently held his

---

[4]W. J. FERGUSON, *I Saw Booth Shoot Lincoln*, p. 13. He had entre of the theatre at all hours.

[5]The portrait measured about two feet each in breadth and length.

[6]Every account of the assassination except that of W. J. Ferguson states that Booth cried from the stage in wild hysteria, "Sic semper tyrannis. The South is avenged." Mr. Ferguson categorically denies that Booth spoke from the stage. His account is so clear and so detailed that it has the value of first-hand evidence. He suggests that the reporters who sent the messages out received their information from Major Rathbone, to whom (in Ferguson's opinion) Booth had hissed the sentence as he wounded him.

yellow mare, mounted her and hastened out of town over the Anacostia bridge. In fact Booth was well out of the way before the panic-stricken audience in the theatre understood what had happened.

The horse he rode belonged to Dr. Samuel Mudd, a widely known and respected rural physician. To his home Booth made his way directly, returned the mare, and received first aid from Dr. Mudd for his broken leg. The physician was wholly ignorant of the crime his patient had committed. His professional labors cost him four years in prison at Dry Tortugas, off the coast of Florida. One of President Johnson's last acts was the pardon of Dr. Mudd (1869).

For six days and nights the fugitive and his accomplice, David Herold, lay concealed in the thickets of Southern Maryland, while a determined army, who surrounded them almost all the time, beat the bushes in a vain effort to find them.

A man named Thomas A. Jones put the fugitives across the Potomac to the Virginia shore (Sunday, April 23). They spent the next day negotiating the deserted rural districts of Virginia from the Potomac to the Rappahannock. The Virginians to whom they applied received them coldly though they did not tell the guilty secret.[7]

They crossed the Rappahannock from Port Conway to Port Royal on the Southern shore in Caroline County. One Daniel Rollins, a water-man, put them both over the river. Booth hired a negro to drive them to Bowling Green, the county-seat, about

---

[7]It is only a conjecture that any of the Virginians knew his identity. I doubt whether any of them guessed that the fugitive was Booth.

fourteen miles away, but when they had traveled three miles the pain in Booth's leg became intolerable, and he ordered the driver to turn in at the homestead of Richard Henry Garrett,[8] near the road.

He introduced himself to the family of his involuntary host as John William Boyd, and in proof of his identity showed his initials J. W. B. tattooed on his arm.

In his own irresistible manner and genial affability that never failed him, he told how he had an argument with a "Yankee in Washington" and, during the fight, stabbed his antagonist, escaped on horseback; but fell from his horse and broke his leg. His hosts did not deny the rites of hospitality for which Virginians have ever been famous.

It was soon bruited that soldiers were coming from Port Royal, looking for the notorious assassin of the President. Booth and Herold had time to escape, but on account of his wounded leg they hid in a tobacco barn near the house. When the pursuers arrived, they asked Jack Garrett, the eldest son of the family, if Booth was hiding at his home. Jack stoutly denied the accusation, but told them a lame man from Washington was in the tobacco barn.

The soldiers at once surrounded the barn and called upon the fugitives to surrender. Herold did so, but Booth, in histrionic style, which was, no doubt, second nature to him, called out:

"Captain, give a lame man a chance. Draw up your men. I'll fight your whole command!"

When this rather unusual challenge was declined, he called to them again:

---

[8] E. C. MONCURE, *Reminiscences*, pp. 64-5; Bulletin Va. State Library, July, 1927.

"Well, my brave boys, prepare a stretcher for me."

They set the barn on fire. Booth appeared in the loft for a moment amidst smoke and flame, and fell just as they shot at him.

The officer had given strict orders that Booth was not to be shot, but taken alive. Whether he shot himself, or was shot by Boston Corbitt, will never be known. For Corbitt, despite orders, looked through a crack, saw Booth crouched in a corner, and fired.

The door was battered in and the dying man dragged out. His wound was under his right ear. He shot Lincoln behind his left ear.

As Booth expired, he murmured,

"Tell Mother I died for my country."

It was seven o'clock Wednesday morning, April 26. His body lay for some hours on the lawn covered with an army blanket.

Some of the soldiers ate breakfast at the Garrett home, and some, under Boston Corbitt, rode to James L. Shaddock's home, a mile away. Corbitt entered unceremoniously and ordered breakfast with the boast,

"I have just shot the man who killed our President."

The troopers forced young Jack Garrett and Daniel Rollins to go with them to Washington.[9]

Booth's corpse was taken to Greenleaf Point on the Potomac aboard the U. S. Monitor "Mon-

---

[9]The author is indebted to W. S. Cash, of Norfolk, Va., for the intimate items above related. He was born and reared on the farm adjoining that of R. H. Garrett, and the items were constantly told by his neighbors and friends in Caroline County, In fact, the Garrett farm was originally a part of the estate of Mr. Cash's great-grandfather, David Stern.

tauk," and secretly buried under the floor of a warehouse at the arsenal.

There have always been those who believed that Booth escaped and that the body was not his. That can hardly be, for he was well identified.

If it was any comfort to his stricken family to believe that he died for "his country," far be it from us to object. "His country," however, was certainly not Virginia nor the South. Every possible effort was made to fasten some part of the guilt upon President Jefferson Davis and other Southern leaders —indefensible political blackmail. Jefferson Davis had had no more to do with the assassination of Abraham Lincoln than he had with the assassination of Julius Caesar. And the stabbing of Caesar, by the way, seems to have been constantly in Booth's mind.

Booth's body was quietly removed to the family plot in Greenmount Cemetery, Baltimore (February 20, 1869) and rests in an unmarked grave.

* * * * *

When Chief Justice Salmon P. Chase gave the inaugural oath to Andrew Johnson, Saturday morning, April 15, immediately after Lincoln's death, he said:

"You are President! May God support, guide and bless you in your arduous duties."

The Southern people knew Andrew Johnson,[10] long, intimately, but not favorably. He was reported to have said to that implacable Radical, Benjamin Franklin Wade, "Treason must be made infamous, and traitors must be impoverished."

Ah! what did that portend?

---

[10]How strangely interwoven the skeins of history. Andrew Johnson was born in Raleigh, North Carolina, the *only* city which yet remained under the Confederate flag.

ARMISTEAD C. GORDON, *Richmond News-Leader*, 12-10-'31: "Jefferson Davis heard of Lincoln's death at Charlotte. He had just arrived from Greensboro, was dismounting, citizens were welcoming him, when the dispatch, signed by Secretary of War Breckenridge, was handed him by Major John Courtney. Mrs. Courtney, the major's widow, told me that her husband heard the President say: 'Oh, the pity of it!' He passed it to a gentleman with the remark, 'Here are sad tidings'."

CHAPTER IV

THE CONFEDERATES RETURN

> Men flung back from dreams of victory and honor,
> glad to have the luck of life and limbs; scarcely
> able to leap over corses that had dragged to die.
> See how they lay! Some as fair as death in sleep,
> with the smile of placid valor and of noble man-
> hood hovering yet on silent lips. These had blood-
> less hands put upward, white as wax and firm as
> death, clasped in prayer for dear ones left behind.
> And of these men there was nothing in their broad,
> blue eyes to fear.
> Yet here they lay dead, dead after a deal of pain,
> with little mind to bear it; and a soul they never
> thought of, gone, their God alone knows whither;
> but to mercy we may trust.
>
> —*Richard Doddridge Blackmore.*

Each Confederate soldier parked his cannon,
sword, musket, ammunition belt, under the beloved
Confederate battle-flag, now forever furled; filled
his canteen (thanks to General Sheridan) and
mounted his horse (thanks to General Grant), if he
had a horse. If he belonged to the infantry, as did
most of them, he placed his parole in his pocket and
began a long and irksome journey homeward through
forest, field and farmland.[1]

---

[1]Never an army disbanded with less disorder. Thousands set adrift without means of transportation; yet not a riot and no thieving. . . . The Confederate army was composed almost wholly of law-abiding lads, drawn from
the farms of the South.

J. WILLIAM JONES, *Reminiscences of Lee*, p. 198: "The conduct of Lee's
soldiers after the close of the war has elicited the admiration of the world."

EASTWARD

If he faced the morning sun he trudged along the very roads he had so recently negotiated. How different the journey now (Wednesday morning, April 12). Alone, and a paroled prisoner; last Saturday he was a Confederate soldier, fighting for his country, home and fireside. The almanac called it four days from Saturday until Wednesday, but to the footsore traveler it was a fragment of eternity. Thousands of his comrades fell, he well knew, during that last frightful week; but he fought it through, to the limit of his strength, and he thanked God for that.

To the rim of every horizon, the landscape bore melancholy evidence of the tornado which so recently hurtled over it and laid a purple ribbon of blood across Virginia from Richmond and Petersburg to Appomattox. It was astonishing how quiet the land lay, but it was the peace of desolation, a hundred miles of scars that evidenced agony, passion, wounds, death and torture worse than death.

The carcasses of dead animals polluted the air. Among malodorous beasts lay human forms. Their lifeless eyes stared into the blue vault of heaven. Their faces were swollen and blackened by decay, begrimed with powder, smeared with blood, but withal so young and once so quick and vital. Some smiled even in death. Some retained horrid evidences of torture, anguish and unendurable pain which wrenched their mutilated bodies before the spirit fled. Their uniforms torn, bloody, muddy,

The bridge at McDowell, Highland County, Virginia, where Stonewall Jackson won his first
strategic victory, May 8, 1862

THE BANKS OF REED CREEK
Wythe County, Virginia, near Wytheville

The thirty-two counties that lie west of the Blue Ridge in Virginia
furnished more than 30,000 men to the Confederate Army. These
sparsely settled counties were literally stripped of their young manhood.''—Page 42.

had once been blue or gray . . . what mattered it now?

Ammunition dumps cluttered the roads, broken wheels, discarded cannon, wagons and ambulances overthrown and mired, muskets and sabres flung about by fighting, cursing, wounded men in mortal combat; or fallen from the feeble grasp of hands a moment since alert and strong.

In the coverts of the forest, the trees stood stark naked, charred, burnt, bark and branches shot away. Death and torture made by man for man had raped the woodlands and chined the gentle hills with lead and fire.

The tender leaves shivered in the south wind[2] as though the spirits of the departed were searching for their mortal tenements of clay. Unclean birds of prey hovered over the former battlefields with hideous croak and ominous cry, and the soldier knew that these foul vultures haunted the spots where the dead lay thickest.[3] In the marish lowlands and along brooks and runlets the mire was still putrid, and the air tainted and heavy, as a breath from the tomb.

But nature was already busy, healing the scars and hiding the hurts of the fever-blistered land. Wild plum trees by the roadside flowered as white as snow, their blossoms pure as a bridal veil. Judas bushes blushed blood-red among their thorns. Here and there purple patches of violets offered their fragrance. Sunbeams lay warm upon the naked

[2]NATHANIEL WRIGHT STEPHENSON, *Lincoln*, p. 415.
[3]MRS. ROGER A. PRYOR, *Reminiscences of Peace and War*, p. 394.

fields and turned the slopes green again despite the double misery of defeat and death.[4]

When the footsore wanderer reached Richmond, some of his comrades had already begun life again, piling bricks, which were still warm, and cleaning the streets, while spirals of smoke rose from acres of ruins.

Libby Prison was a prison still, but behind the sign that hung upon it, "L. L. Libby & Son, Ship Chandlers," Confederate prisoners were now confined. Idle negroes swarmed upon the streets, slept in the sun, sang and danced in the slums, and were fed from the commissary of the Freedmen's Bureau. The revolution was significant. White soldiers, even the crippled, working, and hungry as they worked. The joyous, carefree negroes disdaining work, but well fed.

Norfolk was painted with one graphic touch.[5] "But for the occasional appearance of an idle white vagabond, sauntering along the wharves, gazing wistfully into the water, we would have imagined ourselves in a lost city." Yet Norfolk had enjoyed the benefits of Federal occupation for three years, much of the time under the benign rule of the notorious General, Benjamin F. Butler.

SOUTHWARD

Those who turned southward to the once fair fields of Piedmont Virginia, North Carolina and the

---

[4] The farmers around Petersburg could not plow for the iron which had been shot upon their fields during eleven months.

[5] *Norfolk Journal,* January 6, 1866.

cotton states, tramped along a countryside almost as naked as the Indians left it more than a century before.[6] Where broad acres of tobacco trembled, deep-green and golden, in years of peace and plenty, and stately rows of Indian corn lifted their fronds in martial array, thickets of weeds and underbrush had now unchallenged possession. Where once a modest cottage sheltered the farmer and his growing family, a ruined chimney, like a smoked skeleton, haunted the farm. Instead of romping children, a serpent slunk through the dank wilderness. Poverty, wretchedness, hunger, death and despair clutched the heart of the land.

Homes once prosperous, down their avenues of stately forest trees, were untenanted and falling to decay. The owner was perhaps lying in an unknown grave.[7]

For miles upon weary miles the returning soldier saw not one inhabited homestead, and passed not one human being, black or white. This ruined land, not touched by actual warfare, was devoured by the backwash of war. The returning soldier wondered as he toiled on what scenes would greet him when he reached his home.[8]

The experience of one we know.[9] The camp-

[6]C. G. CHAMBERLAYNE, *Ham Chamberlayne, Virginian*, pp. 332-3.

[7]Gen. Grant wrote Mrs. Grant, May, 1865, "The suffering which must exist in the South next year will be beyond calculation."

[8]E. P. OBERHOLTZER, *Hist. of U. S.*, Vol. 1, p. 56: Sherman's army had swept that part of the South so bare that it was almost without living reminders of human civilization.

[9]HENRY WOODFIN GRADY, *The New South*: "Let me picture to you the footsore Confederate soldier, as, buttoning up in his faded gray jacket, on his parole, he turned his face southward from Appomattox. Think of him as, ragged, half-starved, heavy-hearted, enfeebled by want and wounds, he sur-

followers fled when they heard he was coming, for poltroons are always cowards. In the dooryard, freshly trampled, the carcasses of six dead cows, his cows, lay rotting. Filth unspeakable, piled in the corners of his house, sent forth sickening odors. Decaying flesh and offal drew a million flies that buzzed about. These vermin took possession with the human vermin. Molasses trickled in filthy streams from what had once been library shelves. Glass, once window-panes, and bottles, belittered the floors. The furniture had supplied the camp-followers and their dusky Negro wenches with fuel. One chair remained, the seat cut out with a sabre. One bed remained, propped by broken bits of muskets, "U. S. A." conspicuously carved upon the fragments. Fallen plaster, stained walls, viscid closets, starting weatherboards presented tragic evidence of violence, plunder and decay. Under one window a shallow grave had been hastily dug. Recent rains caused it to sink, and a half-decayed arm and hand protruded from the loathesome soil to welcome the owner of his home when he returned from Appomattox.

Many were the deeds of kindness, unrecorded in history but unforgotten in Heaven. A patriotic matron[10] of Chatham, Virginia, had only a few bushels of blackeyed peas and some corn-meal. As

---

renders his gun, wrings the hands of his comrades in silence, and lifting his tear-stained and pallid face to the graves that dot the old Virginia hills, he begins his slow and painful journey."

[10]Mrs. James Carter, of Chatham; see MAUD CARTER CLEMENT, *Hist. of Pittsylvania Co.*, p. 253.

The homeward journey of Sidney Lanier is described in *The Land of Decision*, SQUIRES, pp. 113-114.

the southbound soldiers trudged wearily along the road, she invited them to partake of this homely fare. "For four or five days these weary and disheartened men passed in procession, unofficered, and many of them hundreds of miles from home. Each guest received a cupful of peas and a small pone to help and cheer him on his way.[11]

Westward

If the soldier faced the setting sun, he had a journey less disheartening. Forest-clad hills lifted the horizon until the dim, far outlines of mighty Blue Ridge appeared against the sky.

These roads led, for the most part, through magnificent forests, thousands of acres of which had never been cleared. In the cool shadows of the uplands and in deep valleys crystal fountains spring from moss-covered rocks, and rollicking little rivulets race down deep, umbrageous valleys. In April the modest anemone offers the delicate perfume of its tiny, white flowers. The wintergreen may be plucked and eaten as tea-leaves. The mountain laurel was not yet ready to blossom, but the trailing arbutus was in flower where the warm sunbeams fell through the intricate thickets of the woodland. The virgins-bower put forth slender fingers. The pines stood stiff and uncompromising. The oaks and chestnuts prepared for another summer. The ash had not decided whether spring had really come, and its limbs were naked.

---

[11]GEORGE S. BARNARD, *War Talks*, pp. 277-284, the diary of one Confederate soldier.

This rugged land, protected by mountain ranges from invasion, had not suffered as the eastern plains. The humble mountain cabins were still inhabited. Old men, women and little children paused in garden patches to welcome the wanderer.

Had General Lee really surrendered? And was he sure it was Robert E. Lee, and not that fool,[12] Fitz? And, in a great army, he didn't happen to meet any man from Amherst or Bedford? They had two boys in the army. Did he know when General Longstreet's men might happen along? The other son was with Mahone. The stranger was welcome to all they had of food, rest and a bed. Sometimes all the cattle and hogs had been stolen, and sometimes they were hidden in the thickest covert of the woods.

The Confederate soldier passed over the Blue Ridge and down the long valleys to his mountain home. Thirty-two counties in Virginia over the Blue Ridge sent 30,000 men to General Lee.[13]

NORTHWARD

The Confederate soldier who left Appomattox by the roads and paths which struck northward, through fields and forest, crossed the James to central and northern Virginia, and found himself beset by increasing difficulties.

---

[12]This from a story Gen. Fitzhugh Lee often told on himself.

[13]W. C. PENDLETON, *Hist. of Tazewell County*: "The Falls Mill neighborhood in Tazewell deserves special mention; 37 men went into the Confederate army, sons of small farmers, only one family owned a slave (one slave). Eight were killed in action, 5 died of camp disease, 13 were wounded, 11 returned safely after the surrender. The County sent nearly 2,000 soldiers into the Confederate army.

The people were hospitable,[14] and gladly divided their starveling store with the soldier, who often bore in his body those scars which proved his valor and his worth. Nature was kind; the gentle valleys were lighted here and there with the pure white petals of the dog-wood. The willows by the noisy little brooks shook out long pendants green, succulent and graceful, their lancets trembling to the touch of the slightest breeze. In the door-yards the lilacs, jonquils and hyacinths were blooming as though the land was happy and prosperous as in days of yore. But when he reached Spotsylvania, Culpeper, Orange, Fairfax and Prince William counties, in which more precious blood was shed than in all the rest of the New World in four centuries, his heart failed him, veteran of many a hard-fought battle though he was. A million men surged back and forth time and again, advancing and retreating, from the Potomac to the James. For four, long years melancholy evidence everywhere revealed the unleashed fury of fratricidal strife.[15] Attila and his horde of Huns had no lesson in unnecessary cruelty, fire and sword, to learn from some of Virginia's in-

---

[14]One soldier wrote: "We found the people along our route obliging, hospitable and disposed to supply us with such food as they had to spare. They helped us on our way and gave us shelter at night."

[15]ALEXANDER H. STEPHENS traveled from Alexandria to Charlottesville months later (Oct. 15, '65), and wrote that the country was "horrible to behold."

WHITELAW REID passed through Virginia in August, 1865, and wrote that every fence was gone for miles and miles. Solitary chimneys stood where there had once been homes; masses of ruins and charred timbers where there had once been villages. "The country seemed absolutely desolate."

vaders. Let General Philip Henry Sheridan[16] speak for himself.

"The whole country from the Blue Ridge to the North Mountain had been made untenable for a rebel army. I have destroyed over two thousand barns filled with wheat, hay and farming implements, over seventy mills filled with wheat and flour, four herds of cattle have been driven before the army, not less than three thousand sheep have been killed and issued to the troops, a large number of horses have been obtained. Lieut. John R. Meigs was murdered near Dayton. For this atrocious act all houses within an area of five miles were burned."

There can be no question that General Sheridan told the truth. A returned Confederate soldier[17] abundantly verifies his report:

"At Scottsville we came upon Sheridan's trail, when his vandal horde came down from the Valley of Virginia. The village was a complete ruin; private and public property had alike been devastated, all put to the devouring flame. Every factory, shop, mill and store was burned. The canal locks were dismantled, records and books were torn and scattered about. The little town lay in its blackened pall like a mourner hopelessly weeping. Upon Sheridan and his gang the shame and infamy of such warfare must rest, a perpetual disgrace. Their work of hatred and extermination went on ruthlessly.

[16]Sheridan's official report quoted by J. LEWIS PEYTON, *Hist. of Augusta County*, p. 229.

E. P. OBERHOLTZER, *Hist. of U. S.*, p. 57: Sheridan and Sherman lead America's Vandals and Huns.

[17]B. W. JONES, *Under the Stars and Bars*, p. 269.

THE WATERFALL

Photo by W. H. T. S.

"The gentle valleys were lighted here and there, with the pure white petals of the dog-wood. The willows by the noisy little brooks shook out long pendants, green, succulent and graceful, their lancets trembling to the touch of the slightest breeze."—Page 43.

They destroyed mills, fences, barns, bridges, homes, crops, stock, and all supplies without mercy and without shame. These things I will record. They are true. I do not wish to stir old hatreds, but all the world should know this record of vandalism;[18] how the fathers were despoiled and the sons impoverished."

The homeward journey of the typical soldier was not always easy, even if he had his parole safely in his pocket. General Lee found it necessary[19] to ask General Grant for the release from prison of many soldiers paroled at Appomattox, and clapped into prison by some ignorant subaltern. He also protested against Federal officers requiring "oaths of paroled soldiers" before permitting them to continue their toilsome way unmolested (April 25, 1865).

And so the Confederate soldier passes into history. Of them, years after, Theodore Roosevelt said: "The world has never seen better soldiers than those who followed Lee, and their leader will undoubtedly rank as, without any exception, the very greatest of all the Captains the English-speaking peoples have brought forth."[20]

II

The desolation of the country, the death of their kindred and friends and the difficulty of the home-

[18] W. E. CARSON, *Historic Shrines*, p. 18: "Pohick Church was used as a stable by Union troops. The old square pews were cut up for firewood and the walls defaced."

[19] HENRY ALEXANDER WHITE, *Lee*, p. 427.

[20] LANDON C. BELL, *Address at Johnson's Island.*

MRS. ROGER A. PRYOR, *Reminiscences*, Chaps. XXV-VI.

ward journey were by no means the most acute
anguish which darkened the homes of Virginia and
the Southland. In the old homestead, sometimes
built in the shadow of great oaks and elms, and
sometimes set beside a pleasant brook or gurgling
spring, a broken and prematurely aged father, a
white-haired mother, a wife clothed in black, and
little children impatiently awaited the soldier's return.

When at last he reached the lane, or stood at gate
or door, joy and gladness, tears of rejoicing, shouts
of welcome, prayers of gratitude that could not be
restrained, buried the sorrows of the past in the
happiness of reunion.

They came straggling in, one by one, for days and
weeks and months[21] after the surrender. But the
joy was often tempered with a searching question,
"Where is your brother?"

They watched and waited long, hoping against
hope.[22] They could not know that on a sloping
plain beyond Saylor's Creek, in a shallow grave on
the ramparts of Petersburg, at Deatonsville or in
the red mud of Appomattox, the man for whom they
hoped, waited and prayed, was sleeping. The homes
of Virginia were filled with gladness . . . and with
grief.[23]

---

[21]One soldier wrote: "I reached home April 18, just nine days after the
surrender, having tramped about two hundred miles."

[22]FANNY MURDOUGH DOWNING:

> "He is taken and I am left;
> And as long as the world and this life remain,
> He will never come marching home again."

[23]Dr. Joseph N. Jones, of Surry County, Va., an aged Virginia gentleman,
not in the army, was thrown in prison and taken to Point Lookout, Md., Oct.
15, 1864. He was incarcerated while Sidney Lanier and John Banister Tabb

Not until that generation passed were the bitter sores healed.

"Norfolk Journal, December 6, 1866, Information is desired by his wife and helpless children of James Eveliegh, Company G., South Carolina Volunteers. He was wounded in April 1865, at Five Forks, and subsequently taken prisoner. Since then he has not been heard from. Any information thankfully received by Mrs. Hannah Eveliegh, Timmonsville, S. C."

For twenty months this widow with her "helpless children" crying for bread and clinging to her skirts watched the lane, the gate, the door by day and night. But James did not come. Multiply this broken heart one hundred thousand times and more beside.

There was a "James Eveliegh" in every county, country-side and village of every Commonwealth.[24] Who can compute the mental anguish, the bitter tears, the broken hearts and the torture the Confederate soldiers brought with their return or their failure to return from Appomattox.

And so the cruel months dragged on, as the sun set day by day in the garish west. Hope slowly faded from ten thousand human hearts, and a black night settled . . . a night that knew no stars.

---

were also prisoners there (see *Land of Decision*, p. 113). He wrote: "I hope that I was of some little service in relieving the sufferings of my fellow-prisoners. About 8,000 died at this prison during the war. The officers were kind, but we were rudely treated by the negro guards. Some prisoners were shot without the slightest provocation. On June 2, 1865, I was released, and arrived at my home the evening of June 3."

[24]P. D. GWALTNEY wrote: "I was captured (after Appomattox) and released July 2, 1865. I reached home (Smithfield, Va.) July 4, not having seen any member of my family for more than two-and-a-half years."

CHAPTER V

THE CAPTAINS DEPART

Thus far into the bowels of the land
Have we marched on without impediment.
—*William Shakespeare.*

The Confederates were by no means the only
soldiers in Virginia. Our roads and highways, streets
and towns swarmed with enlisted men. The Confederate became on the instant a private citizen
"until exchanged," but armies in blue uniforms
remained. They retired slowly northward, leaving
many regiments, with white faces and black, to
hold the Virginians in the stern grip of martial law.
Not for ten years were the last Union soldiers withdrawn from the South![1]

General Grant was in Washington, and the huge
army was gradually withdrawn from Appomattox,
eastward and northward. The largest wing of the
Federal army retreated to Burkeville (Sunday,
April 16), following the tracks of the Southside
Railway. The German Band gave a concert in
the streets of Farmville that day. During the week

[1] FRED L. PAXSON, *Recent Hist.*, p. 5, speaks of the novelty (and one that
people detested) of having garrisons and citadels in every town and bayonets
and sabres at the homes of peaceful citizens, on their streets, at their schools,
places of business and (God help us!) even in their churches.

President Rutherford B. Hayes withdrew the last troops from South
Carolina, April 10, 1877, and from Louisiana, April 20, 1877, twelve years
after the surrender.

these divisions retired to Petersburg, leaving garrisons at Nottoway, Black's and White's (Blackstone) and Wilson.

From Petersburg[2] the army retired to Richmond (May 1-6), passing over the James by the pontoon bridge. Bowling Green (May 9), Fredericksburg and Dumfries (May 12), were passed, and by the middle of May the army reached the Potomac.[3]

II

In the meantime the eyes of the world turned to the plains of North Carolina. Sherman and Joseph Eggleston Johnston signed "a convention," and 37,047 Confederates, officers and men, stacked their arms, furled their flags, parked their cannon, at Greensboro (April 26).

William Tecumseh Sherman followed the victorious army of General Grant. These victorious troops left Raleigh (May 10) for Washington, by way of Richmond. They camped in the fields south of James River, and marched into the city across pontoon bridges laid on the water. All day long they tramped . . . tramped . . . tramped by the Capitol of the Confederacy, "erect, exultant, trained to the highest state of healthy endurance and efficiency." They swung through the streets, bands playing, flags aflutter, with one long continuous

[2]JOSHUA LAWRENCE CHAMBERLAIN, *Passing of the Armies*: "We found the negroes especially unruly." They went into a frenzy, swarming into the homes of the people, demanding food, frightening the women, pilfering all they could lay their hands upon, and threatening to burn houses and barns.

[3]JOSHUA LAWRENCE CHAMBERLAIN, *Passing of the Armies* is interesting, detailed, but not scholarly, and often inaccurate.

cheer. With them went a very caravan of plunder, hundreds of wagons loaded with furniture, jewelry, silverware and other plunder from thousands of homes in the Carolinas, the heirlooms and wealth of two centuries.

General Henry Wager Halleck,[4] who lived in the White House of the Confederacy, where he had recently (April 22) succeeded General Weitzel, cheered them on. Let us follow them through Fredericksburg and Alexandria[5] to the great and final pageant.

The Grand Army, recently withdrawn from Appomattox, passed in brave and inspiring review Monday, May 22, before President Andrew Johnson, General U. S. Grant and the official aristocracy of Washington; senators, congressmen, members of the Supreme Court, of the Cabinet; ambassadors, admirals and generals. They marched with the elastic step of conquerors, brigade followed brigade, division followed division.

It need hardly be said that the vast concourse of spectators along Pennsylvania Avenue were quite beside themselves with triumph, joy and martial enthusiasm. It was a magnificent spectacle. Uncounted thousands of travel-worn and weather-bronzed, athletic soldiers, physically fit, actively intelligent, flushed with the pomp and circumstances of war, intoxicated with triumph and the glory of victory. The patched and bullet-ridden battle-flags, the brilliant stands of new colors, the horse,

---

[4]He was not a friend to General Sherman.

[5]They reached Alexandria and went into camp, Friday, May 19.

B. H. LIDDELL HART, *Sherman*, p. 401. Less than a week after General Grant's army passed.

the cannon and great guns, all maintained in efficiency and perfect discipline.

On Tuesday General Sherman's famous corps followed Monday's martial pageant. These thousands had marched from Chattanooga to the sea, and from the Savannah to the Potomac. They trod the dusty streets to martial music, for the last time— the war was won!

The ovation given Sherman[6] was possibly greater than that accorded Grant the day before. He led his men in person, flowers upon his shoulders, garlands showered upon him by a thousand ardent admirers; flowers, too, about his horse's neck. Behind him came the trophies of war, pillaged from ten thousand homes in the Carolinas; such a procession as the nation had never seen before, and such as we earnestly pray Americans will never see again; horses, mules, goats, chickens, dogs, raccoons, opossums; grinning little darkies, like little monkeys, riding great war-horses, some of them the mascots of regiments; hundreds of other negroes, "contrabands of war." When the parade passed Richmond one soldier played a piano mounted on a wagon. Whether the musician continued his exhibition along Pennsylvania Avenue we do not know.

When General Sherman reached the reviewing stand erected on the lawn of the White House, he dismounted, greeted Mrs. Sherman, shook hands with President Johnson and with each member of the Cabinet until he reached the Secretary of War,

---

[6] B. H. L. HART, *Sherman*, p. 401. Sherman's troops were reviewed Wednesday, May 24. The authorities give different dates: HENRY COPPEE, "the 23rd and 24th."

Edwin M. Stanton, upon whom he deliberately turned his back. It was rude, but Stanton richly deserved it. We quite agree with the scholar who wrote: "Stanton leaves a dark stain on American history,"[7] and with another who said that Stanton played the part of duplicity in Johnson's Cabinet.[8]

Sherman's name has never been forgotten in the Carolinas, as the name of Attila has never been forgotten in Germany. The stories of rapine, fire, pillage and theft; stories of invalids rolled out of beds, rings torn from the fingers of delicate and refined women, of silver stolen, costly furniture broken, heirlooms flung from the windows or deliberately tossed into the flames and a thousand other such details too well authenticated to be denied—all of which we would much prefer not to believe, or to forget.[9]

Long after the war was over and many wounds healed, General Sherman, old and, as always, popular, sat at a banquet-table with Henry W. Grady. In masterly and adroit style the young orator from Atlanta said:

"I want to say to General Sherman, who is considered an able man in our parts, though some people think he is a kind of careless man about fire, that from the ashes he left us in 1864 we have raised a brave and beautiful city; and have builded therein not one ignoble prejudice or memory."

---

[7] B. H. L. HART, *Sherman*, p. 396.

[8] THEO. CALVIN PEASE, *The U. S.*, Chap. XXVI.

[9] JOHN W. DANIEL, *Oration on Lee*, p. 59: "General Gordon, in his public address, declared to the people of York, Penn., 'If a torch is applied to a single dwelling, or an insult offered to a female of your town by a soldier of this command, point me out the man, and you shall have his life.'"

THE PONTOON BRIDGE

"General Lee crossed the James by a pontoon bridge below Mayo's Bridge, which had been burned and rode along Main Street through the burnt district to his home in Franklin Street near Capitol Square, Saturday morning, April 15, 1865." —Page 12.

The Army of the Potomac crossed the bridge, marching into Richmond for five days, May 1-6.

General Sherman, up from Carolina, passed over with his army a week later, reaching Alexandria May 19.—Page 50.

Victors and vanquished have gone now, one and all, to the Judgment Bar of God—and to mercy and forgiveness, let us trust!

III

In striking contrast to the blaze of joy and victory on the left bank of the Potomac, the bitterness, sorrow and desolation[10] on the right bank could not be exaggerated. In the words of our Virginia poet, "Unmerciful disaster followed fast and followed faster." It seemed as though God and man had deserted the proud Virginians in those dark days of tempest and of trouble.

There was only one statesman who found a voice, and only one leader who pointed to a star of hope in the blackness of the night, Alexander Hugh Holmes Stuart, of Staunton. Let us visit him in his colonial and ancestral home on the sloping hillside beside Trinity Church, where he was born (April 2, 1807), six weeks exactly after Robert E. Lee opened his eyes at Stratford. The delicate lad spent a year at William and Mary; took law at the University, recently established at Charlottesville (1827), and was admitted to the bar (1828).

Ante-bellum Virginia was so thoroughly committed to the democracy of Andrew Jackson that she cast her electoral vote, time and time again, against her own sons! It is quite astonishing that William Henry Harrison, John Tyler and Zachary Taylor,

---

[10]Sir Walter Ralegh, the first Governor of Virginia, described Ireland as "a commonwealth of common woe." It was prophetic of Virginia in the Reconstruction era.

See also DON P. HALSEY, *Sketch of Capt. Halsey*, pp. 15-16.

were not elevated to the presidency by Virginia's vote, but in spite of her vote. The wealth, culture and better leadership of Virginia was largely in the Whig camp, but the Whigs were usually a minority by perhaps 10,000 votes.

It is evidence of their prejudice and ignorance that the Congressmen at Washington rung the changes on the "aristocrats of Virginia," the bloated and cruel slave-drivers and secessionists. The fact is that the aristocrats of Virginia and the wealthy class were bitterly opposed to secession. A rich man is always conservative and opposed to any revolution. It was not the rich aristocrats, but the poor devils on the tobacco farms who swung the State into war and proved our ruin. Both Stuart and Lee were aristocrats, rich, Whigs, strong for the Union, and vehemently opposed to Calhounism.

Stuart began his long and splendid career as a delegate to the Young Men's Whig convention at Washington (May 7, 1832). Captain Robert E. Lee was also a delegate. After serving three years in the House of Delegates (1836-1839) Stuart was elected to Congress in the "Tippecanoe and Tyler, too" campaign (1840). He was a presidential elector on the Clay ticket (1844), but Virginia repudiated her own son, Henry Clay, and voted for James K. Polk. Four years later he was a Taylor-Fillmore elector, but again Virginia repudiated her own son and voted for General Lewis Cass.

Nevertheless Fillmore appointed Stuart Secretary of the Interior (1850). Augusta County sent Stuart to the Secession Convention (1861) as a Union man. William Ballard Preston and George W. Randolph with Stuart called upon the newly inaugurated President at the White House, April 12, 1861, at one o'clock.

Abraham Lincoln deliberately snubbed the Virginians, and rebuffed all their efforts for conciliation.[11] In the subsequent debate on secession Stuart pictured the frightful menace that threatened Virginia. With eloquence he urged deliberation, conciliation and delay. He would await a change in the President[12] and in the administration at Washington.

Despite his best efforts and large influence the die was cast, April 17, by a vote of 88 to 55. A change of 17 votes would have held Virginia (and probably North Carolina, Tennessee and Arkansas) in the Union. That President Lincoln, by a sympathetic and conciliatory attitude, could have controlled those 17 votes cannot be controverted. The Lincoln of 1861 contrasts strangely with the Lincoln of 1865.

Stuart would not sign the fatal Ordinance of Secession until Virginia was actually invaded. Then he added his signature, stood with his people and suffered with them.

Now that the Confederate cause was sunk in the "gloom of an eternal night," now that all government was completely paralyzed, now that many of the state's wisest and best leaders rotted in untimely graves, and those that survived were completely discredited, Alexander H. H. Stuart was the first to

[11]This strange conduct, so unlike the Lincoln of later years, was probably due to the unfortunate influence of such radicals as Benjamin Franklin Wade and Edwin M. Stanton, who then seemed to have Lincoln's ear.

[12]Stuart knew Lincoln, though but slightly, in the old days when both were Whigs. Stuart intimated that Lincoln was unfortunate in his advisers at this time.

come to the rescue of Virginia. The agony and horror he had so eloquently foretold and endeavored to avert had befallen, yet his was the first hand to stanch the wounds of war.

A month had not yet passed[13] since the surrender, thousands of wandering and footsore soldiers had not yet reached home, the grand pageant of the returning armies had not yet been staged in Washington, when Alex. H. H. Stuart[14] and others called a meeting of the substantial citizens of Augusta County at the courthouse in Staunton, Monday, May 8.

This first gesture of peace called forth a vigorous and unreasonable protest from the fugitive Governor of Virginia, William Smith, known to his contemporaries as "Extra Billy."

When Richmond was hurriedly evacuated (Sunday, April 2), Governor Smith left by canal-boat for Lynchburg, which he reached Thursday. He pushed southward to Danville, when it became the provisional "Capital of the Confederacy."

After Lee's surrender the Governor (a governor no longer) took refuge in Rockbridge County. A reward of $25,000 was offered for "Extra Billy,"[15] but he was not betrayed, although thousands of Virginians knew his whereabouts.

---

[13]RUDOLPH BUMGARDNER: "In old Augusta the very first movement in the South was organized to reestablish peace between the Northern and Southern states and to restore Virginia to the Federal Union."

[14]ALEX. HUGH HOLMES STUART, born April 2, 1807; died February 12, 1891.

[15]*Through Centuries Three*, SQUIRES, Chaps. CV and CX.

R. A. BROCK, *Eminent Virginians*, p. 383.

JOS. A. WADDELL: "The Governor goes armed with a brace of pistols, and his servant carries a gun or two. He has returned from Staunton to Lexington."

He was greatly displeased with the proposed convention at Staunton, and actually hurried to that town. Sunday afternoon (May 7) he met twenty influential citizens at the American Hotel, and was emphatic and vehement in his protest.[16]

It must be remembered that "Extra Billy" had been a great Democratic leader for many years, and A. H. H. Stuart[17] an influential Whig. Even in the dismal days of calamity the two patriots could not agree.[18] But on this occasion "Extra Billy," in the language of the street, made a fool of himself. When the convention assembled next day, Stuart made the following address:

"The war is over. We must prepare for peace. Guerilla warfare[19] would be worse than useless. Let us demand our rights, reorganize Virginia under the Constitution of the United States, and accept cheerfully and promptly the decisions of the war."[20]

[16]ALEX. H. H. STUART, *Narrative*: "Governor Smith rode to Staunton, twenty-five miles or more, arriving about noon, Sunday, May 7. He met about fifteen or twenty gentlemen about three in the afternoon."

[17]ALEX. F. ROBERTSON, *Stuart*, pp. 152-153.

[18]THOS. P. ABERNATHY, *Dict. of Amer. Biog.*, Vol. XVIII.

H. H. SIMMS, *Rise of the Whigs in Virginia*.

A. C. COLE, *Whigs*: "In person Stuart was over six feet tall, handsome and dignified, serious but affable."

[19]Both Stuart and Lee denounced all suggestions for sniping in the sequestered mountain district after the familiar custom of our Latin-American neighbors.

[20]J. A. WADDILL, *Annals of Augusta*, p. 509: "Monday night, May 8. The county meeting came off today and was attended by many people. A committee was appointed to go to Richmond to ascertain what liberty would be allowed in regard to the re-establishment of the State government. Resolutions were adopted that the contest is now ended and a State Convention should be held."

The day after the Staunton meeting President Johnson issued this proclamation:

"That all acts and proceedings of the political military and civil organizations which have been in a state of insurrection and rebellion within the State of Virginia against the authority and the laws of the United States, and of which Jefferson Davis, John Letcher and William Smith were late the representative chiefs, are declared null and void. All persons who shall exercise any political, military or civil power, authority, jurisdiction or right, by, through or under Jefferson Davis, late of the City of Richmond, and his confederates, or under John Letcher or William Smith, or civil commission or authority issued by them, or either of them, since the 17th day of April, 1861, shall be deemed and taken as in rebellion against the United States and shall be dealt with accordingly."

In this involved English, difficult to follow but not difficult to understand, the President further admonished the faithful to aid Governor Francis Harrison Pierpont "in all lawful measures which he may take for the extension and administration" of Virginia.

On Wednesday of this busy week (May 10) Stuart and a committee[21] called on General Duval,[22] then in Staunton. The General was very polite but replied that his instructions were to "restore order" and to "parole Confederate soldiers." Failing to

[21]The committee was composed of Mr. Stuart, William M. Tate, John B. Baldwin, M. G. Harman and Judge Hugh W. Sheffey.

[22]Isaac Harden Duval was born in Wellsburg, Brooke Co., Va. (now the Pan Handle of West Virginia), Sept. 1, 1824. He volunteered, and was made Major of Infantry May 1, 1861, and became a Brigadier Nov. 1, 1864.

get satisfaction from General Duval the committee traveled to Richmond and interviewed the satrap of the State, in the "White House of the Confederacy." General Halleck[23] adroitly sidestepped the issue and courteously informed the Staunton gentlemen that Governor Pierpont was coming . . . see him!

As the Governor of Virginia was still in Alexandria and did not bring his ambulance loaded with archives to Richmond until two weeks later, the Staunton committee returned whence they came. Let none condemn their effort as an idle gesture. Other large and influential counties followed Augusta in these peace overtures. Though the effort failed, it proves to posterity and the world how anxious the Virginians were to meet any reasonable terms. Stuart, as their leader, was endeavoring to evade the dire dangers which threatened. Unfortunately Governor Pierpont knew less (and was less) even than the military satraps. He arrived May 26, 1865.

The Staunton commissioners awaited developments, and none with a more astute eye upon the horizon than Alex. H. H. Stuart, as we shall see.

IV

The famous Valley of Virginia presented, during the summer of 1865, a scene of utmost desolation. From Staunton to Winchester and Harper's Ferry few trees remained, the fences were gone, the farms were growing crops of briars, nettles and weeds. Almost every landscape had clusters of soldiers'

---

[23]Henry Wager Halleck commanded in Richmond from April 22 to July 1, 1865.

graves—Union and Confederate. Gaunt chimneys everywhere offered pathetic evidence that once a home had stood upon the deserted spot. The land was at peace—the peace of a corpse. Silence followed the rumble of cannon and the shout of conflict; it was the silence of death.

The worst desolation was about the now prosperous village of Stephenson, where the interstate line crosses the Valley. Here about four-fifths of all property, personal and public, had been destroyed. Many who survived were threatened with actual starvation. John Esten Cooke, a talented son of this section, wrote, long afterward: "Is it wrong to remember the past? I think of it without bitterness. God did it—God the All-wise and Almighty for His purpose. I do not indulge in repining nor reflect with rancor upon the issues of the struggle."[24]

Among the soldiers stationed in Winchester at this time were two Presidents of the United States, General Rutherford B. Hayes[25] and Major William McKinley. The young Major was initiated into the Masonic fraternity (May 1, 1865). He returned to Winchester (May 20, 1899), as President, and was received with that cordial hospitality Virginians know so well how to bestow.

---

[24]To the cry of this patriotic Virginian we would reply that it would be wrong, very wrong, not to remember the past. And, while we cannot subscribe to all his philosophy, for we think that the Devil has a hand in all wars, we can but honor so brave a soldier as John Esten Cooke, who could both forget and forgive.

[25]H. J. ECKENRODE, *Hayes*, p. 73, says Hayes' flag was the first to enter the town.

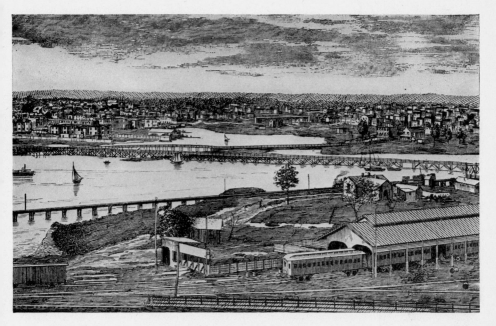

Long after the war was over General Sherman sat at a banquet-table with Henry W. Grady. The young orator from Atlanta said, "I want to say to General Sherman, who is considered an able man in our parts though some think him careless about fire, that from the ashes he left us in 1864 we have raised a brave and beautiful city; and have builded therein not one ignoble prejudice or memory."—Page 52.

Such may be said of Norfolk. The city as it appeared in 1870 is shown above. The city as it appears from the same view-point is shown below. Even before this book is published other buildings will be rising.

CHAPTER VI

FRANCIS HARRISON PIERPONT

I do not pretend to understand Maryland, but if
I understand anything about Virginia, they are as
good-natured, tractable people as any in the world;
and you may do what you will with them by way of
civility. But you will never be able to manage them
in the way you speak of, by hampering and keeping
them under.

—*James Blair.*[1]

President Andrew Johnson issued a proclamation,
May 10, 1865, the day following the mass meeting
at Staunton, as stated:

"To establish the authority of the United States
and to execute the laws within the geographical
limits known as the State of Virginia." All acts of
Confederate days were declared null and void. All
acts signed by Governors Letcher and Smith[2] were
also declared illegal.

All the laws of the Federal Government were declared operative in Virginia. "To carry into effect
the guaranty of the Federal Constitution and a
republican form of State government, to afford the
advantage and security of domestic laws, as well as
to complete the re-establishment of the authority

---

[1]Quotation from a letter of Commissary James Blair to Governor Francis
Nicholson, written in 1700.

[2]John Letcher, Governor of Virginia, 1860-4, and William Smith, Governor,
1864-5.

Through Centuries Three, SQUIRES, pp. 468-485.

Although the President was not a learned man, he should have known
that Virginia was a "Commonwealth" and not a "State."

and laws of the United States and the full and complete restoration of peace within the limits aforesaid, Francis H. Pierpont,[3] Governor of Virginia, will be aided by the Federal Government as far as may be necessary in the lawful measures he may take for the extension and administration of the State Government throughout the geographical limits of the said State."

With the presidential endorsement thus given, Governor Pierpont moved into the plain but dignified executive mansion, which occupies an inconspicuous corner of Capitol Square. He was thrust, by the sensational fall of the Confederacy, into a position of prominence, which was often embarrassing. His record did not commend him to the Virginians. His talents were meagre and his policy necessarily mild and usually colorless.

John Sergeant Wise speaks of him as a "portly, aged man who enjoyed his prominence" and "a kindly, respectable man who was anxious to get the State restored to its constitutional rights," whose consideration for the Virginians, brought down upon him the wrath of the Radicals at the nation's capital.[4]

---

[3]DR. ELLIS PAXSON OBERHOLTZER, in his scholarly histories, spells the Governor's name Peirpont, but we do not know upon what authority.

[4]JOHN SERGEANT WISE, *Lion's Skin*, pp. 189-190.

WHITELAW REID, *A Southern Tour*, p. 319: "The vulgar, drunken governor."

Through Centuries Three, SQUIRES, Chap. CXI.

R. A. BROCK, *Eminent Virginians*, p. 389.

The Richmond Whig: "He has secured for himself a hold on the good will of the Virginians that neither the defamation of malice nor the intrigues of knavery can dislodge."

JOSEPH SEGAR: "A man of ability, character and heart."

Pierpont, now so completely forgotten, was born in Monongalia County, four miles east of Morgantown (January 25, 1814), at present the University town of West Virginia. His grandfather, John Pierpont, came from New York to Virginia in 1770, and erected a blockhouse as protection against the Indians. He married a daughter of Colonel L. Morgan, whose name is retained in the prosperous, mountain city.

The future governor's father, Francis Pierpont, married Catherine Weaver, the daughter of Joseph Weaver, a Pennsylvania farmer, who came up the valley of the Monongahela River into Virginia in 1785.

When the fairies presented this gift to the Pierpont family,[5] Joe Johnson, destined to precede the new-born babe in the gubernatorial chair, was a popular young captain at Bridgeport. Stonewall Jackson, another neighbor, followed Francis into this troubled world some nine years later.

When he was two years old (1814) his father moved to a farm two miles from Fairmont. The growing lad received a good education for the time and place. In 1835 he entered Alleghany College, Meadville, Penn., from which he graduated. He taught school in Virginia and Mississippi, while he diligently read law. When the Baltimore and Ohio was built across the mountains and valleys of Northwestern Virginia, he became their counsel, and he was also active in coal, land and factory properties.

---

[5]HARDESTY, p. 389, has an excellent biography of Governor Pierpont, which we judge is autobiographical.

The young and prosperous attorney married Julia, a daughter of Rev. Samuel Robinson, a Presbyterian clergyman of New York. He had been reared a Methodist. Like the great majority of his fellow citizens in Virginia's great, growing and prosperous Northwest, Pierpont was hostile to slavery. A short residence in the raw and new territory of Mississippi confirmed his natural antipathy against the system.

A staunch Whig, he followed with the great majority of anti-slavery Old Line Whigs into the Republican camp. He served (as did Alexander H. H. Stuart) as a Harrison-Tyler elector, although Virginia voted Democratic.

When the triangular contest of 1860 tore the Democratic party asunder, Pierpont boldly charged that the Breckenridge Democrats deliberately divided the party, to insure the election of Lincoln and afford an excuse for secession. This charge was frequently repeated by John Minor Botts and other Whigs.

When, at last, the fatal ordinance passed the Virginia Convention (April 17, 1861) Pierpont was one of the first, if not the very first, to plan the erection of a "loyal Virginia" in the northwestern mountain land.[6]

A popular convention at Wheeling (May 11, 1861) repudiated the Ordinance of Secession, but adjourned after two days of futile discussion. Pierpont proposed a Committee of Safety, harking back to Revolutionary precedent at Williamsburg. It was his theory that secession automatically vacated all the offices of the Commonwealth.

---

[6] *Through Centuries Three*, SQUIRES, pp. 487-497.

A second convention with representatives from forty counties met (June 11) in the Customs House at Wheeling. Various measures were adopted, and Pierpont was elected "Provisional Governor of Virginia," succeeding John Letcher, who had not resigned (June 25).

The first official act of Governor Pierpont was to inform President Lincoln that Virginia was in insurrection. He requested the Federal Government to suppress the same. As there were fully 100,000 men in battle array, protecting or threatening Washington, we presume that President Lincoln was not surprised at the news from Wheeling! However, he promised to protect "loyal Virginia" and thereby placed the seal of executive approval upon these secessionists, who seceded from the State because the State seceded from the Union.[7]

When President Lincoln discussed the formation and admission of the new State with his Cabinet, three favored it, as a war measure, and three opposed it as unconstitutional and as a virtual fraud. Chase, Seward and Stanton voted for it; Bates, Blair and Welles disapproved.

When the bill came before Congress (December 10, 1862) the House passed the bill to admit the new State (pro 96, contra 55). Lincoln proclaimed West Virginia April 19, 1863, and the new State was admitted June 20, 1863. In Abraham Lincoln's

---

[7]When Senator Waitman Thomas Willey of "Virginia" presented a "Memorial," asking Congress to dismember "Virginia" and form the new State, Senator John S. Carlile opposed the plan as revolutionary and unconstitutional. The Senator was an anti-Confederate Virginian.

career this is his most vulnerable point.[8]   He is said
to have exclaimed, when he signed the bill, "It is a
war measure and will not be precedent in times of
peace."   That was not very honest in Honest Abe.[9]

Francis Harrison Pierpont might have become
the first governor of West Virginia, which he did
so much to create.   Strangely, he preferred to remain "Governor of Virginia."   As Governor Pierpont and "loyal Virginia" had requested the formation of a new State, and as the request had been
granted, Governor Pierpont must needs move without the territory of West Virginia and fix his capital
in "Virginia."

In 1863 a small part of Eastern Virginia was held
securely by Federal forces.   The people of Alexandria, Fairfax and adjacent counties were, and are,
intense Virginians.   It suited President Lincoln,
however, to recognize Governor Pierpont of Virginia
at Alexandria, and it is interesting to watch the
fiction grow slowly into accomplished fact.

The Governor called a State convention[10] (May

---

[8]LYON G. TYLER, Tyler's Mag., Oct., 1928, p. 96 (quoting JAMES C. MC
GREGOR, *Disruption of Va.*).

[9]New Jersey Protest, Tyler's Magazine, Oct., 1931, p. 83: "Against the
creation of new states by the division of existing ones in . . . manner not authorized by the Constitution. . . . And against the right of secssion as admitted by Congress in admitting a new state once a part of Virginia (abbre-
viated)."

[10]SAMUEL W. MC CALL, *Stevens*, p. 269, says that Pierpont assembled twelve
men from fragments of eleven townships out of 149 counties (in the undivided
commonwealth), and called it a "Constitutional Convention of Virginia."
They wrote a "Constitution," had an election and Pierpont was elected Governor, receiving 3,300 votes.   He was proclaimed, in the Market-house of
Alexandria, "I am fond of genteel comedy, but this farce is too vulgar to be
enacted on the stage of nations."
Yet Lincoln endorsed this proposition.

14-15, 1863), at which he was renominated "Governor of Virginia." He was later elected by 3,755 votes, with L. C. P. Cowper, Lieutenant-Governor, and T. R. Bowden, Attorney-General. There were delegates from Alexandria, Norfolk, Spotsylvania, Loudoun, Berkeley, Fairfax and Fauquier counties. Fractions of these counties were "Virginia," Federally speaking.

The "Legislature of Virginia" met at Alexandria, December 7, 1863, six senators and seven delegates. Nothing daunted they met again December 5, 1864, and elected two senators to represent "Virginia" in the United States Senate—John C. Underwood and Joseph Segar. Though President Lincoln recognized Pierpont and his legislature the Congress flatly refused to seat the senators-elect!

During the summer of 1864 Pierpont's jurisdiction was very materially enlarged by the persistent and successful drives and offensives of General Grant. The Confederate defense was shifted from the Rappahannock to the James.

Meantime General Benjamin F. Butler[11] persuaded Norfolk and Princess Anne counties to secede from "loyal Virginia." Secession became the prevailing fashion with our Northern friends in all parts of Virginia; west, north and east. Lincoln, Pierpont and Butler advocated and actually accomplished the secession of various counties from the State. General Butler and three hundred of his friends in Norfolk voted to secede from Pierpont's Virginia

---

[11]T. J. WERTENBAKER, *Hist. of Norfolk*, p. 254: "The bitterness occasioned by unnecessary cruelties of Federal occupation through three years renders 'the name of Butler ever infamous in Norfolk'."

and remain under the benign military government of
Butler. As only sixteen persons voted against
Butler, it is evident that the citizens of Norfolk
(who were really Norfolk citizens) did not vote.

Governor Pierpont appealed to the President
against the General, but the President declined to
interfere, as Butler had much influence with the
press! As Horace Greeley once said, "Abe was
always shrewd."

A week before he was assassinated[12] President
Lincoln authorized General Weitzel to permit the
"gentlemen who have acted as the Legislature of
Virginia" to meet. But the President did not refer
to the pathetic group at Alexandria. He referred
to the Confederate General Assembly at Richmond.
The inconsistency of the whole Federal program
from the secession of Virginia to the end of Reconstruction is amazing. It taxes credulity.

The proclamation of Andrew Johnson quoted
above made Pierpont really Governor of Virginia.
In wartime anything may happen.

Virginia was really a conquered province, although
in Johnson's proclamation the Commonwealth is
guaranteed "a republican form of State government." Francis Harrison Pierpont, in the Executive
Mansion, was, through his entire term, more a
puppet than an executive. A blockade runner, captured during the war, was put at the Governor's
disposal. His family and household effects went
aboard[13] with him and the aquatic moving van

---

[12]April 6, 1865.

[13]W. C. PENDLETON, *Hist. of Tazewell Co.*, p. 631.

Executive Journal, May 23, 1865: "His Excellency, the Governor, in

WILLIAM SMITH
Governor of Virginia, 1846-'49; 1864-'65

Most picturesque of Executives,
A Man of the People,
A Patriot of Patriots,
Aged 65 he volunteered to fight,
A Major-General, C. S. A., in the field,
Called again in seige, blood and fire
To shepherd Virginia,
He served to the bitter end.
An uncompromising Democrat,
He would have none of Whigs
Nor tolerate Whiggery.
He opposed the New Movement
But offered nothing better.
"Extra Billy," to friend and foe,
A Soubriquet he loved,
Stands in bronze
Upon the sward of Capitol Square
And gazes fixedly upon
The scenes he loved.

—Pages 56 and 57

steamed down the Potomac and Chesapeake and
up the James to Richmond, arriving May 30, after
a delightful voyage of four days. Salvos of cannon
were fired in his honor and a military reception
tendered him at the Mansion.

The state officers also came to Richmond from
Alexandria by water, landing at Richmond May 25.
A large concourse of citizens welcomed them. L.
C. P. Cowper, Lieutenant-Governor, was, by virtue
of his office, President of the Senate. The other
officers were T. R. Bowden, Attorney-General;
Charles H. Lewis, Secretary of the Commonwealth;
W. W. Wing, Treasurer, and L. W. Webb, State
Auditor. It was they, we presume, with some
citizens, who arranged the salvos of artillery and
the military reception for His Excellency.

II

President Johnson (May 29) issued a peace
proclamation with amnesty for all who took part in
"the late rebellion" except some thirteen classes!

Among those specifically excepted, and who must
seek personal pardons from the generous Presidential
hands, were such as possessed $20,000 worth of
property. This led to a prompt protest. A number of prominent Virginians[14] called at the White
House in July, and explained that this exception was

---

pursuance of the authority in him vested by the laws of the Commonweath
and upon due information of the suppression of insurrection and domestic
violence within the limits of the Commonwealth, ordered that the seat of
government be restored to and re-established in the City of Richmond from
and after this date; and issued his proclamation accordingly."

[14]The following were appointed at a mass meeting to represent Richmond,
to-wit: J. Alfred Jones, L. A. Lancaster, W. H. Haxall and J. L. Apperson.

unnecessarily severe and tended to halt business recovery. But the President was adamant.

"It was the wealthy men who dragooned the people into secession. I know how the thing was done. You rich men used the press and bullied your little men to force the State into secession." The visitors departed crestfallen. It was impossible! And to this day that false and foolish fabrication is repeated by countless historians, despite the fact that the wealth and culture of Virginia and the South were in the Whig camp, and that the "rich men" did their utmost to prevent secession.

III

June brought sinister developments, which boded ill for State and Nation. The Radical elements of Virginia met at Alexandria (June 12) and declared the conciliatory policies of Lincoln and Johnson would place the State again in the control of "rebels" and secessionists. They advocated that "the Constitution should be amended to confer the right of suffrage, upon loyal male citizens only, and without regard to color."

They[15] condemned Pierpont as too lenient, too sym-

---

[15]S. Ferguson Beach, President of this Radical Convention, evidently sought to capitalize the prejudices of the North and West, especially emphatic after Lincoln's tragic fall, to political advantage.

    1.   Every rebel must be disfranchised.

    2.   Every loyal male should vote, be he black or white.

    3.   Virginia must be reduced to the status of a territory, and kept under bayonet rule for an indefinite time.

These were the chief planks in the platform of those who referred to themselves as "patriotic Virginians."

pathetic and friendly with "rebels" and "traitors" among whom he now lived in Richmond. The Radicals hoped that Congress would regard the Pierpont Government as merely temporary. They waved the bloody shirt frantically to the Radical press of the North and West. They pleaded with the civilized and enlightened people North of the Potomac and Ohio to save the Virginians. Virginia should be reduced at once to the status of a territory. Congress should rule the State with the aid of Underwood, Hawxhurst, Hunnicutt and other patriots. But they must be vigorously sustained by the Federal Army.

It is a short step from Alexandria to Washington. The whole Radical plea sounds so like Thaddeus Stevens—even the very words used—that we judge it was inspired by that eminent statesman.

The day after the Radical Convention at Alexandria spoke for Negro suffrage, a grand jury at Norfolk arraigned Robert E. Lee and Jefferson Davis for treason.[16] The penalty for treason is hanging. The anger and resentment of the Virginians at such a gesture was only equaled by their helplessness.

General Lee wrote General Grant, asking if he was not protected from such persecution by the terms of surrender. General Grant replied very promptly and emphatically that he was, and so notified the President. Andrew was President, but Ulysses was king in 1865. Nothing came of the

[16]G. F. MILTON, *Age of Hate*, p. 192.

indictment but a vast amount of excitement, bitterness and hatred.[17]

Meanwhile, to make bad matters worse, the trial
of those who had aided John Wilkes Booth was going
forward. No less a person than Edwin M. Stanton,
Secretary of War, did his utmost to link Jefferson
Davis and Robert E. Lee with Booth. He even
employed self-confessed perjurers to testify that the
Southern leaders were privy to Booth's plans. "But
it became clear that such schemes were utterly
absurd. No Confederate was ever brought to trial
on the assassination charge."

During this dreadful month of June (22) there was
a near-battle between the Union soldiers stationed
in Norfolk "to protect our republican form of government" and the Negroes, "the wards of the
nation." The soldiers stormed the Negro section
with pistols, rocks and brick-bats, and spread terror
among them, raiding dance-halls, saloons and other
vicious resorts. Next day young Negroes, armed
with bludgeons and cursing the "poor white trash"
in blue uniforms, assaulted the soldiers. The mayor
"requested" General Mann to control his troops and
to prevent further riots.[18]

IV

While Norfolk was seething with disorder, in which
the citizens were merely spectators and victims, the

[17]JAMES BARNES, *The Son of Light Horse Harry Lee*, p. 241, states that the
same day, June 13, General Lee wrote President Johnson, asking for amnesty,
and tendering his oath of allegiance. The letter was completely ignored.

[18]*Norfolk Post*, Jan. 2, 1866, gives details. The Mayor was Thomas C.
Tabb, an influential Old Line Whig before the war.

T. J. WERTENBAKER, *Norfolk, Southern Port*, pp. 256-257.

Governor called the General Assembly into "extra session," June 23, for the regular session adjourned March 7. It was their final meeting.

This august body of three senators and nine delegates in the drawing room of the executive mansion, changed the "Constitution of Virginia" recently adopted at Alexandria, that those who had taken part in the "rebellion" might vote.

The Governor said to them: "It is folly to suppose that a State can be governed under a republican form of government when (in a large area) nineteen-twentieths of the people are disfranchised, and cannot hold office." They passed a resolution commending the pacific policies of President Johnson, and declared his reconstruction measures, "eminently wise, just and proper." In that they spoke well. They made the legal rate of interest 7¾ per centum, raised taxes and declared for a moratorium on debts. At adjournment (June 23) Speaker James Madison Downey congratulated the Assembly: "Virginia is now safe. Whatever they may do to the other States, they can not now saddle Negro suffrage upon us."

But Speaker Downey[19] spake not the sentiment of the three S's who hissed like venomous serpents at Washington, in Cabinet (Stanton), Senate (Sumner), and House (Stevens).

Joseph Segar, the Senator-elect, who had been denied a seat in the United States Senate a year before, declared, in an address at Monumental Hall, Richmond (June 22):

[19]James Madison Downey was speaker and George Tucker, clerk.

"The legislature now assembled, small as it is, has shown much wisdom, generosity and statesmanship. They have admitted the right of suffrage to nearly the whole people. I am in high hope, as the skies seem brightening. With the incubus of slavery removed we shall move forward and attain an eminence not dreamed of in any man's philosophy."

This ominous month of June closed with a meeting of the Unconditional Union Men at Winchester, who, like their brothers at Alexandria, were opposed to any "rebel" voting or holding office; but the Negroes should, one and all, be allowed to vote.

Simultaneously S. Ferguson Beach, Lysander Hall and W. J. Cowing of Alexandria, issued an "Address to the North" (June 30), in which they gave a brief history of "Restored Virginia" and protested the wise and generous attitude of the Rump Legislature. They condemned Pierpont as "totally disloyal" and added that "the Union men of Virginia are now in the position of a conquered people," their only hope being the substantial aid of our loyal government and "our colored population."

There was a municipal election in Richmond (July 25), not important in itself but conspicuous in its repercussions. The Commonwealth's Attorney and keeper of the almshouse were Confederate soldiers. Manifestly the "rebels" were again about to gain control of Richmond! The Federal satrap in the "White House," General John Wesley Turner, set aside the election; yet President Johnson had a month before guaranteed to Virginia a republican form of government!

"Rebels" could not hold office in Richmond. The

Governor took the cue and issued an order forbidding
any Confederate soldier to hold office in Virginia.
It was an earnest of what the Radical Congress had
in store for the South.

During this dreary summer of many calamities
the United States marshals were as busy as bees
libelling the property of "rebels." Valuable realty
was bought in at a fraction of its value by Radicals
and their friends, or simply confiscated. To the
Governor's honor and honesty, be it said, his tact
and diplomacy saved thousands of citizens litigation
which for years followed as an aftermath of Reconstruction.

The state swarmed with "pardon brokers," a
peculiarly vicious form of human vermin. Threatening all manner of vengeance, especially upon the
ignorant, inexperienced or friendless, who had been
guilty of "treason," the "agent," who had "many
influential friends in Congress," would "for a consideration" (a mere matter of fifty dollars or so)
procure a pardon for the "rebel," which would
save him, his family, his home from future trouble.
Once paid the "agent" would likely disappear and
never be seen again except in some other city to
fleece other "rebels and traitors." The victims had
absolutely no redress. But Governor Pierpont did
his utmost to protect the helpless and gullible against
these impostors.

V

Under the benign rule of Federal bayonets the
liberty of the press was entirely suspended. The
Richmond Whig, a liberal paper, and one which

constantly urged the people to accept the inevitable
and make the best of it until the storm was passed,
gave offense and was suspended from July 11 to 26
by General John Wesley Turner. The editor called
President Johnson's thirteenth exception to the
Amnesty Proclamation "heathenish," and the threat
of confiscation "mean and cowardly." "General
Terry suppressed the paper," says Dr. Oberholtzer.
That honor is General Turner's.[20]

The Petersburg News was suspended in June, and
the Richmond Bulletin in October. The Richmond
Examiner, the most pronounced Southern paper,
was not only suspended but the editor, John Mitchell,
was clapped into prison at Fortress Monroe. We
are not writing of Poland under the Czar, but of Virginia under the heel of the United States Army.

General E. O. C. Ord was appointed to command
in Virginia, July 1, 1865. His record was not
assuring. It was he who arrested Colonel McCordle,
an editor, and confined him in a military prison
(November 13, 1867), two and a half years after the
war, because the editor criticized General Ord and
the Radical Congress for their many iniquities. To
be sure that had not yet come to pass, but General
Ord was the same person and, as we suppose, had
the same psychology.

Trouble in Norfolk continued, but not with the
late "rebels." "Shameful outrages" were committed
on the Negroes by the "New York white soldiers."[21]
There were riots almost every day. Two Negroes
were "found dead," dangling from trees. If a Negro

---

[20]*Richmond Enquirer*: "No longer is a free press the bulwark of the state."
[21]E. P. OBERHOLTZER, *Hist. of U. S.*, Vol. I, p. 101.

FRANCIS HARRISON PIERPONT
Governor of Virginia, 1865-'68
Father of West Virginia

"I am satisfied that no state can be governed under a Republican form of government, when three-fourths of the people, embracing the largest taxpayers are disfranchised and denied a voice in making or executing the laws of the state."—Page 90.

appeared on the streets, he was attacked by ruffian soldiers and sailors. There was a reign of terror in the "black districts." Norfolk had been under martial law by the United States Army since May 10, 1862!

During the war, when the women and children of the South were left without their natural protectors, Negroes were "placed on many rebels' farms," said one observer. But when the soldiers returned the squatters fled. "The superintendent of the Freedmen's Bureau" estimates that 70,000 freedmen have been so ejected.

Negro troops in garrison at Wilmington, N. C., caused so much dissatisfaction among the resident colored population that the entire city was in peril.[22]

There were 15,000 vagrant Negroes near Hampton to whom the government issued rations; and 40,000 between Old Point and Newport News. This section presented a picture of desolation. There were no houses, nor fences, nor crops, only one vast common covered with brush and weeds. And to make bad matters worse small-pox raged among the idlers. There were white men, too, with the Negroes, who claimed to be Union soldiers. Virginia has never known so near an approach to anarchy.[23]

At this time many political, church and patriotic meetings in the North and West were fervently singing Julia Ward Howe's "Battle Hymn of the Republic," and saw no irony in the words:

---

[22]Item in *Richmond Whig*, Aug. 1, 1865.

[23]*Richmond Whig*, Aug. 4, 1865; also the Norfolk papers.

"In the beauty of the lilies Christ was born across
the sea,
With a glory in His Bosom, that transfigures you
and me;
As He died to make men holy, let us die to make
men free,
While God is marching on."

As one looks back upon it and considers the intense suffering of the people, the unjust and unreasonable treatment they received, and the provocation everywhere thrust upon them, it is astonishing that they exhibited such self-control.[24]

---

[24]*Richmond Whig*, Aug. 1, 1865: "Only four regiments remain in the Shenandoah Valley under General Torbert, that number of troops being deemed sufficient."

The reporter referred to General Alfred Thomas Archimedes Torbert, who remained in Virginia until Dec. 31, 1865.

The plantation of William E. Taylor, of Norfolk, the area now partly in the Norfolk Naval Operating Base, was seized and held for years by the freedmen, who refused to give up the land, until forced to vacate.

CHAPTER VII

THE WHIG LEGISLATURE

History throws her shuttle to and fro, and, like
an ancient sorceress, weaves an everlasting fabric
from threads as fragile as a spider's web.
—*W. H. T. Squires.*

As the long summer days of 1865 grew shorter,
and the autumn winds took keener edge, the harvests
ripened in the countryside and it was evident once
again that Nature is a generous mother despite
man's inhumanity to man. With the same grim
determination which had won victories on countless
battlefields, and the same unconquerable energy
which had triumphed over previous disaster, the
Virginians bent their backs to burdens, cruel and
heavy to be borne. There was no complaint, for
our people were determined to conquer calamity and
defeat disaster.

A young reporter who journeyed to Virginia
during the summer and fall of 1865—Whitelaw Reid
by name—touched every section of Virginia, and
his candor is compelling.

The South promised a fertile field for "Northern
enterprise." Soon all the banks, railways, stores
and even the plantations, would pass into Northern
hands. "Necessity will begin to pinch" these rebel
owners, and "Northern capital" will have a wonder-

ful opportunity[1] to pluck unheard-of bargains. The
tide of "Northern enterprise" will soon sweep rudely
against the "broken remnants" of the South, and
"new men" will be the order of the day. Not one
word of generosity, kindness nor sympathy, for a
broken and sorrowing people was traced by the
cruel pen of Whitelaw Reid. For cold-blooded
avarice his review of the South has no parallel.[2]

Perhaps it was mere chance, but a Richmond
editor[3] wrote: "There can be no doubt that the
correspondents of the Northern press are a conscienceless set of fellows who manufacture long yarns
about the rebellious spirit of the South, to produce a
sensation in the North. We know of many down-
right falsehoods about Virginia—nothing more or
less—that have been published."

It was abundantly recorded by all observers that
war prices still obtained, and the markets North and
East were open for the necessities and luxuries of
life. Fine profits were to be secured by those frugal
and industrious Southern farmers who could get
their produce shipped. Many such hopes were
realized.[4] The country north of the narrow Potomac

---

[1] ROYAL CORTISSOZ, *Life of Whitelaw Reid*, Vol. I, p. IX. Mr. Reid purchased three large Louisiana plantations. He had "an eye to bargains," and
did not object to a "little profit" gathered from the "misfortunes of the South."
His ventures were financial failures. The prosperity of the South today is not
the result of "Northern enterprise," but of long and hard labor by native skill
and industry.

[2] WHITELAW REID, *After the War* (1866).

[3] *Richmond Whig*, August 8, 1865.

[4] In 1866 a barrel of flour sold for $11.55 in Norfolk, on the average; a
bushel of corn $.98; a pound of middling cotton, $.41; a pound of butter,
$.37; of rice, $.10; of wool, $.50.

was at the very peak of such prosperity as was never before deemed possible.

In the South labor was scarce and difficult to obtain, even if the farmer had the money to pay wages, which he did not have. The worst element among the Negroes left the old plantations. Thousands followed the returning soldiers northward; other thousands drifted to cities and camps and were living in congenial idleness, fed by a generous Government.[5]

In this desolate and sorrowing country there were many causes for gratitude. The fighting had been over for six months now. No longer were loved ones sent home in rude boxes to be buried in the churchyard. No longer came frightful messages of wholesale slaughter from the embattled front. No longer were wounded, shocked and afflicted men sent home to suffer and to die; or, in many cases, to be nursed back to health and strength. From time to time those long absent (and some mourned for dead) arrived from distant States and from long voyages at sea.

Nearly every soldier returned to claim his waiting bride—if unmarried. New homes were being built here and there, mostly cabins, to be sure, but homes none the less. New families were being established. Old homes were being repaired, and fences and barns. Schools were opened for such as could attend.

---

[5] *The New York Nation* reported that the "negroes moved about restlessly, in crowds, like gypsies, from place to place. . . . All over Virginia they were leaving the plantations . . . many believed that by liberty they had acquired the right to the property of their former masters."

The gaunt spectre of hunger faded forever from the fields and farms of the South. In the garden patch and barnyard the returned soldier labored, perhaps with only his hands or a borrowed plow and a mule hired for a day or a week. It was happy toil!

He worked at the very bottom of the financial ladder,[6] but so had his pioneer ancestors, who began with naught but stout hearts, and built a civilization and gathered fortunes. If it had been done before in these same fields, it could be done again.

Whitelaw Reid drew a sad picture of Norfolk. The warehouses were dilapidated (May 1865), the stores vacant and falling to decay. "Elegant residences of prominent rebels, in whose parlors sat the wives of Yankee officers" is part of a sentence which he fails to describe as deliberate confiscation. He admits that the streets swarmed with Negro soldiers and that sutlers were making fortunes. The old merchants and "all rebels are ruined." But the young man did not refer to the constant battles between the Negroes and the soldiers who were stationed in Norfolk. He made no reference to the following general order,[7] still in force:

Norfolk, Va. Feb. 11, 1864.

General Order No. 3.

All places of public worship in Norfolk and Ports-

---

[6]Farm land in Virginia, worth $150 an acre in 1860, could be bought in 1865 for $2 an acre. The best farms in North Carolina could be bought for $1 to $10 the acre. The farmers were destitute of money, seed, tools, stock and fertilizer. They had nothing but a willing heart and hands; many had only one arm, one leg, one eye; others were shell-shocked or carried wounds which never healed.

[7]WALTER L. FLEMING, *Documentary Hist. of Reconstruction*, Vol. II, p. 223

mouth are hereby placed under the control of the provost-marshals of Norfolk and Portsmouth, respectively, who shall see the pulpits[8] properly filled by displacing, when necessary, the present incumbents and substituting men of known loyalty and the same sectarian denomination, either military or civil, subject to the approval of the commanding general. They shall see that all churches are open free to all officers and soldiers, white or colored, at the usual hour of worship and at other times if desired, and they shall see that no insult or indignity be offered to them, either by word, look or gesture on the part of the congregation.

In Richmond there was no railway station; the trains ran down the middle of Broad Street almost to Capitol Square. Passengers loitered in the stores until the train was ready to depart.

Between Richmond and Gordonsville the country was utterly desolate (November 1865). In that entire distance one saw only a dozen fields of poor wheat. Everywhere the homes and farms were abandoned. Breastworks and other evidences of the late war abounded. The trains did not stop at stations, but at piles of debris. Twelve miles an hour was rapid travel. Many men were at work along the roadbed; and some of them still wore ragged Confederate uniforms.

Lynchburg was much more prosperous than Norfolk or Richmond. Half a million in specie was said to be held by Lynchburg banks when Lee surrendered. The city swarmed with representatives of Northern firms looking for bargains. Balti-

---

[8]JOHN DONALD WADE, *Augustus Baldwin Longstreet*, p. 352.

moreans predominated. Many prospectors were seeking mineral land in the mountains of the state. The freedmen had the idea that at New Year (January 1, 1866) the government would take the farms away from their owners and give them to the Negroes. Union soldiers and agents from the North diligently spread that rumor. Lynchburg citizens were now openly for President Johnson.

The trains which left Lynchburg for Southwestern Virginia had, usually, three coaches, with a few freight cars behind them. The first coach was labelled "For Ladies," the second "For Gentlemen," the third "For Colored and Soldiers." All trains were crowded, standing room being at a premium. Nine miles an hour was good time on the Virginia and Tennessee Railway (Norfolk and Western), and even then the train was often derailed.

Among the travelers were many tobacco buyers, cotton buyers and geologists.

II

An election, called October 12, brought 40,000 voters to the polls—an impressive showing, for only those qualified to vote under the Constitution of 1850, the third Constitution, were permitted to register. Many leaders in the late "rebellion," as the congressional orators insisted upon calling the Confederate cause, were under disability for "treason." The congressional orators insisted that it was "treason" to hold opinions contrary to theirs on controverted constitutional questions, debated since 1787.

General Lee[9] earnestly advised all Virginians to take an active interest in public affairs and to vote —but Robert E. Lee could not vote! Thousands were too poor to pay their poll taxes, and other thousands were too discouraged. Their hearts and hopes lay dead with the Confederate cause.

"The people here[10] meant, perhaps once after the surrender, to try to acquiesce in defeat; but now there is an apathy beyond anything you can imagine. No interest is taken in the proceedings of the United States Congress, scarcely any in the State Legislature—apathy everywhere.

"Perhaps some fearless lecturer or clergyman may speak of the old days, the brave men who won immortality for an unsuccessful cause—then you will see faces light up, dull enough a moment before, and read the story of this utter indifference rightly enough."[11]

The General Assembly of Virginia met December 4. It was an able body of men, mostly Old Line Whigs, originally Union men, who had earnestly opposed the Democratic doctrine of secession. John Brown Baldwin,[12] a brother-in-law of Alex. H. H. Stuart, was elected Speaker, and J. Bell Bigger, Clerk.

---

[9]CHARLES FRANCIS ADAMS said of Lee: "From that crown of sorrow (guerrila warfare) he saved the country. He was the one man in the Confederacy who could exercise a decisive influence."

[10]W. GORDON MC CABE, Petersburg, Va., Feb. 17, 1866.

[11]WHITELAW REID, *A Southern Tour*: "It is curious to see with what avidity the Virginians gulp down the praises of their heroic dead."

[12]John Brown Baldwin (1820-1873). "As speaker he showed exceptional ability and his rules of procedure are still in use, and known as Baldwin's Rules."

H. W. HOWARD KNOTT, *Dict. of Amer. Biog.*, Vol. I.

The roll of the General Assembly[13] follows:

Accomac—J. W. Fields, T. H. Kellam.
Albemarle—J. Wood, Jr., W. A. Turner.
Alexandria—T. B. Robertson, J. A. English.
Alleghany—L. T. Mann.
Amelia, Nottoway and Powhatan—G. A. Miller.
Amherst—J. Powell.
Appomattox and Prince Edward—F. N. Watkins.
Augusta—J. B. Baldwin, J. A. Waddell, George Baylor.
Bedford—C. Pate, T. Y. Mosby.
Botetourt—W. E. M. Word.
Brunswick and Greenville—W. H. E. Merritt.
Buckingham and Cumberland—W. M. Cabell.
Campbell—A. J. Clarke, D. A. Wilson.
Caroline—W. R. B. Wyatt.
Carroll—L. F. Woltz.
Charles City, James City, New Kent—W. Martin.
Charlotte and Lunenburg—W. T. Scott.
Chesterfield—A. S. Hancock.
Clarke and Warren—J. S. Davison.
Culpepper and Orange—G. J. Browning.
Dinwiddie and Petersburg—R. P. Atkinson, W. T. Joynes, A. M. Keiley.
Elizabeth City, York, Warwick and Williamsburg—S. Smith.
Essex and Middlesex—M. Garnett.
Fairfax—D. W. Lewis.
Fauquier—J. Marshall, B. F. Rixey.
Floyd—N. B. Moore.
Fluvanna and Goochland—D. W. K. Bowles.
Franklin—F. R. Brown, J. Patterson.
Frederick—J. S. Magill, J. F. Wall.
Giles—A. G. Pendleton.
Gloucester and Mathews—J. T. Seawell.
Grayson—J. W. Parsons.
Greene and Madison—A. W. Graves.
Halifax—W. L. Owen, B. F. Garrett.
Hanover—T. J. Wooldridge.
Henrico—J. J. White, Z. S. Magruder, Franklin Stearns.
Henry—G. W. Booker.
Highland and Bath—R. J Glendy.
Isle of Wight and Surry—J. R. Purdy.
King and Queen and King William—J. H. C. Jones, T. J. Christian.
King George and Stafford—W. H. Hansbrough.
Lancaster and Northumberland—S. L. Straughan.
Lee—W. McDonald.

[13]Fourteenth Annual Report, State Library (1917), pp. 188-192.

Loudoun—R. M. Bentley, W. H. Gray.
Louisa—R. B. Davis.
Mecklenburg—William Townes.
Montgomery—T. D. Childress.
Nansemond—T. J. Kilby.
Nelson—J. M. Harris.
Norfolk City—W. H. C. Ellis, A. F. Leonard, E. T. Hardy, John Goode, Jr.
Norfolk County—L. Hurst, J. C. Langhorne, T. B. Butt.
Northampton—W. J. F. Peed.
Page—J. Long.
Patrick—W. F. B. Taylor.
Pittsylvania—D. C. Ragsdale, W. T. Clarke.
Prince George and Sussex—T. H. Daniel.
Prince William—C. W. C. Dunnington.
Princess Anne—J. O. Morris.
Pulaski and Bland—S. H. Newberry.
Rappahannock—Z. Turner.
Richmond City—T. J. Evans, P. R. Grattan, N. M. Lee, Littleton Tazewell, W. W. Crump.
Richmond County and Westmoreland—J. S. Braxton.
Roanoke and Craig—J. Trout.
Rockbridge—A. Graham, J. McDowell Taylor.
Rockingham—W. G. Thompson, H. B. Harnsberger, J. C. Woodson.
Russell—W. J. Dickenson.
Scott—Z. W. Davidson, G. H. Kendrick.
Shenandoah—J. A. Strayer, T. A. Jackson.
Smythe—V. S. Morgan.
Southampton—P. J. Holmes.
Tazewell—G. W Deskins.
Spottsylvania—C. Herndon.
Washington—C. S. Bekem, J. Teeter.
Wise and Buchanan—H. Riggs.
Wythe—R. Gibboney.

SENATE

President, L. C. P. COWPER

Clerk, SHELTON C. DAVIS

Nathaniel Alexander represented *Mecklenburg, Lunenburg, Nottoway, Brunswick and Greenville.*
Peter Belew—*Shenandoah and Page.*
George W. Bolling—*Sussex, Prince George and Dinwiddie.*
William W. Boyd and Fleming B. Miller—*Alleghany, Bath, Highland, and Botetourt.*
David S. G. Cabell—*Rockbridge and Nelson.*

Dale Carter—*Buchanan, Russell and Tazewell.*
Clayton G. Coleman—*Louisa, Hanover and Henrico.*
Charles L. Crockett—*Wythe, Grayson, Bland and Pulaski.*
Joseph W. Davis—*Washington and Smythe.*
Daniel F. Dulany—*Alexandria and Fairfax.*
James Galt—*Buckingham, Albemarle, Fluvanna and Goochland.*
John H. Gilmer, Robert Ould—*City of Richmond.*
Algernon S. Gray—*Rockingham and Greene.*
William M. Hannah—*Appomattox, Campbell and Charlotte.*
Elisha F. Keen—*Pittsylvania and Halifax.*
Samuel B. Kello—*Isle of Wight, Nansemond, Surry and Southampton.*
Jefferson T. Lawson—*Patrick, Floyd and Carroll.*
John H. Lee—*Spottsylvania, Stafford, Orange and Prince William.*
Francis W. Lemosy—*Norfolk County and Princess Anne.*
Christopher C. McRae—*Chesterfield, Amelia, Prince Edward, Cumberland and Powhatan.*
Nathaniel B. Meade—*Clarke, Frederick and Warren.*
William T. Mercier—*Loudoun.*
Robert C. Mitchell—*Amherst and Bedford.*
George H. Peck—*Giles, Montgomery, Roanoke and Craig.*
Samuel W. Powell—*Accomac and Northampton.*
Robert H. Power—*James City, Charles City, York, New Kent, Elizabeth City, Warwick and Williamsburg.*
William Richmond—*Wise, Scott and Lee.*
Edmund C. Robinson—*Norfolk City.*
Peter Saunders—*Henry and Franklin.*
Phillip W. Strother—*Rappahannock, Fauquier, Madison and Culpepper.*
Warner T. Taliaferro—*Mathews, Gloucester, Middlesex, King and Queen, Essex and King William.*
Nicholas K. Trout—*Augusta.*
Lawrence Washington—*Lancaster, Northumberland, Richmond, Westmoreland, Caroline and King George.*

The presiding officer of the Senate is the Lieutenant Governor of Virginia. L. C. P. Cowper held this doubtful honor (as Governor Pierpont's lieutenant). Shelton C. Davis was elected Clerk.

It became evident at once that hard, cruel and bitter days were ahead for Virginia and the South. Congress met the same day our General Assembly convened. The able and patriotic representatives-elect from Virginia and the South were present, and

denied seats.   It was an ominous proof that Virginia
was not a part of the United States although Virginia
had failed to secede!

L. H. Chandler was elected to Congress from
the Norfolk district, Alexander H. H. Stuart from
the Staunton district, and Daniel Hoge, of Giles
County, from the Southwestern counties.   Charles
L. Mosby of Lynchburg represented that district.
Virginia had eight congressmen-elect in all.[14]

The Whig Legislature, despite discouraging news
from Washington, assumed the burdens and did
their utmost to help the political and economic situation which now confronted Virginia.[15]

Colonel Baldwin, as parliamentarian and speaker,[16]
guided the delegates with tact and urbanity.   A
man of superb physique, forty-five years of age, his
sterling integrity, fine legal achievements, eloquence
and ability, made him one of the most effective
Virginians of his troubled day.   So large a place
does the Colonel fill that his portrait may be briefly
drawn.   His head and brow suggested Daniel Webster, his voice was keen and incisive, rather than
melodious.   His gestures suggested power and determination, rather than grace.   He was a master

[14]ROBERT W. HUGHES wrote editorially, in *The Republic*, Richmond, Va.,
Aug. 2, 1865: "If Virginia sends a representation to Congress against whom
no objection can be urged . . . we think the crisis of Reconstruction can be
safely passed.   If we send a different class of men to Washington, we will be
denied representation," etc.

[15]The Governor nominated William T. Joynes, R. C. L. Moncure and L.
P. Thompson, as judges of the Virginia Court of Appeals, the highest tribunal
in the state.

[16]Baldwin was a member of the First Confederate Congress.

ALEX H. STEPHENS, *War Between the States*, pp. 759-765, gives a memo-
randum of all Confederate legislators and generals.

of constitutional law, devoted to the principles of popular rights. His wit, pathos and invective often overwhelmed his opponents. He had been a powerful Old Line Whig in earlier days. To his convictions he held with Scotch-Irish tenacity; blunt of speech and brusque of manner, he was a man of force rather than diplomacy.

Governor Pierpont's message to the Assembly was temperate and made a good impression. Pierpont was regarded, and justly, as a military usurper. Of that he was himself fully aware.

"I have made every exertion to restore to each man in the State all the rights of a citizen. I have done this under a high sense of duty to my country. The people profess subordination to the laws and allegiance in good faith to the Government, and I believe them to be sincere in their professions. I am satisfied that no State can be governed under a Republican form of government when three-fourths of the people, embracing the largest taxpayers, are disfranchised and denied a voice in making or executing the laws of the State."[17]

These were kind words from Governor Pierpont, but the news that came from Washington caused a black cloud of anxiety to settle over all the South, as we shall see.

---

[17] JOHN PRESTON MC CONNELL, *Negroes and Their Treatment*, p. 120.
PHILIP ALEX. BRUCE, *Rise of the New South*, p. 447.

CHAPTER VIII

THE PURPLE SHADOWS OF DESPAIR

**Hope, withering, fled—
And Mercy sighed farewell.**
                    —*Lord Byron.*

Never has a Congress assembled as the Thirty-
ninth. The members had been elected thirteen
months before, but by our antiquated laws they did
not meet until Monday, December 4, 1865.[1] Enthu-
siastically, joyously, flushed with victory, the floors
of both chambers were filled with gallant men, and
the galleries thronged with brilliant women, gor-
geously gowned, resplendent with jewels. For the
war was won. The South had surrendered. The
sundered nation was reunited with shrapnel and
bayonets. Representatives from eleven Southern
States, which had failed to leave the Union, were
present, ready to take the oath and to support the
Constitution. They were anxious to rebuild a new
and greater nation upon these now altered founda-

---

[1]DAVID SAVILLE MUZZEY, *Amer. Adventure*, Vol. II, describes this meeting
of Congress as one of the most critical in our history, the reactions from which
can hardly be exaggerated.

tions. All agreed that slavery and secession had died upon an hundred battlefields.[2]

The representatives of the South had no place in the exuberant and vibrant rejoicing, for our people were shrouded in shadows of disappointment and despair. Disaster followed hard upon the heels of disaster. Calumny with tireless tongue was busy. Press and politicians never wearied proclaiming the baseness of all Southern "rebels."

Eight million Americans, with high hopes dashed, lived and labored under the cruel heel of military despotism. The only participation the Virginians and other Southern people had in the government of the United States was the privilege of paying taxes. Taxation without representation had again become the fate of Virginia!

In the House of Representatives the Speaker, Schuyler Colfax, of Indiana, rapped the gay assembly to order and the opening prayer was said. God knows they needed prayer if ever a Congress did! Edward McPherson, of Pennsylvania, Clerk of the House, who owed his position to Thaddeus Stevens, also of Pennsylvania, called the roll. One by one each of the eleven states, which had failed to secede, was omitted.

When Tennessee was not called, Horace Maynard, congressman-at-large and a close personal and political friend of President Andrew Johnson, likewise a citizen of Tennessee, demanded that he be enrolled. The obsequious clerk said nothing. He looked at

[2]BENJAMIN H. HILL: "There was a South of slavery and secession—that South is dead. There is a South of union and freedom—that South, thank God, is living, breathing, growing every hour."—Address in New York, 1866.

his master, Thaddeus Stevens, seated immediately in front of him, his aged and haggard face grim, colorless, bitter, relentless and determined.

Stevens made no sign. McPherson made no sign. Ah, that silence was pregnant with disaster for eight million people, who thought they were protected by the Constitution of the Republic.

At this critical juncture James Brooks, of New York, demanded an explanation. Why was Tennessee omitted? "If Tennessee is not a State," he cried, "and has not been a State in this Union, and is not loyal to the Union, and if the people of Tennessee are aliens and foreigners, by what right does the President of the United States usurp a place in the White House?"

That scathing question was not answered. And it has never yet been answered. In its brief compass, it contains the logic, or lack of logic, of the dismal era we know as "Reconstruction."

The Honorable James Brooks did not know a dark secret, which all the world knows now: namely, that Thaddeus Stevens, with uncanny foresight and diabolical cunning, called thirty ultra-Radicals to Washington, Friday, December 1. They discussed and denounced the President's efforts to heal the wounds of war, and carry Abraham Lincoln's policies into effect. They laid diabolical plans to thwart all efforts making for reconciliation and peace. No representative from any Southern State should be seated. A gentlemen's agreement was made that neither chamber should admit a "rebel" unless the other chamber agreed. By this simple but effective manipulation the more Radical House controlled the less Radical Senate.

Furthermore, Stevens in the House, Sumner in the Senate, and Stanton in the President's Cabinet were to stand together until the South was sufficiently punished for "rebellion" and "treason."

Next day the regular Republican caucus assembled. Thaddeus Stevens had the resolution ready. It was adopted without debate and without a single dissenting vote! The ultra-Radicals now controlled the huge Republican majority in Congress.

Machiavelli was a novice in craftiness and cunning beside Thaddeus Stevens. To our sorrow be it written.

To make the chains doubly secure it was moved that all Republicans be bound by the decision of the caucus. Also carried. The trap was now completely sprung.

Thaddeus Stevens[3] was master of the ultra-Radical minority in the House of Representatives; and, by virtue of the caucus, master of the House, and by virtue of the gentlemen's agreement master of the Senate, and by the control of the Congress master even of the President in the White House, whom of all men he most hated and determined by means, fair or foul, to degrade from his high office and thrust out in shame and disgrace.

There sat in the Thirty-ninth Congress fifty senators from twenty-five States, of whom thirty-nine were Republicans and eleven Democrats. In the

---

[3] S. E. MORRISON, *Oxford Hist. of U. S.*, Vol. II, pp. 333-334, gives a brief but impartial character sketch of Stevens and Sumner.

House of Representatives there were one hundred and forty-one Republicans and forty-three Democrats.

If the eleven Southern States were readmitted, as President Johnson earnestly desired and expected, their twenty-two senators would likely be Democrats, and then there would be thirty-three Democratic senators and only thirty-nine Republicans.

If the South sent up fifty-eight Democratic representatives, then the Democrats would have 101 votes against 141 Republicans.

They argued that the Republicans had won the war, and it was only fair that they should enjoy the rich spoils of office, undisturbed. They also recalled the immediate past. The Democrats had practically monopolized "the best government on earth" since the days of Andrew Jackson. Now the Republicans proposed to have their turn. They were determined that "copperheads" (Northern Democrats) and "rebels" (Southern Democrats) should not unite to jeopardize their grasp upon the power and patronage of government.

In the meantime Thaddeus Stevens was determined to force Negro suffrage upon all the States, North, West and South. He would use the Union League and Freedmen's Bureau to break the influence of the Southern white leaders over the freedmen, and he would bind them in one great mass to the Radical wing of the Republican party. By so doing, not only would the Republican party maintain a huge and permanent majority in the nation, but the ultra-Radical element would wield the whip-hand over the entire party.[4]

It is astonishing that such a gigantic conspiracy could have been forced upon millions of intelligent Americans. For ten years Stevens[5] and his conspirators carried their program to completion, and sank this nation to the nadir of scandal and disgrace, and left a legacy of prejudice and hatred not yet entirely eradicated.

II

The most accurate portrait of this potent politician has been painted by the pen of Claude G. Bowers in "The Tragic Era." This deformed and dissipated misanthrope, warped in body and mind, became master of the destinies of the nation by virtue of the bullet of John Wilkes Booth.

He was born in Danville, Vermont (April 4, 1792), to a shiftless father, said to have been a cobbler and wrestler, who soon deserted mother and son. From birth one of the child's limbs terminated in a mass of shapeless flesh. Sensitive to a degree, bitter because of his poverty and his deformity, envious of those happy, because he was not, cursed with an ambition which knew no restraints of honesty nor virtue, he especially hated "aristocrats," because he

---

[4]The only method by which a permanent Radical party could be organized in the South was to give the freedmen the vote and (so long as it could be done) withhold the vote from all ex-Confederates. There was intense prejudice against Negro suffrage in the North. Eli Thayer wrote: "If they come North, we do not want them and would not endure them." Yet many were willing to give negroes the vote as a means of punishing the late "rebels."

Connecticut voted down negro suffrage (1865), pro 27,217; contra 33,489.

[5]CARL RUSSELL FISH, *Development of Amer. Nationality*, p. 413, describes Stevens as "a remorseless hater of the South."

was not to the manner born. This dark-browed
and sullen child developed an immense capacity for
hatred.

His devoted mother labored to the limit of her
strength to give Thaddeus an education. He graduated at Dartmouth (1814), came South and, by a
strange freak of fate, selected Bel Air, Maryland,
the native place of John Wilkes Booth, as his home.
He soon removed to Lancaster, Pennsylvania, and
became a neighbor, though not a friend, of James
Buchanan. Even in these early days he was known
to his neighbors (for he had no friends) as a rude,
boorish, lonely man, a misanthrope.

He began his hectic political career as an ardent
supporter of the aristocratic and wealthy John
Quincy Adams, and as an inveterate foe of Andrew
Jackson, who, like himself, once poor and friendless,
was forced by bitter circumstances to fight his way.
Strange are the inconsistencies of human nature.
Still it is to remember that Adams was of New
England, even if aristocratic, and that Jackson was
of South Carolina, even if plebian.

Stevens won a seat in the Pennsylvania Legislature, and turned his first fury against the Masonic
fraternity, "a secret, oath-bound, murderous institution that endangers the continuance of republican
government." For years he denounced all Masons
and bent every effort to have the lodges "investigated" and destroyed by law.

He helped prepare a new Constitution for the
State (1836), but vehemently denounced the instrument because it did not permit Negro suffrage.

When Daniel Webster brought forward overtures

of peace to the distracted country, Stevens turned against him with the gentle statement: "I could cut his damned heart out"—and he would have done so with pleasure.

Before he entered Congress he was an inveterate gambler. An editor wrote, "All his life he has been known as a scoffer at religion and a reviler of sacred things." A senator who knew him well called him a "debauchee in morals."

A mulatto woman, Lydia Smith, was his housekeeper, and we suppose, his most loyal friend. Her husband, a negro barber, died, and Lydia became the mistress of his homes in Lancaster and Washington. She cared for him with docile, patient and affectionate loyalty. It was she who soothed his dying bed, and buried him among the negroes of Lancaster when he died.

Lydia Smith, a mulatto servant, is the only woman whose influence has added two amendments to the Constitution of the United States.

Thaddeus Stevens' career in Congress began at the mellow age of fifty-seven (1848). Though a Whig, he fought Henry Clay and his compromise measures, especially the Fugitive Slave Law. His sullen hatred was transferred from the Masons to the Southern slave-owners.

In 1859 he was again returned to Congress, when fierce sectional and anti-slavery feeling swept the North. Like many Old Line Whigs he joined the new Republican party. And, of all Republicans, he most hated and berated Abraham Lincoln! He denounced him as a weakling, trimmer, clown, peanut-politician and vulgar opportunist. He denounced John Brown, too, and cried, "Damn him, he ought to hang!" His was a viper's tongue and a devil's temper. James G. Blaine described him "as somewhat unscrupulous as to his political methods, somewhat careless in personal conduct, somewhat lax in morals."

When the war was won, and Booth's bullet removed Abraham Lincoln, a queer freak of misfortune made this misanthrope the most powerful leader in the United States. He would dispatch a million Federal bayonets, if necessary, to make the South a fire-swept desert. He would crush any man who attempted to thwart him, and trample any contract under foot. The Constitution was nothing but a scrap of paper. "Conscience?" he cried; "Throw conscience to the devil. Stand by your party." It was he who pushed the impeachment of the President of the United States, and by one vote only did he fail in this gigantic conspiracy of folly and wickedness. This was the aged and feeble man, tall, thin, cadaverous, with hatred stamped upon every line of his dark brow and cruel mouth, this was the domineering, arrogant, sullen, revengeful dictator who held the clerk of the House, Edward McPherson, under his eye when the Thirty-ninth Congress convened.

The affable and dapper speaker of the House, Schuyler Colfax, just reelected to succeed himself, and soon to become Vice-President of the United States, ruled that any change in the roll of the House as read by the clerk was out of order. These are his shameful words:

"The attitude of Congress is as plain as the sun's

pathway in the heavens. The door having been shut in the rebels' faces is still to be kept bolted."

As the Speaker was sustained by an overwhelming majority, there was nothing for it but acquiescence. The Southern representatives-elect (85 of them— eight from Virginia) returned to their respective homes. Month by month the dictator and his fellow conspirators unfolded their plan for the punishment and humiliation of the South, and the impeachment of Andrew Johnson for the crime of defending the Southern people and upholding the Constitution of the United States.

III

Among those who came to the Thirty-ninth Congress from Virginia was L. H. Chandler, who filled a position of some importance in those troubled times. Born in Maine, he made his home (1850), his reputation and a career in Norfolk. He was an able lawyer, a successful politician and a staunch Unionist. His loyalty to the Federal cause was promptly, generously rewarded when he was appointed United States District Attorney for Eastern Virginia. All parties, Democrats, Whigs, Confederates and Unionists, united to elect him to Congress (1865). Though it anticipates the story, we may add that he estranged his Southern and Conservative friends by becoming a Radical; but he estranged his Radical friends by being too conservative. The riot of a convention at Petersburg (1868) howled him down. Radicals of the Wells type would have none of him. He was at constant odds with Dr.

Bayne, Norfolk's negro Solon, whom we will meet again. In an effort to conciliate the negroes, Chandler made a speech from the Court House steps (July 4, 1868). "He began with a bitter address, abusing the white people of Norfolk, who ostracized him after his defection to the Radicals. He advocated the equality of the races, whatever that means, and wished white and colored children to sit and play, side by side, in the public schools."[6]

Whitelaw Reid described him as "a nervous, restless, black-haired Virginian" who cordially supported Pierpont and believes that "loyal men," even if in a minority, should rule the Commonwealth.

The tragic death of Mr. Chandler called forth the profound sympathy of all his neighbors, without regard to political affiliations. He disappeared mysteriously from his residence in York Street (April 6, 1876), and eleven days later his body was found in the harbor. He had mental trouble, and it was generally supposed that he drowned himself. He had "regained the confidence and friendship of many former acquaintances, who had been estranged on account of political differences."[7] He was buried from Old St. Paul's Church, by the rector, Rev. Dr. Okeson.

[6]T. J. WERTENBAKER, *Norfolk, Southern Port,* p. 264.
[7]H. W. BURTON, *Hist. of Norfolk,* p. 167.

CHAPTER IX

CONGRESSIONAL RECONSTRUCTION

The outrages, and humiliations worse than outrage, of the period of so-called Reconstruction, which were actual servile dominations.

—*Charles Francis Adams.*

Thaddeus Stevens[1] was determined to thwart and discredit President Johnson and to render his policy of peace and tranquility nugatory.

Having kept Southern representatives out, his second move was even bolder than his strategic elimination of all Southern Democrats. He persistently proclaimed that with the Congress and not the Executive rested the power to reconstruct the lately seceded States; with Congress rested the right to decide when, where and how a State (which had attempted but failed to secede) should be readmitted to a Union it had not left. Stevens moved that a Committee of fifteen, six senators and nine representatives, be appointed, to whose care all matters pertaining to the reconstruction and readmission of the "rebel" States be referred. This Committee was also charged to "consider the conditions of the so-called Confederate States, and with reporting by

---

[1] WHITELAW REID, himself a Radical, declared that Thaddeus Stevens was "foremost of all in Reconstruction." That statement no one doubts.

bill if any were entitled to be represented in Congress, and until that time no member to be received."[2]

The bill was passed by large majorities, December 4, 1865, the day Congress met. The senators who served upon this Committee, and whose names must go down to posterity on this roster of disgrace, were James W. Grimes, of Iowa; Ira Harris, of New York; Jacob Merritt Howard, of Michigan; George Henry Williams, of Oregon; Reverdy Johnson, of Maryland, and William P. Fessenden, of Maine.

The nine representatives were Thaddeus Stevens, of Pennsylvania; Elihu Benjamin Washburne, of Illinois; Justin Smith Morrell, of Vermont; Henry Grider, of Kentucky; John A. Bingham, of Ohio; Roscoe Conkling, of New York; George Sewell Boutwell, of Massachusetts; Andrew J. Rogers, of New Jersey, and Henry T. Blow, of Missouri, a native of Southampton County,[3] Virginia.

Senator William Pitt Fessenden, of Maine, was chairman of this powerful Committee. Of the senator it is said, "He wrote its celebrated report, pronounced one of the ablest state papers ever submitted to Congress. It vindicated the power of

---

[2] It will be noticed that Stevens had no more respect for grammar than he had for logic or for the Constitution of the United States. This sweeping resolution officially repudiated Abraham Lincoln and his policies. It set aside the government Lincoln had established in several Southern states.

[3] *The Land of Decision*, squires, p. 169: "This sequestered county, which produced General George Henry Thomas, U. S. A., and General William Mahone, C. S. A., and John Young Mason, also gave the world Henry T. Blow (July 15, 1817-Sept. 11, 1875). In his fourteenth year the family moved to St. Louis, and he graduated from a local University. Successful in business and in politics, he served four years as a Missouri state senator, and was appointed minister to Venezuela by President Lincoln (1861). From 1863 to '67 he sat in the House of Representatives. He later became minister to Brazil (1869-'71).

Congress over the rebellious States, showed their
relations to the Government under the Constitution
and the law of nations and recommended the constitutional safeguards made necessary by the rebellion."

We gladly quote these complimentary words.
Lincoln referred, once, to Fessenden as "a Radical
without the petulant and vicious fretfulness of many
Radicals." Was Abe, we wonder, thinking of Thaddeus?

It is noteworthy that Fessenden and not Stevens
was called to the chair. For that small kindness
we should be grateful. But Fessenden's was a
mailed-fist. Let him speak:

"There is nothing better established than the
principle that the conquerors have the power to
change the form of government, to punish, to exact
security and take entire charge of a conquered
people."

The Senator was certainly candid, and with him
we quite agree that the Radicals did completely
"change the form of Government";[4] they did punish
and take charge of a conquered people. Evidently
the brilliant Senator never heard of such documents
as the Declaration of Independence and the Constitution of the United States. With a graceful wave
of his hand, he consigns to oblivion all interpretations
of those documents, debated by America's ablest

---

[4]It is of compelling interest to historians that Senator Fessenden admits
the Radical subversion of the Government of the United States by the War
Between the States. It has always been the contention of the South that the
Confederate States fought for their constitutional rights, as guaranteed by that
instrument. Evidently Senator Fessenden endorsed the Confederate contention that Federal victory was by conquest and invasion, and not by Constitutional right.

statesmen since the Continental Congress first discussed them.

But there is a higher authority than the Committee of fifteen. It is the statement "By their fruits ye shall know them"; and no historian can deny that the fruits of the labors of this Committee were years of tyranny, force, riots, murder, poverty, anguish, cruelty, injustice, shame, disgrace and sorrow, not for a few political leaders but for eight million innocent and law-abiding people through ten frightful years. Two-thirds of a century has now passed; all are long since gone, victors and vanquished, to their eternal rewards, but the seeds scattered by the hands of the Committee of fifteen, even to this late day, bear still a harvest, though a diminishing harvest, of sectional hatred, racial feeling and fratricidal strife.

Senator Fessenden was an able man, but the program of congressional reconstruction was hatched in the fertile brain of Thaddeus Stevens, who still dominated the Committee. He probed the wounds of war. He was determined that the hurts of the Nation should not heal. His hatred of all men and things Southern was as intense as it was malevolent. He would grind the "Southern aristocrats" into the dust and eternally damn them. Every white man in the South was "an aristocrat." The Southern States were not fit to have a place in the Union. "Massachusetts is better able to govern Georgia than Georgia is to govern itself," was a gentle axiom he preached and really believed.

The program of congressional reconstruction, as

forged out by the Committee of Fifteen, was thorough and comprehensive.

I.   The States should be reduced to the status of territories.

II.   And territories are governed by the Congress.

III.   The Congress must be controlled by the Republican majority.

IV.   And the Republican majority must be controlled by the Radical minority.

V.   Under no circumstances must any Southern senator nor representative be admitted—certainly not before July 4, 1870.

VI.   And when the Southern members are finally admitted they must represent, not the taxpayers, but the voters.

VII.   All who fought, aided or sympathized with the Confederacy, should not be allowed to vote.

VIII.   Except the Negroes who protected the farms, women and children, and who largely fed the Southern armies; all Negroes should vote.

IX.   And the nation should provide a farm for each of them.

X.   These farms were to be confiscated from the white owners.   No rebel should be allowed to own more than $20,000 worth of property.

XI.   The slaves were to become the lawmakers and masters of their masters, and the masters were to become the political slaves of their former slaves.

XII.   If the rebels objected to this program— there was the army.   And what is an army for?

II

It was of Stevens, his Committee of Fifteen and their plans and purposes that John Warwick Daniel eloquently said: "I need not go to foreign shores to seek instances of mental subjugation. When the Confederate War closed its bloody pages, we beheld set on foot the most tremendous scheme of intellectual oppression that modern history has known. The Constitution was altered,[5] that the bravest and best of our citizens might be ostracized by law; and new constitutions far severer and wider-sweeping in their disfranchisements than the amended Federal instrument itself were imposed upon the conquered States. While the intelligent master was stricken down, the rude untaught slave was elevated to the highest places of government. While in many States the native white citizen could not vote, hold office, practice a profession, teach school, preach a sermon, marry the adult, baptize the infant, or bury the dead with religious rites, the seditious alien and ignorant slave ruled and ruined.

"While the conquerors' henchmen sang paeans to liberty and independence, the desolate captives of the South lay in bondage. In magnanimity may

---

[5]WOODROW WILSON, *Hist. of U. S.*, pp. 268-269, states that there was no Constitution during the Civil War. Upon unproved suspicion of disaffection to the Union cause, many suffered prosecution and persecution. Judges were incarcerated, civil officers imprisoned, members of the Maryland legislature were thrown into jail. Editors were silenced, "peace meetings" broken up with rioting, the prisons were filled with peaceful citizens who had no opportunity to secure a trial. Not even the ordained ministry, in the House of God upon the Sabbath, was free to preach or pray if suspected of disloyalty to the Lincoln administration.

we forgive those who struck down the liberties of the white race, made us strangers in our homes, turned us over, bound in shackles, to the tender mercies of our slaves, inflamed with bad passions, by wicked and unscrupulous men, who came here to make spoil of our adversity. But let no American citizen ever forget the doer or fail to execrate and denounce the unjust deed. They who did this were tyrants and we should ever hate the tyrant as we hate hell pains.

"These were the only rebels the war produced; rebels against the Constitution, rebels against their race, rebels against their kith and kin, rebels against liberty and against mankind. No, not rebels. God forbid that I should so desecrate the great and glorious name of Rebel, the highest and grandest name in history save that of Saviour. That name which Washington and America wreathed with the halo of victorious valor; which Lee and the South wreathed with the lustrous crown of vanquished martyrdom. They were not rebels. They were traitors. But forgive them. Let them pass."[6]

The Committee of Fifteen and their program, planned the addition of no less than three revolutionary amendments to the Constitution of the United States; the upbuilding of a Radical party in the South; the rewriting of twelve Constitutions for as many great States, West Virginia and Tennessee included. They planned the political persecution of huge masses of the population, systematically and consecutively. Their tyranny would reach from

---

[6]JOHN WARWICK DANIEL, *Speeches*, p. 143.

the capital to the smallest village in "the damn rebel provinces" (to quote a gem from one of Stevens' addresses). It was an articulated program, followed, step by step, beginning with the Radical caucus called by Stevens, Friday, December 1, 1865, and continuing until President Hayes recalled the last uniformed and bayonetted soldiers from the South, long after Stevens was dead. It is a drama of iniquity, intrigue and treachery.

Many different kinds of people, influenced by many motives, were united behind Stevens and the Fifteen in the Reconstruction era.[7] Many were interested in bargains, Southern railways, factories, municipal and other values which (in Southern poverty and misery) might be picked up at a mere fraction of their value.

Again, many suffered, and keenly, during the War Between the States, and could not forget their sons and brothers who fell—a frightful harvest of death, through four bloody years. Should not these be avenged?

But perhaps the most powerful and influential class of all were the politicians who were determined that the Democrats of the North and border States and the "rebels" of the South should be kept out of power, just so long as it could be done.

---

[7]THORNTON KIRKLAND LATHROP, *Seward*, p. 414: Those who balked at the Radical program were reminded that the Constitution guarantees every state a "republican form of government." This fiction was approved by no less an authority than Chief Justice Chase, who failed to define a "republican form of government."

III

Many and potent voices were raised against Stevens and his policies. Lewis D. Campbell, long an Old Line Whig and influential leader in Ohio, cried out passionately: "The question is whether the impractical Radical zealots, who seem to be instigated by the devil and fatally bent on mischief, shall gobble us all up and run us on their infernal train to national perdition."

Daniel Wolsey Voorhees, "the tall Sycamore of the Wabash," who served in the House during the war (1861-65) and later (1869-73), and spent his last years as an influential senator (1877-91), spoke in no uncertain accents:

"No State can sunder connection with the Federal Union except by total subversion of our system of government. The President's enemies assail him with the masked face of friendship and the treacherous sword of Joab. (This reference was to Secretary Edwin M. Stanton). It is safer to rob a corpse than to pick the pockets of the living. Stevens maintains that the war to restore the Union was an utter failure . . . the war is over but the Union is still rent in twain! Confiscation in Stevens' mouth means plunder for Stevens' purse."

In a speech of unexampled bitterness and vindictiveness, Thaddeus Stevens addressed Voorhees, in the House of Representatives, December 18:

"The Union can only be saved by the Republican party, and the Republican party can only be saved by the Radical element. Southern representatives must be excluded. If the South were admitted they would send up twenty-two Democratic senators and fifty-eight Democratic representatives—and behold the rebels would again control the nation with the 'weak-kneed Republican in the White House.' The foolish idea that this is a white man's country is as atrocious as the infamous sentiments that damned the late Chief Justice (referring to Taney) to everlasting shame and I fear to everlasting fire.

"If the Democrats, Copperheads and Rebels once get control of this nation, they will likely repudiate our national debt, or add the rebel debt to ours, and the people will be crushed beneath the intolerable burden.

"The national debt, forced on us by the rebels, should be paid by the rebels. All Southern land and property should be confiscated for that purpose. The vanquished deserve to be stripped. The very foundations of the South should be broken up and relaid. Do not let them come back here until they yield to all our demands. Every negro adult should be given forty acres of land and a mule,[8] and the rest of the Southern plantations should be sold for ten dollars an acre." From the funds thus obtained Stevens would "pension all disabled and those ruined by this villainous war."

Some one referred to Stevens' policy as "revolutionary."

"It is intended to be revolutionary," he cried. "It is far easier and more beneficial to exile seventy thousand rebels than to expatriate four million natives to the soil, who are loyal to this government." He would tax export cotton, and thus break the back of the cotton farmers. He would "build a penitentiary for eight million people and hold them

---

[8]JOHN SPENCER BASSETT, *Hist. of U. S.*, p. 603, describes in detail "Forty Acres and a Mule."

down at the point of a bayonet." "If they undertake to come here, we will shoot them down."

It is not strange that the Chicago Times urged President Johnson to arrest Thaddeus Stevens and Wendell Phillips as incendiaries.

IV

On the last day of January, 1865,[9] the House of Representatives passed a joint resolution, previously enacted by the Senate, now the Thirteenth Amendment to the Constitution. It reads:

"Section I. Neither slavery nor involuntary servitude, except as punishment for crime whereof the party shall have been duly convicted, shall exist within the United States, nor any place subject to their jurisdiction.

"Section II. Congress shall have power to enforce this article by appropriate legislation."

It is quite astonishing that a single vote was registered against this amendment, but fifty-six voted "No," one hundred and nineteen "Aye," and eight did not vote at all.

When the result was announced the House went wild with enthusiasm. The spectators joined in the celebration, tossing up hats, handkerchiefs and umbrellas. Hundreds of ladies in the galleries joined in the plaudits which added color to the sensation.

Mr. Ingersoll, of Illinois, finally got the floor and cried, "In honor of this immortal and sublime event, I move that the House adjourn." It was carried by one hundred and twenty-one to twenty-four.

---

[9] Seventy days before General Lee surrendered.

The Thirteenth Amendment was sent down to the States and adopted by three-fourths of them, Virginia[10] being one. When it suited the Radicals to count Virginia's vote, it was counted; when it did not suit them to count Virginia's vote, it was not counted . . . an excellent illustration of American honesty and integrity in 1865-70.

The Secretary of State, William Henry Seward, of New York, proclaimed the Thirteenth Amendment, December 18, 1865. Delaware and Kentucky never did adopt this amendment. Strangely enough, the very day Seward proclaimed the Amendment, Thaddeus Stevens made his bitter and revolutionary speech against admitting the Southern congressmen, which has been described above.

---

[10]JOHN WILLIAM BURGESS, *Reconstruction*, p. 55: "Virginia was one of the States announced by William H. Seward as having adopted the XIII Amendment."

If Virginia was not a State, how could the Secretary of State count Virginia's vote? If Virginia was a State, why were not her representatives seated in Congress, and why was she denied all other constitutional privileges?

BLAIR NILES, *James River*, Chap. 24.

WM. JOS. SHOWALTER, *Virginia, National Geographic Magazine*, April, 1929.

ALLEN NEVINS, *Thaddeus Stevens, Dict. Amer. Biog.*

CHAPTER X

AN OMINOUS YEAR ENDS

We stand among the crowding ghosts of many
miserable years.
—*Charles Dickens.*

As the long, dismal and troubled year, 1865, drew
slowly to a close, the Virginians might well have
taken an inventory. Many homes were happy,
even if a widowed mother, or infirm father garlanded
the graves of their dead. It was estimated that
one hundred and five thousand young men—more
than one-seventh of the total white population[1]—
were either disabled or lay rotting in untimely graves.
These noble youths, the flower of Virginia, begotten
of the best blood on earth, were cut down in the
prime of manhood. They were the hope of the
future, the stay of the feeble and aged, the potential
husbands and fathers of the generation yet unborn.[2]

Those who remained, despite poverty, persecution
and proscription, did not lose their morale. Splendid

[1]In 1860 the population of Virginia was 1,047,411, white; 58,042 free colored, and 490,865 slaves (West Virginia's area included). In 1870 the population of Virginia was 712,089 white and 512,841 colored. The population of
West Virginia was 424,033 white and 17,980 colored.

[2]Through this troubled year the remains of young Confederate heroes
were brought from battlefield or trench every day, and laid in a family plot
with Christian burial. The columns of the local press were filled with such
notices.

WALTER HINES PAGE, *Life*, p. 2.

men were they, though clothed in faded and battered
uniforms but little better than rags. They walked
the earth like heroes, erect and manly. Every gesture said: "I am native here, and to the manner
born." They knew that they were still the lords
of the land.

The Revolution left Virginia a desert,[3] and Bacon's
Rebellion reduced the colony to the verge of extinction.[4] Yet Virginia survived; she would again
negotiate her troubles and solve her difficulties and
her problems. What had been done could again be
done.

The typical Virginian in 1865 was a farmer. He
lifted his eyes to the majestic sweep of a forested
slope; he saw the dew-drops glisten in the morning
sun and the shafts of light penetrate the thick foliage
of the forest; he heard the happy birds in the woodlands. The brooks murmured their way over mossy
stones as in the happier days. The long day's work
done, he rested, and the evening star swung like a
censor in the blue vault of heaven. He prayed that
here he might live to labor and to love, to claim his
promised bride, to rear his family and at close of
day to leave Virginia for his Home Eternal.

He recalled the widely quoted words of General
Lee . . . Virginia needed her sons now more than
ever before. He had offered his life for the constitutional rights guaranteed the Commonwealth, and
he had been spared, though all but life was taken.
Yet, with life and the good land, he would carry

[3] *The Land of Decision*, SQUIRES, p. 10.
[4] *Through Centuries Three*, SQUIRES, pp. 221-225.

bravely on and wrest prosperity again from the generous soil.

The young Virginian knew that he must walk wisely and circumspectly. One word or even gesture might be used by the human vermin who spied constantly upon him to clap him into prison or confiscate his land. Whitelaw Reid[5] reported the case accurately: "The rebels must walk in a certain path, or be suppressed by the military authority."

The young farmer dared not allow a band, braid or button to show upon his faded uniform—else he would be arrested as a "traitor." In Norfolk the provost-marshal gave notice to arrest such offenders. Sometimes Negro soldiers in bright, blue uniforms would stop the ex-Confederate and, with great ceremony, cut off the Confederate button (or a button that the large, black patriot claimed might be a Confederate button) with a glistening sabre. In Richmond the buttons were allowed if cloth-covered.

There was always an undefined fear, a vague dread, lest worse befall, which haunted the land like an horrid spectre . . . and with reason. The threat of confiscation was ever present.[6] Millions of dollars worth of private and personal property had been taken or ruthlessly destroyed during the war. Many leaders, like Thaddeus Stevens and Charles Sumner, openly demanded the confiscation of all

---

[5] WHITELAW REID, *A Southern Tour*, p. 320.

[6] W. E. WOODWARD, *Meet General Grant*, p. 379. The Freedmen's Bureau degenerated into a rapacious corps of human vultures, each agent having an eye on rich land that might be picked up at a fraction of its value, or might be acquired without price.

THE PILOT BOAT VIRGINIA

The pilot boat "Virginia" which for many years standing off the headland of Cape Henry welcomed every ship inbound.

* * * *

The ancient Record Book of Norfolk Borough has this minute:

"At a Common Council held this 1st day of April, 1754, the Honorable Robert Dinwiddie, Esqr., His Majesty's Lieutenant Governor and Commander-in-Chief, this day presented to the Borough of Norfolk a very handsome silver Mace, which was thankfully received."

This rare Colonial relic, the only such Mace possessed by an American city, has escaped destruction and theft. During the Revolution Mayor Paul Loyall buried the Mace in a garden at Kempsville, Princess Anne County. During the War Between the States, Mayor William Lamb buried it under a hearth on the second floor of his residence, 240 W. Bute Street, where it remained until the dangers of Reconstruction passed.

It is now on exhibition in the vault of the National Bank of Commerce during banking hours, in a crystal case provided by the bank.

THE NORFOLK MACE

Southern property.   Certainly no rebel should be allowed more than $20,000 worth; the valuation to be made by martinets imported for that purpose. Federal soldiers constantly assured the negroes that the plantations, and even the homes of the rebels, would soon be turned over to them.

"The freebooter,[7] pilferer, low sneak and cowardly robber had begun their despicable trade, which soon became so widespread in the South.   These detestable camp-followers must have been numerous in the Northern army.   Within three days after the close of hostilities the sharks, robbers, thieves, oppressors and insulters began their work as avant couriers of the carpet-baggers, who figured so largely in politics a few years later."

It is exceedingly interesting to read the editorials of the Norfolk press in 1865.   Their guarded language and fine self-control leave volumes unspoken.   Their devotion to the South and her ideals were adroitly unexpressed.   John Mitchell was still in prison at Fort Monroe, because of his outspoken editorials in the Richmond Examiner.[8]

"I suppose you have seen an account of the suppression of the Richmond Examiner?   It was the boldest paper in the State except the Petersburg Index, the editor of which, Lieutenant Keiley, of

---

[7] B. W. JONES, *Under the Stars and Bars*, p. 279.   This statement is too well authenticated to be discounted as mere prejudice, or an exaggeration.

[8] BASIL L. GILDERSLEEVE, in a sonnet to the memory of J. M. Daniel, late editor of the *Richmond Examiner*, has these lines:

"'Twas better thus to die,
Than live to see this swarm of crawling things
And burn with words that must remain unspoke."
—*Fugitive Poems of Virginia*, p. 299.

Mahone's Brigade, has already spent a week or two in Castle Thunder. I have been up before the provost-marshal once," wrote W. Gordon McCabe, a Confederate colonel, who was now a schoolmaster.

There was no Magna Charta in Virginia from 1865 to 1870, and no Constitution in the home of Patrick Henry, George Washington, Thomas Jefferson and John Marshall.

Flags were stretched across the streets, and if a woman[9] declined to walk under them, she was arrested and fined for being a "traitor."

II

These radical agents, spies, professional informers[10] and managers of the Freedmen's Bureau collected every sensational tale of disorder, disloyalty or crime, and sent it to the Radical press as indisputable evidence of a disloyal, unrepentant and undefeated South.

The Southern people were only awaiting a chance

---

[9]The Federal soldiers found it impossible to subdue the women of the South. If an officer appeared on the sidewalk, the women would cross the street, through dust, mud or traffic. General Terry reported to Washington that he was hissed by the women as he drove through the streets of Richmond. At Liberty (now Bedford), Virginia, the soldiers complained that the women would leave a pew in Church if one of them entered it. They would not walk under the National flag, but around it.

[10]T. J. WERTENBAKER, *Hist. of Norfolk.*

The streets of Norfolk were crowded with idle men and boys, vagrants, sailors, camp-followers and countless hundreds of negroes, both men and women. The disreputable section was alive with notorious dance-halls, saloons, gambling-parlors and dives of every description. There were almost daily fights between the negroes and soldiers. Hold-ups and burglaries were of nightly occurrence. Norfolk had been under martial law since the Confederate troops retired, May 10, 1862.

Land of Decision, SQUIRES, p. 58.

to rise again, destroy the nation, re-enslave the
blacks. If Federal bayonets were withdrawn, these
fiery rebels would murder every Union soldier and
assassinate every Union sympathizer. The Southern
people were lazy, degenerate, passionate, shiftless,
domineering, bloodthirsty aristocrats, unbowed and
unbroken. They must be humiliated, kept for
years under an iron heel, made to acknowledge their
crimes and become really civilized like the people
up North. The best way to civilize and Christianize
the South was to disfranchise all the "rebels" and
enfranchise all the freedmen.

Thousands and thousands of such items from
every part of the South, published daily for a decade,
in all parts of the North, made a profound and permanent impression. So persistent were these malicious falsehoods and so convincing (for they could
not then be answered) that one hears them quoted
to this day.

"Jeff Davis," wrote George Washington Julian
(November 4, 1865), in Indiana, "I would hang him
in the name of God. What an outrage that Lee is
unmolested—hang him too. I would hang liberally
while I had my hand in. I would give the land to
the Negroes and not leave a rebel enough to bury
his carcass in."

The agents of the Freedmen's Bureau were especially diligent in this malicious propaganda. If
the South was readmitted to the Union, their representatives would unite with the "Copperheads" in
the North and control the government. Then
slavery would be reinstituted, and the fruits of
victory lost. William Lloyd Garrison, of Massa-

chusetts, had this in mind when he declared, "I know that at the South the powers of hell are still strong and defiant, resolved upon doing whatever evil is possible in a spirit of diabolical malignity."

Such constantly reiterated reports added fuel to the Radical flames. But the propagandists were able to forget important items. They did not report that a negro regiment from Baltimore had a riot, which might have been described as a battle, with the white soldiers of the 20th Regiment of New York, during which some were killed, many wounded and a reign of terror was given Norfolk's law-abiding citizens.[11]

The "New York Tribune" seemed to be especially hospitable to detailed accounts of every outrage practiced upon freedmen and for all the iniquities of the rebels. But the Tribune's neighbor, the "New York World," sprang to the defense of the South. The "World" was a Copperhead sheet, as everyone knew . . . so its opinion and its news must be discounted.

So great was their indignation that the citizens of Richmond, in a mass meeting, denounced the Radical press of the North for their constant and bitter attacks upon the people of the South. They would not submit to the libels repeated and reiterated until, it seemed to their readers, that the lies must be true. The South asked only peace, justice, fairness and a chance to live and be loyal to the Union. They fought bravely to the bitter end, and surrendered in good faith—why this endless persecution?

---

[11] *Norfolk Post*, files for December, 1865.

The citizens of Lynchburg found their voice. In a meeting at Dudley Hall, the last day of September, they drew up strong resolutions of loyalty. They had made an honest fight, they had surrendered in good faith, and now they asked only peace and justice as loyal citizens of the United States. Copies of these resolutions were sent President Johnson and Governor Pierpont.

Lynchburg seemed to have been the boldest of Southern cities. Soon after the surrender a meeting for women was called in the Second Presbyterian Church, to memorialize President Johnson in behalf of ex-President Jefferson Davis. General Newton Martin Curtis,[12] then commanding in Lynchburg, forbade the meeting! A lecture on "Chivalry in the South," by H. Pollard Rives, was also forbidden. The citizens met on Washington's Birthday (1866), and endorsed President Johnson's policies. Soon after this, April 9, 1866, the troops were withdrawn from Lynchburg.

The resolutions of Lynchburg[13] and Richmond seemed useless. The slanders and libels of the Radical press were as vindictive as ever. Yet it is to congratulate those Virginians who found their voice.

There were occasional outbreaks, as at Memphis and New Orleans, but on the whole the dignity, sobriety, self-control, energy, self-possession and discipline of the Virginians and the other Southern

---

[12]He came to Lynchburg, July 1, 1865, to hold Southwestern Virginia in subjection, and was mustered out January 15, 1866. This order to the women is his only service now remembered in Virginia.

[13]Annual Cyclop.—1867.

people under the lash of such libel, petty tyranny and constant irritation; of such calumny and tissues of lies, retailed for political purposes, is on the whole astonishing. The Virginian is usually portrayed in fiction as volatile, high-strung and impulsive; exactly the reverse is true. The typical Virginian is a Saxon of peaceful, quiet and dignified demeanor, slightly reserved, as is his British cousin.

Every falsehood carries its own retribution. Every lie returns to torment the liar. Those who are too radical always defeat their own purpose. Many and increasingly potent influences were at work to heal[14] the hurts of war, and usher in an era of better feeling.

Henry Ward Beecher cried: "It is said that if admitted to Congress the Southern senators and representatives will coalesce with Northern Democrats and rule this country. Is this nation, then, to be dismembered to serve the ends of party?"

Other influential voices spoke for the South. Editors, senators and even President Johnson pleaded for charity and justice. Such men as James E. Campbell, of Ohio; Thomas Andrews Hendricks, of Indiana; Chief Justice Salmon P. Chase, William H. Seward, now Secretary of State, had kindly words and keen sympathy for the suffering South.

Could the civilization which produced Washington, Marshall, Jefferson, Madison, Monroe, Clay, Scott, Taylor; the Harrisons, Lees, Blairs, Bentons

---

[14]WILLIAM LANDER WEBER, *Southern Poets*, p. 215, describes the philanthropy of the women of Baltimore, in the poem "Kind Hands," by SEVERN TEACKLE WALLIS. A great fair given by the women raised $165,000 which was used to supply the farmers of the South with seed, so that they might the sooner become self-supporting. (See Wallis' *Works*.)

and an innumerable host equally as distinguished, be so debased as Garrison, Thaddeus Stevens, Charles Sumner, Edwin Stanton, Benjamin F. Wade and Julian declared?

Was not Abraham Lincoln born in Kentucky, and George Henry Thomas in Virginia, and David Glasgow Farragut in Tennessee? Without these three would the war ever have been won?

III

The greatest factor, the one unanswerable argument, was the diligent, thrifty, honest, silent and disciplined man who labored from dawn to sunset six long, hot days, in fields of cotton, corn or tobacco. "Thrift, diligence and economy were practiced by the women, as industry, energy and determination were practiced by the men," wrote one shrewd observer.

General Lee wrote Walter Herron Taylor at Norfolk: "Tell them (the ex-Confederate soldiers) they must set to work and if they can not do what they prefer, then let them do what they can. Virginia needs all their aid to sustain and recuperate her."

General Lee[15] also wrote former Governor John Letcher: "All should unite in honest effort to obliterate the effects of the war, and to restore the blessings of peace."

---

[15] R. E. LEE. Letter to his daughter (1867), *Life of Lee*, p. 253: "You must bear in mind that it will not be becoming in a Virginia girl now to be fine or fashionable. Gentility as well as self-respect requires moderation in dress and gaiety. While her people are suffering you should practice self-denial and show sympathy in their affliction."

"Lee formally applied for amnesty[16] and the restoration of civil rights within two months of his surrender." His application was ignored, and he died (1870) a prisoner on parole. But while General Lee[17] had no vote, the right of suffrage was conferred upon all the negroes in the state, even the most ignorant and brutal.

During this year General William Henry Fitzhugh Lee, the son of Robert E. Lee, called familiarly "Rooney" Lee, raised a crop of corn on an ancestral farm in New Kent County. The fine old residence upon the estate, called The White House, was burned during its occupation by Federal troops, so "Rooney" Lee made his home in an outbuilding.

In every neighborhood the ex-Confederate soldiers did as Robert E. Lee advised, and followed his noble example as well as his precept. Like General "Rooney" Lee, General Edward Johnson farmed his acres in Chesterfield County. General Samuel Jones managed his farm near Mattoax, Virginia. General Lunsford Lindsay Lomax was a farmer until he was elected president of the Virginia Polytechnic Institute at Blacksburg, Virginia. General Thomas Taylor Munford became a large and prosperous planter, and General William Booth Taliaferro tilled his ancestral acres in Gloucester County. General James A. Walker, one of Stonewall Jackson's ablest lieutenants, "returned to his home in Pulaski County[18] and immediately went to work, putting in

[16]CHARLES FRANCIS ADAMS, *Military Studies*, p. 336.
[17]DON P. HALSEY, speech on bill to provide a statue of Lee to be placed in the Capitol at Washington (1903).
[18]*Confederate Military History*, Vol. III, p. 679.

Photo by H. C. Mann

THE ROAD HOMEWARD

"The soldier returned from Appomattox, a youth though a veteran, glad of life and limb for he had seen his comrades fall on every side like autumn leaves. Standing on his parental acres, in the shadow of the pines, he lifted his eyes to the rising sun. His fathers had won this land by sweat and blood before the days of Bacon's Rebellion, and had defended his home from British invasion and he knew that in all the world there was no land so fair as Virginia."—Page 131.

a crop of corn with the two mules he brought home"
from Appomattox, thus fulfilling General Grant's wish
expressed at the time of the surrender. General
Reuben Lindsay Walker, "after participating in
sixty-three battles and other combats," returned to
his farm.

As all the world knows General Robert E. Lee
became president of Washington College,[19] which he
managed with conspicuous ability until laid to rest
under the rostrum of the University Chapel.

Charles Scott Venable filled the chair of mathe-
matics at the University of Virginia for many years;[20]
Matthew Fontaine Maury was a professor at Virginia Military Institute, on the classic hilltop just
beyond Washington College. Colonel W. Gordon
McCabe established a famous school for boys at
Petersburg, Virginia. General Raleigh Edward Col-
ston opened a military academy for boys at Wilmington, North Carolina. General Richard L. Page became superintendent of the public schools of Norfolk.

Many distinguished officers turned, or returned, to
the practice of law. Both Generals Jubal Anderson
Early and Henry Alexander Wise became famous
advocates at the Richmond bar. General Wise won
distinction as an author. General Eppa Hunton
opened his office at Warrenton. General William
Henry Fitzhugh Payne and General William Terry
became advocates, the latter leading the bar at
Wytheville.

Colonel Walter Herron Taylor became a banker,
financier and philanthropist in his native city, Nor-

---

[19]Now Washington and Lee University, Lexington, Va.
[20]LYON G. TYLER, *Cyclop. Va. Biog.*, Vol. III, p. 160. From 1865 until 1896

folk. General John Echols' career, in his native town of Staunton,[21] was as a financier.

Major James Barron Hope became famous as an editor, poet and author. General Thomas Jordan became an editor and author in New York. General Armistead Lindsay Long, frequently quoted in these pages, is remembered as an accurate historian; for years he was chief-engineer of the James River and Kanawha Canal Company. General Dabney Herndon Maury is remembered as an author and historian.

General William Mahone[22] returned to the building of railways. General Walter Husted Stevens built a valuable railway in Mexico. General Carter L. Stephenson became distinguished as an authority in civil and mining engineering. General William Carter Wickham took over the Virginia Central Railway (Chesapeake and Ohio) and rebuilt it, as General Mahone rehabilitated the Norfolk and Western—two of the great railway systems of the country to this day.

General George Edward Pickett developed an insurance business in Richmond, and General Henry Heth engaged in the same business in the same city. General Patrick T. Moore and General Beverly Holcombe Robertson also turned to insurance. General Thomas LaFayette Rosser became an executive of the National Express Company.

The fates ordained that eight[23] Confederate sol-

---

[21] ALEX. F. ROBERTSON, *Stuart*, p. 268-70.

[22] *Land of Decision*, SQUIRES, Chap. XI.

[23] *Through Centuries Three*, SQUIRES, pp. 517-567. A brief biography of each of them is given in this book.

diers, of different ages and ranks, should become Governors of Virginia: General James Lawson Kemper, Colonel Frederick William Mackey Holliday, Colonel William Evelyn Cameron, General Fitzhugh Lee, Captain Philip Watkins McKinney, Colonel Charles Triplett O'Ferrell, Private James Hoge Tyler and Private William Hodges Mann (the two last mere youths in the Confederate battle line).

These were the leaders, and, like them, the entire Confederate army disappeared after the surrender to take up similar activities. This simple but significant item explains the gradual solutions of all Southern problems (and no civilized nation ever faced more), on one hand; and the enormous increase of wealth, culture and prosperity the South achieved before that strenuous generation passed away.

The young farmers heard the news on court day, or at church, or in town. They knew that the cities were being cleared, the deserted homes and farms rehabilitated, rails were again being laid in all parts of the state. On July 11 a train from the North reached Richmond[24] . . . the first to arrive since April 18, 1861, the day after the fatal Ordinance of Secession was passed. The rails on this and all the roads were rusted, the bridges burned, and travel dangerous. These passengers crossed the Rappahannock at Fredericksburg by ferry. They left Washington 9:00 a. m. Tuesday, and arrived in Richmond at 5:00 p. m. Wednesday. During the summer and fall the trains were crowded with

---

[24]*Richmond Whig*, Aug. 2, 1865, promised that travel to Washington by rail to Acquia Creek and thence by boat to Washington would soon be opened.

curiosity hunters, sight-seers, speculators, pardon-brokers, Southern politicians, carpet-baggers and job hunters. A visitor from New York made the trip from Richmond to Lynchburg in thirty hours. The train crept cautiously along, sometimes attaining nine miles an hour. By October 5th service from Lynchburg to Chattanooga by way of Bristol was announced. The fare was from five to eleven cents per mile, according to accommodations.

There were two daily trains from Petersburg to Lynchburg[25] on the Southside Railway (now the Norfolk and Western). At High Bridge the passengers took an ambulance for a mile-and-a-half drive around the bridge. Six miles from Lynchburg the passengers were transferred to a canal boat. This was "not a very good line, and our cars were indifferent and passengers frequently complained of the inconvenience." But the service provided some revenue, and so helped the company to effect many needed repairs. General William Mahone, of the Norfolk and Petersburg, was elected President of the Southside Railroad, December 7, 1865.

The night before the surrender General Lee is reputed[26] to have said, "Well, it is over and forever. The wise thing is to accommodate ourselves to the new order, go home and go to work."

General Mahone was much impressed by the statement, remembered it and followed it to the letter. He returned to Norfolk and to the rebuilding of the Norfolk and Petersburg Railroad. He found it in deplorable condition, the foundations damaged, roll-

[25]HELVESTINE, in N. and W. Magazine, Vol. I, No. 3.
[26]NELSON M. BLAKE, *Mahone*, p. 72.

ing stock gone, organization completely disrupted
and all capital dissipated.   Despite all obstacles he
put such energy into the task that by February 19,
1866, he had trains running on schedule.   The
Southside Railway extended from Petersburg to
Lynchburg, 123 miles, and it had acquired the
nine mile road from Petersburg to City Point.   This
modest railway was built in 1837, and is the oldest
link in the great system now known as the Norfolk
and Western.

The Southside Railway had been a life-line to
the Confederacy during the siege of Petersburg and
Richmond.   When it was returned to its former
owners by the Government, July 28, 1865, it was a
complete wreck, an elongated ruin.   During the fall
of 1865 the trains would run when they could, and
the passengers were transferred to ambulances when
gaps in the track made it impossible for the train
to pass.

During the summer of 1865 the Virginia Central
endeavored to make a schedule from Richmond to
Staunton and the Orange and Alexandria operated
trains its whole, short length.

On the water rival steamboat companies adver-
tised trips to Baltimore and other points and were
said to "swarm in James River."   By the end of the
year one might travel from Richmond to Mobile on
an unbroken line of rails.

All over Virgina men were at work rehabilitating
the lines and making repairs.   The telegraph lines
were being restrung and improved.   By July messages were received from New York and were being
sent to all the larger cities of the South.

Mail service from Washington to Richmond was begun, July 31; but it was almost Christmas before a letter might be sent to Charleston, S. C., or to Florida points.

It argued well for the future that within six months after the surrender sixteen new banks were opened in Virginia.[27]　Considerable support came to these institutions from Northern capital.

General Wade Hampton advised his neighbors in South Carolina to "devote their whole energies to the restoration of law and order, the reestablishment of agriculture and commerce, the promotion of education, the rebuilding of our cities and dwellings, which have been laid in ashes."

Norfolk began a system of public schools before the war (1857).　During Federal occupation General Benjamin F. Butler demanded that every teacher take an oath of allegiance to the Federal government. He insisted that white and colored children be educated in the same rooms, side by side.

Norfolk Academy was used as a hospital; but renovated and reopened in October, 1865, as a school.

"The Norfolk Virginian" began publication November 1, 1865, and its policy was to urge patience, moderation and self-control in the trying situation now confronting state and nation.　James Barron Hope began publication of "The Journal,"[28] January 1, 1866.　Norfolk was excited over the question of an issue of bonds to build modern water-works, at

---

[27]In the entire South 35 were organized by Oct. 31, 1865.

[28]It became, after a few years, "The Norfolk Landmark," and, after half a century of service, was merged with the "Virginian-Pilot."

a cost of $500,000. After a heated campaign the progressives won (pro 451, contra 149), but the proposition could not be financed until 1872. In the meantime the citizens used private cisterns and private and public wells, the largest of which was at the corner of Main and Nebraska Streets.

In Richmond the burnt district south and east of the Capitol Square was rapidly rebuilt, and the edifices were "much handsomer than those destroyed."

Radical senators and congressmen maligned the South in bitterest invective, and hostile editors dipped Radical pens in vitriol and produced endless diatribes of falsehood.[29]

The soldier returned from Appomattox, a youth though a veteran, glad of life and limb, for he had seen his comrades fall on every side like autumn leaves. Standing on his parental acres in the shadow of the pines he lifted his eyes to the rising sun. His fathers had won this land by sweat and toil, and he knew that in all the world there was no land so fair as Virginia.

IV

Of the millions who toiled, labored and hoped for better things,[30] there was one young Confederate soldier who, when the war broke out, left his two motherless children with relatives, marched away from his farm, four miles north of Durham, North

---

[29]JAMES FORD RHODES, an historian by no means partial to the South, and very unfair, we believe, to President Johnson, wrote that revolutions usually become too radical, and that three men, President Johnson, Thaddeus Stevens and Charles Sumner were chiefly responsible.

Mr. Rhodes overlooks Edwin M. Stanton.

[30]EDWARD A. POLLARD, *The Lost Cause*, p. 743.

Carolina, and enlisted.   When he returned he found
that Federal troops had removed or destroyed everything that could be removed or destroyed.   He had
his barren land, one half-dollar, two blind mules and
two orphaned boys.   With these he began again.
His name was Washington Duke, and one of the
two little boys was James Buchanan Duke.   When
James Buchanan Duke died, October 10, 1925, he
left the largest endowment for educational and eleemosynary institutions which has ever been given at
one time in all human history.   Southern wealth was
destroyed, and Southern institutions were destroyed,
but Southern manhood has triumphed over every
disaster.[31]

---

[31]There was much loud but futile emigration talk during 1865.   To Mexico,
Cuba, Brazil, New Zealand and Australia the pessimists advised the Confederate
soldiers to go.   Robert E. Lee stood like adamant against such wild schemes.
Those who talked so wildly gradually settled down to work, others who actually
left the country in almost every case returned.

THOMAS CARY JOHNSON, *Life of Dabney*, pp. 299-327.

BURTON J. HENDRICK, *Walter H. Page*, p. 14.   Reconstruction worse than
war.

GEORGE W. BAGBY, *Old Virginia Gentleman*, poem, "After Appomattox."

ARMISTEAD C. GORDON, *Virginia Portraits*, "W. Gordon McCabe."

GEORGE S. BERNARD, *War Talks*, pp. 10-23.

CORNELIA PHILLIPS SPENCER, *Last Ninety Days of the War*, p. 267: "More
than one-seventh of the graduates of the University of North Carolina fell in
battle before October 1st, 1863."

BOOK TWO

DECEMBER 4, 1865—NOVEMBER 6, 1866

CHAPTER XI

THE VAGRANCY ACTS

Alas, too well we know
The pain, the penitence, the woe
That passion brings down on the best
The wisest and the loveliest.

—*Thomas Moore.*

The new year, 1866, began ominously for Virginia. "Fitful fortune in her darkest mood turned to us a frowning face."[1] Despair clutched at the hearts of our people. Forty-nine "witnesses" were summoned to Washington from this State to testify as to the condition of Virginia. Now Virginia is not a long, long way from Washington. Almost every building has windows from which the dim, blue heights over the Potomac may be seen. Fully half the inhabitants of the District are Virginians. One of the Committee of Fifteen was a native Virginian, another a native of Maryland. Nevertheless, Virginia was to be "investigated." Forty-seven of the forty-nine witnesses were Radicals; many of them ultra-radicals. The other two were Robert E. Lee, then President of Washington College at Lexington, and Judge William T. Joynes, of Petersburg, a supreme justice of Virginia.

The ratio, 47 to 2, gives an excellent idea of the

[1] PHILIP ALEXANDER BRUCE.

Committee's fairness and impartiality. The testimony was precisely as expected. The overwhelming majority made oath that the Virginians were a brutal, blood-thirsty, arrogant people, proud, bitter, unbroken and unconquered. When the Federal troops were withdrawn they would butcher all who opposed them. No invectives were too strong, no adjectives too severe, to describe the fierce barbarians living just over the Potomac. Among those who testified were Gen. John Wesley Turner, of New York, of the Army of the James; Judge John C. Underwood, whose name runs like a malediction through our Reconstruction history; Gen. Alfred Howe Terry, whom we will often meet again; Lewis McKenzie, of Alexandria, a member of Congress for two months from "restored Virginia" (1863); John F. Lewis, of Augusta, a pronounced Unionist, who would not sign the Ordinance of Secession; Col. Orlando Brown, chief of the Freedmen's Bureau for Virginia; George S. Smith, who replied to the question, "If left to themselves what would the Virginians do with the Negroes?"

"They would entirely extirpate them from the face of the earth. They would commence with the Union men, and then they would take the Negroes."

General Lee[2] testified that the Virginians were entirely loyal to the United States, and wished only the opportunity to live in peace.[3]

---

[2]JOHN ESTEN COOKE, *Life of Lee*, pp. 471-485, gives in full the questions asked General Lee and his replies.

[3]LANDON C. BELL, *Robert E. Lee, an Address*, pp. 24-27.

General Lee's extended letter to Lord Acton (quoting Acton's correspondence, Vol. I, pp. 302-305).

Judge William T. Joynes, of Petersburg, a member of the Whig Legislature then sitting in Richmond, stated that the General Assembly was entirely loyal and anxious for the restoration of peace and harmony between the sections lately at war, and between the two races.

But what were they among so many?

II

The Whig Legislators in an effort to protect the law-abiding citizens of Virginia from the multiplying criminal classes passed several vagrancy laws. The slums of our cities and towns were filled with idle freedmen, petty criminals and many vicious whites, the flotsam and jetsam that every revolution brings to the surface.

The Norfolk Journal (March 6, 1867) has this item: "It is very gratifying to learn that the destitute Negroes in Yorktown and vicinity have been brought to the attention of the Freedmen's Bureau in Washington. There is an immense surplus of this Negro population in that section, which, while scarcely maintaining a bare existence by most precarious means, is a constant dread to the farmers and citizens. Bands of desperadoes organized with ringleaders have robbed the farmers and threaten the lives of those who resist them. Every store between Hampton and Williamsburg has received a visit or two from these marauders. General Howard ordered the bands to be scattered around the country."[4]   One must protest Gen. O. O. Howard's method of scattering "criminals around the country," but that is not our story.

It is significant that General Terry came to Richmond from the committee room in Washington with enthusiasm inflamed, and nine days after the vagrancy act, he annulled it, January 25, 1866. Yet the General was supposed to be in Richmond to "protect a republican form of government." The act passed by the Whig Legislature was dropped at once . . . Virginia was not a republic in 1866, but a conquered province. The satraps were the military commanders, and behind the satraps was the Reconstruction Committee of Fifteen, under the scowl and lash of Thaddeus Stevens.

In the Senate the will of the Committee was potent with such radical leaders as Charles Sumner, of Massachusetts; Ben Wade, of Ohio, and Zachariah Chandler, of Michigan. One can not escape the conviction that, with this political background, "the gallant Terry"[5] was playing politics as he spoke one word for the wandering, idle, thieving Negroes and two for the Reconstruction Committee before whose frown the soldier trembled. "The ultimate effect of the statute will be to reduce the freedmen to a condition of servitude worse than that from which they have been emancipated—a condition which will be slavery in all but name. It is therefore ordered that no magistrate, civil officer or other person shall

---

[4]GENERAL FRANCIS JAY HERRON reported that the freedmen were moving en masse to the military posts instead of laboring in the fields, the only place in which they could make an honest living.

[5]JOHN SERGEANT WISE so calls him.

in any way or manner apply or attempt to apply the provisions of said statute to any colored person in this department."

No doubt there were those, especially if far removed, who believed that the vagrancy acts of Virginia and the South were intended by the bloodthirsty "rebels" to reinstate slavery in form and in fact. But General Terry could not have been one of them, for Terry was a shrewd observer, thoroughly conversant with the local situation. At politics this gallant soldier was not an amateur.

The vagrancy act as passed by the Legislature of Virginia—the same Legislature which had just approved the Thirteenth Amendment—was a good and necessary, law,[6] and Terry knew it. The effect of it was not to reintroduce slavery, but to protect honest and sober citizens in the "department," and Terry knew that. The law applied to whites as well as to Negroes, and he knew that. Such laws were upon all the statute books of all the States, and Terry knew that. To abrogate the law in such a high-handed manner was to encourage idleness, vice, thieving and immorality; and the effect of his proclamation was to place the bayonets of the United States Army behind the criminal class, and by the same token jeopardized the life and property of every honest citizen in Virginia, black or white, and the General knew that!

The radical press praised Terry. Editorials fell

---

[6]CHARLES and MARY BEARD, *Rise of American Civilization*, Vol. II, p. 117: "Former masters through state legislatures restored a kind of servitude by means of vagrancy and poor laws."

This statement is certainly not true, in spirit nor in fact.

hot and fast throughout the North and West. The blatant, blood-thirsty, impenitent Virginians were endeavoring to re-enslave the wards of the nation, but were checked by General Terry!

A Chicago editor declared that he would prefer to make the State of Mississippi "a frog pond" rather than allow the vagrancy acts of that Commonwealth to be enforced. And yet there always have been vagrancy acts on the statute books of Illinois and every other state!

Neither General Terry nor the Radical press were at all concerned about the life, liberty, property, nor welfare of the honest law-abiding, hard-working farmers or merchants, their wives and children.[7] The Radical press did not tell their readers that the Legislature of Virginia legalized the marriage of Negroes, and made their offspring legitimate. They did not mention that no contract should be binding upon any ignorant man, black or white, until and unless the terms were read to him and explained in simple language by a disinterested magistrate.

Nor did they tell that all distinction between the two races in crime were now abolished, that the old slave codes and other discriminations were cancelled. Nor that Negroes were now allowed to give testimony in court, like other citizens, previously denied them. Nor did they tell that all the white men and many women and children labored in the fields from sunrise until dark to rehabilitate the farms and raise foodstuffs while thousands of freed-

---

[7]JAMES J. MC DONALD, *Old Virginia*, pp. 168-178.

men wandered aimlessly about, fed by the Freedmen's Bureau, and quarreled and fought among
themselves as to which should get the choicest fields
and fattest farms when the Government confiscated
the rebels' land and turned it over to the former
slaves.

The Legislature of Virginia under the superb
strategy of John B. Baldwin promptly and effectively
answered the gallant Terry by reconsidering and
expunging the vagrancy laws and by a resolution
that declared slavery in all forms whatsoever, forever
abolished in Virginia (February 6, 1866). But
gallant Terry took no notice of that and the Radical
editors did not think it worth while to mention it.

The scenes in the tragedy of Congressional Reconstruction evidence a closely-articulated program,
manipulated with a fine, Italian hand. Nothing was
left to chance. There was to be a new Congress,
the Fortieth, elected November 6, 1866. On the
franchise of that autumnal contest Radical Reconstruction would be endorsed or vetoed. Hence the
bloody shirt must be flung to every breeze in village,
town, city and countryside from Maine to California.
Rebels, slave drivers and all traitors must be kept
constantly and conspicuously before the public
until the election was passed.

Johnson's policy (which was Lincoln's policy) of
amnesty, conciliation and reunion must be buried,
the deeper the better, under an avalanche of votes.
Throughout the shifting scenes of this memorable
year (1866) the coming election must not be forgotten . . . it was never absent from the cunning
calculations of Radical politicians.

Less than two weeks after the "investigation" of
Virginia's "condition," the Virginia Radicals met in
Alexandria (February 5), John Curtis Underwood
presiding. These "loyal" patriots implored Congress (meaning of course the Committee of Fifteen
and the dictator, Thaddeus Stevens) to establish a
territorial government in Virginia. The Pierpont
government at Richmond was too mild. Pierpont
was no longer "safe," although it was Pierpont's
hand which had, to a degree, carved the new State
of West Virginia from Virginia and left this Commonwealth rent asunder for all future time.

They urged that the Freedmen's Bureau be
strengthened, enlarged and made more efficient.
These patriots begged that the freedmen be made
full citizens of the United States with franchise,
although the Constitution provides expressly that
each State must decide for itself who shall be permitted to vote. As Thaddeus Stevens already had
the Freedmen's Bureau bill and the Civil Rights
bill in his pocket one can not escape the conviction
that Underwood and his fellow patriots at Alexandria were directly and expressly inspired . . . in
their resolutions and opinions.

III

The Freedmen's Bureau was established in 1865
to aid the freedmen in the South. It was a politico-
eleemosynary institution, the ideals of which were
worthy. Nor could a better man have been found
to place at the head of this organization than General

Oliver Otis Howard.[8] (May, 1865). Eleven assistants, all of them officers in the Union Army, served under General Howard. Virginia was under the fostering care of General Orlando Brown.

The powers granted the officers of this Bureau resembled the Spanish Inquisition.[9] If, in the opinion of the Bureau's agent, any freedman was denied "full equality" the agent (and there was an agent for each Southern county) acting as judge and jury combined had the authority to "impose a fine or sentence." The decision of the agent was not to be executed by courts of law, but by Federal troops!

Senator Lyman Trumbull, of Illinois, brought this "Bill of Enormities"[10] before the Senate (January 11). After two weeks it was passed by strictly party vote. The House readily passed it and sent it to Andrew Johnson.

At this opportune time[11] (February 7), Frederick Douglass, the Negro agitator from Michigan, led a group of Negro Radicals to the White House and asked President Johnson to save the Negro race by giving them the suffrage. The President replied

---

[8]WILLARD GLAZIER, *Heroes of Three Wars*, pp. 357-360.

[9]HOWARD K. BEALE, *Critical Year*, pp. 157-159. The officials of the Freedmen's Bureau and the officers of the Union Leagues kept close contact with the Radical politicians. It was not uncommon for these professional troublemongers to arouse resentment, and then interpret the resentment as evidence of rebellion and treason, for which they could impose such fines as they pleased. And all such "evidences" were carefully preserved and cruelly used.

One young officer reported that he was not willing to search the homes of law-abiding Southern people, and turn them out of their homes and beds. He declared that the Bureau officials provoked their victims to say "disloyal" things about the government, and then fine or imprison them for the remarks made.

[10]So characterized by Edward Bates, of St. Louis, Missouri, the Attorney-General in Lincoln's cabinet.

[11]"February 27," OBERHOLTZER.

courteously, that the franchise under the Constitution must be handled by each State. He thought
also that it was a mistake to hurry such matters
along and feared that such methods would do the
race more harm than good.[12]

Douglass became much excited, argued and ex-
postulated, shouting vociferously. The President
interrupted to say that he was not debating the
question, but giving his opinion. Douglass then
rudely turned his back and cried: "The President
sends us to the people, and we will go to the people."
By "the people" he meant Thaddeus Stevens and
the Radical politicians in Congress, who had (as we
imagine) coached Douglass. For the Negro Radical
at once took the stump, making "grossly abusive
speeches" all over the country, denouncing the
"Rebel in the White House." The Chicago Tribune
declared editorially, "The Negro has more ability,
logic and eloquence than the President and a better
right to vote."

Three days later a committee from the Legislature
of Virginia visited the President (February 10). He
told them he was in favor of the prompt readmission
of the States.[13] In fact the war had been waged to
keep the States in the Union. He would never
acknowledge that Virginia had been legally out of
the Union. "The government," he added, "has

---

[12]He "wanted no contest between the races," which would lead to the
extermination of one or the other.

[13]President Johnson contended that taxation without representation
repudiated the corner-stone principle of American institutions. It threw all
our Revolutionary history into the discard. He insisted that the Union must
be preserved, with the dignity, the rights and the essential integrity of all the
states unimpaired.

taken hold of one extreme and with the strong arm of physical power has put down the rebellion. Now as we swing around the circle of the Union, we find the counterpart or duplicate of the same spirit . . . this other extreme, which stands in the way, must get out of it."

This is an involved sentence, far from clear, by which he meant that the Union had been saved from ultra-Southern secessionists, and must now be saved from ultra-Northern abolitionists (or radicals).[14]

IV

The President promptly vetoed[15] the Bill of Enormities (February 19). The "Spy in the Cabinet," as Edwin M. Stanton was called, declared that he was "disappointed at the President's obstinacy." But what better could one expect from a "rebel" and an East Tennesseean, born in Raleigh, North Carolina?

Johnson deliberately accused the Reconstruction Committee of promoting the most diabolical scheme in our history, a conspiracy against great masses of our people, debated and decided largely in secret

---

[14]GENERAL FULLERTON said of this bill, "It fosters disunion rather than cures and heals."

GENERAL GRANT criticized the bill and its agents as "dishonest and incapable." It caused constant disturbance and unjust discrimination.

GARRETT DAVIS of Kentucy called the bill "an enormous outrage and a monstrous measure."

The bill provided for the employment of a regiment of paid spies, all bitterly antagonistic to the President and his policies. Some 3,000,000 acres of land were to be given to "freedmen and loyal refugees in the Gulf States, 40 acres to each," at such rentals as the agents of the Bureau fixed.

[15]The bill passed the Senate (pro 137, contra 33) February 3.

session, whose object was the complete subversion
of the laws and the Constitution of the United
States. He would not sign a bill which placed all
the white people in the South completely at the
mercy of petty officials, giving to them unlimited
power to fine and to incarcerate innocent victims
and to enforce it by the Army. Instead of bringing
peace and harmony, such a bill would inflame class
and race and sectional hatred—and, in the end, do
more evil than the war now happily ended.

News of Johnson's veto brought great joy to the
conservative press and people.[16] Virginia heaved a
sigh of relief.

"Nothing so good nor important has, in our
opinion, occurred since Lee's surrender," came to
the White House from Rochester, New York. The
Radicals were furious, but Thaddeus Stevens quietly
awaited a favorable opportunity—in four months it
came.

---

[16]JOHN W. WAYLAND, *History of Rockingham County, Virginia*, p. 159. A
mass meeting at Harrisonburg approved the President's veto and urged that
it be sustained.

CHAPTER XII

AN UNFORTUNATE WASHINGTON
CELEBRATION

Hope, like a candle long-lighted, burned low in
many hearts and cast vague shadows of dread.
—*W. H. T. Squires.*

The Republicans had many and just reasons to
be proud of their new party's record. Springing
into the political arena in the Fifties the young
giant gathered into its arms almost all the Old Line
Whigs, which party really expired with Henry Clay.
With extraordinary wisdom and acumen the Republicans aligned themselves with the intense hostility to slavery, everywhere developing, and the
equally intense nationalism which developed most
rapidly in the great and growing states of the West,
a double master-stroke.

Under the superb leadership of Abraham Lincoln
the Republican party won the war, settled the
question of secession forever in America and liberated
the slaves of the entire world by direct action and
indirect moral influence. With victory for the
Union cause there came to the North and West such
a tide of commercial and industrial prosperity as no
people had ever before experienced.

As a political force the old Democratic party was
practically dead. But it was saved from complete

extinction by the radical excesses of its powerful young rival. For no sooner was Republicanism completely triumphant than it split into two antagonistic factions, grappling for place and power. The leader of the conservative Republicans, although himself once a Radical, was the President of the United States, Andrew Johnson, a native of Raleigh, North Carolina, and long a veteran in State and National politics. A Southern man, an ante-bellum Democrat, an ardent anti-slavery leader, an intense Unionist, he was placed on the ticket with Abraham Lincoln to make that ticket "national" instead of "sectional." No one ever supposed that Johnson would move into the White House.

The radical wing of the Republican party had three outstanding leaders in 1866—Thaddeus Stevens in the House of Representatives, Charles Sumner in the Senate, and Secretary Edwin M. Stanton in the Cabinet. This remarkably able and astute triumvirate held the entire Republican party in leash and almost succeeded in impeaching the President, "the Rebel in the White House," as they delighted to call him.

They failed, Stevens died, and the rising star, General Ulysses S. Grant, took control of the national party (1868); but that carries us far ahead of our story.

II

The Republican hosts gathered in the City of Washington to celebrate both Washington's birth and their splendid series of political victories.

The cleavage between radical and conservative

Republicans was not as yet deep; nor had their quarrels passed beyond compromise. Many of the wisest hoped to hold the great and victorious party intact. Had they succeeded, the Democratic party would likely have ceased to exist. February 22, 1866, is one of the strategic dates in the political history of America; although, we dare say, that not one who participated in the event realized the immense significance.

After a great demonstration at Grover's Theatre, and eloquent speeches by Montgomery Blair, Green Clay Smith, Senator Thomas Andrews Hendricks (an Indiana Democrat) and "Sunset" Cox,[1] the jubilant Republicans took up a march to the White House, to serenade the great leader of Republicanism, the successor of Abraham Lincoln, the President of the United States. They would congratulate Andrew Johnson upon his sturdy adherence to the Constitution, upon his herculean efforts to unite a divided nation, heal the wounds of war and hold intact the Grand Old Party (still so young). These marching patriots were not "Rebels" (Southern Democrats); they were Lincoln Republicans, with some Northern Democrats.

Responding to this call from two thousand ardent friends, Johnson appeared upon the balcony and in the dim and uncertain light of that frosty February night spoke for one hour with intense emotion.

He would retain our Glorious Union, not tear it asunder. He had fought to maintain it, and he would fight again. He was a citizen of Tennessee,

---

[1]Samuel Sullivan Cox of Ohio.

a native of North Carolina, but he was not a secessionist, nor a "Copperhead" and not an advocate
of slavery. The war was over. The South had
surrendered, in good faith, almost a year ago.
Slavery was dead; and Calhounism as dead as
slavery. Why is the nation not united? Why do
we deny the very doctrine of "No taxation without
representation," upon which this Government was
founded? And deny it to one-third of the United
States?

As he spoke the crowd gave him an ovation.
They frequently interrupted him with cries, "Give
it to them, Andy," "Hit 'em again."

The President referred to current threats to
assassinate him.[2] African slavery is dead, but
America now faces a new form of slavery, "An irresponsible central Directorate" are trampling our Constitution under foot, seeking their own selfish and
sinful ambitions. They dictate to Congress; they
decide who shall and who shall not be seated in Senate
and House. They order Congress to obey their
wicked behests. They are determined to hold eleven
great States out of the Union. The States fought
for four years to leave the Union. They failed.
Now a handful of conspirators and traitors, posing
as patriots, persecute millions of their peaceful fellow
citizens, trample them under feet, tax them, but

---

[2]There was a Radical in Congress, named Loan, from Missouri, described
by CLAUDE G. BOWERS, *Tragic Era*, p. 157, who accused the President of the
assassination of Lincoln. "An assassin's bullet, directed by a rebel hand, and
paid for by rebel gold, made Andrew Johnson President."

GENERAL BENJAMIN FRANKLIN BUTLER introduced a resolution in the House
to investigate the connection of President Johnson with the assassination of
Lincoln!

deny them representation, and make them outcasts and aliens in the land of their fathers.

As he spoke the cheering crowd surged nearer. Andrew Johnson was for forty years a powerful speaker. No man in public life knew better how to sway the passions of the crowd. He was at his best on the stump. His short and heavy-set figure, his rugged and swarthy face, lit by the flare of candle-light, his thick, black hair touched with gray, his brilliant, black eyes, shining through heavy and shaggy eye-brows, his strong, pugnacious mouth, the countenance of a man at once strong and obstinate, his searching voice, his slow but very effective speech, his faulty grammar and indifferent diction . . . he looked the plebian that he was, and did not look the master of men, which he also was. His fearlessness, for America never knew a braver man, his intense, moral earnestness, his convictions of duty, and his stern and indomitable will moved his hearers to enthusiasm, almost frenzy.

So intense was the reaction that one stentorian voice called from the crowd: "Name those traitors!" The President hesitated for a moment. It was but a moment, and then cried: "Thaddeus Stevens, Charles Sumner and Wendell Phillips."

Instantly the reporters hurried to headquarters. The telegraph wires burned and next morning the country was aflame with sensational news!

Woodrow Wilson[3] calls this speech "Johnson's Declaration of War," and such it was. Of course, the Radical press from Maine to California opened

_____

[3]*History of the United States.*

their heaviest batteries upon the "Rebel in the White House."

On the same eventful evening, February 22, 1866, a huge Republican assembly at Cooper's Union in New York was addressed by William H. Seward, Secretary of State, Postmaster-General Dennison, Henry J. Raymond and David Dudley Field. These stalwart Republicans would not vote to persecute the South. Lincoln's policies were Johnson's policies. Johnson's policies were the policies of righteousness, justice and peace. Both patriotic and economic motives demand that one-third of the United States be fully and completely brought back into the Union. No Anglo-Saxon people ever will submit to bayonet rule.[4] One hundred guns, a salute of peace and good-will, were fired in New York that day, and every discharge as it echoed over the metropolis was cheered.[5]

But the Radicals were ready with a counter-stroke. Johnson became the target for the most vicious and systematic campaign of vituperation ever launched in America. No libel was too bold, too false, too absurd or too unreasonable to be hurled upon him. His political acts were derided, his private character attacked, even the sanctity of his home was ruthlessly invaded.

Johnson's declaration of war split the Republican party from stem to stern. Henceforth the politicians were Radicals or Conservatives. As the years passed the Radicals became less radical, and the Conserva-

---

[4] The *London Times* said, "Not Mr. Johnson, but the Constitution of the United States is now in danger."

[5] OBERHOLTZER, *History of the United States*, Vol. I, p. 169.

tives either returned to the Republican camp or
joined the Democrats.

III

It is interesting to note how the invisible and intangible skeins of life and destiny are interwoven.
When Johnson made his speech Horace Greeley was
at his desk in the "Tribune" office, the newspaper
that rightly claimed to be the leading Republican
journal in America. Would Horace Greeley ever
become the candidate of the Democrats for the
presidency? Wait only six years.

A quiet and able lawyer living in bachelor quarters
in lower New York, Samuel J. Tilden, will carry the
Democratic banner to victory in ten years and be
elected President of the United States, by Democrats
and Conservative Republicans.

There was a 29-year-old lawyer in Buffalo, New
York, also a Democrat. His name was Grover
Cleveland; and the "mugwumps" (Conservative
Republicans) will send him to the White House in
eighteen years. On and on through the rolling
years our echoes come and go, and the event most
unlikely is sure to happen.

As for President Johnson, he has been vindicated.
However fierce the assaults of contemporary partisans may be, the cold and calculating verdicts of
history are almost invariably correct. Fierce heat
warps the judgment of men, but time and equity
weigh acts and the actors on the stage of life. Posterity is rarely deceived. Sooner or later every lie
and every libel is correctly labelled. More and more
history has taken the measure of this man who did

his utmost to carry on Lincoln's policies in Lincoln's tolerant spirit.[6] More and more his stalwart honesty, his unswerving conviction to duty and his courage in defense of those principles he knew to be right are appreciated.

More and more those who hounded him, persecuted and maligned him have sunk into the quagmire of shame and disgrace. None rise now to do them reverence though honor, influence, wealth and success shone brilliantly upon them at the time.

IV

Congress passed a law (March 2, 1886) by which two rich and beautiful counties in the Valley of Virginia, Jefferson and Berkeley, were lost to Virginia.[7] They form the "Eastern Panhandle" of West Virginia. It was part of the punishment meted to Virginia eleven months after the Confederate armies had made an honorable surrender and in good faith. The dismemberment of Virginia was now complete.

---

[6]JAMES TRUSLOW ADAMS, *The Epic of America*, p. 285, refers to the "vindictiveness" of Stevens and the "fanaticism" of Sumner. These unfortunate leaders made impossible the reconciliation of the sections for which Lincoln hoped and prayed.

GEO. H. HAYNES, *Dict. Amer. Biog.*, gives an accurate pen portrait of Senator Sumner.

[7]EDWARD W. DOUGLAS, *Boundaries of the United States*, p. 145. The boundaries of West Virginia.

Chapter XIII

CIVIL RIGHTS AND CIVIL WRONGS

Men seldom, or rather never for any length of
time and deliberately, rebel against anything that
does not deserve rebelling against.
—Thomas Carlyle.

Undismayed by such intangible reactions as the
verdict of history the Radical element pushed their
plans for further punishment of the South with
astonishing perseverance and success. President
Johnson's Declaration of War and his unavailing
efforts to bring some help and protection to the
people of the South were utterly unavailing.

Senator Lyman Trumbull, of Illinois, though a
Conservative Republican, pressed for the passage of
this bill as early as February 2, 1866. It came up
in the House of Representatives and was, of course,
passed (March 11), and went to the President to
receive his anticipated veto.

The Civil Rights Bill had a fine and fair name, as
innocent a name[1] as ever masked any legal iniquity.
Its provisions were worse, far worse, than those of
the February Freedmen's Bureau Bill of Enormities,
killed by the Presidential veto for the nonce. This

---

[1] S. E. FORMAN, *Our Republic*, p. 517, describes the Bill.

Act should have been called the Military Tyranny
Bill, for such in fact it was, and such it was intended
to be in effective use and widespread operation.

President Johnson's veto[2] brought this monstrosity
promptly back to Congress, March 27.

In his veto message President Johnson argued that
the States, not the nation, decided who should be
citizens. Furthermore, the Union was composed
of thirty-six States, yet eleven of them were uncon-
stitutionally denied their rightful seats in Congress.
It was not in his judgment "sound policy" to confer
the rights of citizenship on 4,000,000 colored persons
just rescued from slavery. "Can it be reasonably
supposed," he asked, "that they possess the requisite
qualifications to entitle them to all privileges and
immunities as citizens of the United States?"

It was another long step toward centralization
and it will "resuscitate the spirit of rebellion and
arrest the progress of those influences which are
more closely drawing around the States the bonds
of union and of peace."[3]

Congress passed it over the President's veto,
April 9, 1866 (pro 33, contra 15), in the Senate.
The galleries, which were crowded, broke into applause. Senator Garrett Davis, of Kentucky, was
indignant and cried, "Vagabond Negroes hovering
over this Capitol like a black cloud should be sent

[2]In vetoing this bill President Johnson wrote: "My stand has been taken,
my course is marked. I shall stand by and defend the Constitution against
all who may attack it, from whatever quarter the attack may come. I shall
take no step backward in this matter."
  EDWARD A. POLLARD, *The Lost Cause*, p. 748.
[3]RICHARDSON'S *Messages and Papers*, Vol. VI, p. 407.

to work instead of asking government alms for their race and such purposes."[4]

President Johnson gave this interview to the correspondents of the foreign press: "The Radicals know nothing of the South nor of the Negroes. The South will treat the Negro more kindly than these abolitionists if they will let the South alone."

The Civil Rights Bill[5] carried ten major provisions, some of which were just and fair, and some not only invited but actually put a premium upon fraud, robbery and crime.

I. All citizens, except Indians, have the same right to hold and enjoy property as all other citizens.

II. Anyone who tries to deprive any citizen of any right commits a misdemeanor.

III. Federal courts alone, not State courts, may try such cases.

IV. Officers of the United States courts or of the Freedmen's Bureau and "special agents" are to execute this Act.

V. Any officer who refuses to execute this Act may be fined.

VI. Resistance to this Act is penalized by fines and prison sentences.

VII. Generous fees accrue to those who enforce this Act.

VIII. The President may send "special officers"

[4]CLAUDE G. BOWERS, in *The Tragic Era*, describes the negroes who packed the galleries of Senate and House, who hissed, groaned or applauded at will; or, perhaps, as the signal was given from the floor.

[5]JOHN SPENCER BASSETT, *History of the United States*, p. 606, describes the Civil Rights Bill at length and in detail.

to any place where acts against this law are "likel
to be committed."

IX.   The President may use "special agents," the
army, navy and militia to enforce this Act.

X.   Appeal from injustice may be made to the
Supreme Court.

II

This is the Civil Rights Bill which turned loose a
horde of special agents, Radical spies, upon the South
and practically declared war upon a peaceful people
who had surrendered in good faith.

By an irony of fate this monstrosity[6] of martial
law became a law April 9, 1866, one year to the day
after General Lee surrendered.   But what a year
of shame, sorrow, persecution and disgrace!

The crafty manipulation and astute unfolding of
the Radical program are astonishing.   Stevens[7] and
his lieutenants drew one bow after another from
their well-filled quivers.   Each shot was admirably
timed.   Each made a sharper, deeper and a more
deadly wound in the prostrate South.

But the people of the North and West, honest,
God-fearing and sympathetic folk, must be "educated" by judicious Radical propaganda, else they
would not tolerate this conspiracy.   They must
especially, be informed how cruel, lazy, ignorant,
unsubdued, stubborn and obdurate "the aristocratic

[6]*Detroit Free Press* (March, 1866) said the Radicals were motivated "by
what they thought would perpetuate" their power with not a "single emotion
of solicitude for the black race."

[7]On Stevens' theories see CHARLES WARREN, Supreme Court, Vol. II,
pp. 448; also 471; also 488.

rebels" are. They must be made to hate the South
. . . and the more the better.

The Radicals were masters of practical psychology.
They understood the country, the press and the
people. Stevens did not move too fast, but just
fast enough.

December brought the repudiation of Presidential
reconstruction and the appointment of the Committee of Fifteen with dictatorial powers. During
January the South was "investigated" and each
"witness" added something to the indignation of
the nation as the "rebels" were defamed.

February brought forth the Freedmen's Bureau
Bill of Enormities and March produced the Civil
Rights Bill. No slight obstacle such as a Presidential veto, nor the unconstitutional character of
an act foiled or thwarted the Radical conspirators.

Nothing the Radicals had done made the Southern
people so angry as the Civil Rights Bill. In their
righteous indignation our fathers forgot that no
law is stronger than public opinion behind it. They
could not be expected to foresee that the Civil
Rights Bill and the Fourteenth Amendment were
harmless. National enactments change with every
passing shift of public opinion, but the laws of
nature never.

III

The freedmen of Norfolk with their friends from
the vicinity had a great parade, April 16, to celebrate the Civil Rights Bill. Before the day was
done Robert Whitehurst and his stepmother, Mrs.
Charlotte Whitehurst, were "deliberately murdered

by the infuriated and drunken mob." John Whitehurst, a brother, was dangerously wounded, William
Moseley, a policeman, and his son were severely
beaten. W. Turner was wounded by a sabre thrust.
Mark Bennett, a Negro, was killed. Lawrence
Hampton, a small boy, was bayonetted by another
Negro in the procession. The celebration was
staged by "some renegade white men still in our
midst."[8]

Three days later a white man was severely beaten
by two Negroes. The Negroes were not arrested
but the bleeding white man was sent to the Hard
Labor Prison by Major P. W. Stanhope. These
riots caused much indignation, particularly when
Major Stanhope declared that if his command was
menaced by white men he would arm the blacks to
assist him in carrying out his orders.

The effect of the Civil Rights Bill in Norfolk is
here given, not for the importance of the riot, but
as typical of the reaction throughout the South.
Nor was the North free of riots. Six hundred Negroes
instituted a reign of terror in Washington under the
shadow of the Capitol.[9] The Radical press did not
report it, or deliberately discounted the riot. But
fear and unrest spread throughout the North, es-

[8]H. W. BURTON, *History of Norfolk* (1876).

[9]The Union armies, whose withdrawal from the South has been described,
were followed by thousands of freedmen, of both sexes. These camp-followers
were called "a black fringe around the army." It was said at the time that
fully 30,000 freedmen were, after the war, living in the congested slums of
Washington.

Of course there were also thousands of colored soldiers and sailors, who
were immensely popular with their own people. Many of these were undoubtedly awaiting the generous gift of "forty acres and a mule" from the
government. See RHODES, *History of the United States*, Vol. V, p. 811.

pecially in those cities to which large numbers of
Negroes were now migrating.

In Memphis, Tennessee, 24 Negroes were killed in
a riot. During the summer 150 Negroes were killed
or wounded by the police of New Orleans in an
effort to curb a riot in that city—a political riot.

And yet as one looks back upon it, the order
maintained and the self-control of the Southern
whites is astonishing. The men of the South did
not blame the Negroes for their political troubles.
Practically every colored man and woman in the
South labored day by day for, under and with the
white farmer, or his wife. The kindliest feelings
existed in millions of instances. Only when Radical
agents and alien activities intervened were there
race conflicts. The typical Southern man has the
most generous feeling for the typical Negro. And
the typical Negro finds in the typical white man a
neighbor and friend. Only in the zone of political
and social equality were riots and bloodshed developed.

We suppose that nowhere else on earth two totally
different races live and labor so peacefully side by
side as the white and colored races of the South to
this day. Much credit belongs to the white and
equally as much to the Negro.

The Southern citizen knew exactly who would
wreck the economic fabric[10] of the South carefully

10 *Norfolk Journal*, Editorial, June 28, 1869: "An Appeal to Our Colored
People: We are glad to see that all over the state colored associations are
forming for the support of the expurgated Constitution and Gilbert C. Walker
(Conservative), and against the slavery of the Loyal Leaguers. . . . Colored
People of Virginia, we are rejoiced that you are beginning to find those men

built during three hundred years. It was the Radical politician who for place and power was willing and anxious to ruin that he might rule.[11]

IV

Not content with their triumph in passing this, the most drastic punishment that could be devised under the Constitution, the Radicals determined to write the Civil Rights Bill into the Constitution as the Fourteenth Amendment. And so they did, although it took two full years to force it through the reluctant States. Many of the Southern States, including Virginia, were compelled to pass the Fourteenth Amendment. If the State declined to do so it would be kept indefinitely under military rule.

But time is a great physician and carries a healing touch. The Fourteenth Amendment modified the fiercer, Radical provisions of the Civil Rights Bill.

---

out, those stragglers who have come here to make money out of you. . . . They have been cheating you long enough. . . . If you have been deceived by them thus far, it is *their* fault. If they do so hereafter it is *your* fault." (This editorial is a full column in length.)

[11]So late as June 7, 1869, during an election in Washington, D. C., long under the benign influence of Radical legislation, a serious riot occurred. Police and negroes battled in the "Second Ward," stones, pistols, clubs, razors and other weapons played their part. The marines were held in readiness to quell the rioters; but, fortunately, the police held the situation without assistance.

MRS. MAUD CARTER CLEMENT, *History of Pittsylvania*, p. 254, gives an illuminative illustration from Southern Virginia:

"A man named Lehigh from Pennsylvania became sheriff of Pittsylvania County, who defaulted costing the taxpayers $30,000.00. A carpet-bagger from Maine named Tucker was commonwealth's attorney, and was very active in inciting resentment among the negroes toward the white people. For such minor offenses as pig and sheep stealing Lehigh would have the culprit hung up by the thumbs for two hours, with suffering almost beyond endurance." These facts cannot be controverted.

General Amnesty had pardoned many "rebels." Most of the freedmen were working peacefully in the fields by the time the Amendment was proclaimed and the Freedmen's Bureau soon ceased to exist.

During this dark and dreary month of March, when such ominous and sinister clouds hung over our people, a rainbow, the emblem of hope, appeared unexpectedly — and from the powerful Supreme Court.

The case was argued from March 6 to 13. The prisoner who was charged with "giving aid and comfort to the rebels," was defended by General James A. Garfield, David Dudley Field and Jeremiah S. Black, who made (as was said at the time) one of the ablest arguments ever heard in the Supreme Court chamber. Mr. Black addressed the Court without referring to a note or book, and yet presented such an array of reference and such research, with such force and eloquence, that he astonished and bewildered those who heard him. Constitutional liberty, he declared, not Milligan, was his client! The great cause of human liberty hung upon the court's decision.[12]

The Court held that President Lincoln's military tribunals were illegal. The Court declared:

"No graver question was ever considered by this court, nor one which more nearly concerns the rights of every American citizen . . . The Constitution of the United States is a law for rulers and people, equal in war and peace, and covers with the shield of its protection all classes of men, at all times and

---

[12]For an erudite description of this celebrated trial, see CHARLES WARREN, *The Supreme Court*, Vol. II, p. 426, and following.

under all circumstances. If suspended, we fall into anarchy or despotism. Martial law can never exist where the courts are open." The decision was rendered April 3, 1866, only three weeks after the argument.

Henceforth military commissions and trials were illegal in America! The delivery of this opinion was hailed with gratitude in the South. The Radicals turned upon the Supreme Court the same storm of "invective and opprobrium" which they focussed upon the President. They declared that the Court had joined hands with the Executive to destroy Congressional Reconstruction and to protect "rebels."

The Springfield (Mass.) Republican said it rejoiced that the decision would end the "senseless clamor for the military trial of Jefferson Davis and other rebel leaders."

Thaddeus Stevens was livid with rage. He shouted that it would "turn loose murderers upon the lives and liberties of the loyal men of this country."

The Richmond "Enquirer" rejoiced that the ark of American liberty and justice remained unpolluted by the political filth of the time.

CHAPTER XIV

JEFFERSON DAVIS

Gone gray with the sorrow of days
And leaden nights of despair.
—*Virginia Taylor McCormick.*

President Andrew Johnson issued a proclamation, April 2, 1866, that the Civil War was now officially concluded "except in Texas."[1] If President Johnson had possessed any sense of humor—and he did not—he might have issued the proclamation one day sooner: April Fool's Day. The War Between the States terminated really, if not officially, April 9, 1865, when Robert E. Lee surrendered.

The reason for the President's absurd proclamation was not difficult to find. The Freedmen's Bureau, which furnished thousands of Radical henchmen salaries they had not earned, was to terminate its charitable activities "one year after hostilities ceased." The Radicals in Congress and their henchmen all over the South wished to make their employment indefinite, which was one reason, and a potent reason, for Stevens' "Bill of Enormities"

---

[1]ALBERT BUSHNELL HART, *Chase*, p. 341.

President Johnson issued a supplementary proclamation August 30, 1866, that the war had ceased "in Texas" also.

vetoed in February. The President by his proclamation April 2, 1866, was serving notice to the nation that the brethren of the Bureau would be out of a job in a twelvemonth . . . but they were not, as we shall see.

II

Three days after this political Peace Proclamation (April 5) word was received from France that Louis Napoleon, the Emperor of the French, would withdraw troops sent to aid the Emperor Maximilian in Mexico.[2] Ah, what tragic fates awaited the two Emperors.

III

From these distant scenes the Virginians were soon brought home to their own problems and perils. May, like each succeeding month in this dismal and dreary year, brought a plethora of trouble.

Despite the decision of the Supreme Court in the now famous "Milligan Case," despite the reiterated opinions of the ablest attorneys in the country that Jefferson Davis was no more guilty of rebellion and treason than one million men who had convictions (and the courage of their convictions), the aged, broken and feeble man was kept a close prisoner in Fortress Monroe. He was denied a trial and also bail. In short, the army and politicians were de-

---

[2]HERBERT INGRAM PRIESTLEY, *Mexican Nation*, Chapter XXI, gives much light on this strange chapter in our history.

W. E. WOODWARD, *Meet General Grant*, declares that Grant had an idea of uniting the Northern and Southern armies, placing Longstreet in command of the former and Sherman in command of the latter, and marching into Mexico to end the "Empire" with one vigorous stroke.

termined to make the late President a martyr and a symbol of the suffering South. To the South he became a martyr to a lost cause, to the North he was the arch-rebel.

From his cell he was brought to Norfolk under heavy guard, May 8, a year after he was captured, and denied a trial or bail by the notorious John C. Underwood, a man whose name is a malediction in Virginia.

The facts of Davis' case were then well known, now they are forgotten.

Just before the evacuation of Richmond, President Davis and the Confederate government officials took train to Danville[3] which served for ten days as the Confederate capital. From Danville Davis moved to Greensboro, North Carolina (April 14). After a brief conference with Generals Joseph E. Johnston and P. G. T. Beauregard, who assured him that further resistance was useless, Mr. Davis journeyed to Charlotte (April 18). There he heard of Lincoln's assassination. He made his way southward as best he could with Mrs. Davis and a small party of friends, leaving Charlotte April 26, but he was captured at a camp in the pinewoods of Georgia near Irwinsville, May 10, by a cavalry force under Lieut.-Col. Pritchard[4] of General James

---

[3]MAUD CARTER CLEMENT, *History of Pittsylvania.* President Davis, his cabinet and many departments of the fast-dying Confederate States, reached Danville, Monday, April 3, and remained until Wednesday, April 12. The stately mansion of Major William Sutherlin was used as the Capitol and a brick school building, built in 1801, was used by the departments. President Davis received the news of the surrender at the Sutherlin mansion.

[4]Of the Fourth Michigan Cavalry.

H. Wilson's command.[5] The prisoners were taken first to Augusta, Georgia, and thence aboard the U. S. S. "Clyde"[6] to Fortress Monroe which was reached May 22,[7] where he was confined in Casemate No. 2.[8]

The casemates, although above ground, are artificially subterranean, and are dark, damp and altogether unhealthy. Davis was no longer a young man, born June 3, 1808, now 57 years of age. The strenuous life of the last four years left an indelible mark; yet he lived to a peaceful old age (dying December 6, 1889).

IV

The day after his arrival General Nelson Appleton Miles, in command of the fort, had Captain Titlow, with two blacksmiths rivet a pair of irons on Mr. Davis' ankles.

---

[5]ARMISTEAD C. GORDON, *Richmond News-Leader*, 12-10-31.

"General Wilson abruptly and rather indelicately introduced the subject of reward offered by the President of the United States for the arrest of Mr. Davis, and the charge against him of complicity in the assassination of Mr. Lincoln, inquiring whether he had heard of it. 'I have,' was the answer, 'and there is one man who knows it to be a lie.' 'By one man,' rejoined Wilson, 'I suppose you mean some particular man.' 'I do,' answered Mr. Davis. 'I mean the man (Andrew Johnson) who signed the proclamation; for he knows that I would a thousand times rather have Abraham Lincoln to deal with as President of the United States than to have him'.'"

[6]The other prisoners aboard the "Clyde" were Alexander H. Stephens, Vice-President of the Confederacy; John H. Reagan, Postmaster-General; Clement C. Clay, General Joseph Wheeler, William Preston Johnston, R. F. Lubbock and Burton Harrison.

[7]Some authorities say May 19.

[8]LOUIS PENDLETON, *Alex. H. Stephens*, p. 343.

Mr. Stephens was arrested May 11. When he met Jefferson Davis aboard the "Clyde" their greeting was not cordial, nor was it unfriendly. Captan Kelly of the "Clyde" delivered Mr. Stephens to Captain Fraily of the U. S. S. "Tuscarora." He was taken to Fort Warren and paroled October 12, 1865.

The ex-President was thoroughly aroused and asked,

"Has General Miles given that order?"

"Yes."

"I would like to see General Miles."

"Impossible; he is leaving the fort."

"Then I ask you to wait until General Miles returns to the fort!"

"I can not wait," Captain Titlow replied.

"That is an order which no true soldier would give. It is their intention to torture me to death. I will not submit to indignities by which it is sought to degrade in my person the cause of which I am a representative."

The Captain insisted that he must obey his orders.

"I am a soldier," Davis replied, "and I am a gentleman. I know how to die. Let your men shoot me at once."

As he spoke Mr. Davis stepped backward against the walls of the dark casemate, in the position of those who are to be shot after a court-martial.

Captain Titlow ordered the blacksmiths to rivet the irons and chains upon his ankles. When the smith attempted to do so, Mr. Davis threw him off so violently that he fell to the floor. The smith was so angry that he raised his hammer to strike Mr. Davis dead, but the Captain interposed and ordered him to drop his hammer. One of the sentinels then aimed his musket at Mr. Davis and cocked it. "You must not fire," said Titlow. The Captain then brought in four strong unarmed men, who quickly overpowered Mr. Davis and held him down until the irons were placed.

Those details set the country by the ears. The Southern people were quite beside themselves with anger and indignation. The Copperhead press of the North was almost as angry. The reaction was so intense and so unfavorable to the Radicals that Secretary Stanton telegraphed General Miles (May 27): "Please report whether irons have or have not been placed on Jefferson Davis. If they have been, when was it done, and for what reason, and remove them."

We have no wish to judge Edwin M. Stanton,[9] but in our opinion it shows the contemptible smallness of the man, a method of side-stepping his responsibility and of throwing popular odium on a subordinate. Miles was made the "goat," to use the vernacular.

Miles replied that the irons were placed to prevent him "running away." The utter absurdity of Mr. Davis, who could not escape a detachment in the pinewoods of Georgia, "running away" from Casemate 2 at Fortress Monroe where he had an officer and sentinels guarding him day and night, not to mention the garrison on war-footing and the United States Navy in Hampton Roads—the reply of Miles is as contemptible as the telegram of Stanton.

The postmaster-general of the Confederacy, John Heninger Reagan, who was with Mr. Davis when

[9]These are Stanton's instructions to Miles:

"Major-General Miles is hereby authorized and directed to place manacles and fetters upon the hands and feet of Jefferson Davis and Clement C. Clay whenever he may deem it advisable, in order to render their imprisonment more secure."

he was captured, was also brought to Old Point. On that same ship also came Senator Clement C. Clay, who, "conscious of his innocence of any connection with Booth," unwilling even to seem to fly from justice, went deliberately to General Wilson in Macon, Georgia, and surrendered himself.

Stephens and Reagan were sent North to Fort Warren aboard the U. S. S. "Tuscarora." Senator Clay was confined in a casemate near Davis.

While the Democrats and Moderate Republicans were exasperated at the treatment of Davis, the Radicals demanded his blood. General Benjamin Franklin Butler in 1860 had voted, as a great Democrat, through fifty ballots to make Hon. Jefferson Davis the Democratic nominee and elect him President of the United States.[10] Butler now demanded that both Davis and Lee be hanged! The "hideous cross-eyed beast" (as one Southern woman described the General) could not be expected to remember his enthusiasm for Jefferson Davis six years before.

Schuyler Colfax (later Vice-President of the United States) told an applauding crowd in Virginia City, Nevada (June 26, 1865), "If there is justice left in this country we will see him hanging between heaven and earth and he is not fit for either."[11]

As the months wore away, and excitement subsided, and especially as all efforts to trace any con-

---

[10]ROBERT GRANVILLE CALDWELL, *History of American People*, p. 471' calls Davis the "recognized successor of Calhoun."

[11]Before Lincoln was buried or Davis captured (namely, April 16, 1865), Andrew Johnson, Z. Chandler, B. F. Wade and B. F. Butler agreed that Davis if captured "should be summarily punished by death."

Life of Chandler, p. 281.

nection between Mr. Davis[12] and John Wilkes Booth proved utterly abortive, the persecution of the captive became less severe. He was removed (October 2) from the casemate and placed on the second floor of Carroll Hall, a location at once brighter and more comfortable.

Over and over again Mrs. Davis wrote President Johnson, from Canada, beseeching him to permit her to visit, aid and console her husband. The letters at first were not even answered, for Andrew Johnson by his own statements was not "a gentleman born," and was proud of it. In this item he proved it plainly enough. At last, however, Mrs. Davis was permitted (May 3, 1866) to go to her husband for daily visits under parole.

The treatment that Davis received at Fortress Monroe brought him a popularity which he had never before enjoyed, and a modicum of it remains. During the war he was about the most unpopular man in the Confederate States, and much of it was deserved. Jefferson Davis was a gentleman and a statesman of some ability. But he was surely a poor executive, whose administration his most ardent admirers find it difficult to commend. Some patriotic societies moved rather by zeal than good judgment, prevailed upon the legislature of Virginia to make his birthday a State holiday. Virginia has too many State holidays and this is one of them.

[12]ARMISTEAD C. GORDON, *Richmond News-Leader*, 12-10-31:
"Even the Confederates in prison were heard from. The officers confined at Fort Warren signed with General Ewell a letter to General Grant, expressing to 'a soldier who will understand,' their detestation of Booth's horrible crime. The commandant of the fort, Major William Appleton, added a note, testifying to their deep sincerity."

The attitude of the South was well-expressed by a memorial presented to President Johnson[13] asking that Mr. Davis be released: "He was elevated to his high position by our suffrages and in response to our wishes. If he is guilty, so are we. . . . Let not the retribution of a mighty nation be visited upon his head, while we who urged him to his destiny, are suffered to escape."[14]

[13]*Confederate Records of Georgia*, Vol. IV, p. 430.
[14]BISHOP CHARLES B. GALLOWAY, *Tribute to Jefferson Davis*: "He earnestly advocated the Crittenden Compromise" (1861).

CHAPTER XV

THE FOURTEENTH AMENDMENT

The philanthrophy of the Virginians toward the negro race is best proved by figures. The Virginians at great pecuniary sacrifice set more slaves free than eleven great states with eight times her population.[1]
—*W. H. T. Squires.*

The dreary month of May, 1866, brought much sorrow and anxiety to the hearts of patriotic Virginians. To them "all endeavor seemeth worse than vain."[2] A week after Judge Underwood at

[1]The Eighth Census of the United States.

	White	Free Colored
Population of Virginia (including West Virginia)..............	1,047,411	58,042
Population of Maine....................	626,952	1,327
New Hampshire...........	325,579	494
Vermont.................	314,389	709
Massachusetts.............	1,221,464	9,602
Rhode Island.............	170,668	3,952
Connecticut..............	451,520	8,627
Illinois....................	1,704,323	7,628
Indiana..................	1,339,000	11,428
Iowa.....................	673,844	1,069
Michigan.................	742,314	6,799
Wisconsin................	774,710	1,171
California................	361,353	4,086
Kansas...................	106,579	625
Minnesota................	171,862	259
Total..............	8,984,557	57,776

EMERY E. CHILDS, *Hist. of U. S.*, p. 33, states that in 1774 there were 6,464 negroes in Connecticut and 3,761 in Rhode Island. What became of them and their offspring through 90 years?

[2]CHARLES WASHINGTON COLEMAN, *Virginia Writers of Fugitive Verse* (Gordon), p. 291.

Norfolk refused either to try Jefferson Davis, or release him on bail, and sent him back to Fort Monroe, a convention of Unconditional Union men gathered at Alexandria. As the first political meeting since the surrender it is of importance.

Alexandria is very near Washington, the headquarters of American Radicalism. Over the convention presided a Virginian, very widely known in his day, but now completely forgotten, a picturesque and petulant politician, John Minor Botts.

Let us journey to Alexandria and attend this unique assembly. Let us look carefully at the president, for he throws a shadow, rather dark than otherwise, across three generations of Virginia's State politics. Powerfully built, with gestures always suggestive of force, will-power and aggressiveness, he was a born fighter, a masculine leader, untiring and (if the truth must be told) contentious to a degree.

Botts possessed a violent temper and there was one word of three syllables which never failed to raise a very tempest in his manly breast, and that word was "Democrat."

His father, Benjamin A. Botts, a brilliant lawyer, was one of Aaron Burr's counsel. John Minor, whose mother was Jane Tyler, was born at Dumfries, but the family soon removed to Richmond. Both parents perished in the disastrous Richmond Theatre fire (1811). The education of two surviving boys was directed by relatives and at the early age of eighteen John was admitted to the bar, after six weeks of private study.

He began his checkered and stormy political

career as a stout Calhoun Democrat, opposed to the high tariff and the United States Bank policy of the second Adams. But in the reign of the great Andy, John Minor Botts bolted (1834) and was henceforth a stout contender in the Whig ranks. He served six years (1833-39) in the State legislature, and was elected to Congress by his neighbors of Richmond and vicinity (1839–43) and again for one term (1847-49).

Botts bitterly opposed John Tyler, whom he considered a traitor to Whig doctrine, he opposed the annexation of Texas and the Mexican War as tending to extend slavery and disrupt the Union. He was now as intensely anti-Calhoun as he had previously been pro-Calhoun.

The Democrats had no foe so bitter as he. Standing stoutly beside Henry Clay he aided the Great Pacifier in the compromise measures of 1850.

The most valuable service John Minor Botts brought to Virginia was in the Constitutional Convention of 1850. He lent his aid to many constructive reforms.

When the Whig party disappeared in the fifties, Botts, like Alexander H. H. Stuart and many other Old Line Whigs, joined the Know-Nothing or American party. He was an active campaigner against Henry A. Wise, whom he insisted upon calling "Unwise Henry Wise."

Unsparing in his criticism of Governor Wise in the John Brown episode, he insisted that the whole affair was a "Democratic conspiracy" to create sympathy and votes for the Calhoun doctrine of secession.

Botts could always see a conspiracy in the acts of his political opponents. In Lynchburg (October, 1860), a month before Lincoln's election, he made a sensational campaign speech in which he declared that the Democrats deliberately split their party between Douglas and Breckenridge in order to elect Lincoln, force secession, and form a Southern Confederacy. There have been many besides Botts who believed something of the sort. If there was any truth in it, it will now never be known.

He was a violent anti-secessionist candidate for the Secession Convention of 1861, but failed of election. Botts created another sensation when he declared that President Lincoln offered to recall the fleet sailing to Fort Sumter, if John B. Baldwin and the peace commissioners would persuade the Secession Convention to adjourn. Baldwin categorically denied the statement before the Committee of Fifteen in 1866.

When the war began Botts retired from public life and lived as quietly on his farm near Richmond as could such an aggressive man. But talk the old Whig must, and talk he did. And Botts never talked in a ladylike manner, one may be sure of that.

Before daybreak on the morning of March 2, 1862, Botts' home was surrounded. He was arrested by order of President Jefferson Davis and marched to a Negro jail in which he was confined for eight weeks. We have often wondered whether Jefferson Davis thought of that while he was at Fort Monroe.

This persecution by the Confederate authorities can not be justified. Botts was a thorn in the flesh. He was to the Confederates what Clement L. Vanlandingham was to Ohio and the Federals.

This unhappy politician moved to Culpeper County. Pierpont offered to elect him Senator from "Restored Virginia" (1864), but Botts declined the empty honor. This is he, a Radical but mild, honest but contrary, exceedingly unpopular, who presided at Alexandria, an old man now but a fierce fighter still, violent in speech, thundering in full voice, shaking his powerful frame and head, denouncing the abolitionists of the North and the "rebels" in the same breath—as eccentric as was Botts it would have been fortunate for Virginia if his large and capable hands could have held control from more shifty Radicals. Botts lost the crown of Virginia's eternal gratitude to a patriot far abler, namely Alexander H. H. Stuart. Botts was a politician not a statesman. Stuart was a statesman not a politician. No statement is further from the truth than "A statesman is a dead politician." Many and many a successful politician is no statesman though he be as dead as King Tut.

The increasing strength of the Radical element at Washington, and their control of national affairs encouraged Botts and his friends in this State to effect the regular organization of the Republican party.

A resolution was quickly passed "that no reorganized State government of Virginia should be recognized by the Government of the United States, which does not exclude from suffrage and holding office, at least for a term of years, all persons who have voluntarily given moral or material support to rebellion against the United States; and which does not, with such disfranchisement, provide for the immediate enfranchisement of all Union men without distinction of color."

The convention wished Congress to terminate the administration of Governor Francis Harrison Pierpont. To be sure, he was an original Republican, but of late he had become too conservative, and too friendly with "rebels." They further requested "that the Hon. John C. Underwood, the faithful patriot and distinguished jurist, who had always adhered to the Government with a fidelity which no flattery could seduce, no bribery corrupt, nor fears intimidate, be selected as said provisional Governor."[3]

This platform was all politics with not a scintilla of statescraft nor judicious foresight. The very men who sat under the gavel of John Minor Botts will turn upon him and rend him in less than fifteen months; and throw him upon the political scrapheap forever.

II

Not content with placing the Civil Rights Bill in the code of national laws, Congress determined to write it into the Constitution as the Fourteenth Amendment.

The Reconstruction Committee of Fifteen knew that the President would veto the amendment and were not sure they could pass it over his veto, so

[3] *Annual American Encyclopedia*, 1866.

WILLIAM ASBURY CHRISTIAN: "The greatest curse at this time visited upon Richmond was the judge of the United States District Court, John C. Underwood."

a "joint resolution" embodying the chief features of the Civil Rights Bill was introduced the last day of April by the Committee. The House of Representatives passed it, May 10, the day Judge Underwood refused to try or admit Jefferson Davis to bail. It was long debated in the Senate but passed, June 8, in modified form. On June 13, the House accepted the Senate's amendments and it went to the States for adoption or rejection. Nevertheless the President sent a message (June 22), in which he expressed his emphatic disapproval of the proposed amendment.

It was finally ratified by three-fourths of the States and proclaimed by the Secretary of State, William H. Seward, two years later (July 28, 1868).

It is interesting to note that this amendment was rejected by Delaware, Kentucky and Maryland. California never acted upon it. New Jersey and Ohio passed it, and then reconsidered and voted against it. As there were thirty-six states in the Union (counting the Southern States not represented), the amendment must receive twenty-seven votes.

Congress had little respect for the Constitution in 1868, so Congress decided that the amendment was passed and ordered it proclaimed. Congress forced Virginia, Mississippi and Texas, on pain of continuing indefinitely under bayonet rule to adopt the XIV Amendment. Violence and chicanery are written into this now defunct paragraph of the Constitution.[4]

---

[4] *Harper's Encyclopedia*, "Constitution."

ALEX. H. STEPHENS, *War Between the States*, p. 642, gives an adequate idea of the opinion of the Southern people anent such procedure.

CHAPTER XVI

THE FREEDMEN'S BUREAU

**Arbitrary power is most easily established on the
ruins of liberty abused to licentiousness.**
                    —*George Washington.*

The Freedmen's Bureau, as organized by the Congress in 1865, was to close its books one year after
the end of the War Between the States. The President's absurd proclamation that the war was ended
"except in Texas," April 2, 1866, gave the Bureau and
its long list of salaried agents one more year of life.
Thaddeus Stevens' Bill of Enormities pushed through
the Congress in February made the life of the Bureau
indefinite. Even the Radicals with their close
organization and their "whip" did not venture to
pass the Bill of Enormities (Freedmen's Bureau
Bill) over the presidential veto.

But the Bureau was an important part of Radical
organization. It furnished them with the choicest
arguments for keeping the Southern States out of
the Union, for giving the freedmen votes and for
disfranchising the cruel and crafty "rebels."

The entire South heaved a sigh of relief when this
enormity was dropped in February, but the South
did not take the correct measure of Radical purpose
and determination. With the heat of June, and

the approaching adjournment of the Congress the
Freedmen's Bureau Bill was brought up in both
Senate and House as a "joint resolution."

In order to make it less objectionable the life of
the Freedmen's Bureau was limited to two years
from the date of passage and there were other minor
changes.[1]

The gentle reader must remember the congressional
election in November, 1866. In November, 1868,
somebody was going to be elected President of the
United States. Evidently the Bureau must be
continued and the "special agents," spies and reporters must by all means be kept in the South until
both elections were safely won.

The bill passed. The President returned it (July
16) with the expected veto. He declared that the
Bureau reestablished slavery in another form. The
profits from the system were merely transferred from
the former masters to the pockets of Radical officials.

The President had detailed and authentic information from Generals James Barrett Steedman and J. H.
Fullerton, distinguished officers in the Federal Army
and Northern men that the Bureau officers were "a
radical close corporation," devoted to defeating
Johnson's policies. They were "incompetent," often
"corrupt" and some had been arrested for their
offenses. The two generals thought that these
Bureau agents "demoralized the Negroes" and promoted "bitterness between the races." Its good
work was already ended.

The President said in his veto message, "In nu-

[1] GEORGE WILLIAM WILLIAMS, *Negro Race in America*, pp. 379-381, gives the
text of the Act *verbatim*.

merous instances the Bureau was used by its agents as a means of promoting their individual advantage, and that the freedmen are employed for the advancement of the personal ends of the officers instead of their own improvement and welfare."

It cannot be denied that the Freedmen's Bureau was, and was intended to be, a gigantic political organization. The multitude of officers, agents, organizers, teachers, nurses and other employees on the payroll of the National government swarmed like a plague of locusts on the South—then back again in person or by report to convince the Northern people how wicked, rebellious, stubborn and immoral all Southern people were. It was said of Carl Schurz that he "treasured every idle word and idle gesture to libel the white population of the South," and there were thousands like the imported Prussian Radical.[2]

As soon as the veto was read it was passed by the usual two-thirds majority and became law.[3]

The disappointment of the South was keen.

---

[2]Carl Schurz was of all leaders the most contentious. He was born in Liblar, graduated at Bonn, and became a German Radical and insurrectionist at Bonn. He had to flee his native land. First in Switzerland, then in Paris he was a "rebel." He drifted to Philadelphia and then to Wisconsin. Instantly he became as radical in America as he had been in Germany. All his campaigning before 1860 was in the German tongue among German-Americans. He was made a Major-General. As the only battles he took part in were Second Manassas, Chancellorsville and Chattanooga, three overwhelming Confederate victories, he could not have received his appointment for military prowess or ability.

He bitterly opposed the Senate, he bitterly opposed General Grant as President, he bitterly opposed the Republicans after serving in President Hayes' Cabinet, and he bitterly opposed James G. Blaine. His capacity for controversy was extraordinary.

[3]E. P. OBERHOLTZER, *History of the United States*, Vol. I, p. 181.

For two more long years these "agents," swarming over the South as "guardians of the freedmen," with power to make their contracts, settle disputes with their employers and interfere in all affairs, political[4] economic, even domestic, must be endured.[5]

II

Tennessee was knocking at the doors of the Congress for readmission. It had of all the Southern States the largest minority of Union citizens during the war. One-third of its people bitterly opposed slavery and secession. They were carried into the Confederacy against their will. In no part of the United States was there such bitter fratricidal strife as in the mountains and valleys of Eastern Tennessee. It is really quite astonishing that no proposition was seriously advanced to divide the State as Virginia had been divided and erect a new Commonwealth in the eastern section.

[4] ROSCOE LEWIS ASHLEY, *American History*, p. 441, admits that the agents found "rich picking" in the impoverished South.

H. A. HERBERT, *Why the Solid South*, Chapter 1.

[5] W. W. SCOTT, *History of Orange County*, pp. 160-163.

"There was not seed in the county sufficient to pitch a crop, nor money wherewith to buy. The Freedmen's Bureau was constituted by the conquerors; and satraps with soldiers' straps and brass buttons were sent to every county to look after the slaves. The Negroes were organized into Union Leagues and depraved white men did their utmost to inflame them to riot and tumult. To the credit of the Negroes, be it said, many of them continued orderly, respectful and industrious."

It should be remembered with gratitude that the citizens of Baltimore offered to furnish seed on credit if a crop were raised. Every one then took fresh heart and went to work.

HUNSDON CARY, *Some Observations*, p. 10: Under the Freedmen's Bureau Virginia was divided into eight districts, each under an Asst. Quartermaster; and these districts were in turn divided into sub-districts under the command of military officers.

The President was, of course, anxious for many and for personal reasons to have his State again represented. But there was bitter opposition. The Radicals who hated Andrew Johnson were little disposed to look upon the readmission of his State with favor.

Then Tennessee, with two votes in the Senate and eight in the House, was almost certain to send up some Democrats and Conservative Republicans. They might disturb the huge majority necessary to pass the radical program over presidential vetoes. Yet once again, Tennessee, if admitted, would give encouragement to other Southern States and establish a precedent; evidently the door must be shut upon the Tennesseans so long as possible.

As soon, however, as the Fourteenth Amendment was proposed "Parson" Brownlow, the Governor of Tennessee, a vindictive Radical, called the Legislature to Nashville (July 4, 1866).

Every effort was made to hold a quorum together and to force Tennessee to adopt the Fourteenth Amendment (although Tennessee was not a part of the United States according to Radical logic). By fair means or foul a quorum was counted amid "some of the most violent and irregular scenes in the parliamentary history of America," and under Brownlow's "scourge of scorpions" a vote for the amendment was counted.

The Congress was weary, the weather was hot, the election was coming and the nation was growing restless. To the startled Senate the Secretary read this telegram from the desk:

"Nashville, July 19, 1866.
"Hon. J. W. Forney,
"Secretary United States Senate,
"Washington.

"We have fought the battle and won it.   We have ratified the constitutional amendment in the House— 43 voting for it, 11 against it, two of Andrew Johnson's tools not voting.   Give my regards to the dead dog of the White House.

"W. G. Brownlow."

Next day Edgar Cowan, a fearless and independent Republican from Pennsylvania, rose in the full strength of his manhood, towering six feet four inches, and delivered this phillipic:

"This is the first time in the history of the Senate, unquestionably, that such a dropping as this has fallen from so foul a bird into this chamber, and it is the first time, I think, in the history of this chamber, that members of this body would sit patiently by and not vindicate themselves from the charges of being accessories to such vituperation.   And this is published with joyful acclaim by an officer of this body, published in the very sanctuary of American decency."

The Senator was mistaken only in this.   There was no decency as there was no justice in the Government of the Country in 1866.   Those who do evil to others, themselves become the victims of the evil they do.

John A. Bingham,[6] a conservative member of the Reconstruction Committee of Fifteen, moved to re-

---

[6]W. H. Barnes, *History of the 39th Congress*, Chapter 20.

consider the relation of the State to the Federal
Union. When adopted he offered as a substitute:
"That the State of Tennessee is hereby restored to
her former, proper, practical relation to the Union,
and again entitled to be represented by senators and
representatives in Congress, duly elected and qualified, upon their taking the oaths of office required
by existing laws." The House passed the substitute
July 20 and the Senate July 21.

The President responded with his signature and a
message of approval read to the Representatives
July 24, "amid much ironical laughter." Some of
the State's congressmen were present and were permitted to take their seats.

The two Senators-elect were Joseph S. Fowler
and David D. Patterson.[7] No objection could be
found to Fowler, but Judge Patterson was the husband of Martha, the daughter of Andrew Johnson!

Instantly the Radicals were in arms. Judge Patterson had officiated on the bench in Eastern Tennessee under a "rebel" government. The Senate
passed a joint resolution to the effect that he was
not eligible to a seat in that honorable body, but
the House disagreed.

Finally on the last day of the session, and almost
the last hour, Judge Patterson was allowed to take
the oath and was seated.[8] The first session of the
Thirty-ninth Congress then adjourned, and that

---

[7]JAMES G. BLAINE, *Twenty Years of Congress*, Vol. II, Chapter 3.

[8]It will be noticed that Senator Bingham's Resolution readmitting Tennessee to the Union quotes the very words used by President Lincoln three
days before his assassination, "restored to her proper, practical relation to the
Union." Tennessee was admitted on the Lincoln theory, as the other Southern

was the only good thing the Thirty-ninth Congress did. It was a Congress of "many and violent iniquities." If from December to July they passed one act that was helpful, tolerant or constructive this pen has been unable to detect it.

This Congress goes into history as the worst, except the Fortieth. The cruelty, avarice and fanaticism of those men must ever remain a foul blot on the pages of American history.

The Virginians heaved a sigh of relief when Congress adjourned and hoped that the worst was over. . . . In that hope, unfortunately, they were sadly deceived.

States should have been. Infinite suffering, sorrow and bitterness through the nine remaining years would have been avoided if the other ten States had been so received. Unfortunately, such was not the case.

The State Suicide theory of Charles Sumner was absurd to a degree, and as eccentric as the scholar who begat this unscholarly progeny.

The Radical theory, that the States should be reduced to the status of territories, which finally prevailed, accepted as authentic the Confederate theory that their secession was legally accomplished and that they had become conquered provinces by sheer force, as Poland was conquered by Russia or Gaul by Rome. That theory substituted a Union pinned together by bayonets and cemented by blood for the Union of 1789, pinned together by mutual respect, regard and cooperation and cemented by cordial political friendship, for the mutual advantage of all.

Under Lincoln's simple theory the 101 counties of Virginia should have been reunited to West Virginia, and the undivided Commonwealth would at once have become an integral part of the Union. Had this been done the standing fraud that West Virginia was created by the consent of Virginia would have been eliminated, and the Commonwealth would have been one today having been saved the political persecution of Reconstruction.

The simplicity, clarity and genius of Lincoln were never more conclusively shown than when he proposed that simple, just and equitable reestablishment of the sundered Union.

CHAPTER XVII

THE BLOODY SHIRT CAMPAIGN

The blood of men,
And the tears of women.
—*William Makepeace Thackeray.*

We have never had a campaign like it before or since. Pray that America will never have another! There have been campaigns—thousands of them, of every conceivable kind—and some are well remembered; like the "Tippecanoe and Tyler, too" campaign of 1840, the Lincoln-Douglas-Breckenridge-Bell campaign of 1860, the Tilden-Hayes campaign of 1876. But for fire and frenzy the Bloody Shirt Campaign of 1866 passes them all.

It was not a presidential year, but a by-election to select the members of the Fortieth Congress. The issue was "Radicalism" versus "Andy Johnsonism." We recall no other congressional election which was heralded by no less than four national conventions; such was the excitement.

The Conservative Republicans (as early as June 25) called to Philadelphia, "the City of Brotherly Love," all patriots, including even Democrats and "rebels" to sit in a National Union Convention, August 14. So great was the crowd expected that a "Wigwam" was built on Girard Avenue, to seat 10,000 people—and it was taxed to capacity. At high noon a grand procession filed into the large spaces. Governor James Lawrence Orr, of South Carolina, entered upon the arm of General Darius Nash Couch, of Massachusetts. And ever after the editors called it the "Arm-in-Arm Convention."

The band played "Yankee Doodle" and the Southern delegates stood on their seats and cheered. The band played "Dixie" and the "Yankees" stood longer and cheered louder.

The convention put forth its political creed. No State could be at one and the same time in the Union and out of it. They extolled a President who courageously upheld the Constitution and labored to heal the hurts of war.

A telegram came from the President and was read in a very tumult of enthusiasm. "The people must be trusted and the country will be restored," he said.

Henry J. Raymond, an influential Conservative of New York, cried in impassioned voice, "Slavery is abolished and forever prohibited." Judge Yerger, of Mississippi, called up from the floor:

"And nobody wants it back."

Governor William Alexander Graham, of North Carolina, called from his sector, "That's true of North Carolina and of all the South." A large banner was unfurled:

"All the States have an equal and an indefeasible right to a voice and a vote."

Senator Jas. Rood Doolittle, of Wisconsin, presided and, pleading pardon for the pun, we will add that it was indeed a Do-Little Convention.

It takes votes not cheers to win elections. Tennessee was the only Southern State with a vote. And again: The enthusiasm and the shouting were too evidently made-to-order. The truth is, it was almost impossible to grow enthusiastic over Andrew Johnson. He lacked that indefinable but requisite quality called "tact."

The Radicals had an organization like a Macedonian phalanx, Stevens, Sumner, Stanton, Wade, Butler, Chandler, and were flattering General Grant the uncrowned king of America. If they could capture Grant . . . and they did!

The Radicals had the press and the Bloody Shirt. The Conservatives were disgusted with the everlasting waving of the Bloody Shirt. But the Radicals never tired. It was at once the cheapest and surest way to win.

II

The Arm-in-Arm Convention was a pink tea to the Radical counterstroke. They, too, met in "The City of Brotherly Love" (September 3), and called it the Southern Loyalist Convention. It was not a large gathering, but what it lacked in numbers it made up in fire and frenzy.

Our friend John Minor Botts was conspicuous. Botts opposed unlimited suffrage for men, but the other Radicals from Virginia differed with Botts. James W. Hunnicutt offered a resolution declaring for the enfranchisement of all men except "rebels."

He said it was the only safe course for Virginia and the nation. George Tucker agreed with Hunnicutt. Finally the convention voted 66 to 8 in

favor of universal suffrage without regard to color.
But no "rebels" must under any circumstances be
allowed to vote.[1] Parson Brownlow was up from
Nashville, Governor Henry C. Warmouth from New
Orleans and Algernon W. Tourgee came from North
Carolina. Anna Dickinson, "a lady orator" of
Abolition days, was very much present, and Fred
Douglass, the Negro orator of Michigan; Theodore
Tilton, the erstwhile friend of Henry Ward Beecher,
soon to become conspicuous in the Beecher scandal,
and many others such.

For five days they remained in Philadelphia
"where freedom was proffered and pledged by the
Fathers of the Republic," these "representatives of
eight millions of people" asked their friends and
"brothers in the North for protection and justice."
They implored the Congress to keep in subjection
"the contrivers of the Rebellion."

The New York World described the convention
and insisted upon calling it the "Bogus Southern
Convention." The World said they were "self-
appointed, representing nobody but themselves,"
and that they were "mean whites" and "ribald
fanatics." The New York Herald called them
"mongrels," "black and tan conventionists," and a
"miscegenation crowd." In the convention James
Speed,[2] of Kentucky, who had just resigned as
Johnson's Attorney General, called his recent chief
"The Tyrant of the White House," who had "pardoned some of the worst rebels."

---

[1] HAMILTON JAMES ECKENRODE, *Reconstruction in Virginia.*

[2] JAMES SPEED wrote Edwin M. Stanton, August 4, 1866, that the rebels
were now planning to make Robert E. Lee or Jefferson Davis a King!

The convention condemned such Copperhead Commonwealths as Kentucky and Maryland, which opposed Negro suffrage. They begged for "national and appropriate legislation enforced by national authority," meaning of course, the United States Army.[3]

III

But the "City of Brotherly Love" was not the only center of political propaganda. The great Middle West must be touched, and the men who fought the battles of the Republic must be aroused. So a "Soldiers and Sailors Convention" met at Cleveland, Ohio, September 17. The policies of the President, his efforts to unite the country and bring peace, were again extolled by such conservatives as Generals Hugh Boyle Ewing, Geo. Armstrong Custer, Jno. Ellis Wool, Jas. Barrett Steedman, Geo. Bibb Crittenden, Gordon Granger and Lovell Harrison Rousseau.

General Wool, remembered in Norfolk, to whom Major Lamb surrendered this city, March 10, 1862, spoke of the Radicals as "revengeful partisans with a raging thirst for blood and plunder who would leave their country a howling wilderness for want of more victims to gratify their insatiable cruelty."

General Nathan Bedford Forrest, the famous Confederate leader, sent a telegram from Memphis. The Radicals were at this time demanding that Forrest be hanged along with Davis and Lee.

---

[3] *Philadelphia Ledger*, September 3-9, 1866.

IV

As the Conservative Republicans had a Soldiers' and Sailors' convention, the Radicals must have one also. They met at Pittsburgh a week after the Conservatives adjourned at Cleveland. Before this assembly Benjamin Franklin Butler, also well if not affectionately remembered in Norfolk, made a fantastic and lurid speech, in which he called for a rope to hang Jefferson Davis and Robert E. Lee, as traitors. There was a huge torch-light procession, an abundance of flags and oratory and abuse of the Rebel-in-the-White-House and all "rebels" in the South.

V

President Johnson accepted an invitation from Chicago to lay the corner stone of a monument to Stephen A. Douglas. Unfortunately he made the tomb of Douglas the excuse for a huge presidential stumping tour. He would "swing around the circle" from Washington to Chicago, and swing back again in another great sensational arc. No decision President Johnson ever made was more unfortunate.

He and his party, which included General Grant and Admiral Farragut, journeyed to Baltimore, were cordially received, and hurried on to Philadelphia. Both in Philadelphia and New York his reception was all that could be desired. There were parades, orations, bands, decorations and applause without end.

The party traveled up the Hudson in the "River Queen," as big cannon reverberated along the shores and pretty ladies in huge skirts waved handkerchiefs and flags. Handsome cadets paraded at West Point and the Governor welcomed the visitors to Albany. The patriots of Niagara Falls entertained them at an elaborate ball, and Buffalo and Erie were cordial.

But when the party reached Cleveland, the home of Benjamin Franklin Wade, President of the Senate, a rabid Radical and the politician who would succeed Johnson in the presidential chair should he die or be impeached, the atmosphere thickened with storm clouds. Here he was rudely interrupted, and the thugs and dregs of the city were hired, the Conservative press declared, by the Union League, to interrupt and mob the President. While we do not know who planned or paid for the disgraceful reception accorded him, it is admitted that as he began to speak the bullies also began,

"Why don't you hang Jeff Davis?" one cried. And another, "You are a liar."

The President, unfortunately, answered these antagonists. He called for the man who said "liar" to come up and face him. Of course the thug did not appear. Johnson then cried, "This eye has never seen the face this heart has feared." It was true. His faults and weaknesses were many, but there never lived a more courageous man than Andrew Johnson.

The Radical press all over the country made the most of the Cleveland incident, exaggerated it and undoubtedly encouraged other cities to follow Cleveland's shameful precedent. They did.

At Oberlin, a seat of education and culture, he

was snubbed. At Elyria, Ohio, the station and streets were hung with black flags. At Norwalk, Ohio, he asked why he could not speak to the citizens without being insulted. At Detroit he likened the thugs to dogs yelping at his heels.

At Chicago the ceremony was carried through and Johnson then visited the tomb of Lincoln at Springfield. At Alton he went aboard the "Andy Johnson" and floated to St. Louis.

The reception he received at St. Louis was worse than the Cleveland riot. As he addressed an immense crowd from the portico of the Southern Hotel one stentorian voice cried, "Judas."

"If I am Judas, what of Thad Stevens, Wendell Phillips and Charles Sumner—are they Christs?"

The further the tour continued the worse it got. At Indianapolis the President was actually hooted off the platform. "Shut up," they cried, "we do not want to hear you." "Traitor." In the riot one man was killed and many were wounded.

Theodore Tilton referred to him in the "Independent" (supposed to be a religious paper) as "the basest citizen of the republic, though its Chief Magistrate."

They visited Louisville and came up the river to Cincinnati; then to Pittsburgh where again he was actually hooted off the platform as at Indianapolis.

Johnson's "swing around the circle" was worse than a tragedy; it was a blunder.

When at last he reached the welcome privacy and seclusion of the White House, the election, though two months off, was won. The only question was the size of the Radical majority.

Horace Greeley, of the New York Tribune, "watched with a feeling of national shame the coarseness with which the President had turned a solemn journey to the tomb of a celebrated American into the stumping tour of an irritated demagogue."

The Philadelphia Press thought his speeches will be read "with black brows and fiery eyes by an insulted people."

The Nation (N. Y.) said his speeches were "vulgar, egotistical and occasionally profane, full of coarse abuse of his enemies, and coarser glorification of himself." The Cleveland (Ohio) Leader spoke of his "bitter political harangues all of which were insults to his Radical hosts."

But is it not strange that none of the Radical editors had a word of condemnation for the thugs and rioters who were paid to fill the best seats and hector the President of the United States, and a Republican President at that?

As the people of Virginia, who once hated the name of Andrew Johnson, read of the unfortunate reaction, their hearts died within them. They knew that worse things were now in store for the prostrate South, and worse than their worst fears befell.

CHAPTER XVIII

THE RADICAL TRIUMPH

The eternal stars shine out
As soon as it is dark enough.
—*Thomas Carlyle.*

As the days shortened in the autumn of 1866 the campaign was on in full swing, a campaign of un-exampled bitterness and vindictiveness. General John A. Logan shouted to applauding audiences, "There is but one way to treat the rebels, take a torch in one hand and a sword in the other and sweep over their territory." Carl Schurz declared that the "Rebel-in-the-White-House" was worse than Judas Iscariot or Benedict Arnold. And again: "If there is any man who ought to hang it is Andrew Johnson." When United States Senators, scholars and major generals use such language, it is no wonder that the crowd at the saloon, on the street corner and in the back country was wrought to white heat of fury.[1]

Grant advised that colored troops be mustered out of service as quickly and quietly as possible, as they were particularly distasteful to Southern

[1] I am sorry to say that so fine a man as JAMES RUSSELL LOWELL wrote (North American Review, October, 1866) that the President had a "vulgar mind and that mind a Southern one."

people; but Schurz, our gentle Prussian statesman, insisted that they be retained as garrisons in the South "to impress upon them the Negroes' freedom." Senator Zachariah Chandler, of Michigan, boldly declared, "The rebels have only changed their leader and their tactics. Then it was Jeff Davis, now it is Andy Johnson. The white-livered rebels mean to overthrow your Government."

Thaddeus Stevens told his neighbors at Lancaster, Pennsylvania (September 7, 1865), and frequently repeated the sentiment that "the lives, liberty and property of the belligerents of the South" were in the hands of the voters to do with as they pleased. Jewett declared in New York that all "Southern people are a dirty and contemptible race unfit for any share in government and inferior to their own Negroes." He stumped Indiana with speeches violent, even incendiary. He delighted to tell and retell blood-curdling stories of Southern depravity and cruelty. The only hope for the nation was to confiscate all the rebels' property, give the Negroes the right to vote, and force the issue with bayonets and bullets. Charles Sumner told applauding audiences in New England that he had no faith "in the repentance of rebel devils." He declared, "By the assassination of Lincoln the rebellion vaulted into the Presidential chair. Who can doubt that the President is the author of these tragedies?" He also favored indefinite military occupation of the South.

A radical orator of Tiffin, Ohio, openly asserted that the President was Booth's partner in the murder of Lincoln. At Toledo, Ohio, a man shouted in a

torchlight procession, "We'll hang the G—— D——
traitor!"

The campaign reached an apex of passion, prejudice and violence.[2]   Hatred was fanned into furious
flames. The propaganda of the Radical minority
was skillfully, adroitly and persistently handled by
tongue and pen. The worse made to appear the
better reason. Every appeal to reason, justice,
conciliation or calm thought was eternally damned
to perdition. America has never before nor since
seen such devilish ingenuity, conscienceless libel,
such wholesale calumny.

Every Southern man was a blood-thirsty monster,
every Democrat a copperhead snake and a traitor
to his country, and every Conservative Republican
a white-livered scoundrel; and the greatest of these
was Andrew Johnson, the Radical Republican who
turned Conservative and a Rebel-sympathizer.

The President, as brave as a lion, dared to say,
April 2, 1866, "The idea of muzzling the press[3] and
tying the tongues of the people of the South after
the manner of suspicious tyrants and the Holy

---

[2] B. W. JONES, *Beneath the Stars and Bars*, p. 268.

"How fortunate, then, that none could lift the veil, which concealed beneath its lurid and slimy folds the horrors, wrongs and humiliations of the
decade, now known as the miserable 'reconstruction' days; the decade of the
carpet-baggers, the renegade and the negrophile."

[3] OLIVER P. MORTON gave the voters of Indiana this classic: "Every un-
regenerate rebel calls himself a Democrat, every bounty-jumper, every deserter,
every sneak who ran away from the draft, calls himself a Democrat. Every
man who murdered Union prisoners, who burned steam-boats and Northern
cities, who contrived hellish means to scatter yellow fever, is a Democrat.
The Democratic party is a common sewer and a loathsome receptacle."

SENATOR ZACHARIAH CHANDLER of Michigan reechoed: "Every man who
murdered and poisoned and stole was a Democrat."

Inquisition! A people should be allowed to grumble
who have suffered so much. They would be unworthy the name of men if they did not respect the
brave officers and men who have suffered with them,
and honor the memory of their gallant dead who
sleep in a hundred battle-fields around their homes."
But such kindly words found no place in the angry
and violent crowd. Wendell Phillips cried, "Let
us pray God the President may continue to make
mistakes. Congress should impeach the Rebel in
the White House."

Georges Clemenceau, a young French reporter,
wrote to Paris, "The Sumners, Stevenses and
Phillipses are the finest men of the nation." And of
the South he said, "Nothing will bring the South
back into the fold. The whole region has become
impossible as a dwelling place for Union men. In
some places blacks are still bought and sold by a
people long slave-holding has demoralized."[4]

II

As the young Frenchman knew nothing of the
South, it is evident that he merely retailed information furnished so generously by the Radicals.

When the votes were counted and the country
awoke November 7, the Radicals had swept the
country. The success of the Bloody Shirt Campaign
was even beyond the Radicals' most optimistic
hope.

---

[4]The student of political psychology will be interested in BENJAMIN J.
LOSSING, *History of the United States*, pp. 719-739, in which almost every statement made concerning the South and its leaders is false in fact and inaccurate
in detail. Lossing wrote poor history, but excellent partisan propaganda.

For one item the country was drunk with war-prosperity.[5] Cheap money flowed hither and yon like water in streams never failing. When all were so rich and so happy, why change?

The Radical organization had almost complete control of the railways, now very much in politics and destined to stay in politics for fifty years. The telegraph lines, banks, newspapers, factories, big business and to a great extent the churches were solidly behind the Congress. The executives and legislatures of every Northern and border State, except two, were against Johnson and for the Congress. The huge army vote and all enlisted men and all who were growing rich from innumerable contracts . . . all were for the Radical Congress.

The Democrats, Copperheads as they were always called, who wished to aid the President, and who for their own purposes wanted to bring back the ten Southern States as soon as possible were completely discredited.[6]

In 1864 Lincoln carried New York by a slim 7,000 majority. New York was full of Copperheads. In this election the Radicals doubled Lincoln's majority.

Michigan rolled up a 39,000 majority, Wisconsin 24,000, Illinois 56,000, and so it went throughout the country.

---

[5]HARRY FLOOD BYRD, *Scribner's Magazine*, June, 1928, p. 685, gives a brief statement of the effects of Reconstruction in the state.

[6]HOWARD K. BEALE, *Critical Year*, p. 406: "The Radicals forced their program upon the South by an evasion of issues and a clever use of propaganda, in an election where the majority of the voters would have supported Johnson's policies had they been given a chance to express themselves in an issue squarely joined."

When the Fortieth Congress meets, March 4, 1867, the Senate will have 42 Republicans and 11 Democrats.

It seemed that the nation turned thumbs down. Andrew Johnson, his Southern policies and Presidential Reconstruction were evidently repudiated. The nation gave a clear mandate to Stevens, Sumner, Stanton, Wade, Butler and Chandler. As the Southern people read the news their hearts and hopes sank into deeper despair. Our fate is the fate of Hayti, they declared.

Simon Cameron, of Pennsylvania, speaking in Harrisburg, cried: "I did not believe that low white from the South was fit to be President. If I were a lawyer I'd be the first to impeach him, and put him out."

As the student of American political history looks back upon the lurid, turbid campaign of 1866, he will find it, perhaps, not so much a repudiation of Andrew Johnson as a potent example of powerful, political propaganda. It is astonishing how people can be led, merely by the process of repetition. Repeat a falsehood often enough and one comes to believe it . . . keep on repeating it and the world about you comes to believe it. But when that falsehood meets the cold and critical scrutiny of posterity, history will likely give a true verdict. Every falsehood carries on its back its own repudiation.

Our fathers, in their despair, facing a Federal soldier at every corner, and looking into the muzzle of a gun at every cross-roads . . . could not guess that in the Bloody Shirt Campaign the tide of vituperation, falsehood, passion and prejudice reached its flood. They little reckoned that from this time the tide would ebb, slowly and painfully at first, with much delay and many disappointments; still, as each year passed, it brought to the nation and to the South that common sense and sanity which has saved America in every crisis as it has also been the salvation of the Anglo-Saxon race for twelve centuries.[7]

III

More than twenty months had passed since Lee surrendered and the Southern soldiers had returned to their homes. There was peace throughout the Southland except where the soldiers, black and white, their "missionaries" and agents, the Freedmen's Bureau and the carpet-baggers stirred up race hatred, incited riots and filled their ignorant wards with foolish fancies and impossible dreams.[8] But the trouble was wholly imported. Nevertheless

[7]"What a gloom, a foreboding, a sadness rests over the land! Who can tell but that a worse disaster than defeat awaits us. Shadows deepen everywhere. All is despondency, apprehension, fear. There is no life but a stupor, a dazed unrest, a silent looking about for the proverbial silver lining on the dark cloud. But we looked in vain"—a contemporary description of Eastern Virginia.

[8]A large delegation of colored soldiers called on the President at the White House, October, 1865, and he admonished them to be honest, law-abiding, industrious. He advocated morality, self-control, temperance and thrift.

It is quite astonishing that zealous Wendell Phillips was instantly and vigorously in arms. He denounced the Rebel-in-the-White-House for such an address and declared that "future historians" will hold Andrew Johnson up to the "indignation and scorn of the world."

But the "future historian" has come more and more to honor President Johnson, and Wendell Phillips, that prince of agitators, has shrunk to smaller statue with each passing year.

the future was dark and clouds, heavy with impending doom, seemed banked upon every horizon.[9] The government was to the Virginian a military despotism of the worst type, from which there was no appeal and no escape. The civilization of three centuries seemed doomed to extinction. Ireland and Poland were to be envied in 1866. The President demanded one thing, Congress something else. President and Congress were united against the South, but united in nothing else, and at war each with the other. Congress was united against the President, but united in nothing else. The factions within the Republican party were constantly at each others' throats. Wise men, like General Sherman and President Johnson, predicted a second civil war!

IV

But in his home and fields the Virginian was happy. God was good and Nature kindly. The worst element of the freedmen had gone from the farms and were now congested in the slums of the cities. War-prices still obtained, what little the farmer had to sell, when he could get it to market.[10]

The North and West were rolling in such a riot of luxury as no people had ever before enjoyed. Money was as plentiful as the leaves of the forest. Some of it was coming South, and the Virginian hoped that more would come—and it did.

[9]It was ever a bitter reflection that these emissaries who did so much harm were on the pay-roll of the National government, supported by all tax-payers, the South included!

[10]Cotton and tobacco brought splendid, though falling prices, since the war ended.

The military satrap, General Schofield, was gentle, kindly-disposed and very popular in Virginia. The very quarrels between President Johnson and the factions of the Republican party might redound to the benefit of the South—and they did.

In Virginia the Whigs and Democrats still hated each other as cordially as ever . . . but they had fought together in the Confederate army, and they were now ready to unite and save Virginia.

Improvement there was in our economic condition, even if there was no improvement in matters political.[11] The railways were running their trains again, there were steamboats on the rivers, the mails arrived and departed even if much delayed. Thousands of pardons had been issued by President Johnson and signed by Secretary Seward for those who took part in the "late rebellion." Here and there excellent people were moving from the North and West into the South, and bringing new money, new enterprise and new hope to the desolate countryside.

V

And so we come to the end of the troubled year 1866. Perhaps the part of Virginia that felt the shock of war and defeat least of all was the "Empire of the Cumberlands, protected because sequestered.

---

[11]In 1938 Senator Millard E. Tydings of Maryland said: "In the dark days of the Reconstruction era following the Civil War, men in Maryland and in other states of the nation had to walk between lines of fixed bayonets to register their choice for national representatives. The force then used was silent, represented only by soldiers who, acting upon the orders of the little coterie then in control of our national government, sought to apply the lash of retribution to the impoverished people of the war-torn and devastated lands of the Old South. . . . "

The last Confederate flag[12] that fluttered to the breeze in Virginia was lowered two weeks after General Lee's surrender, at Cumberland Gap. Its defenders disappeared along the paths and through the mountain ravines to their cabin homes. Since that long distant day profound peace has blessed this favored land. The gigantic upheaval of the World War with its wrecks and hazards brought to this people a great rise in prices.

The westerning sun of each summer's day slipped behind the steep summits of the Cumberland range. A thousand deepening tints of rose, orange and amber touched the dark forest of oaks and pines which climbed the rugged slopes like giants in battle array.

The evening clouds caught and held the rare glory of the sunset, until at length the colors faded into that sombre gray which heralds approaching night. The stars peeped forth dimly and timidly in the pale sky as the shadows darkened on the purple peaks and grew black in the coves and valleys.

May the God-given benediction of peace and happiness; and the blessing of strength, purity, honesty and well-being continue upon the people of Virginia on mountain and plain beside the flowing rivers and the restless sea; until the light of the last day fades and mankind awakens to the glory of resurrection dawn.

---

[12]JOHN FOX, JR., *The Army of the Cumberland.*

BOOK THREE

NOVEMBER 6, 1866—DECEMBER 11, 1867

CHAPTER XIX

RIFTS IN THE STORM CLOUDS

Th' oppresive, sturdy, man-destroying villains
Who ravaged kingdoms, and laid empires waste,
And in a cruel wantonness of power,
Thinned states of half their people, and gave up
To want the rest.
                                    —*Samuel Blair.*

Despite the calamity which befell the South in the Radical triumph, November 6, 1866, the typical Virginian who bided his time and waited for a better day, might discern blue rifts in the storm clouds.[1] The President, stubborn as the hickory forests from which he came, was still at the helm. The potent Supreme Court of the United States still remembered that a document called the Constitution was the foundation of our Government.

And now another rift of blue, a kindly gesture, a hand lifted in blessing, to remain through the unnumbered years; and it came to the South from Massachusetts. Far above the pecuniary value of the gift were the lessons and the moral influence of George Peabody's great benefactions. After all,

---

[1] *Norfolk Journal* (January 2, 1867): "The survey for a railway from Newport News to Richmond is now completed."

IBIB (January 3): "Never in history have so many bales of cotton been received here as in the latter part of 1866; a minimum estimated at 45,000 bales (some say 65,000). The market is active, and the price for middling is about 33c a pound."

not every man in Massachusetts was a Charles
Sumner or a Ben Butler!

George Peabody was born in Danvers, Massachusetts, February 18, 1795. Francis Peabody, the
first of the name, an English Puritan, came over in
1635. George went to work at the tender age of
eleven. As a lad of seventeen he managed a store
in Georgetown, D. C., for his uncle, John Peabody.
At nineteen he opened a dry goods house in Baltimore with Elisha Riggs as his partner. They soon
had branches in Philadelphia and New York.[2]

George was still a young man, 34, when he took
over the chain of stores. A few years later (1837)
he moved to London and established a banking
house of international reputation. His first large
benefaction was a tidy $200,000 donated the State
of Maryland.

In 1851 he gave the first "Fourth of July Dinner"
in London. The Duke of Wellington was one of
his guests. Queen Victoria sent her portrait and
one of Prince Albert, her husband, to decorate the
dining hall.

He founded libraries at Danvers and North
Danvers, his native town (1852). He visited America
(1857) and founded the Peabody Institute at Baltimore, to which he gave more than a million dollars,
first and last. He wished London's poor to live in
better homes and gave sums in seven figures, from
time to time, to help build them.

---

[2] J. L. M. CURRY, *George Peabody*, pp. 1-75. An excellent portrait of Mr.
Peabody as the frontispiece.

During the War Between the States when Federal bonds sank to unprecedented figures, George Peabody's heavy investments in them strengthened Federal credit and his wealth soared with the collapse of the Confederacy.

During the hectic year 1866, now closing, he visited America again, giving large sums to Harvard and Yale. He placed $2,100,000 (increased three years later to $3,500,000) in a fund for education in the South. And it was to be used (not wholly) largely for the education of poor and orphaned white children. A helping hand for the arrogant "rebels" and their children and orphans!

The benefaction came in the midst of the Radical campaign (in October) and was the first substantial gesture of sympathy, help and appreciation the South received. It touched the heart of the South where the name of George Peabody will never be forgotten.

The sands of his life were almost run, for he died in London, November 4, 1869. George Peabody was the first of that increasing company of philanthropists who have used their great wealth, not for self-indulgence, but as a trust for mankind. Gladstone said of him, "He taught the world how a man may be the master of his fortune and not its slave." George Peabody often confessed to his intimate friends that his disposition was "naturally parsimonious," and he gave from a sense of "benefits conferred upon him by Divine Providence." His benefactions were the largest in human history to his time.

II

Recalling the disaster of 1866 James Barron Hope[3] wrote: "Upon reviewing the year we look upon a checkered scene, in which the dark portions far exceed the bright. How many hopes have been utterly ruined! Let us thank our Creator for the blessing of Hope. Without it what would be our life?"[4]

The following picture of Lynchburg was drawn by the pen of William Asbury Christian: "The effects of Reconstruction were now everywhere apparent. Commerce was paralyzed. Stores were vacant; the tobacco business seemed ruined, and property everywhere declined in value. The outlook was indeed serious. Efforts made to revive Lynchburg were without success. Reconstruction thwarted every move. The soldiers here were a rowdy, rough and drunken set, continually fighting with the Negroes[5] and creating general disorder. Robberies were of nightly occurrence.

Substantially the same testimony is given for Norfolk.[6]

[3] *Norfolk Journal*, January 1, 1867.

[4] BEVERLEY D. TUCKER'S poem "Christmas, 1866," gives a faithful picture of the psychology of that dismal holiday:

> Tho the battle may be over,
>   Yet its horrors still remain;
> Tho the cannon's voice is silent
>   Still we hear the clanking chain;
> And the graves of sleeping heroes,
>   And the exile's lonely hours
> Warn us that the days of pleasure
>   But resemble faded flowers.

[5] The Negroes had an intense antipathy for the Northern soldiers. See T. J. WERTENBAKER, *History of Norfolk*, pp. 257-259.

[6] H. W. BURTON, *History of Norfolk*, 1865-9.

During November General Phillip H. Sheridan
wrote the President: "The South is impoverished,
and the probability is that in two or three years
there will be a total transfer of landed property.
The North will own every railroad,[7] every steamboat, every large mercantile establishment and
everything that requires capital." This optimistic
prophecy was never fulfilled, despite the suffering
and poverty of the South.

Misunderstanding was the chief cause of the war,
and it was even more pronounced during Reconstruction. The typical citizen in the North did
not know Southern conditions. In the South the
situation was similar. To Southern people every
"Yankee" was a black Republican, when as a
matter of fact half of them were normally Democrats. And every "Black Republican" was a Radical, when as a matter of fact comparatively few
were Radicals; as comparatively few were Abolitionists before the war.

The ordinary and average citizen of the North
was kindly disposed towards the South, once the
fighting was over, and more especially as the tragic
assassination of Abraham Lincoln faded from memory.

---

[7] *Annual Cyclop*, 1866.
Governor Pierpont advised the sale of Virginia's share of stocks and bonds
in the following railways which the taxpayers had helped to build:

    The Virginia and Tennessee Railway
    The Southside Railway
    The Norfolk and Petersburg Railway
    The Richmond and Danville Railway
    The York River Railway
    The Orange and Alexandria Railway
    and the Virginia Central Railway

The face value of these securities aggregated $15,000,000 more or less.
No governor ever gave this Commonwealth worse advice.

Congressional Reconstruction, with its heritage of sorrow, hatred, riot, vindictiveness and hard-feeling, which has not even yet entirely disappeared, was a conspiracy deliberately planned and astutely executed.

To make bad matters worse the crops for the year 1866 were not so good; cotton was especially poor, and the price was, of course, constantly falling now that peace had come. The Radical Congress added yet one more bit of persecution by placing a Federal tax of three cents upon every pound of cotton. This outrage upon a prostrate and poverty-stricken people by a nation in full swing of super-abounding prosperity was positively Satanic in refined cruelty and iniquity. Ah, we had plenty of taxation without representation and no protection and no funds during Reconstruction.

III

There began at this time a double movement of population, unheralded; and to which no historian, as far as we have observed, has alluded. Yet these silent forces, which have continued with increasing volume to this day, have wielded an immense influence on the people and the attitude of Virginia, the South, and the nation.

Even before the surrender of the Confederate armies, the freedmen[8] of this State began moving northward. Year by year the number of young colored persons of both sexes migrated until in the last decade (1920-30), the census showed an actual

---

[8]J. P. MC CONNELL, *Negroes in Virginia*, pp. 48-49:
"In the neighborhood of Norfolk, Fort Monroe and Yorktown, about 70,000 negroes congregated during the war."

loss of 40,000 Negroes in the population of Virginia, through the decade, despite a large birthrate. The proximity of Washington, Baltimore, Philadelphia, New York and even Boston and Buffalo, the ease of travel and especially the high wages to be obtained in normal times has acted as a magnet. The older Negroes have usually remained. New York is today the largest African city in the world, and every train, bus and boat adds to the number living there.

The other movement has proven the greatest blessing to Virginia and the South. Uncounted thousands[9] have come to Virginia from the North and West, people of property, wealth, culture and intelligence. They found magnificent farms, colonial homesteads, railways, factories, and innumerable bargains for sale. The poverty of the broken South was an opportunity they wisely embraced. Many of the most prominent and influential citizens of Norfolk, Richmond, Roanoke, Atlanta, Birmingham, and especially in Florida are men whose fathers and grandfathers were of Northern or Western birth. The presence of the freedmen, employed all over the South for crude labor, discouraged the immigration among us of the laboring classes from the North. In almost every case those who came to make their homes in the South, to rear their families here, were men of wealth, culture and refinement. These two movements have made the race problem a national, no longer a sectional, problem; and have brought an increasingly valuable element into the heart of Virginia and the South.

---

[9]HENRY W. GRADY: "We have learned that one Northern immigrant is worth fifty foreigners and we have smoothed the path southward."

CHAPTER XX

THE STORM CLOUDS THICKEN

**I am disgraced, impeached and baffled here
Pierced to the soul with slanders' venomed spear.**
—Shakespeare.

The program of Reconstruction which was legalized by the Radical Congress and could be carried
out only with the aid of Northern bayonets was
motivated by many desires, some noble, some sordid.
The better motives were generally Utopian and
visionary, while the evil ones were practical and
decisive.

This is the criticism of David Saville Muzzey, a
native of Lexington, Massachusetts (born 1870), a
brilliant author, profound scholar and an accepted
authority in American history. Holding no brief
for the South, his conclusions will likely represent
the verdict of posterity.

The new year 1867 brought to Virginia the darkest
days in our history.[1] The worst was about to
befall. Many who loved the Commonwealth better
than life believed the radical measures would crush

---

[1] JOHN O. CROWN, poem, "Confederate Soldiers":

"You plod with weary feet
Into the deepening gloom of the unknown,
Where the vanquished wander, when hope's stars are gone."

our civilization and that the fate of Hayti awaited Virginia.

The two legislatures, which held in their hands the thread of our political destiny, met the same day and hour, December 2, at noon. The Thirty-ninth Congress assembled for its second session in the Capitol at Washington. It was to expire March 4, 1867. The Whig General Assembly met for its second session in the State Capitol at Richmond. It also was to expire March 4, 1867.

This is the last service the Old Line Whigs, as a political party, rendered the people of Virginia, and, so far as we know, the last appearance of that fine and able party of patriots in the politics of America. This Whig legislature received a thoughtful and reasonable message from Governor Francis Harrison Pierpont. He reminded the Virginians of the overwhelming endorsement given the Radicals at the polls a month before. He urged timely submission to the will of the Congress. The new Congress which would convene March 4 next would certainly be as radical, as unreasonable, as vindictive and as harsh as the present Congress. Opposition to Radical policies was worse than useless.

He suggested the further modification of the vagrancy laws. Though good and necessary, the Radicals were constantly making powerful appeals to the prejudices of the North and West based upon these laws. He earnestly advised Virginia to adopt the hated XIV Amendment and reenter the Union, following the example of Tennessee. If the Assembly refused to adopt the XIV Amendment, other and more drastic punishments would be laid upon Virginia; and, in the end, the State would be forced to adopt it. Why not now?

The Fourteenth Amendment was a monster with five heads: (1) All persons born in this country are citizens and have an equal right to life and property. That was very fair. (2) If any State denies any class of male citizens a vote the representation of such a State in the Congress and the Electoral College shall be reduced proportionately. That was unfair as all paid taxes. (3) No "rebel" shall hold any office, Federal or judicial or local. That was an outrage. The "rebels" surrendered in all good faith two years before. (4) All States must pay their share of the United States debt, bounties and pensions included, but must repudiate all "rebel" debts, and must not be reimbursed for the slaves set free. That was punishment. The Southern people, despite their poverty during the post-war decades paid, first and last, an immense sum in pensions to those who robbed, despoiled, maligned and maltreated them. (5) Force shall be used to grind this Amendment into such "rebels" the Radicals think need it. This was military tyranny, worthy the Huns.

II

Virginia was fortunate in her commander, John McAllister Schofield. His reign, which might have been as despotic as Attila's, was reasonable, just and mild, though firm. He was a fine type of Conservative Republican. Like Governor Pierpont he advised the Legislature to adopt the Fourteenth Amendment and apply for admission to the Union. He feared "more radical reconstruction" if the Legislature declined. General Schofield visited Washington soon after the Congress assembled. He interviewed "leading Republicans," who gave it as their personal opinion that the State would be readmitted if the Virginians would adopt the Amendment.

No less an authority than Salmon P. Chase declared, "Prompt ratification would have assured complete restoration in my judgment." John Sherman said practically the same, and James G. Blaine declared that many congressmen felt morally bound to admit those States which accepted the Fourteenth Amendment. He wrote: "The Republicans of the North were deeply concerned as to the fate and fortune of the colored population of the South. Only a minority were ready to demand suffrage for those recently emancipated, and who were presumably unfit to be entrusted with the elective franchise.[2] That privilege was indeed still denied them in a majority of the Northern States, and it seemed illogical and unwarrantable to expect a more advanced philanthropy, a higher sense of justice from the South than had as yet been attained by the North."[3]

[2]GEORGES CLEMENCEAU, *American Reconstruction*, p. 35.
"Johnson wants the States to decide the question of Negro suffrage. The Radicals want national action—Sumner advocates Negro suffrage (in order to create in the Southern States a voting faction of unquestionable loyalty)."
[3]Congress voted to admit Colorado and Nebraska, provided they permit all races to vote, except Indians. They had no Negroes, but many Indians! The bill was vetoed by Johnson.

When this matter came up the pride of Virginia was touched. The General Assembly refused by a vote of 20 to 0 in the Senate and 74 to 0 in the House of Delegates to adopt the Fourteenth Amendment (January 9, 1867).

Practically all the historical authorities, including our Virginia historians, condemn the Virginians for this high-spirited decision as impolitic. They contend that the State would likely have been readmitted to the Union had we humbled our pride, and the three subsequent years of bayonet tyranny would have been spared us.

Perhaps it is presumptuous to dispute so many and such weighty authorities; but we rejoice that the General Assembly had the courage of their convictions, standing as they did in the midst of the ruins of war and Reconstruction. We rejoice that they put their principles above expediency. They evidenced to posterity that, despite the threat, tyranny and persecution, they did what they believed to be right. They stood like adamant by Andrew Johnson as Andrew Johnson stood by them. They would not and did not adopt this iniquitous amendment,[4] until all choice and freedom were denied them.

To be sure there came a time when Virginia was forced to adopt the Fourteenth Amendment and the Fifteenth with it . . . but under duress, and

---

[4]JOHN WILLIAM BURGESS, *Reconstruction*, p. 55: "No matter how speedily Virginia adopted the XIV Amendment and all other conditions she must remain under military tyranny until the XIV Amendment was adopted by a sufficient number of States to become a part of the Constitution."

by the grace of the United States Army, not of free volition.[5]

As for the contention that the Radical Congress would have admitted Virginia, as Tennessee was admitted, we do not believe a word of it, despite the testimony of such giants as Salmon P. Chase and James G. Blaine.

There were many roads through the tangled morass of Reconstruction, but all led exactly to the same destination.

The influence and set determination of Thaddeus Stevens, Charles Sumner, Benjamin Franklin Wade, Benjamin Franklin Butler and others of like kidney, their prestige and power, immensely enhanced since the November elections (1866), their plan to control the South by giving the freedmen the franchise and by disfranchising the "rebels," the constant threat to confiscate the property of the "rebels" and to take over the plantations, railways, factories and other utilities at a mere fraction of their value, their well paid army of Freedmen's Bureau agents, providing innumerable jobs for petty politicians; their conspiracy to impeach Andrew Johnson and elevate Benjamin Franklin Wade to the presidency of the United States; when one considers all this, one is bound to conclude that no United States senators or representatives would under any circumstance be admitted to the Congress from the South.

Thaddeus Stevens declared to the members of the House of Representatives amid laughter and cheers

---

[5]Some Virginians advocated the XIV Amendment, as R. W. HUGHES, *Papers*, p. 16: "In 1867 he thundered against the follies of slavery, secession, useless war and the rejection of the XIV Amendment."

that he had previously been a "Conservative," but that since the recent election he had become a "Radical." The nation had endorsed the Radical policy, and he proposed to see that it was carried out root and branch. This sardonic humor was by no means an idle threat. The Radical policies of 1865 and 1866 were mild beside the policies of 1867; and even as the Congress assembled, Stevens had the Military Reconstruction Bill, which he would force through the Congress, in his pocket.

President Johnson's message to the Congress was simple, sound and forthright. He presented "the evil estate of the nation to the chief authors of its woes."[6] He urged the readmission of the ten Southern States, but his plea fell upon deafened ears. He made no reference whatever to the proposed Fourteenth Amendment and his silence on this sore subject cried aloud throughout the land against it. He plead that the Congress "consummate the work of restoration and exert a salutary influence in the reestablishment of peace, harmony and fraternal feeling." Unfortunately peace, harmony and fraternal feeling were the last reactions the congressmen of the "Congress of Many Iniquities" desired.

III

Events moved rapidly with the Congress, and always from bad to worse, as it seemed to the South. A bill was promptly introduced to grant the franchise to Negroes in the District of Columbia. The

---

[6]GEORGE FORT MILTON, *Age of Hate*.

District did not have the large urban population it has since acquired. But during the war and more especially since the surrender, great numbers of the freedmen had followed the armies northward and lived in the squalid and crowded slums of Washington. The House passed the bill December 14 (114 pro, 54 contra). Any officer who rejected a Negro's vote at the polls was liable to a fine of $500 or a year in prison, or both. Charles Sumner cried with characteristic enthusiasm to his fellow Senators: "As you once needed the muskets of the colored men, you now need their votes."

The President vetoed the bill (as Congress expected) and the Congress passed it over his veto (as the nation expected). The inconsistency of those members of Congress who voted for colored franchise in the District when their own States and constituencies had repeatedly rejected the measure need not be pointed out here. Even General Grant, who had not yet gone over to the Radical element, wrote (January 4, 1867), that it was "contemptible business for members of Congress whose States excluded Negro suffrage," to vote for it in the District of Columbia.

At this time only six States permitted the Negroes to vote, namely, Maine, New Hampshire, Vermont, Massachusetts, Rhode Island and New York. Only New York had a considerable Negro population. Connecticut voted down the proposition by substantial majorities. Negro suffrage had been emphatically rejected by such extremely Northern States as Michigan and Minnesota. Kansas and Ohio voted it down.

Sumner wrote of the President in January, "Our only purpose in retaining him a day longer is to compel him to fill the measure of his shame by draining to the very dregs the cup of bitter, blasting humiliation that will be held remorselessly to his lips; until, together with his own, he complete the degradation of his accursed section."

There is a law of retribution[7] which runs like a golden thread through life. "With what measure ye mete it shall be measured unto you again." Sumner who would thrust out President Johnson in shame and disgrace will in four short years find himself practically expelled from the Republican party, excluded from all places of honor and influence. Proud, vindictive Charles Sumner will soon become a friendless and embittered old man, no longer seated in the place of power he had once held. He who conspired to humiliate President Johnson and his accursed section (meaning the South), will himself become the victim of political conspiring. *Sic transit gloria mundi.*

---

[7]JAS. FORD RHODES, *History of United States*, Vol. VII, p. 287.
DAVID S. MUZZEY, *The American Adventure*, Vol. II, Chap. I.
JAS. TRUSLOW ADAMS, *American Tragedy*, p. 389.
S. E. MORRISON, *Oxford History of United States*, p. 345.

Chapter XXI

THE SHERMAN-SHELLABARGER BILL

O haughty tyrannous man, injustice breeds injustice: curses and falsehoods do verily return always
home; wide as they may wander. All anarchy, all
evil, injustice is by the nature of it, dragon's teeth,
suicidal and cannot endure.

—*Thos. Carlyle.*[1]

The year 1867 is remembered as the blackest, the
most dreadful in the long history of the Commonwealth. It began a sequence of sinister events with
a celebration of the Proclamation of Emancipation
by the freedmen of Norfolk, who had as their guest
the Radical politician, the Rev. James Hunnicutt.
In an incendiary address he denounced Governor
Pierpont and the Legislature of the State. He insisted that the freedmen's only hope of remaining
out of slavery was the Radical majority in Congress.
The celebration was noisy and violent, but the police
did not interrupt.[2]

The Rev. James W. Hunnicutt aspired to the
role in Virginia that Parson Brownlow played so
sensationally in Tennessee. But he was not of
Brownlow's ability. As we will meet the cleric
often again, a word of introduction is necessary. He

---

[1]THOS. CARLYLE, *History of the French Revolution.*

[2]*Norfolk Journal*, January 2, 1867, reports the celebration in full. It
makes interesting reading after seventy years.

lived for years in Fredericksburg and published a religious paper there. He had owned slaves and voted for the Ordinance of Secession. This he explained he did unwillingly. After the war he was as ardent a Unionist as John Minor Botts. But Botts and Hunnicutt did not agree. Botts was too conservative. Hunnicutt was at this time the most Radical leader in the State unless Judge Underwood deserved that unwholesome honor.

The New York Tribune, the leading Republican paper in America, said (April 12, 1867): "To organize a campaign on the Hunnicutt plan is to abandon any hope of a permanent Union party in the South. We can not afford to array the white against the black or the black against the white." The New York Times said, "Hunnicutt and such as he are unceasing in their endeavors to organize the blacks as a party that shall hereafter control Southern affairs and with this view they teach the superiority of the Negroes as a race over the white."[3]

II

When Congress returned after the Christmas holidays (January 3, 1867), Thaddeus Stevens had a paper in his pocket, and a double purpose in his heart. The feeble and aged man dedicated his remnant of life to two major activities. He knew that his time and strength were short. He pro-

---

[3] He declared that he was working for the damnedest revolution the world ever saw.—c. g. bowers, *Tragic Era*, p. 200.

horace greeley spoke of "agitators like Mr. Hunnicutt of Virginia, whose zeal is bitter and abusive."

posed to erect five provinces on the ruin of ten great States in "the accursed section," as Sumner called the South. The South was to be held in subjection by the armies of the United States until the freedmen were given votes and the "rebels" were disfranchised in the land of their fathers. His other set purpose was to impeach the President of the United States and drive him from the White House.[4] Is not Andrew Johnson now the worst of rebels and traitors? Is he not a native of the "accursed section," born in North Carolina, a citizen of Tennessee?

In his first purpose Thaddeus Stevens succeeded temporarily and partially; in his second he failed by one vote . . . and died (August 11, 1868). His two plans were really one. For if twenty Southern Senators came to Washington Andrew Johnson would never be impeached!

III

On the day the Congress convened,[5] January 3, Stevens unfolded his first paper, a bill to provide a drastic military government for the ten "so-called Confederate States," abolishing their "pretended governments." The Fourteenth Amendment, which everyone of them voted down (Virginia six days later) is too easy a basis for the readmission of the

---

[4]HAMILTON JAMES ECKENRODE, *Hayes*, p. 79: "The madman, Thaddeus Stevens, was chairman of this inferno."

CHARLES RANSDELL LINGLEY, *Since the Civil War*, p. 18. There were many who believed with James M. Ashley of Ohio and Benjamin F. Butler that Johnson was somehow implicated in the assassination of Lincoln.

[5]LLOYD PAUL STRYKER, *Andrew Johnson*, p. 417 and following.

rebel Commonwealths. He demanded measures more drastic, more thorough and more comprehensive.[6]

"The old man's energy[7] was astonishing. Vindictivenss seemed to animate him." He trembled with excessive hatred and pushed on despite the seventy-five years which lay behind him . . . a life not of angelic purity.

The bill was referred to the Reconstruction Committee of Fifteen, of which, of course, Stevens was the most influential member. It came back to the House in February. A General with sufficient troops was to be placed in charge of each of the five military districts. District No. 1 was what remained of the once powerful Commonwealth of Virginia; No. 2 was the two Carolinas; No. 3 was Georgia, Florida and Alabama; No. 4, Mississippi and Arkansas; No. 5, Louisiana and Texas.

Let us hear the aged apostle of Radicalism: "For two years the Southern States have been in a state of anarchy. For two years the loyal people of those ten States have endured all the horrors of the worst anarchy of any country. Persecution, exile and murder have been the order of the day within all these territories, so far as loyal men are concerned, whether white or black; and, more especially, if they happen to be black. We have seen the best men, those who stood by the flag of the Union, driven from their

---

[6]SIDNEY ANDREWS, *The South Since the War*, p. 339: "Hell has laid her egg, and right here it hatched."

[7]At Lancaster, Pennsylvania, in a speech delivered September 7, 1865, Stevens declared for the confiscation of Southern property and the use of the private wealth thus secured to pay "not only Northern pensions, but three-fourths of the whole Federal debt as well."

homes and compelled to live on the cold charity of a cold North. We have seen their loyal men flitting about everywhere, through your cities, around your doors, melancholy, depressed, haggard, like the ghosts of the river Styx, and yet we have borne it with exemplary patience. While we were praising the rebel South and asking in piteous terms for mercy for that people, we have been deaf to the groans, the agony which have been borne to us by every Southern breeze from dying and murdered victims."[8]

He closed this libel of eight million people by exclaiming, "Tomorrow, God willing, I will demand the vote."

As this Military Reconstruction Bill made bayonet rule indefinite, James G. Blaine and John A. Bingham attempted to secure amendments which would place an end to the military despotism, but they were voted down. The House passed Stevens' bill February 13 (109 pro, 55 contra).

When smiling Schuyler Colfax announced the result, Stevens cried in exultation:

"I wish to ask, Mr. Speaker, if it is in order for me now to say that we endorse this language of good, old Laertes: 'Heaven rules as yet and there are Gods above'?"

Speaker Colfax smiled upon his pugnacious and triumphant fellow Radical and replied:

"It is in order, Mr. Stevens."

A profound and accurate historian, who is not at all partial to anything of or from the South, has

[8]*Congressional Globe*, February 7, 1867.

this to say: [9]"Stevens carried his bill through an unwilling House. A minority of his party opposed it. Military rule is distasteful to Americans. He carried it by sarcasm, taunts, dragooning and cracking the party whip. There had been no such scene in Congress since "Douglas carried his Kansas-Nebraska Bill through the Senate." Mr. Rhodes is wrong only in his last sentence. There had never before and there has never been since such another shameful scene in the nation's legislative halls. And let all true Americans hope that the like will never again be seen in this land; where, for a time, "government of the people, for the people and by the people" had perished from the earth!

The Senate passed[10] the iniquitous bill Sunday at 6 in the morning, February 17, by a vote of 27 to 4. The Senate, however, improved the bill and it was not so drastic. The amendments were offered by Senator John Sherman[11] of Ohio, the brother of General William Tecumseh Sherman, and Samuel Shellabarger, also of Ohio. That is why this monstrosity has gone into history as the Sherman-Shellabarger Bill (which it was not), instead of the Thaddeus Stevens Bill, which it was. This infamy should be known by the name of the man who begot it.

[9]JAMES FORD RHODES.

[10]HOWARD K. BEALE, *Critical Year*, p. 112.

[11]JOHN SHERMAN, *Recollections*, p. 316, gives this interesting schedule:

February 13. The Bill came from the Representatives.

February 16. Sherman's less radical substitute was adopted (pro 29, contra 10).

Senator Sherman gives the text of the Bill in full, pp. 316-317.

The bill came to the President on Washington's birthday (February 22). He laid it before the Cabinet, all of whom advised a veto, except Edwin M. Stanton, always consistently anti-Southern.

Perhaps at that busy time neither the President nor Congress remembered that Andrew Johnson, one year before to the day, "declared war" on the Radicals and specifically named Stevens, Sumner and Wendell Phillips in his speech at the White House. The Radicals of his party had heaped many punishments upon him since then; and more and greater humiliations were now in the offing.

IV

Of course the President vetoed this Military Monstrosity, designed to keep one-third of the nation under military rule; and to force Negro suffrage upon them . . . two years after "peace" had come with Lee's surrender.

"I would sever my right arm from my body before I would sign such a monstrous Bill," he declared to his Cabinet.

The veto, in 20,000 words, was returned March 2. The Thirty-ninth Congress was to expire two days later. Without hesitation and without debate Congress passed Stevens' "Sherman-Shellabarger Bill," over the Presidential veto. It became law the very day it was returned from the White House. When so announced the galleries burst into applause.

But public opinion was now swinging away from Radicalism. The Bloody Shirt Campaign was largely forgotten. There were newspapers which printed the passage of this Bill in broad, black lines of mourning. They declared that Liberty was dead; the Republic no longer existed. The United States had become a military despotism.[12]

It can not be stated too often nor too emphatically that the people of the North and West did not hate the South. They did not regard Virginia as "an accursed section." They did not wish to punish nor persecute the South. Americans, like all Anglo-Saxon peoples, detest military rule. The people will not tolerate it. Reconstruction, as this narrative has made manifest, was a political conspiracy astutely manipulated by the Radical leaders in the Congress.

Senator Willard Saulsbury[13] of Delaware spoke the sentiment of multitudes when he declared: "I would not touch the paper that Bill is written on! It is an unclean thing—the foulest document in American history." He was right. It was the foulest law ever passed by any legislative body in America. The shadow of glistening bayonets and of uniformed troopers now fell over every home, farm, village, factory, in ten great States . . . which no

---

[12]"Revolutionary?" Thaddeus Stevens had cried to an audience in Lancaster, Pennsylvania. "It is intended to revolutionize the principles and feelings of the people. . . . It is easier and more beneficial to exile 70,000 proud, bloated and defiant rebels than to expatriate four million laborers, native to the soil and loyal to the government."

[13]WILLIAM ARCHIBALD DUNNING, *Reconstruction*, p. 93. The preamble of the Bill declared that "no legal state governments, or adequate protection for life and property existed in the rebel States."

In that sentence, which was false, Congress deliberately reversed both Lincoln and Johnson. They praised Lincoln to the heavens, but they repudiated his plans and condemned his policies.

longer existed. No less an authority than John William Burgess declared the act the most brutal ever submitted to the Congress by any committee.

General Sherman wrote his brother, the Senator, January, 1867: "If the President be impeached and the South be reduced to territories the country will, of course, relapse to a state of war or quasi-war. And what good it will do passes my comprehension."[14]

The Senator answered the General: "Three years ago the Southerners hated you and Johnson most of all men. Now your advice goes further than any two men in the nation." He suggested that General Sherman advise the South to accept the situation and make the "best of it."

Yet General Sherman was mistaken. There was no rebellion in the South, despite this tyrannical and unnecessary political persecution. We insist that no people in history ever exhibited more superb self-control, or more real heroism, under the lash of calumny and tyranny.

Many influential voices were raised in behalf of the South. The New York World was especially emphatic. It declared, "If the South should resist marshal law they would be fighting in as righteous a cause as any in which a patriot ever drew his sword." The Albany (New York) Argus said, editorially "The President has vetoed the Bill by which Congress, setting aside the Constitution and all the traditions of American liberty and the theory of representative government, has proclaimed martial

[14] *Sherman's Letters*, p. 288.

law, and Negro suffrage, the proscription of whites from the ballot-box, and the exclusion of the South from the Union.

"The Bill had for its object to disfranchise the South, to obliterate the boundaries of states—to repudiate past legislation—to create political dependencies upon which all the experiments of arbitrary and oppressive government might be tried. Apart from every other consideration the bad faith implied in these transactions from the South is sufficient grounds for the veto.

"The armies of the South surrendered on terms that were at once recalled by the victors. They disarmed under assurance of forbearance and fair treatment. Their surrender was complete and unreserved, and they did not hesitate to abolish and forbid slavery, to astigmatize the Confederate debts, and to assume their share of the Federal obligations. But every concession, each of which was declared to be the last, was followed by fresh demands, and even the humiliating constitutional amendment is regarded as insufficient in its exactions, and this new device is invented. Even it is not final. But it is so ingeniously framed as to make the ultimate concession of representation to the States optional to the congressional majority.

"The President has vetoed this infamous enactment, and he has done right. The demagogues who control Congress menace him with impeachment for his recusancy and threaten to pile upon the South still further insults and wrongs. Let them do it. The madness of the hour is to be cured by its excess.

Let the Impeachment Bill come. Let the Confiscation Act which Stevens threatens be produced. Let the deposition by which Butler threatens to precede the trial of the President be attempted. The conspiracy which seeks to perpetuate the usurpation at Washington by cancelling the existence of ten States, by overruling others, by corrupting all; and which for the purpose clothes an instrument with the executive power, the purse and the sword will end by revolting the good sense of the people of all States.

"It is here, at the North, to the aroused and indignant masses of our free people that we look for the demonstration of sentiment and that exertion of power which will sweep these plotters from place, in the very midst of their schemes, and at the moment of expected fruition."

So large a place has the Reconstruction Act of 1867 filled in the history of Virginia and the South, and so profound, far-reaching and potent have been the reactions from it through three generations that the measure shall be described in some detail.

The Sherman-Shellabarger Bill seemed to endorse the theory of state suicide.

President Lincoln held that secession was illegal, hence Virginia had never left the Union. The war was waged with individuals who were personally in rebellion. That was, of course, fiction; but it was logical. The Sherman-Shellabarger Act gave the lie to all that Lincoln taught. Virginia no longer existed—it was a territory, in which there were no citizens. Yet when the Radicals wished to count

Virginia's vote for the Thirteenth Amendment, it was counted! And the debt of the old State, with interest mounting every day and compounded, did not die with the State, but Secretary McCullough demanded that it be paid to the last farthing—partisan passion and financial juggling have no conscience and recognize no logic!

In order for the territory, previously two-thirds of Virginia, to be re-admitted to the United States, to re-assume the control of its own local affairs, to be rid of a harsh and alien military government and to have representation in the national Congress:

The State must adopt a new constitution.

The constitution must be prepared by a constitutional convention.

The members of the convention must be elected by all the male citizens, over twenty-one years of age, without regard to race or color, except "rebels." No "rebel" had a vote.

The new constitution must provide for Negro suffrage. No "rebel" would be permitted to sit in the constitutional convention. And the constitution must disfranchise all "rebels."

The new constitution must be adopted by a majority vote in the State. It must also be adopted by Congress as satisfactory.

The legislature of the State (which did not exist) acting under a constitution (not yet adopted) must endorse the Fourteenth Amendment. And the senators and representatives sent to Washington from the "rebel" States must take the iron-clad oath which read as follows:

"I . . . , do solemnly swear that I have never voluntarily borne arms against the United States, since I have been a citizen thereof; that I have voluntarily given no aid, countenance, counsel, or encouragement to persons engaged in armed hostility thereto; that I have never sought nor accepted nor attempted to exercise the functions of any office whatever, under any authority or pretended authority, in hostility to the United States; that I have not yielded a voluntary support to any pretended government, authority, power or constitution within the United States, hostile or inimical thereto; and that I will support and defend the Constitution of the United States against all enemies, foreign and domestic, etc."

The Sherman-Shellabarger Bill would fill a volume of 20,000 words. It was "utterly destructive of all those great principles of liberty and humanity for which our ancestors shed so much blood." It was an enactment for which every American has a right to hang his head in confusion and shame.[15]

---

[15]CHARLES WARREN, *The Supreme Court in U. S. History*, Chap. XXX, is the most valuable, concise and accurate discussion of Reconstruction that we have seen.

CHAPTER XXII

THE FORTIETH CONGRESS

No sword bites so fiercely as an evil tongue.
                                    —*Sir Philip Sidney.*

The Fortieth Congress, elected by the Bloody
Shirt Campaign of November, 1866, assembled
March 4, 1867, a moment after the Thirty-ninth
Congress adjourned. The outgoing Congress had
been radical enough in all conscience, but the new
Congress was even worse. The President and the
South looked to them with dread and dismal fore-
bodings . . . unfortunately they were not deceived.

The opening was like a far echo of that brilliant
assembly staged fifteen months before, when the
Thirty-ninth Congress convened. Again the beautiful women were present, the flashing diamonds, the
magnificent silks, the huge hoopskirts and billowing
crinoline. Again the Senate desks were banked
with gorgeous, exotic flowers, and again the persistent hum of happy voices filled the spacious
chambers, the smiles, suppressed laughter and
friendly salutations; as if it were a splendid ball.
The congressmen made a brave show, well-tailored
and attired in tight trousers and tall silk hats of the
period, the kid gloves and boutonniers. Military
uniforms, stripes and epaulets were not so much in
evidence as in 1865.

A minute after the Congress of Many Iniquities adjourned, Hon. Schuyler Colfax, of Indiana, quite appropriately called "Smiler" Colfax, rapped for order and the Fortieth Congress was assembled.

Again a prayer was said, and God knows both country and Congress needed prayer if ever a nation or a legislature did.

Again the obsequious clerk, Hon. Edward Mc-Pherson called the roll.

Again all Southern States except Tennessee were omitted; but now the omission caused no surprise.

Again Hon. James Brooks, a Democrat of New York, demanded to know by what authority the clerk omitted ten great States. But his protest was now perfunctory. . . . It was ancient history.

Again the smiling "Smiler" Colfax was elected Speaker of the House. Let none discount the "Smiler's" pleasant smile. He smiled his way to the Vice-Presidency of the United States before he sank into well-deserved oblivion.

The personnel of the new Congress was substantially the same as the old, but there were some new faces. One we have met often before in this narrative and we must meet often again . . . we regret to say. The crossed eyes, strutting stride, emphatic uniform, proclaimed the Honorable Benjamin Franklin Butler, whose memory lingers unpleasantly in Virginia even after three generations. The General represented a Boston constituency. One who watched him narrowly wrote: "A terrible face, it looks like a pirate's . . . a strong, unscrupulous, cruel face; a low, wide head, crossed eyes, the hatchety Roman

nose, the thin lips which make a combination powerful and pitiless." This quotation is not from a Southern pen, but from the "Independent," a Radical
paper supposed to be a religious journal, dated March
14, 1867. It seems that the new Congressman was
not more admired in the North than in the South.[1]

In the Senate only four Johnson or Conservative
Republicans retained their seats. There were only
seven Democrats . . . Copperheads, as they were
usually called. The Senate is judge and jury combined when a President of the United States is impeached. And it's on the cards. Thaddeus Stevens
is not yet ready to move, but he is getting ready. It
takes two-thirds of the Senate to impeach a President. Thad adjusted his ill-fitting wig. It can be
done. It shall be done!

The previous president of the Senate, LaFayette
Sabine Foster, of Connecticut, must be retired.
The next president of the Senate will become President of the United States, if Andrew Johnson should
die or be impeached. That is not the succession
now; but it was then.

The candidate for the office which loomed so
large among future possibilities was Senator Benjamin Franklin Wade, of Ohio, who had been in the
Senate since 1851; and was known as a rabid
Radical. There have always been those who believed that Ben Wade arranged the rude reception

---

[1] Of Butler, his fellow ultra-Radical, Thaddeus Stevens, said: "A false
alarm, superficial, weak, impracticable—in short a humbug." This is the
only opinion of Thaddeus Stevens the South wishes to applaud.

CARL RUSSELL FISHER, *Dictionary of American Biography*: "He was hardly
more hated in Louisiana than by the conservative elements of both parties in
Massachusetts because of his radical proposals."

President Johnson received in his home town of Cleveland, when the President was virtually mobbed. Let us hope it is not true.

As Wade was the only candidate he was elected, and the news was received in the South with grave foreboding. From such a President may the good Lord deliver us; that was the prayer of the South . . . and it was answered!

There were those who said that James G. Blaine declared openly on the floor of the House, "There will be no impeachment by this Congress. We would rather have the President than the shally-wags of Ben Wade." Blaine denied that he said it. Stevens declared that he heard him . . . let it pass. All were Radicals together.

II

The Fortieth Congress remained in session only three months primarily to pass a Supplemental Reconstruction Bill, although the Bill of March 2 had no less than 20,000 words. The long law failed to provide the method by which the Military Monstrosity was to be put into practical operation. The Supplemental Bill passed March 12 supplied the defect. By it the generals in charge of the "Military Districts"—once States of the Union—were to register the lawful voters before September 1, 1867. They were also to appoint days for the election of delegates to the Constitutional Conventions of the ten States. No "rebels" of course must be registered, nor allowed to vote. And certainly no "rebel" should be allowed to sit in the conventions.

This Supplemental Monstrosity was pushed through the House of Representatives in two hours! One could not believe it, if it were not abundantly authenticated. These two monstrous bills struck liberty dead in the land dedicated to liberty. One generation sacrifices all for a great principle—and the next cuts it up root and branch without protest and without debate!

Sumner once remarked that great empires are built upon the ruin of small states. He was correct, but we did not know that America was an "empire."

The Senate debated the bill for a week. It meant in plain English: "Accept Negro suffrage; or remain indefinitely under martial law." Finally it passed the Senate, Tuesday, March 19, 1867.

Of course President Johnson returned it with his veto (March 23). It was passed over the veto immediately, without comment and without debate.

Though Congress would not hear the President, future generations will listen to his calm and dignified appeal:

"When I contemplate the millions of our fellow citizens of the South, with no alternative left but to impose upon themselves this fearful and untried experiment of complete Negro enfranchisement, and white disfranchisement, it may be, almost as complete—or submit indefinitely to the rigor of martial law, without a single attribute of freemen, deprived of all the sacred guarantees of our Federal Constitution, and threatened with even worse wrongs, if any worse are possible, it seems to me that their condition is the most deplorable to which any people can be reduced."

The nation and the Southern people understood
perfectly that Negro suffrage and white, "rebel"
disfranchisement were now to become a part of their
punishment.[2] It was the price they must pay for
the folly of secession and the misfortune of defeat.

Senator John Sherman wrote: "The whole idea
of giving votes to the Negroes is to create just that
many votes to be used by others for political purposes."

Parson Brownlow, of Tennessee, did not hesitate
to declare from the hustings, "We want loyal Negroes
to vote down disloyal traitors."

Senator J. M. Howard wrote Charles Sumner
(November 12, 1865), "Colored suffrage will give all
possible security whatever the Northern people
may do to their own blacks."

III

Virginia was, of all the Southern States, the most
fortunate in her general.[3] John McAllister Schofield, commander of "District No. 1," was a loyal
Republican, but not a Radical. He was also a

---

[2] *New York Times* (March 12, 1867): "The Southern people must now
choose between the Sherman plan of Reconstruction and the Stevens plan of
confiscation."

[3] JOHN WILLIAM BURGESS, *Reconstruction*, p. 248. The military commanders
were reasonable. The common soldiers from the North made many friends.
They did not like the black soldiers and usually protected the whites against
"brutal blacks in blue." It is even said by those who have every opportunity
to know, that many Union soldiers doffed their uniforms on election day,
went to the polls and voted the Democratic ticket.

In Norfolk there are many good citizens, the sons of Union soldiers and
sailors, who married in the city and remained as permanent and valuable
citizens.

gentleman. His sympathy was with those he ruled. When he took charge as "Commander of Military District No. 1"[4] (March 13), he issued a tactful address.

"The undersigned appeals to the people of Virginia and especially to magistrates and officers to render the necessity for the exercise of this power as slight as possible by strict obedience to the law and by impartial administration of justice to all classes."

As much must be said henceforth of General Schofield, who was really our Governor, a sketch is presented.

John McAllister Schofield, born in Chautauqua County, Western New York, September 29, 1831, was at this time still a young man of 35. He graduated from West Point (1853) some fourteen years before. His military service, which was not brilliant, was mostly in Missouri. He accompanied Sherman on his famous march through Georgia.

General Schofield defeated General Hood at Franklin, Tennessee (November 30, 1864), and his reward was a promotion, major-general. He joined General Sherman in North Carolina and was with him when Johnston surrendered (April 26, 1865).

President Johnson sent him to France to negotiate the Maximilian diplomatic troubles, and (August, 1866) when he returned, he was assigned to command the Department of the Potomac. He re-

---

[4] *Land of Decision*, SQUIRES, pp. 170-175.

WILLIAM ARCHIBALD DUNNING, *Essays*, p. 144, names the satraps of Virginia (District No. 1), Schofield, Stoneman, Webb and Canby.

mained in Richmond[5] until May, 1868, when he was called to Washington to succeed Edwin M. Stanton as Secretary of War, after the collapse of the Impeachment Conspiracy (June 1, 1868).

General Schofield's authority under the Sherman-Shellabarger Act was greater than that of a Russian Czar.[6]

"His will was to take the place of all law."

"He was bound by no State laws."

"He might make a criminal code of his own."

"Everything was a crime which he chose to call a crime."

"All persons were condemned whom he pronounced guilty."

These quotations are from President Johnson's veto message.

He was also authorized to deputize his power to subordinates, and make them despots like himself—if he chose to do so.

No English-speaking people since the Norman Conquest have groaned under such despotic laws.

To assist General Schofield in inflicting the Sherman-Shellabarger military tyranny upon Virginia there were 2,087 soldiers in twelve camps

---

[5]GENERAL SCHOFIELD said: "The terrible oppression of the Southern people embodied in these acts of Congress has hardly been appreciated by even the most enlightened and conservative people of the North.

"Only those who actually suffered . . . can ever realize their full enormity."

WILLIAM ARCHIBALD DUNNING, *Essays*, p. 151, describes General Schofield's tact and moderation.

[6]JAMES G. GARFIELD said of the Sherman-Shellabarger Bill that it was "written with a steel pen made out of a bayonet."

scattered here and there through the State. The largest camp, 1,031 troopers, was at Richmond.[7]

[7] *Richmond Times* (March 12, 1867): "Never before have our citizens been subjected to such insults as they received yesterday from the Negro soldiers, who arrived here Saturday. In different sections of the city they fought among themselves, or with the white soldiers, and with Negroes. Insults were offered also to women and children. But the crowning insult was offered to our General Assembly. About 2:30 P. M. some twenty Negro soldiers in closed ranks and with bayonets, commanded by a burly Negro, marched around the Capitol in which the legislature was in session and cheered for the Union and the Shellabarger Bill."

MARY NEWTON STANARD, *Richmond*, Chap. XXXV, for contemporary items of unquestioned accuracy.

CHAPTER XXIII

THE WILD MONTH OF MARCH

Every wanton and causeless restraint of the will
of the subject, whether produced by a monarch, a
nobility, or a popular assembly is a degree of tyranny.
—*Sir William Blackstone.*

The wild month of March, 1867, is memorable
in our annals for many events of lasting significance, international and economic, political and
domestic. The most radical of congresses was busy
writing laws to place an iron hand upon the prostrate South.

Taking advantage of our Civil War, Napoleon III
landed a small army in Mexico (1864). Grant and
Lee were at that time in a terrific life and death
struggle. The Mexican Republic was overthrown.
The President, Benito Pablo Juarez, a full-blooded
Indian, a patriotic statesman and soldier of ability,
was driven into exile.

The Mexicans "voted" to establish an empire
with Archduke Maximilian, the brother of the Emperor of Austria, on the shaky throne. Of course,
the "election" was merely a smoke-screen for invasion and quasi-conquest.

When Lee surrendered Maximilian and Carlotta
were fairly well-established in authority, by French
bayonets and gold. When America was again

united (technically, if not really), Seward suggested to Napoleon in tones so mild as to be almost apologetic that the United States really could not permit a French Empire across the narrow Rio Grande.

Many statesmen, General Grant among them, were in favor of more emphatic measures. Grant ordered Philip H. Sheridan to move 52,000 troops across Texas to the border (August, 1865). Secretary Seward gradually used stronger words to the French Court; until, in March, 1866, our ambassador told Napoleon, frankly but politely, that the American people demanded French evacuation.

The beautiful and popular Empress Carlotta hastened to Paris (August 6, 1866) and besought Napoleon to support Maximilian for the five years he had originally promised. Napoleon refused. In grief and despair Carlotta appealed to the Pope. "At her third audience with the Pope her excitement was uncontrollable and her reason fled."[1]

The last French troops sailed with Marshal Bazaine, March 12, 1867, leaving Maximilian to his fate; notwithstanding that the Marshal insisted that the Emperor return with him. Juarez soon captured Maximilian. He was tried, condemned and shot (June 19, 1867), despite Seward's effort to save him.

---

[1]GAULET, *Fin d' Empire*, quoted by James Ford Rhodes.

In 1867 the Pontiff was Pius IX, Giovanni Maria Mastai-Feretti, of Senigallia, who reigned from 1846 to 1878.

Francois Achitte Bazaine, born at Versailles, February 13, 1811, made Marshal, 1864, entered Mexico in 1865 and married a wealthy Mexican lady. He withdrew from Mexico in March, '67. In the Franco-Prussian War he was shut up in Metz and surrendered an army 173,000 strong (October 27, 1870). Arrested and tried for treason he was condemned to death, but the sentence was commuted to twenty years in prison. He died in 1888.

II

In this same wild month of March Russian America was transferred to the United States for $7,200,000 paid the Czar. The treaty was signed at four o'clock in the morning, March 30—the very day the Fortieth Congress blessed the country by adjourning. Many called Alaska "Seward's Folly." The Radical Republicans, who did not like the Secretary's conservatism, were especially indignant that such a "huge sum in gold" should have been "squandered" on a "vast area of rocks and ice." But posterity knows Alaska as "Seward's Wisdom." Who can compute the immense value of Alaska to this country, directly and indirectly, since the Czar retired from North America?

III

From the ultimate climes of Alaska and the lofty mountains of Mexico, we must return to the heat and dust of Virginia's fetid and putrid politics under the gentle rule of the United States Army. The Radicals of Virginia were well organized and were ready to leap to their task . . . a task congenial, and one which promised large plunder and rich political rewards.

A week after General Schofield was appointed commander of "District No. 1," a call went forth for a Radical convention to be held in Richmond at the African Church, April 17, 1867. Six names were signed to the summons: Lysander Hall, John

Hawxhurst, Burnham Wardwell, Louis McKenzie, James H. Clements and W. R. Smith.

Unwittingly this convention assembled on the sixth anniversary of the Ordinance of Secession! Forty-nine counties sent up 210 delegates, of whom 50 had white faces and 160 black!

The meeting was not a love feast. The rivalry of two factions threw the proverbial monkey-wrench into the machinery, and the white and colored patriots were soon at each other's throats. The Rev. James W. Hunnicutt, whom we will often meet in these black years, was out to defeat John Minor Botts.

Hunnicutt needed no introduction to the citizens of Richmond.

"This city was having trouble[2] with the worst class of Negroes. There had been a riot at Chimborazo where the Negroes had a camp in an old Confederate hospital. Wardwell and Hunnicutt, two white men, were making incendiary speeches to them, inciting them to violence. They organized a company 500 strong, and drilled every night with muskets and sabres at Navy Hill. General Terry ordered them to disband." This occurred a year before the Constitutional Convention.

The Convention was soon organized; G. W. Hawxhurst was elected president and Lewis McKenzie and J. W. Hunnicutt, vice-presidents.

Hunnicutt evidently held the whip-hand. The Negro orators, and they were many, were violent,

---

[2]WILLIAM ASBURY CHRISTIAN, *History of Richmond*, p. 279.

arrogant and abusive. Their most popular theme was the immediate confiscation of "rebel" property.[3]

The meeting adopted six resolutions:

1. They thanked Congress for Reconstruction.

2. All classes, races and colors were invited to cooperate with the Radicals.

3. The Convention demanded full and equal rights for both races, indiscriminately, to courts of law, public and private schools. They wished lower taxes and lower interest rates.

4. All men were declared free and equal. (This clipping from the Declaration of Independence had here an application Thomas Jefferson never dreamed of, we dare say.)

5. All patriots were admonished to stand by their party.

6. They appealed to the "laboring classes" to vote the Radical ticket.

John W. Hunnicutt was master of the situation, and the situation was literally and metaphorically black. In a violent speech he declared that "the rebels have forfeited all their rights and we will see that they never get them back." Immense applause. Many other menacing doctrines, equally revolutionary, were urged.

On the second day the Convention moved from the African Church on East Broad Street to Capitol Square, for many years the rendezvous of Rich-

---

[3] *New York Times* (March, 1867): "Confiscation admits of only one interpretation. It is the equivalent of general spoilization, anarchy and bloodshed. The men who go about familiarizing the Negroes with the demand should be dealt with by the military commanders as incendiaries."

mond's wealth and culture. The calm eyes of
George Washington looked down that spring day
upon a very riot. Black men and white, speaking,
shouting, cat-calling and jeering. They cheered for
Thaddeus Stevens and for the Sherman-Shellabarger
Bill, which had indeed put the bottom rail on top
(long a favored expression). They called for the
confiscation of the white rebels' property, and
shouted damnation for the "Rebel-in-the-White-
House" and all rebels outside.

Now that no election was in the offing the Northern
press had cooled off. Diatribes against the South
were much softened. Even the New York Tribune
came forth with this paragraph from Horace Greeley:

"To organize a campaign on the Hunnicutt plan
is to abandon any hope of a permanent Union party
in the South. We cannot afford to array the white
against the black or the black against the white."

Yet Mr. Greeley did not seem to realize, for all
his immense intellect, that every step the Congress
had taken for eighteen months encouraged that
plan and program.

The New York Times said, "He and such as he,"
referring to Hunnicutt, "are unceasing in their endeavors to organize the blacks as a party that shall
hereafter control Southern affairs, and with this in
view they teach the superiority of the Negroes as a
race over the white." Was not that the logic of
Congressional Reconstruction? Was it that the
North could not see it—or did not want to see?

IV

The Conservative Republicans were not blind to the situation.[4] They sent a "missionary" to Virginia to help the Botts faction draw the rein on Hunnicutt and make the Republican party respectable, if not popular, in Virginia. The "missionary" was no less a person than distinguished Senator Henry Wilson, of Massachusetts, destined to become (1872) Vice-President of the United States. He made a very tactful speech in Richmond, appealing to the Old Line Whigs to build a Union party in the South.[5]

Senator Wilson stood upon the front portico of the Capitol, where the long southward stoop has since been built, and where the governors of Virginia now take the oath of office, each quadrennium, and deliver their inaugural addresses. The distinguished Senator looked down upon a sea of faces in the Square, fully 6,000 of them—but most of them were black! That was not the audience he came to address. It was noticed that he had no compliments for the President. He also insisted that the Sherman-Shellabarger Military Tyranny Bill was "good and needed by the entire country."

[4] *New York Herald* (April 20, 1867): "When designing white politicians undertake to fill the heads of Southern blacks with the notion of free farms from the confiscation of the estates of 'landed monopolists', they are sowing the dragon's teeth which will fill the land with armed men and scenes of slaughter."

Boston Post (April 30, 1867): "The condition of the South requires forbearance and encouragement. The zealots who excite strife that they may reap personal and party advantage are moral and political traitors and should receive punishment due hypocrites and promoters of dissension."

[5] This visit was made to Richmond April 22, 1867.

Secession, war, defeat, disaster, and destruction had been Virginia's bitter portion. And whence came these dire calamities? From Democratic rule.

He called upon the "best men of both races" to cooperate for the restoration of peace, harmony and good-will. He invoked the memory and the spirit of that great Virginian, Henry Clay, whose calm marble eyes gazed steadfastly upon him across the fresh green lawn of the Square.

Governor Pierpont introduced the Senator and followed his address with a few practical but wholesome words. He advised his colored auditors to "go to work," for all prosperity is based upon labor, thrift and honesty.

Well would it have been for Virginia if men like Wilson, Botts and the Old Line Whigs could have saved the nascent Republican party from Hunnicutt, Hawxhurst, Underwood and their fellow Radicals. But the event proved their effort vain.

Two years later, namely, July 24, 1869, Senator Wilson gave this very enlightening interview to the New York "Independent":

"The Legislature[6] was in session when the Reconstruction acts were passed. Governor Pierpont was exceedingly anxious to build up a Republican party which would grant equal rights to both races, schools for colored children, as well as white, and an enlarged plan for internal improvements.

---

[6]The Legislature at Richmond struggled with many and difficult local problems, especially the rehabilitation of business and finance.

Governor Pierpont said in his message (March 4): "I think the only proper mode of recovering safety and tranquility to the State is for the Legislature, on the basis of the acts of Congress, in good faith, to carry out the require-

"The Governor, with perhaps thirty members of the Legislature, invited the writer to visit Virginia and address the people on the policy of Reconstruction. . . .

"We met in the Governor's house and discussed the proposed organization of the Republican party. It was stated that about forty members of the Legislature were ready to join in the movement.

"About the middle of April delegates from fifteen to twenty counties held a meeting and organized a Republican party. The proposition that a State-wide convention be held to complete the organization was unwisely rejected. . . .

"Another effort was made for harmonious and united action, sponsored by the Union League of Philadelphia, which was joined by the Union League of New York and the Reconstruction Club of Boston. Charles Gibbons, of Pennsylvania; Boker,[7] of Philadelphia, the poet; John Jay[8] and Colonel Van Buren,[9] of New York; Francis W. Bird, Charles W. Slack and other prominent men made a pilgrimage to Richmond for that purpose.

"A meeting was held at the home of the Governor and all parties were heard, conservative and Radical, white and colored. These speeches consumed five

---

ments of the law and adapt ourselves to the new state of affairs at once . . . the fortunes and happiness of a million people may depend on your prompt action. . . . May a Merciful God grant peace to our distracted State and give confidence to a desponding people."

Annual Cyclop, 1867.

The Legislature wished to attract immigration to our vacant lands and appointed General Daniel Ruggles of Fredericksburg to encourage same. They adjourned April 29.

[7] Charles Henry Boker, author, who had recently published "Poems of the War." Later United States Minister to Turkey and Russia.

[8] John Jay, one of those who organized the Republican Party in New York State, later United States Minister to Austria-Hungary.

[9] Abraham Van Buren, the son of President Martin Van Buren, who won distinction as an officer in the Mexican War.

hours. Next day the committee urged harmony and insisted upon the cooperation and unity of action for both races. We were especially anxious to secure the support of prominent leaders in Virginia.

"At last all agreed to a State convention, and several gentlemen of large political influence came to Richmond to aid in the organization. These were repelled. The leaders seemed determined to keep the reconstruction party conveniently small. They succeeded in keeping thousands of good men out of the Republican party. They were among the first in their efforts to divide the new party.

"There can not be the shadow of a doubt in the minds of those acquainted with the affairs of Virginia in the spring and early summer of 1867 that a wise, earnest and unselfish effort made at that time to organize a reconstruction party would have succeeded. A constitution could have been adopted, a delegation to Congress seated and Virginia would likely last year have given a large majority to General Grant. I believed then and believe now that a liberal, just and unselfish policy would have made Virginia a strong, loyal Republican State."

In these words the eminent Senator explains the failure of Botts, the success of Hunnicutt and Underwood and the hopelessness of the Republican party in Virginia from that day to this. As Senator Wilson plainly shows, it was not the wisdom of the Democrats but the unspeakable folly of the Radicals that lost Virginia to the Republican party.

Chapter XXIV

THE TRIAL OF JEFFERSON DAVIS

Days of my youth, ye have glided away;
Hairs of my youth, ye are frosted and gray;
Strength of my youth, all your vigor is gone;
Thoughts of my youth, your gay visions are flown.

Days of my youth, I wish not your recall;
Hairs of my youth, I'm content ye should fall;
Thoughts of my youth, you have led me astray;
Strength of my youth, why lament your decay?

—*St. George Tucker.*

During this dreadful spring, two years after the surrender, every cloud upon the political horizon of Virginia cast a shadow yet blacker and more threatening. A more inopportune time and place to bring the ex-President of the Confederacy from his prison in Fortress Monroe could not have been chosen. And a judge more cordially hated by the Virginians could not have been found.

While Davis lay in casemate No. 2, a villain by the name of Conover admitted that he lied (for a consideration) when he claimed to have proof that Davis and other "rebels" were privy to the assassination of President Lincoln. This testimony produced an immense sensation throughout the North. Here were leading politicians, generals and members of the Cabinet, paying a perjurer to swear away the life of Jefferson Davis! More and more conservative opinion condemned such methods. The Copperhead press spread the news in the largest type the paper would carry! Radical propaganda and the bloody shirt experts were ready, they declared, to use all the powers of hell to hang innocent victims! The New York World constantly referred to Davis as the "Martyr of Fort Monroe."

James T. Brady,[1] a brilliant attorney, appeared before Judge Underwood in Richmond (January 5, 1867), and insisted that President Davis be heard and tried. The Judge and the government at Washington were determined that Davis should not be tried, and should not be bailed.

To quote Dr. H. J. Eckenrode, "The government did not try him; it did not want to try him. A trial must have aired constitutional principles and in court the Union might not have come off so well as on the battlefield. Davis' lawyers were ready and might have come uncomfortably near proving that secession was legal . . . whatever it might have been otherwise."

After the Bloody Shirt campaign of 1866, the nation cooled off and many insistent and influential voices throughout the North and West condemned the Government's continued persecution of Davis. Even the Radicals, who hated him, realized that persecution was making Davis a martyr not only in the eyes of the South, but in the opinion of the civilized world.[2]

---

[1] James Tropham Brady (1815-1869), of New York, of whom it was said: "His arguments were put with such tact, his statements were so lucid and candid, and his appeals so eloquent and impressive that he almost invariably carried judge and jury with him." He was sent to the Gulf States to investigage the administration of Generals Butler and Banks there, but Brady's report was not made public!

[2] *Land of Decision*, SQUIRES, Chapter VI.

Americans believe in fair play. Why was a trial
denied Jefferson Davis? Dr. John Joseph Craven,
the physician of Fortress Monroe, a Union officer
and a loyal New Jersey Republican, wrote a book
and many letters referring to Davis as "an illustrious
statesman, a pure and noble-hearted Christian
gentleman," who suffered unceasingly, who could
not sleep more than two hours at a time, who was ill
of dyspepsia and neuralgia, and constantly afflicted
by boils and carbuncles. His friends were not
allowed to see or even write him. Letters from
Mrs. Davis were intercepted and read before they
were delivered.

So unfavorable was the reaction that followed
Davis' early imprisonment that President Johnson
removed General Nelson A. Miles (September 1,
1866). Davis called Miles "a miserable ass," and
we fear his estimate of Miles was accurate.

A wealthy merchant in Baltimore volunteered to
raise two million dollars bail for Davis "in five
hours," if the Government would release him on
bail. The Government did nothing.

Two full years of "peace" had now passed. Evidently something must be done. The situation was
growing acute.

Judge Underwood opened the Federal Court in
Richmond May 6, 1867. He is remembered in
Virginia as the most vindictive Radical, the most
unscrupulous carpet-bagger, by whom Virginia was
ever afflicted.[3] Negroes served on his jury, for the

---

[3] *Richmond Whig*, August 1, 1865, carried this news item: "Mr. McVeigh,
of Alexandria, whose property has been confiscated by a decree of Judge Underwood and a portion of which it is said is occupied by the Judge, denies that

first time, six of them. To this mixed jury he delivered this classic (May 7):

Address to Jury

"Gentlemen of the Grand Jury:

"The circumstances surrounding us demand devout thanksgiving to Almighty God that we, the friends and representatives of the United States, who last year were threatened with destruction and hunted by assassins in this city for attempting to execute the laws of our country, can now meet in conscious security under the wings of the starry banner which our patriotic Congress has raised for our protection; and we are permitted to meet in this building of everlasting granite, so emblematic of the power and strength of our Government, standing alone and unharmed amid the general conflagration that swept, as with a besom of destruction, all around it.

"And what solemn associations are suggested by reflecting that in the very rooms we now occupy dwelt the fiery soul of treason, rebellion and civil war, and hence issued that fell spirit which starved,[4] by wholesale, prisoners for the crime of defending the flag of our common country, assassinated colored soldiers for their noble and trusting labors in the behalf of a Government that had as yet only promised them protection, burned towns and cities with a barbarity unknown to Christian countries, scattered yellow fever and smallpox among the poor and help-

his conduct has any taint of treason and feels confident of his ability to prove that the proceedings against him are unjustified."

[4]JOHN WARWICK DANIEL, *Speeches*, p. 299: "With 60,000 more Federal prisoners in the South than there were Confederate prisoners in the North, 4,000 more Confederates than Federals died in prison. A cyclone of rhetoric cannot shake this mountain of fact."

less and finally struck down one of the earth's noblest martyrs to freedom and humanity.[5]

"Another subject of thanksgiving is presented in the very constitution of your body, furnishing ocular evidence that the age of caste and class cruelty is departed, and a new era of justice and equality, breaking through the clouds of persecution and prejudice is now dawning over us.

"And strongest of all, that this city of Richmond should be the spot of earth to furnish this gracious manifestation. Richmond, the beautiful and abandoned seat of the rebellion looking as comely and spacious as a goodly apple on a gilded sepulchre where bloody treason flourished its whips of scorpions; Richmond where the slave trade so long held high carnival; where the press[6] has found the lowest depth of profligacy; where licentiousness has ruled until probably a majority of the births are illegitimate, or without the forms of law; where the fashionable and popular pulpit has been so prostituted that its full-fed ministering gay Lotharios generally recommend the worship of what they most respected —pleasure, property and power. But we are reminded that 'where sin aboundeth grace may much more abound.' And in the light of recent changes, may we not hope a material and moral future for this city of Richmond in strong contrast with its awful and aesthetic past, and in harmony with the salubrity of its climate, the poetic beauty of its scenery and the magnitude of its water power. I am truly gratified to find so many gentlemen of public and private worth upon the present jury."

---

[5] S. A. ASHE, *Tyler's Magazine*, April, '29, pp. 270-273, on efforts to hire false witnesses to prove the connection of Lee and Davis with the assassination of President Lincoln.

[6] WHITELAW REID, a young Radical who saw nothing good in the South, visited Richmond (November, 1865), and wrote: "The newspapers of Richmond throughout the war were in many respects the ablest on the continent," and he admitted that the editorial ability abided still.

The same day Underwood delivered this diatribe in Richmond, Edwin M. Stanton, Secretary of War, submitted a letter from L. H. Chandler, of Norfolk, to the Attorney General of the United States, asking "an order upon the commandant at Fortress Monroe, directing him to surrender Jefferson Davis to the United States Marshal," if the Federal Court so desired.

President Johnson gave the order at once and Judge Underwood summoned Jefferson Davis to appear (May 10). This Friday, May 10, was further signalled by a race riot in Richmond, during which several policemen were severely injured. General Schofield hurried to the disturbed district in person and ordered the excited Negroes to disperse. They refused, and he called out a regiment to quell the rioters.

Saturday, May 11, Z. Haywood,[7] a Radical "missionary," was arrested, charged with inciting the Negroes to "acts of violence and insurrection." The same day a policeman attempted to arrest a drunken and riotous Negro and was mobbed, beaten and fired upon. Again General Schofield sent troops to assist the police in keeping order, and found it necessary to place guards and sentinels throughout the city.[8]

---

[7]ZEDEKIAH HAYWOOD, of New Hampshire, like Thaddeus Stevens an alumnus of Dartmouth, claimed to be a philanthropist. His philanthropic activity consisted largely in urging the freedmen to claim their "full rights," in all places at all times. He especially demanded that the colored people should be allowed to sit with the whites in street cars, trains, restaurants, theatres, churches and all places of public assembly. One of his exhortations was, "It is useless for me to advise you what to do; for great masses usually do what they have a mind to."

[8]*Through Centuries Three*, SQUIRES, pp. 497-501.

This condition was by no means confined to
Richmond. Congressional Reconstruction brought
such blessings as riot, arson, murder and bloodshed.

II

Saturday morning, May 12, President Davis,
dressed in a mixed black suit, accompanied by
Mrs. Davis, General Burton,[9] of the United States
Army, Dr. Craven, the physician, and Burton
Harrison, his secretary,[10] left the Fortress, bidding
many of the soldiers there, his personal friends, a
cordial farewell. Aboard the "John Sylvester" the
party traveled up the James, reaching Richmond
about six o'clock. They repaired to the Spotswood
Hotel, the proprietor of which assigned Mr. and
Mrs. Davis the same rooms they occupied when he
came to Richmond as "President of the Confederate
States" in 1861.

Mr. Davis had never been popular in Richmond,
or in Virginia. He was about the most unpopular
man in the South during the War Between the
States . . . and we fear his lack of popularity was
deserved. All was now changed. Disaster and
suffering brought him tributes which had not been
his in happier days. Friends, flowers, gifts and
messages of affection overwhelmed the "prisoner."

At eleven o'clock, Monday, May 13, he was
escorted to the courtroom, previously the Depart-

[9]Henry S. Burton (1818-1869), a veteran of the Mexican and Civil Wars,
now stationed at Fort Monroe.

[10]The father of Fairfax Harrison, President of the Southern Railway and
of Francis Burton Harrison, Governor-General of the Philippines (1913-'21).

MRS. BURTON HARRISON, *Recollections Grave and Gay*, pp. 265-270, gives two
long letters written by her husband describing the trial of Jefferson Davis.

ment of War, C. S. A., on the site of the present
postoffice building in Richmond.

An eye-witness wrote:

"As he entered the densely-crowded courtroom
with his proud and lofty look, every head reverently
bowed to him and a stranger would have sworn that
he was the judge and Underwood the culprit."
President Davis entered leaning on the arm of
General Burton, who succeeded Miles as commanding
officer at Fortress Monroe. With them was Charles
O'Conor, of New York, perhaps the most brilliant
lawyer in the country, who volunteered to defend
President Davis. He was a fine representative of
millions of people in the North who were not vindictive Radicals. William B. Read, a distinguished
attorney from Philadelphia; George Shea, Randolph
Tucker, Robert Ould and James Lyon . . . such an
array of legal luminaries as few judges have ever
faced, were present.

The Government of the United States was represented by William M. Evarts[11] and L. H. Chandler,
of Norfolk.

The arrival of Horace Greeley, editor of the New
York Tribune, formerly a leading Radical, now
present as a voluntary bondsman, caused a real,
though subdued, sensation.

Judge Underwood mounted the bench and in his
low, nasal, cracked voice, so well known and cordially
detested in Virginia, delivered a voluntary address
on the wickedness of rebellion and the sin of treason.

---

[11]A year later William M. Evarts was called to defend President Johnson
in his impeachment trial before the Senate.

Mr. Davis did not hear him, apparently, and the lawyers sat quietly through the monologue.

When the Judge finished, Charles O'Conor stated that his client was present and desired to be tried.

Mr. Evarts replied that the Government of the United States was not ready for the trial.

Mr. O'Conor[12] then moved that his client be admitted to bail in a sum to be fixed by the honorable court.

The "honorable court" named $100,000. Sixteen men came forward promptly and signed the huge bond, and the first signature was "Horace Greeley."

The others on this roll of generosity and honor were Augustus Schell, of New York; Aristides Welsh, of Philadelphia; David K. Jackson, also of Philadelphia; William H. McFarland, Richmond; Richard Barton Haxwell, Isaac Davenport, Abraham Warwick, Gustavus A. Meyers, William W. Crump, James Lyons, John A. Meredith, William H. Lyons, and James Thomas, Jr., all of Richmond; John Minor Botts and Thomas W. Boswell, of Virginia.[13]

"The Marshal," Judge Underwood ordered, "will discharge the prisoner," at which deafening applause broke from the crowd, shouts of joy, hats, canes, handkerchiefs, fans, were waved and thrown about. A crowd estimated at two thousand who stood

---

[12]DAVID B. PARKER, *A Chautauqua Boy*, who was the United States Marshall at Richmond, and was present, but whose recollections do not seem always to have been accurate, describes Charles O'Conor (whose name Parker spells O'Connor) as tall, straight, athletic. His white hair, "soft complexion, large, luminous black eyes made a very striking appearance."

That night Mr. Greeley and Garrett Smith spoke to a large and representative audience in the African Church.

[13]DAVID B. PARKER, *A Chautauqua Boy*, p. 121, speaks of "Garrett Smith" and "Vanderbilt" signing the bond. There were but sixteen names. Greeley

outside, unable to gain entrance, took up the cheering. The Boston Advertiser, speaking of the event said, "The cheer that went up when he was released told the story of the city's heart—it was jubilant and defiant. The ovation given Davis was for intensity and heartiness, such as Boston perhaps never gave anybody nor any cause."

President Davis has not, as yet, been tried, as General Lee has not yet been pardoned. Davis' case was postponed from time to time until December, 1868, when it came again before Judge Underwood sitting with Chief Justice Salmon P. Chase, in the Circuit Court of Virginia. They heard arguments for quashing the indictment. The Chief Justice favored granting the motion. It need hardly be said that the unspeakable Underwood opposed it. A few days later President Johnson's Proclamation of General Amnesty was so comprehensive that it covered the case of the ex-President. During the February term (1869) an order "nolle prosequi" was entered and the sixteen bondsmen were released.

In 1876 a bill passed the House of Representatives removing all political disabilities from Confederates. I am sorry to say that James G. Blaine secured an amendment to the bill expressly excluding Mr. Davis. Three years later (1879) he was again specifically excepted in a bill to pension all Mexican War veter-

remarked to Parker after he signed his name, "I expect to be abused for this, but it is for the country's good."

When Jefferson Davis offered his hand to Mr. Greeley, Greeley declined to acknowledge it, and passed out. If that statement is correct, it does Mr. Greeley no honor. Such rudeness could never be justified.

ans, this by the grace of Senator Zachariah Chandler, of Michigan.[14]

III

The night after his release, May 13, Mr. and Mrs. Davis returned to Norfolk aboard the "Niagara" and were met by A. F. Leonard,[15] long one of Norfolk's most influential citizens, distinguished as an editor, poet, statesman and philanthropist.

They were entertained by Mrs. Cornelia Taylor, who lived near A. F. Leonard in Freemason street. Major R. C. Taylor, a friend of President Davis, drove the guests about the city. Norfolk friends crowded the spacious parlors of the Leonard and Taylor residences until Mr. and Mrs. Davis again boarded the "Niagara" (at ten in the evening) for New York. They traveled to Canada, England and France, and finally made their home in Memphis, Tennessee, where Mr. Davis was president of a life insurance company.

At the time Senator Chandler had his name struck from the roll of Mexican pensioners, Mrs. Dorsey left him her modest but comfortable home at Beauvoir, Mississippi, where he resided until his death December 6, 1889.

Richmond requested Mrs. Davis to bring the remains of President Davis to Hollywood. He was

[14]w. mac donald, *Zachariah Chandler, Dict. Amer. Biog.*: "By methods openly partisan and despotic if not actually corrupt he obtained control." The Senator from Michigan was born December 10, 1813, and died November 1, 1879.

[15]william s. forrest, *History of Norfolk*, pp. 287 and 361-364. Abram F. Leonard was long an influential citizen of Norfolk. He advocated the construction of the Norfolk and Petersburg Railway, but he was especially influential as an editor and poet. Two excellent poetic selections are given in the history quoted above.

interred near Presidents Monroe and Tyler who sleep beside the swiftly flowing James.

"Noble are the words of Cicero when he tells us 'It is the first and fundamental law of history that it should neither dare to say anything false, nor fear to say anything true, nor give any just suspicion of favor or disaffection.'

"No less a standard must be invoked in considering the life, character and services of Jefferson Davis.

"He organized a nation more populous and extensive than that for which Jefferson wrote the Declaration of Independence; and was the Commander-in-Chief of armies many times greater than those which Washington commanded.

"He swayed Senates and led the soldiers of the Union—and he stood accused of treason in a court of justice.

"He saw victory sweep illustrious battle-fields— and he became a captive.

"He ruled millions—and he was put in chains.

"He created a nation—he followed its bier—he wrote its epitaph—and he died a disfranchised citizen.

"But though great in all vicissitudes and trials, he was greatest in that fortune which, lifting him first to the loftiest heights and casting him thence into the depths of disappointment, found him everywhere the erect and constant friend of truth. He conquered himself and forgave his enemies, yet bent to none but God."[15]

---

[15]The opening sentences of an address delivered to the General Assembly of Virginia, in Mozart Academy of Music, Richmond, January 25, 1890, at the request of the Assembly. JOHN WARWICK DANIEL, United States Senator from Virginia (1887-1910).

See also CHARLES WARREN, *The Supreme Court*, Vol. II, pp. 421 and 485-87.

CHAPTER XXV

MANY MISSIONARIES IN OUR MIDST

One master passion in the breast
Like Aaron's serpent, swallows up the rest.
—*Alexander Pope.*

During the spring, when the roses bloom in profusion, memorial days were observed in all parts of Virginia. Services were held in churches, addresses delivered in cemeteries, hymns were sung, and flowers scattered upon the soldiers' graves.

The unknown soldier was never forgotten, although that name was not used. After a battle, the dead were hurriedly laid in long trenches, or pits, often by the hundred, and sometimes by the thousand. These graves were blanketed with flowers on memorial days.

The Federal Government cared for those who fell in the Union cause. But it was left to surviving comrades, and especially to devoted women, to care for Confederate graves. Trembling hands and tear-dimmed eyes laid the flowers on the graves of Northern soldiers, also, for in the cold embrace of death all men are brothers.

Frances Miles French's popular poem, "The Blue and the Gray," was inspired when the matrons of Columbus, Mississippi, laid garlands upon the graves of Union soldiers.

"By the flow of the inland river,
    Whence the fleets of iron have fled;
Where the blades of the grave-grass quiver,
    Asleep are the ranks of the dead.

*   *   *   *   *

"No more shall the war-cry sever,
    Or the winding rivers be red;
They banish our anger forever,
    When they laurel the graves of our dead."

It has been claimed that the first organization to keep memorial day "in perpetual memory" was effected by the women of Petersburg under the leadership of Mrs. William T. Joynes,[1] who called them into conference May 6, 1866, and suggested that June 9 be observed. Before the war Petersburg was a wealthy city, a tobacco mart of international importance, but on June 8, 1866, only two or three uncertain "carriages" remained. These were loaded with flowers, and the women and girls of the city, in simple white dresses, followed as a band played the Dead March. Surviving Confederates and other citizens fell in behind the procession. It was pathetic in its simplicity, sincerity and genuine grief. One good woman had written an anthem, but it was not sung, as uniformed soldiers, black and white, loitered about and were alert to detect "rebellion" and "treason." As the anthem might give offense the familiar hymn, "Guide Me, O Thou Great Jehovah," was substituted. Prayer was offered, the flowers scattered and the mourners

---

[1] A. P. HILL CAMP, *Roster*, p. 56.
The Hollywood Memorial Association of Richmond also claims priority.
MRS. ROGER A. PRYOR, *Reminiscences*, pp. 404-406.

returned sadly to their homes. Fortunately the soldiers did not find it necessary to interfere.

In the spring of 1867, memorial days were observed throughout Virginia and the South.[2] Each community chose its own date for the celebration. When Memorial Day was observed in Macon Georgia (April 26, 1870), Sidney Lanier[3] made an address, "Retrospect and Prospect," which is still remembered and quoted.

General and Mrs. Ulysses S. Grant, their daughters and a party of friends visited Richmond, Saturday, May 18,[4] 1867, and made an excursion to the battle-field of Cold Harbor in Hanover County. How peaceful now this countryside twice drenched with human blood! The Virginians never ceased to appreciate General Grant's courtesy to General Lee at the time of the surrender. He also opposed the use of Negro soldiers in the South and on numerous occasions befriended Virginia and the South, as we shall see.

---

[2]HENRY TIMROD composed a matchless "Ode" to the memory of the dead in Magnolia Cemetery, Charleston, South Carolina (1867):

> "Sleep sweetly in your humble graves,
>   Sleep martyrs of a fallen cause.
> Though yet no marble column craves
>   The pilgrim here to pause.

*   *   *   *   *   *

> "Stoop, angels, hither from the skies
>   There is no holier spot of ground,
> Than where defeated valor lies
>   By mourning beauty crowned."

Southern Literary Readings, L. W. PAYNE, p. 154.

[3]*Land of Decision*, SQUIRES, p. 119.

[4]DAVID B. PARKER, *A Chautauqua Boy*, p. 110, relates that he accompanied the party to the battle-field. He mentions the General's daughter "Nellie" as one of the party.

President Andrew Johnson and Secretary of State
William H. Seward visited Richmond two weeks
later (June 1), stopping at the famous Spotswood
Hotel. The city officials extended the hospitality
of the city to both parties of distinguished guests.

II

June was a busy month in Virginia and the busiest
of Virginians was the Honorable John Minor Botts.
This eccentric but experienced and determined
politician set himself to build a respectable, nay, an
aristocratic, Republican party on the Old Line
Whigs as a foundation. For the Whigs of Virginia
loved the Democrats as the Devil is said to love
holy water. Botts had no place in the black and
tan convention of April 17, 1867, which was all of
Hunnicutt and none of Botts.

So it came to pass that Brother Botts called a
new convention for July 4 in Charlottesville, to be
attended by all the aristocratic and wealthy planters
of Albemarle.[5] He persuaded no less than three
hundred, some very distinguished citizens, to sign
the "call." These Old Line Whigs were ready to
accept the new order in State and Nation. They
agreed that bad conditions might be ameliorated.
They hoped to save the State from such Radicals as

[5]JOHN H. GILMER, *War of Races*, a letter, reprinted July 29, 1867, as a pamphlet says:

"Passion and prejudice, selfish propensities and avaricious invectives, ambitious schemes and party frenzy have all conspired to madden public men and alienate the people from each other."

This letter is a powerful invective of the Albemarle movement; and yet, as one reads it seventy years after date, Dr. Gilmer, though accurate and logical, is not wholly practical, diplomatic, nor convincing.

Underwood and Hunnicutt. They would build a
Conservative Republican party, the "best men of
both races" cooperating. "The best men of both
races" became a popular catchword, and was a bid
for popular support. The black Radical element
were conspicuously, one might say, ostentatiously,
ignored.

The Republican leaders at Washington realized
that the new party in Virginia, from which they
hoped to receive many benefits, and perhaps even
some future electoral votes, was about to be rent
asunder while it was aborning. The Reconstruction
Committee of Fifteen took a hand. The Union
Leagues of Philadelphia, New York, and even distant
Boston also took a hand. It is quite astonishing
how narrowly the Virginians were watched. It was
said that this breach in Virginia "threatened to disturb the harmony and unity of the party not only
in Virginia, but through the South."

III

A conference assembled as the guests of Governor
Pierpont in the ample drawing rooms of the Executive Mansion, June 11. Fifty Republican leaders
talked it over.[6]

Among those present were Senator Henry Wilson,
of Massachusetts; General C. W. Strong and John
Jay, of New York; H. H. Coolidge, C. W. Slack, R.
M. Morse, Charles H. Gibbons and George H.
Boker, of Philadelphia.

[6]Union League Club of New York.
Report of the Richmond Convention, June 11-12, 1867, Library of Congress.

The discussion was opened by Judge Underwood. Botts, Hawxhurst, Hunnicutt, Pierpont, Beckley and L. H. Chandler took part.

Hunnicutt defended his black and tan convention of April 17, as good and regular. Botts declared that if the Democrats ever again obtained control of Virginia, which he fervently prayed the Almighty to forbid, they would immediately reenslave the Negroes.

The leaders met at the Ballard House, the second day. Charles H. Gibbons, of Philadelphia, took the chair. It was announced that a fund of $1,500 would be raised in New York to organize Union Leagues in Virginia.[7]

This ill-assorted and wholly uncongenial gathering finally agreed to abandon the proposed convention at Charlottesville, July 4 (as a concession to the Radicals), and to annul the Richmond convention of April 17 (as a concession to the Conservatives), and to hold a new convention of all parties in Richmond, August 1. At that time a platform would be adopted and a regular party organization effected. The gathering closed with an enthusiastic meeting at the African Church, the night of June 12.

During July, John Minor Botts was busy with his cultured Whig friends, and Hunnicutt was just as busy lining up the Radical element.

The Albemarle leaders put forth this manifesto, July 1:

"Having consented in good faith to the reconstruction of the Southern States under the Sherman-Shellabarger Bill, we consider ourselves as bound in

[7] *New York Tribune,* June 15, 1867.

honor to the unconditional maintenance of the Union in these States, and we regard the welfare of Virginia and of the other Southern States as requiring that our people should cooperate with the party that will give us protection for life and property, and believing that the Republican party of the United States alone has the power to give us protection, we desire to cooperate with them."

Meetings were held and delegates elected in Louisa, Amelia, Charlotte, Smythe, Pittsylvania, Prince Edward, Halifax, Buckingham, Rappahannock, and perhaps other counties. If Botts had succeeded, the political history of Virginia would have been different from that day to this. But the success of Botts meant the end of Hunnicutt, and no one knew that better than the Radicals.

Botts favored enfranchising those colored citizens who were honest, thrifty taxpayers and were really assets to their neighbors and respective communities . . . exactly what Abraham Lincoln proposed long before. Manhood suffrage was coming whether the South liked it or not. It was, therefore, the part of wisdom, reasoned the Old Line Whigs, to accept limited suffrage for the freedmen, and make it a premium, an incentive and a blessing to them and to the Commonwealth, instead of allowing it to become a curse. After all is said, they argued, the intellect, wealth and culture of any community will rule, no matter who votes and who does not. All of which was wiser than the Virginians of that day realized.[8]

---

[8]Registration proceeded all summer long. 70,000 were disfranchised, and did not attempt to register; 120,101 whites registered and 105,832 colored voters.

CHAPTER XXVI

VIRGINIA'S DARKEST DAY

AUGUST 1, 1867

**The souls of the Virginians were driven hither
and yon in the darkness like the gulls on the shores
of the Chesapeake, when a frightful storm is brewing.**

—*W. H. T. Squires.*

The Radicals of Virginia were determined to
confound John Minor Botts, his aristocratic Whig
friends and their constructive, conservative measures.

Lewis Lindsay, a negro attorney of Richmond, the
most able colored leader in the state, made a sensational speech in Charlottesville (July 2), in which he
told the white people exactly what the freedmen demanded, and were going to have, namely, a fair and
equal division of all offices and honors, social recognition, a Negro governor, senators, congressmen and
State legislators. The freedmen were forty percent
of the State's population, and would cast forty
percent of the votes. Henceforth all legislative
committee and honors must be divided between the
white and colored citizens in that proportion.

The reaction to Lindsay's demands may readily
be imagined.[1]

---

[1]HAMILTON JAMES ECKENRODE, *Virginia During Reconstruction.* Johns
Hopkins Studies, pp. 73-80.

Fredericksburg News files of August, 1867.

Richmond Enquirer files of August, 1867.

Norfolk Journal files of August, 1867.

As though the anxiety and perplexities of the Virginians were not sufficient, the Congress added a third Military Reconstruction Bill, July 19, 1867, to strengthen and enforce the military tyrannies of March 2 and 23. The new law gave the Military Commanders full power in their respective Districts to remove any State officer, fill the vacancies thus made, and to require all candidates for all offices to take the iron-clad oath.[2]

The last day of July found busy Botts in Richmond with his platform in his pocket. It was a typical Botts product. It whirled verbal thunderbolts against secession, rebellion, treason and the Confederate debt. . . . Then he advocated the vote for all ex-Confederates "except the leaders." None knew precisely who the "leaders" were. That made no difference.

August 1 dawned over a feverish State and city. Hunnicutt was ready. The convention met in the African Church, a huge barn-like structure on Broad street near the famous Monumental Church, not far from the Capitol. The Negroes were up with the sun. The street was jammed with a happy, jeering crowd as black as the coast of Dahomey. They awaited the opening of the doors, the mob growing every moment. At eleven, they surged into the huge building and packed it to capacity. Only fifty white Radicals got in. When John Minor Botts and his co-operators arrived, they found two thousand outside demanding entrance.

[2] WILLIAM ARCHIBALD DUNNING, *Essays*, p. 154.

DAWN OVER CHESAPEAKE

"The happy day of deliverance came as peacefully and as quietly as the dawn that lights the rippling waters of the Chesapeake." —Page 281.

Photo by H. C. Mann

Hunnicutt won by sheer numbers and the right of mob law. He told his triumphant followers that it was only necessary to re-adopt the platform of the April Convention . . . they wildly and joyously adopted it. There was no system, no order. It was simply a huge happy mob, immensely enjoying the new and rare delights of citizenship. Were they not now politicians and statesmen?

The great crowd who could not get in adjourned to Capitol Square for a mass meeting. This overflow elected John Hawxhurst, of Alexandria, a close friend of Underwood and Hunnicutt, chairman. A motion that Honorable John Minor Botts address the mass meeting was howled down with emphatic derision.

Botts and his aristocratic co-operators were impotent spectators of the degradation of Virginia. The machinery and organization of the Republican party in this State slipped from their grasp. Botts' platform remained unfolded in his wide, large pocket.

Why Botts and the Old Line Whigs did not organize a convention of their own and appeal to the National Republican party on the one hand and the better elements of Virginia on the other for recognition and support (as General Mahone did so successfully at a later date) does not appear.[3]

Botts was out-maneuvered, out-generaled, and whipped at his own game. This was the second time in six months the Radicals tricked him. Evidently he was too old to learn.

---

[3]That night a mass meeting was held at which Mr. Botts read his platform and made an address, but it was a futile gesture. His platform may be read, *verbatim*, *Annual Cyclop*, 1867—"Virginia."

It was the closing scene of a tempestuous life, the sands of which were running low. He faded completely from the political picture. Eighteen months later he died at his home in Culpeper. His body was brought to Richmond (January 10, 1869) and lay in state in the Senate chamber. John Minor Botts sleeps on Shockoe Hill not far from Chief Justice John Marshall.[4]

II

But we must return to the African Church and the sable convention within it. Hunnicutt, Underwood, and Hawxhurst were for the time masters of Virginia. No doubt the soul of Thaddeus Stevens rejoiced. Dr. Bayne, an influential Negro delegate from Norfolk, wished all "rebels" permanently disfranchised. Hunnicutt did not wish it, but Dr. Bayne and his colored friends pushed it over. He then moved to adjourn. He wanted the convention to "wind up like a Georgia camp meeting—with a general jollification." Again Hunnicutt objected. He had other matters, mostly for Northern and Congressional consumption. But Bayne had his way and the jeering crowd dispersed.

The Confederate soldiers and sympathizers watched these shifting scenes narrowly.[5] They had no vote. More than a thousand Federal bayonets gleamed in Richmond's mid-summer sun. The Vir-

---

[4]WILLIAM ASBURY CHRISTIAN, *History of Richmond*, p. 302.

[5]HORACE GREELEY had this unkind and unreasonable thrust in the *New New York Tribune:*

"The rebel States have adopted a do-nothing, accept-nothing policy, pro-

ginians were patient and orderly. "Wait until we get our chance." In two years it came, but they were long, hard and disheartening years, none the less. The Virginians hoped that this, the worst, was a prelude to the better—and it was. The extreme Radicalism of Hunnicutt, Hawxhurst and Underwood proved their political suicide.

There was certainly one young man[6] in Virginia who read the future with the sagacity of a sage, General John McAllister Schofield, and he was a Republican, a veteran of the Union army and the monarch of "District No. 1"; that is Virginia.[7] He knew that such unnecessary, gratuitous shame and humiliation were never before inflicted upon a proud people, who had made a valorous fight, and an honorable surrender, trusting to the integrity and the political justice of their former foes, only to be shamefully maligned and vindictively punished in the nation their fathers established.

As one looks back upon the black scenes of August, 1867, it is to marvel at the magnificent self-control of a million proud Virginians, men of culture, intelligence and experience. Their discipline and restraint are worthy the best traditions of the Saxon race, from which they sprang.

---

fessing to have no choice in the matter, except to tire the loyal people into acquiescence to their original demand for representation without any conditions and irresponsible control over the future of the blacks. Probably we can stand it as long as they can."

That editorial was unworthy Horace Greeley.

[6]DON C. SEITZ, *The Dreadful Decade*, p. 40.

[7]He divided the state into sub-districts, June 3, and appointed commanders over the same, "furnished with sufficient military force to enable them to discharge their duties."—*Annual Cyclop*, 1867.

Their blood boiled with righteous indignation, but there were no riots, no unlawful assemblies, no murders, no secret arming or drilling and no dark threats.

III

Over and over again the Confederate leaders and the press,[8] especially General Lee, counselled patience, forbearance and passive resistance. Over and over again the old leaders prophesied the dawn of a better day.

The Virginians understood their colored neighbors, none better.[9] They did not blame the Negroes, but they poured forth the vials of impotent wrath upon scalawags and carpet-baggers, who were using the colored vote for private and political purposes.[10]

These Virginians watched the shifting scenes north of the Potomac; such shameful scenes in the Capitol of the United States as the ante-bellum years had never known. They saw a President of the United States publicly and repeatedly mobbed by a fanatical faction of his own party. They heard that President say that he expected at any time to fall as Lincoln fell by the bullet of an assassin. They heard General William T. Sherman predict

[8] *Annual Cyclop*, 1867.

"The Commanding General notified Charles H. Wynne of the *Richmond Times* that he censured an editorial on 'A Black Man's Party in Virginia,' as an intolerable insult to all Union soldiers, and no less to the Confederates. He wished the press to foster peace, not to stir up strife."

[9] JOHN ESTEN COOKE, *History of Virginia*, p. 508.

[10] SAMUEL EAGLE FORMAN, *Our Republic*, pp. 531-533, discusses carpet-baggers and scalawags. The former were "mostly unscrupulous adventurers," and the latter, who as natives, were more hated than the alien carpet-bag brigade. Scalawag is a "scaly sheep."

another Civil War, which would be a war between citizens, not between States. They heard threats, as of anarchists, against the Supreme Court of the United States, they saw a great nation sinking into frightful financial, political and partisan corruption.

The Virginians never made a finer record than when they lifted themselves out of the terrors of Reconstruction, took charge of their own affairs, re-entered the Union—all without the slightest excitement, without firing a shot, without bloodshed, without even a threat of violence! It was superb.

IV

The happy day of deliverance which came as peacefully and quietly as dawn lights the rippling waters of the Chesapeake, was yet two years deferred. The Richmond Enquirer sounded a clarion call (August 3):

"The disgusting and loathsome exhibition of the past week[11] demonstrated to the plainest intellect that the fate of Hayti awaits Virginia if, through apathy and indifference, the Caucasian majority in this State permits the African minority to obtain control of the Government. Completely demoralized and corrupted by the infamous renegades who have affiliated with them, a large portion of the Negroes are now inaccessible to reason. If there

[11]It is to recall the words of HENRY E. SHEPHERD, *Lee*, p. 261:

"Despite the record of affluent horror, of blood and of torture, with which romance, fiction and professional libel have invested the story of Southern slavery, we affirm that a richer harvest of crime, defilement and abasement, of remorseless cruelty, and political debauchery followed in the train of Negro enfranchisement during a single year than marked the record of slavery during two Centuries."

were not, fortunately, a large majority of white men to whose instincts of race and interests we may be permitted to look hopefully, our prospects would be no better than those of Hayti when French radicalism kindled in that unhappy land the fires of servile insurrection. . . .

"The recent hideous Radical carnival[12] in this city, like a fire-bell at midnight, should arouse every honest white man in Virginia to a sense of danger."

This extreme pessimism was natural, no doubt, but the bold editor failed to take into consideration those hidden but potent counter-currents which eventually bring every evil to a disastrous end. Every iniquity carries with it the seeds of its own destruction.[13]   There is a solution for every problem.   Like rivers that drag themselves along, and wander hither and yon, how aimlessly!   Lost in a wilderness of coarse marsh-grass, bound by sprawling, green pocosons, their devious way is desolate and discouraging.   But never river, great or small, failed to find the parent sea.   So in the affairs of men; patience to bide delay will usually bring freedom of life and action.

---

[12]JAMES ELLIOTT WALMSLEY, *Jno. Minor Botts, Dict. Amer. Biog.*
[13]PHILIP ALEX. BRUCE, *Rebirth of the Old Dominion*, Vol. II, pp. 115-119.

CHAPTER XXVII

THE UNION LEAGUE AND KU KLUX KLAN

Whoever is right the persecutors must be wrong.
—William Penn.

The twelve weeks which intervened between the adjournment of the Radical Convention and the day set for the election (August 2-October 18) tried the soul of those who loved Virginia and were concerned for the welfare of her people.[1] The freedmen entered fully and completely into the contest. Not only were they slaves no longer, not only citizens who could come and go at pleasure, not only the nation's wards and often pensioners, but now they had a vote—a vote denied the great majority of white citizens, employers and former masters. The bottommost rail was topmost.

Unfortunately for the freedman, he repudiated his old master and his present employer, if he had one, to follow Radical leadership. A responsible system of manhood suffrage, placing a premium upon thrift, stability and integrity, might have been made a blessing. But when the freedmen accepted almost unanimously the doctrines of the most extreme Radicals, only trouble could come of it.

---

[1] A convention of ex-soldiers and sailors was held at Richmond, September 25, Henry Horatio Wells presided. But the soldiers and sailors were not Confederates.

The Freedmen's Bureau, so thoroughly organized that it touched the life and the cabin of every Negro, supported a great army of teachers, preachers, nurses, visitors and other agents in every part of Virginia. They taught the Negroes that they owed all their present blessings and their future security to the Radicals, and the Radicals must be supported. If the Conservative Republicans or the wicked Democrats ever got control of the Government, every Negro would be forced back into slavery, worse than ever before. The Negroes naturally believed it, and the falsehood was so thoroughly ingrained that they never forgot it.

General Oliver Otis Howard, the commander-in-chief of the Freedmen's Bureau, visited Norfolk once (August 1868). He addressed the colored citizens at the Bank Street Baptist and Bute Street Methodist Churches. He gave them sound and reasonable advice about going to work, making good homes for themselves and their children and living sober, industrious and honest lives. The audiences were disappointed that he did not speak of confiscation, "forty acres and a mule," which they still hoped to receive, and the other glittering promises of what the Government proposed to do for them.

The right hand of the Freedmen's Bureau, in matters political, was the Union League. That was the master-stroke of Radical political diplomacy. If that organization were not so serious and so fraught with danger, it would be humorous—and it is wholly interesting.

After the War Between the States many veterans

THE FRINGE OF GREAT DISMAL

Photo by H. C. Mann

"There is always a solution to the problem. Like rivers that drag themselves along and wander, hither and yon, how aimlessly! Lost in a wilderness of coarse marsh-grass, bound by sprawling, green pocosons, their devious way is desolate and discouraging. But there never was a river, small or great, be obstacles what they may, that failed at last to find the parent sea. So in the affairs of men, one must move by patience and circumspection and often bide delay, but all come forth at last to freedom of life and thought and action. —Page 282.

in Northern cities organized Union Leagues,[2] as social, military, fraternal, political and altogether innocent societies. There were national organizations and local branches. As soon as Congress granted the franchise to the Negroes, the Union League naturally entered the South. Here was real "missionary" territory.

In Virginia the organization was entrusted to white leaders of ability. The clubs met at night in secret and sequestered places. The ritual was chiefly concerned with the education of the freedmen— how to vote "right." Whom to vote for, and above all, whom to vote against. They must be good party men and stick to their friends.

Their only friends were in the Republican party, not the Andrew Johnson, or the Governor Pierpont, or the Botts Republican party; but the Hunnicutt-Underwood Republican party. It was they who would protect them from the fierce Democrats just waiting a chance to pounce upon the poor Negroes and enslave, or perhaps murder them.

Strictest secrecy was enjoined and the elaborate and often gruesome ritual was conducted in total darkness. The most terrible oaths were administered in compelling fashion. The initiation was thrilling. The old members marched about the new members, groaning, moaning, crying, rattling chains, with subdued shrieks of agony. The kneeling victim's blood was frozen with terror in his veins—but, once in, it was entrancing.

---

[2] WALTER L. FLEMING, *Document, History of Reconstruction*, Vol. II, Chapter VII, for history of the Union League.

When the lights were lit a simple lesson was given about good Radicals and bad Democrats and "traitors." Once initiated, the Union Leaguers were now in direct contact with the ruling powers of the great Congress—Stevens, Sumner, Stanton, and other great and good men. In fact, the Union Leaguers knew many and valuable secrets hidden from the haughty, white "rebels," "copperheads," and other "traitors," so long their cruel masters.

So astutely managed were the Union Leagues and Freedmen's Bureau, that of 93,145 Negro votes cast in October, 1867, only 638 in all Virginia were cast for the Conservative candidates.

General Orlando Brown came to Richmond soon after the war (June 15, 1865), as head of the Freedman's Bureau. The Grand Deputy of the Union League in Virginia was General Edgar Allan; and the General did his work thoroughly, although there came a time, as we shall see, that the General parted company with his Radical friends.

Despite the oaths, the secrecy and the sequestered places of meeting, the Virginians knew perfectly what was going forward.[3]

II

If the Radical "missionaries" chose to play upon the ignorance, superstition and gullibility of their wards, the white men would do the same. The Ku Klux Klan was the Anglo-Saxon reply to the Union League.

---

[3]The ruins of a beautiful colonial church, near Bacon's Castle, are a monument to the Union League During the excitement of the Reconstruction era it was burned by an incendiary. The ruined walls, ivy covered, remain and the cemetery is in use to this day.

When the Ku Klux rode the Negroes were terror
stricken[4] . . . and they had reason for their terror.
The young white men were out for business, and it
was business of a serious nature. There was danger
abroad, and the Ku Klux trooper intended to take
no chances.

The Invisible Empire had local dens, over which
a Cyclops ruled. There were gradations of office,
as in an army, from the Grand Wizard down; Genii,
Dragons, Hydras, Furies, Goblins, Night-Hawks
and other fascinating titles. Their methods were
usually harmless, even humorous, but if the harmless method was not sufficient, more drastic per-
suasions were forthcoming.

One Dragon met a Negro who had become too
insolent. He asked for a drink with the casual remark that water was hard to get in hell and he
hadn't had a drink since he was killed in the battle
of Manassas. In fact, he had just dug his way up.

A Cyclops, on another occasion, told a Negro, in
confidence, that his grave was on a battlefield,
and a road had been built over it, and that he had
to scratch like hell to get through the gravel. It is

[4]DON C. SEITZ, *Dreadful Decade*, pp. 25-27.

THEODORE CALVIN PEASE, *The United States*, Chapter XXVI.

The Klan restrained the freedmen from allowing their new liberty to lead
them into a "reign of violence."

FREDERICK LOGAN PAXSON, *New Nation*, p. 51. Congress kept the soldiers
garrisoned in the South to see that the freedmen were protected, yet they
were unable (and often unwilling) to control the white men.

JOHN SHERMAN, *Recollections*, p. 315.

"The outrages of the Ku Klux Klan seemed to me to be so atrocious and
wicked that the men who committed them were not only unworthy to govern
but unfit to live."

That is a very pronounced and sensational charge from the patron of the
Sherman-Shellabarger Bill, who does not give his opinion of the Union League
and League "missionaries" in the South.

astonishing how promptly successful the Ku Klux Klan was in its time.[5]

The Union League lasted only two or three years, but the Ku Klux Klan and similar organizations continued for many years. Queerly enough those most energetic and enthusiastic for the Union League were the loudest in condemnation of the Ku Klux Klan. All such methods are dangerous and only justified when all legal efforts fail, and the law is impotent.[6]

The white population, in the meantime, was paralyzed. The Committee of Fifteen and their allies made it plain that no "rebels" and "traitors" would be allowed to vote in any election in the South. Not only those who bore arms to resist the invasion of the State, the destruction of their property and the protection of their hereditary rights were "rebels," but those who had in any way aided or sympathized were also "rebels" and "traitors." In short, all the white people from the Potomac to the Rio Grande were rebels and traitors, and nearly all the blacks, too. Had not the Negroes protected the plantations and largely fed the Confederate armies and actually served the soldiers as helpers. But that item was never once mentioned. To "aid" and "abet" was quite pardonable if the "rebel" or "traitor" was African! Only Anglo-Saxons were disfranchised. Such was the logic of Reconstruction.[7]

---

[5]The Ku Klux Klan was never so active in Virginia as in the Gulf States— it was not necessary.

[6]It should be remembered that England, Scotland, Ireland, France and every civilized nation has had recourse to the same methods under sufficient provocation.

[7]WILLIAM ARCHIBALD DUNNING, *Essays*, p. 220, states that it was assumed

If any white man had any doubt anent disfranchisement, and surely none had, the Radicals in Congress pushed through another emphatic act (July 9), requiring a "test oath" of every voter.

One might register, and 120,101 white men did so, but 44,017 did not venture to vote. Some 105,932 Negroes registered and only 12,687 failed to vote; if the figures given are accurate, and that we much doubt.

The white people, though a majority, had no organization, which was natural. The moral effect of defeat, the ever increasing hostility of Congress, the bitterness and vindictiveness of the Northern press, the set determination of the Radicals to humiliate all "rebels" and "traitors," to make them "know their place," to hold them out of participation in all government, national and local, and to hold over their heads like the sword of Damocles the threat of confiscation—these and many other reasons discouraged the white majority. Many leaders were dead, maimed or discredited.

The Virginians knew that the two wings of the Regublican party were now at each other's throats.

United so long as Lincoln lived, so long as the war fever and enthusiasm lasted, they were now the bitterest enemies. It was wise to await the decision of the contest. It must be remembered that a Federal bayonet glistened in the sunshine at every corner in our "Military District." In ten great States, more than two years after the total and com-

that the negroes could take this oath, "though such an assumption is irreconcilable with notorious facts as to the conduct and sympathy of the blacks during hostilities."

plete surrender of the Southern armies in good faith, 19,000 soldiers of the regular army were on duty at 133 camps (September, 1867). They awaited "a call to quell insurrections, and enforce every injunction, even the most trivial and petty persecutions of the hated white aristocrats."[8] The military authorities did not hesitate to remove civil officers, judges and magistrates, and to set aside the enactments of the Legislature or the verdicts of the courts.

As the election came nearer, excitement, though subdued, was intense. A great political meeting was again held in the Capitol Square (October 13). Even the tobacco factories closed as all the help had gone into politics! The meeting was a great Radical success.

There were intense speeches by Hunnicutt, Underwood and an Irishman named James Morrisey, and two Negroes (Lewis Lindsey and James Cox), all of whom were elected to represent Richmond in the Constitutional Convention.[9]

The conservative Republicans attempted to hold a meeting in order to nominate their ticket, but an excited mob of Negroes broke in and the gathering ended in a riot.

III

When at last election day arrived, Federal soldiers, fully armed, were stationed behind all the ballot boxes, and those who came as peaceful citizens to vote had the privilege of looking into the business end of a musket. This was the democratic form of

---

[8]DAVID SAVILLE MUZZEY, *History of the United States*, Vol. III, p. 17.

[9]*Land of Decision*, SQUIRES, p. 245.

government, furnished 8,000,000 American citizens
by such statesmen as Stevens, Sumner, Stanton,
Butler and Wade, a republic in name only,[10] a military despotism of the worst possible type, covering
one-third of the area of the United States. General
Schofield had 2,529 soldiers in Virginia at this time;
1,031 at Richmond and the remainder stationed at
eleven strategic points through the State,[11] although
two and a half years had passed since there had
been an hostile shot or a threat of armed resistance
in the whole South.

As though, in Heaven's name, one day were not
enough, General Schofield prolonged this election
through three days, October 22, 23, 24, 1867. William
Asbury Christian, a trustworthy authority, makes
the statement that the ballots cast in Richmond
October 22, the first day, gave the Conservatives a
majority. But by voting three days the Radicals
secured the majority. The reason for a three-day
election has never been explained.

As might have been forecast the Radicals won a
complete victory. Of the 105 members elected to
the proposed convention, 72 were Radicals and of
the Radicals 25 were Negroes. There were 38
Conservatives, some claimed by both sides. Some

---

[10]WOODROW WILSON, *History of the United States*, Vol. V, Chapter I.

[11]MATTHEW FORNEY STEELE, *American Campaigns*, p. 588.

"In August, 1867, the U. S. Army numbered 53,962.

"In 1869, it was reduced to 34,000.

"In 1870, 30,000."

WILLIAM ADDLEMAN GAUSE, *History of United States Army*, p. 301:

"Equally distressing was the situation in the former Confederate States.
About 19,000 Union soldiers were distributed through 134 posts in the erst-
while Confederacy," to support carpet-bag and Radical partisans.

Compare p. 244.

107,342 voted for the Convention, and 61,887 opposed it.[12]

To vote against the Convention was useless, as it was the will of the conqueror, and the only means by which the State could get rid of military rule and again take her place in the Union. "I think there can be no doubt in the minds of those who reflect that conventions must be held in the Southern States under the Sherman Bill; that the people are placed in a position where no choice in the matter is left them, and it is the duty of all who may be entitled to vote to attend the polls and endeavor to elect the best available men to represent them and act for the interests of their States. The division of the people into parties is to be greatly reprehended and ought to be avoided by the willingness on the part of everyone to yield minor points in order to secure those which are essential to the general welfare. Wisdom dictates that the Convention should be cheerfully submitted to by the citizens of each State, who should unite in carrying out its decrees in good faith and kind feeling." The Virginians submitted, not cheerfully, nor with any enthusiasm.

Sometimes in the affairs of men the worst happens for the best. Such seems to have been the case with this October election. The worst befell; and it had two diametrically opposite reactions.

---

[12]WILLIAM ARCHIBALD DUNNING, *Reconstruction*, p. 111, states that very frequently the registrars encouraged the blacks and did all in their power to discourage white men to register and vote.

The Radicals were elated, so elated that Hunnicutt[13] was arrested in Charles City County for inciting the Negroes to armed insurrection and bloodshed. The long arm of the military satrap intervened. Schofield was no friend of Hunnicutt . . . but the Radicals of Washington must not be offended. Hunnicutt was released on bail.

IV

As the Radicals became more violent and dangerous, the white people determined to protect themselves. The Ku Klux Klan was riding. Many employers dismissed those Negro employees who were too Radical. The Northern press was very perceptibly cooling off and Congress had adjourned. The leaders of Virginia, ante-bellum Democrats and Old Line Whigs, united at last. They quietly laid their plans to save the Commonwealth, and within eighteen months they succeeded.

[13]*Annual Cyclop*, 1867. The incendiary speech was made September 27 at Elam Church. He was arrested November 25, charged with inciting insurrection.

Chapter XXVIII

VALOR'S EFFORT VAIN

In vain doth valour bleed,
While avarice and rapine share the land.
—*John Milton.*

The enfranchisement of the freedmen and the disfranchisement of all "rebels," with the election machinery completely in the hands of the Radicals, reinforced by the bayonets of the United States Army, enabled the Radical element to carry the election of their candidates in all doubtful districts. The personnel of the Constitutional Convention elected that doleful October day, will be described in detail below. But there were many other elections held in many other States during the fall of 1867. They showed a marked reaction against the Radicals and their iniquitous policies.

California, Connecticut, Kansas, New Jersey, New York, Pennsylvania, Kentucky and Maryland went Democratic.[1] The previous Radical majorities in New England were much curtailed. In Ohio a constitutional amendment granting franchise to the Negroes was rejected by 50,209 majority. Lewis D. Campbell declared "the party that planted itself

---

[1] The Democrats of New York City kept a cannon firing at intervals for two days to celebrate this victory.

squarely on Negro suffrage in Ohio was overwhelmingly defeated wherever that issue was squarely raised."

New Jersey, Kansas and even distant Minnesota decisively rejected Negro suffrage.

There resides in all Americans a sense of justice and fair play.[2] Anger is abnormal and temporary. The Radicals waved the bloody shirt so furiously in 1866 and appealed so dramatically for vengeance against the wicked Southern slave-drivers and rebels that they swept the country. But that method failed when repeated in 1867. The outrageous extravagance of the government, the insults heaped upon the President of the United States, the needless and cruel political persecution of the South, influenced men of sober second thought, more and more, against Radical policies. In all of which the Democratic, or "Copperhead" press was very active.

Such metropolitan papers as the New York World came forth every day with scathing editorials, which handled the Radical program in no gentle manner. For a generation the New York World was the champion of the South, and had an immense circuction throughout the Southern States, nor was it less influential in such doubtful States as New York, New Jersey and Connecticut.

The shock of the Radical triumph in Virginia, and the consequent dangers to our civilization, the sweep of the Democratic and Conservative victories in the North and West, convinced those Virginia

---

[2] E. BENJAMIN ANDREWS, *History of United States*, Vol. IV, Chapter XI. The learned authority packs into this chapter so many errors, and so much mistaken information, that his history is little better than cheap and partisan propaganda.

statesmen who astutely watched their opportunity,
that the time for action had arrived. The shrewdest
observer in Virginia was the able, experienced and
patriotic Whig leader in Staunton, Alexander H. H.
Stuart. Again he stepped forth and determined to
save Virginia, for Virginia has never known a finer
patriot.

II

Democrats and Whigs must bury the hatchet.
So far as national affairs were concerned the Whig
party was as dead as Henry Clay, who had been
sleeping for seventeen years under the sod of Kentucky. The executive committee of what had once
been the potent Democratic party and a similar
committee of the Whigs called a convention of
Conservative Virginians in Richmond, December 11,
1867, irrespective of party.

The response was prompt and gratifying. The
Virginians moved quietly, almost secretly. Machinery, long neglected, was again put in motion.
The Radicals, flushed with triumph and busy with
their plans to control the State, must not be aroused.
The Northern press and national Republican party,
most especially, must not be excited. During November, 800 representative Conservatives were
chosen from all the counties of the State.

When they assembled, December 11, they represented the wealth, intelligence, and noblest traditions of the Commonwealth. Nearly every one
of them was "disfranchised by act of Congress."[3]

---

[3]JOSEPH ADDISON WADDELL, *History of Augusta County.*
RICHARD LEE MORTON, *History of Virginia*, Vol. III, p. 115.
ALEX. H. H. STUART, *Restoration of Virginia*, p. 18.

Let us visit this important convention and glance over the roster: Robert Mercer Taliaferro Hunter, Secretary of State in Jefferson Davis' Cabinet; S. McDowell Moore, an influential Whig leader from Lexington; Marmaduke Johnson, a member of the secession convention of 1861; Wood Bouldin, an ardent Unionist and Whig leader before the war; Raleigh T. Daniel, long a distinguished Whig leader in Richmond; Thomas Jefferson Randolph, son of Governor Thomas Mann Randolph and his wife, Martha, elder daughter of Thomas Jefferson; James Lawson Kemper, later Governor of Virginia (1874-78); Thomas Stanley Bocock, a member of Stonewall Jackson's staff and Speaker of the Confederate House of Representatives; Henry K. Ellyson, an experienced Richmond attorney and political leader; Robert Old, awarded a prison term by order of Edwin M. Stanton and acquitted as soon as he could secure a trial; T. S. Evans, long a member of the House of Delegates for Richmond; Thomas Stanhope Flournoy, once a Whig candidate for Governor of Virginia; John B. Baldwin, frequently mentioned in these pages; John Letcher, the War Governor of Virginia (1860-64); James Barbour, influential in the constitutional convention of 1850; William H. McFarlane, who signed President Davis' bond; Robert S. Preston, Cincinnatus W. Newton, of Norfolk, George W. Bolling, tenth in descent from Powhatan, and many others as influential and distinguished.[4]

---

[4]"The aristocrats of Virginia usually got what they wanted."—ELBERT HUBBARD.

Alexander H. H. Stuart was unanimously called to the chair, in assuming which he said:

"At the close of the war we were assured that upon the repeal of the Ordinance of Secession, the repudiation of the Confederate debt and the emancipation of the slaves, we would be restored to our rights in the Union; but, instead of these promises being fulfilled, a policy has been inaugurated which places the Southern States under the control of our inferior race. We are met to appeal to the North not to permit the infliction of this disgrace upon us. Our rights may be wrested from us, but we will never submit to the rule of an alien and inferior race. We desire, further, to perfect our organization so that all who wish this to be a white man's government may be able to act in concert and by one vigorous and united effort save ourselves from ruin and disgrace."

A platform, of six planks was adopted. It was an appeal to the better element of the North, both press and people, even more than to Virginia.

I. The Virginians have no wish, purpose, or desire ever to restore slavery, directly or indirectly.

II. Virginia wishes to be restored as promptly as possible to her rightful place in the Union. To all Virginians secession is now as dead as slavery.

III. The Virginians claim the protection, rights and privileges guaranteed by the fathers in the Constitution of the United States.

IV. The Virginians protest that the subjection of the white to the black race, under any circumstances is "abhorrent," and dangerous alike to State and nation.

V. The Virginians have the kindest feelings for the freedmen, but insist that this country must be governed by the white race.

VI. The Virginians are anxious for the restoration of peace, unity and good will.

During the second day (December 12), the Convention heard Robert Mercer Taliaferro Hunter. He deplored the political situation, and was much concerned with the danger of Negro suffrage, but he alluded with fine hope and confidence to the ability of the manhood of Virginia to meet and solve the problems as they arose.

It was tactful and diplomatic to invite Secretary Hunter to a place on the program. As a Democrat he was as popular as Stuart among the Old Line Whigs. Hunter was the United States Senator for Virginia when the State left the Union in 1861. He became Secretary of State in President Davis' Cabinet. After the surrender he was clapped into prison, released on parole and had just been pardoned by President Johnson.

It was an hopeful sign for Virginia when such a Whig as Stuart was willing to labor side by side with such a Democrat as Hunter.

An elaborate organization was effected—too elaborate, we suspect. A central committee of thirty-five, with headquarters in Richmond, was to cooperate with local organizations in each of the eight congressional districts.

These eight hundred men realized fully (none better than they) that a long, hard, bitter, difficult and even dangerous struggle was impending, but they did not hesitate if our civilization could be saved. They hoped to avoid Negro suffrage, to defeat the Radicals in their effort to control Virginia, to secure the readmission of Virginia and to regain representation in Congress. In this program they failed—but ultimately succeeded.

The prospect now before Virginia was dark, indeed. But Nature was still kind, even if man was cruel. From turmoil and strife the Virginian might turn to the peaceful forested slope, where long shadows fell softly from the lofty fringe of the pines, and lengthened with the slowly setting sun. Perhaps a thrush in the thicket lifted a flute note of cheer. Perhaps the waves that lapped the selvage of yellow sand and broke with a murmur reminded him that many a fierce storm had beaten these shores and torn through the woodland, but after every storm there is peace.

BOOK FOUR

December 11, 1867—January 1, 1869

CHAPTER XXIX

THE CONSTITUTIONAL CONVENTION

Probably never before in the history of the Anglo-Saxon race had civil government sunk to such a state of impotence as this; or had been brought into such absolute contempt.

—Philip Alexander Bruce.

It would be impossible to find a greater contrast than was offered by the eight hundred patriotic leaders of Virginia assembled in Richmond December 11, on the one hand; and the Constitutional Convention then meeting in the hall of the House of Delegates on the other hand.

William Asbury Christian is justified in this scathing sentence, "Never had such a disreputable convention met within the borders of this city. It seems mockery to call a crowd like this a Constitutional Convention."

The shame and the iniquity which called that mob into legal existence rests not with Virginia. It is one of the many crimes against representative Republican institutions for which the Congress of Many Iniquities must answer at the bar of history. This "Convention" was the child of the Reconstruction Force Bill, passed March 2, 1867, and of the tyranny called an election held the preceding October. The record of Congressional Reconstruction should bring a blush of shame to every American. Alexander H. H. Stuart said, "Such stringent restrictions were imposed upon the eligibility of members that much the larger number of men of intelligence, education, and experience in public affairs were effectually excluded from participation in its deliberations."[1]

The Convention was called to order, Tuesday, December 3, 1867, at ten o'clock in the hall of the House of Delegates, in the historic and beautiful Capitol of Virginia, the same chamber within whose walls the Ordinance of Secession had finally been adopted less than seven years before: James H. Platt, of Petersburg, acted as temporary chairman, and called upon Reverend James Mitchell to offer prayer. Charles H. Porter, of Norfolk, nominated the notorious John Curtis Underwood, now of Richmond, as President of the Convention. Joseph T. Campbell representing Washington and Smythe Counties nominated Reverend Norval Wilson, of Frederick County, and J. T. S. Taylor, of Albemarle nominated Judge Edward K. Snead of Accomac. Judge Underwood was elected, receiving 64 votes; Mr. Wilson received 33 votes, and Judge Snead 3.

In assuming the chair Judge Underwood made a characteristic speech, abounding in expressions of humility, and phrases of great verbosity.

General Schofield sent a message, wishing them well and transmitting various orders from the War Department. He also submitted letters of protest from many parts of the State, in which the honesty

---

[1] Debates and Proceedings of the Constitutional Convention of 1868.

of the election of various members, whom they asserted had been counted in, was questioned. It was asked that such members be refused seats in the Convention.

Fourteen of the Radicals were Virginians, thirteen came from New York, and one from each of the following States or foreign nations: Pennsylvania, Ohio, Maine, Vermont, Connecticut, South Carolina, Maryland, District of Columbia, Ireland, Scotland, Nova Scotia, Canada, and two Englishmen.

Of the fourteen white Virginia Radicals, some had voted for secession, others had been in the Confederate service, others were old men whose sons had been in the Confederate army, hardly one had a Union record. A large proportion of the Northerners and foreigners had drifted here in some non-combatant capacity.

A shrewd observer of the constitutional convention wrote[2]: "The members vary in color from mulatto to blackest African. One colored man is said to be an Indian of almost pure blood, his person is quite impressive and his deportment is eminently respectable. Some five or six Negroes aspire to statesmanship, and discuss the most difficult questions with all the complacency of Daniel Webster." The Indian was Peter G. Morgan, of Petersburg.

"The official reporter is giving an utterly false version of the debates. He makes an eloquent speech of a meaningless string of words.

---

[2] *Staunton Spectator*. The author is probably Joseph Addison Waddell, who with Powell Harrison represented Augusta County.

J. A. WADDELL, *Annals of Augusta*, p. 519.

"The white Radicals are a motley crew, some with little more intelligence than the Negroes. They come from the lowest ranks of the people. Their leaders, with two or three exceptions, are Northern men who came to Virginia with the Federal army as petty officers, clerks, sutlers, etc. Some are ex-Freedmen's Bureau employees out of employment. They are now jubilant to receive eight dollars per day from the State Treasury; and happy in anticipation of the fat offices they will get by the same votes which sent them to the Convention.

" 'Dr. Bayne' would not hesitate to take a seat on the Court of Appeals." He takes a prominent part in all discussions. Small of stature, as black as an African could be, he was born a slave, escaped as a boy to Boston where he learned dentistry. He makes his home in Norfolk, which he now "represents." One of his speeches was reported, as follows:[3]

"The cullud race, Mr. Presi-dent, hab allus been leaders in all de gret rebolutions of history. And dey do say dat it was de black man what druv Jeff Davis out of dis here Richmond. Certun it is dat a negro, so-called, led . . . now he didn't follow, you mind dat . . . now he led de attack on de British sodjers on State Street, dat's in Boston whur I come frum. Dis was de beginnin' of de Rebolution, and ef dat black man haddent led de white men on ta victory, I specs dat dere wouldn't hav been no Rebolution-war, and you would all be still a-groanin' under de British yoke."

---

[3] *Norfolk Journal,* January 13, 1868.

A neighbor of "Dr. Bayne," William Hodges of Princess Anne County, familiarly known as "Specs," wore a great shock of gray hair and ornamented his nose with huge silver-rimmed spectacles. "Specs" was a native Virginian who lived for a time in New York. He had a great way of removing his shoes and propping his enormous feet on his desk. His attitude always suggested comfort and complacency.[4]

One of the ablest delegates was a Negro lawyer from Richmond, Lewis Lindsey, whom John S. Wise said was originally one of John Minor Botts' slaves.

Judge John C. Underwood,[5] the president, was decidedly the most influential member of the body. So marked was his influence that Virginians to this day refer to the assembly as the "Underwood Convention," and to its product as the "Underwood Constitution."

John Sergeant Wise, who knew him well, if not favorably, has drawn his portrait.

A fantastic, aged, feeble, frail, cadaverous, round

---

[4]It is interesting to note that under the Sherman-Shellabarger Bill the negro was given the right to vote on the vexed question of the negroes' right to vote!—w. e. woodward, *Meet General Grant*, p. 377.

[5]william asbury christian, *History of Richmond*, p. 309, says of Underwood:

"There was one judge in Richmond whom the most daring would not accuse of any delicacy of feeling nor consideration. Few would be so rash as to charge him with being afflicted with any sense of justice. There had been a big swindle of the United States government revenue stamps by some carpet-baggers. When the case was called Underwood renewed his abuse of Richmond to his own evident delight and the disgust of the people." Many recalled the words of the great John Marshall: "The worst curse with which an angry God can afflict a people is a vicious, venal or corrupt judiciary."

shouldered, old man with long snaky hair and beard always untrimmed, a voice weak and drawling, to which the members for the most part paid no heed. He represented (or mis-represented) Richmond, and was fond of likening himself to Chief Justice John Marshall who represented Richmond in the first two Constitutional Conventions.

This anomaly called forth a protest from John Reuben Thompson:[6]

> "Virginia, how sad is thy case!
>   How degraded thy judgments impartial,
>   When Underwood sits in the place
>   That once was adorned by a Marshall!
>   We say it with reason that Fate
>   Was cruel, if not undiscerning,
>   To give Knavery, Pedantry, Hate
>   For Goodness and Wisdom and Learning."

Underwood was a contribution from New York. President Lincoln appointed him United States District Judge at Alexandria, and he never made a worse appointment; one that does his memory no honor. It is to hope that "Honest Abe" did not know him.

The Virginians prefer to remember President Lincoln for his many superior, generous and excellent qualities; but with his head of gold were feet of iron and miry clay.

Judge George L. Christian[7] once wrote: "We would fail to do justice if we omitted a passing notice of Judge John C. Underwood, and the ignoble and contemptible part played by him. He fled the

---

[6] *Land of Decision*, squires, p. 245.
[7] *Through Centuries Three*, squires, p. 512.

city, too cowardly to remain, and his conduct was
in keeping with his whole judicial career. We say
without fear of contradiction that if Abraham
Lincoln had done nothing else to discredit him as a
man, the nomination of such a creature as Underwood and his approval of the act creating West
Virginia, establish his unfitness for his office."

Dr. Lyon G. Tyler[8] pays his tribute to Underwood:
"He was bitterly denounced in the South on account
of his violent and unbecoming partisanship, and was
forced to defend suits brought against him on account of his decrees sanctioning confiscation."

The Richmond Enquirer (November 7, 1865) has
this item: "Judge Nutt's farm near Alexandria,
and Dr. Bowen's farm, sold by decree of Judge John
C. Underwood, are to be delivered up to Judge Underwood, Governor Pierpont and Mr. Downey, the
purchasers under the confiscation sale. It now appears that the principal properties sold under Judge
Underwood's decrees in and around Alexandria were
purchased by himself[9] and those connected with
him in the high position he holds at a fractional
part of their value.

"Rumor says, and I have not heard it doubted,
that Judge Underwood during the rebellion obtained
permission to raise a regiment of Negroes in Alexandria, which he succeeded in getting at a low price,
which regiment he turned over to one of the Northern

---

[8] *Cyclop. of Virginia Biography*, Vol. III. See p. 259.

[9] AESCHYLUS wrote five centuries before Christ: "Whether one sit or
walk or lie at ease, unseen and voiceless, Justice dogs his steps, striking athwart
his path from right or left nor what is foully done doth night conceal, whate'er
thou doest some god beholdeth thee." If true of a layman how much more
true of a judge upon the bench!

FOREST, SAND AND SHORE

"The prospect now before Virginia was dark, indeed. But Nature was kind, if man was cruel. From turmoil and strife the Virginian might turn to the peace of the forested slope where long shadows fell softly from the lofty fringe of the pines, and lengthened with the slowly setting sun. Perhaps a thrush in the thicket lifted a flute note of cheer. Perhaps the waves that lapped the selvage of yellow sand and broke with a murmur reminded him that many a fierce storm had beaten these shores and torn across the woodland, but after every storm there is peace."—Page 300.

Photo by H. C. Mann

States at a large advance, thereby realizing a large
sum of money with which he has been buying up
the property confiscated by himself[10] under his own
decree, in fee simple."

Judge Underwood cultivated a smooth and gentle
manner, the amiable smile and puritanic humility
of Uriah Heep. He suggests the familiar quotation,
"as mild-mannered a man as ever scuttled a ship."

Like Thaddeus Stevens, Underwood demanded
the confiscation of the rebels' property. He evidently believed that every Virginian was a conscienceless tyrant, and the Negro a downtrodden
brother. It was his God-given duty to humiliate
the rich and elevate the poor. It need hardly be
said that the Virginians loathed him and still shudder
at his name.

There were some men of character on the floor of
the Convention.[11]   Among the Radicals Judge Edward K. Snead, of Accomac, whom Dr. Eckenrode
calls the ablest debater in the Radical camp, was a
man of reasonable and moderate opinions.   General
Edgar Allan, Chief of the Union League in Virginia;
Charles H. Porter, who was born and died in Cairo,
New York (1833-1897), whom Norfolk sent twice to
Congress (1869-1873); John Hawxhurst, of Fairfax
County; David B. White, a tall man with eyes that
suggested a rat as he looked from a thickly-bearded
countenance; Major Orrin E. Hine, a staunch Union
army officer who bought a farm in Fairfax County

---

[10]The instance of the McVeigh property in Alexandria has previously been
cited.

[11]JOHN SERGEANT WISE, *The Lion's Skin*, pp. 210-217.
An account and description of the Convention.

and evidently intended to make Virginia his home, were among them. Hine's word was respected and his opinions carried weight. The Major was a man of stern convictions and force. So determined was he to disfranchise all "rebels" that he drew a rebuke from the administration leaders at Washington. An influential Northern editor[12] said:

"The most prominent advocate of hatred, race-equality and white subversion was an ex-preacher from South Carolina, James W. Hunnicutt, who is now editing a paper for the Radicals in Richmond, 'The New Nation.' Logic and consistency do not disturb Brother James. Once he owned slaves. He had voted for secession. He deserted the army, it is claimed. Now his influence is most dangerous in Virginia. When the rioting, hungry, idle, ambitious Negroes were loafing about the saloons and infecting the countryside, it was he who cried, 'There is corn and wheat, flour and bacon, turkeys, chickens, wood and coal in the State. The colored people will have them before they starve'."

This statesman, clergyman, editor and orator was also aged, also bearded, also active and also influential. It was his ambition to vault into the gubernatorial chair. From that crowning calamity a kind Heaven preserved the Commonwealth.

---

[12] *New York World*, January 2, 1868.

CHAPTER XXX

THE CONVENTION ADJOURNS

They mix the fire of the moral sentiment with personal and party heats, with measureless exaggerations, with the blindness that prefers some darling measure to justice and truth.
—*Ralph Waldo Emerson.*

A small but determined group of Conservatives fought the Radical majority with the ferocity of tigers. They knew, though hopelessly outnumbered, that upon their shoulders rested an immense responsibility. They blocked the Radical majority at every turn. A statesman[1] paid them this tribute, well-deserved:

"These young men fought a good fight, but found themselves powerless to resist the torrent of malignity and radicalism which swept everything before it."

The Commonwealth owes them an eternal debt of gratitude. Unfortunately they lacked experience and legislative skill. Perhaps they answered their antagonists too often; and talked, at times, when silence might have been better. It has been said that they injured their cause by impulsiveness and imprudence; but they surely had great provocation. They struggled to preserve Anglo-Saxon civilization, and used every device to irritate, confuse and rout

[1] ALEXANDER H. H. STUART.

their opponents. Sometimes they patronized the freedmen; sometimes they appealed to their better instincts; and sometimes berated them.

Their chief strategy was to divide the Radicals against themselves. Throwing their votes now this way and now that, they blocked their agenda.

They attended each meeting fully armed, prepared for whatever might happen. If they died, they would die like men. Fortunately, the riot of a Convention never came to bloodshed, although at times it seemed imminent.

The most aggressive and vigilant leaders were John Lawrence Marye, Jr., born in Fredericksburg (1823), a successful lawyer, who served in the State Legislature (1863-65). He later became Lieutenant-Governor of Virginia (1870-73). His career ended, 1902, as one of the most popular leaders in Virginia. With him were James C. Southall (1827-97), of Charlottesville, an able editor, educator and author; Eustace Gibson, of Giles County; the Reverend Norval Wilson, of Frederick; James M. French, of Tazewell and Bland; J. C. Gibson, of Fauquier; William H. Robertson, of Nottoway, and Jacob N. Liggett, of Rockingham.

II

The Constitutional Convention had a visitor, January 14, 1868, who was very much at home in this ill-assorted mob of constitution-makers, the notorious Benjamin Franklin Butler.

When a motion to hear General Butler was made, such strenuous and determined objection was offered

by the Conservatives that a near-riot ensued. Points
of order, personal privilege, motions to adjourn, all
manner of amendments were hurled at the Chair,
but were laid aside. Even after General Butler
entered the hall there was violent opposition. Five
closely-printed pages[2] are given to the story of the
General's reception. Had the General been a gentleman, he would not have pressed his pompous person
on a minority so antagonistic.

He gave the Convention at least one item of wise
counsel. He advised them to follow the old Constitution of 1850, and build upon it. For that we are
willing to applaud him.

He urged that all Negroes be allowed to vote, and
that all Confederate soldiers or sympathizers, officeholders, Confederate or State, bankers, merchants,
railway executives; in short, all men with white
skins (except of course recent arrivals from the
North) be disfranchised.

The General had very advanced ideas on taxation.
The arrogant and aristocratic landowners should be
taxed until their backs were broken, and all incomes
of more than $1,000 should be taxed. As few whom
he addressed had either land or incomes the General
was heard with applause. But the poll taxes should
be lowered so that the very poorest might vote!
The General indulged now in unfathomable vague-
ness, now in rodomontade. His address makes
difficult reading.

Judge Underwood wanted all Negroes to vote,
and all women except, of course, those who had in
any way aided the Confederacy.

[2]Proceedings of the Constitutional Convention of 1867-1868.

Governor Pierpont and General Schofield frowned upon such extreme Radicalism. The longer they lived in Richmond, the more conservative they became. Then, too, the Northern press was watching and reporting. The Conservative Republicans, the Johnson followers, and the Northern Democrats, cried aloud at these Richmond outrages. The war had been over now three years and the desire for peace and amity was widespread.

Perhaps the most wholesome influence, which sought to reunite our distracted country, was the plodding, silent but influential business man. It is notorious that politicians defer to business, great or small. The business interests of the North demanded peace, fraternity and good-will. Insurance companies were doing an immense business in all parts of the reviving South. Manufacturers had countless millions at stake. Wholesale merchants were seeking new markets. There was not a train, boat, or road into the South without these missionaries of business, penetrating even the most sequestered corners. Their reports, their letters and especially their order-blanks, demanded peace. They knew that the South had been libelled, that the bloody-shirt had been waved too relentlessly. Like General Grant, business cried "Let us have peace."

III

No one can tell how long the amateur constitution-makers would have lingered at their agreeable task had not General Schofield forced a cloture. He gave notice that no bills would be paid after April 6.

The patriots were drawing eight dollars the day from the treasury of this State to recompense them for their arduous labors, but when the funds ceased, their altruistic efforts for the Commonwealth also ceased.

General Schofield visited the Convention and addressed them before adjournment. He insisted that the paragraph disfranchising practically the entire white population of the State, the tax-payers and the citizens of education and culture, be stricken out. Also he thought it unjust that no "rebels" be allowed to hold office if their constituents chose to elect them.

This appeal to the justice and wisdom of the Convention was useless. As soon as the General's back was turned, the Radicals denounced him for his intrusion and interference. Bayne and Lindsey were especially emphatic and offensive in their remarks. Dr. Bayne said:[3]

"I ain't gwine ter be timidated by no gineral. Dat would be a pretty thing to go home an say dat dis here Convention was skeered of a gineral."

It happened that there were visitors present at the time, men of culture and education from the North. They were amazed that the Congress of the United States forced such humiliation upon a proud people in the name of "a Republican form of government."[4]

---

[3] *Norfolk Journal*, April 20, 1868.

[4] WILLIAM ARCHIBALD DUNNING, *Essays*, p. 143.

The generals and armies were sent into the South "to protect all persons in their rights of person and property." This quotation is from the Reconstruction Act of March 2, 1867.

"The black speakers scold and hector their white associates, whom they suspect of an indisposition to toe the mark. Some of the latter cower and cajole to conciliate them. Other white men are evidently restive.

"It seems incredible that this should occur in Virginia—full-blooded cornfield Negroes as grossly ignorant, superstitious and bestial as their contemporaries in Hayti and Dahomey."

Twenty-five Negroes, recently slaves, sitting in the midst of forty-five white men, on a footing of political (if not social) equality, taking a verbose share in all discussions. Of the whites only fourteen were scalawags, native Virginians, the others were unsavory adventurers from the ends of the earth . . . and behind them, from first to last, was the gleam of Federal bayonets. The Congress of the United States was responsible, cowering under the lashing tongue and obedient to the will of Thaddeus Stevens. It was impossible, but true!

Of the freedmen Schofield wrote Grant: "They can neither read nor write; they have no knowledge of law or government; they do not even know the meaning of the freedom already given them."

The Conservative members of the Convention issued an address to the people three days after adjournment (April 20); one paragraph reads:

"The convention organized by electing a New Yorker (the despised John C. Underwood) president. A native of Maryland (George Rye) secretary. An Irishman, resident of Baltimore, was elected stenographer. The assistant clerk was from New Jersey.

GILBERT CARLTON WALKER
Provisional Governor, 1869-'70
Governor of Virginia, 1870-'74

An engaging Personality,
An handsome Physiognomy,
An Apollo in Form and Physique,
A Beau Brummel, a Chesterfield,
A Colonel, U. S. A.,
A delightful Carpet-bagger,
A fine Campaigner,
A fluent Speaker,
But not a Saint.
Had he the intellect of Mahone
Or the character of Stuart.
No heights had been to high for him
Even with his short-comings,
Many and conspicuous.
He aspired to the Vice-Presidential
Nomination with Sam'l J. Tilden
But aspired in vain.

—Chapter XXXIX.

Two Negroes were appointed chaplains. Even the boys appointed as pages, with one exception, were Negroes or sons of Northern men or foreigners. The clerks of the twenty standing committees, with two or three exceptions, were also Northern men or Negroes."

Alexander H. H. Stuart has aptly described the Convention in one sentence: "The Convention was mainly composed of ignorant and excited Negroes, led by greedy adventurers from the North, popularly-known as 'carpet-baggers' and a few recreant natives designated 'scalawags'." He said also, "The publication of this monstrous instrument filled the public mind with horror and dismay."

The editor of one of the boldest papers[5] in the entire South, came to the front with this editorial:

"We do not intend to mollify Radical wrath by a base surrender of the cause of Virginia. We will cling to her in her fallen fortunes with the love of loves. We will turn upon her enemies with the hate of hates. There are crises in human affairs when whosoever would save his life shall lose it."

This was a true reflex of the Virginia spirit; and a prophecy, though the courageous editor did not then realize it. Nothing could be further from the truth than the statement sometimes made that during Reconstruction the Virginians "lost their morale." Everything else was lost except that invincible spirit which has never forsaken the Virginians in the three centuries of their varied history.

[5] *Petersburg Index.*

IV

The Constitution was cumbersome and unbalanced. Some of its provisions were impossible. Many were quietly changed from time to time. It instituted a public school system modelled after those of New England, which has since become the pride of the Commonwealth. The Negroes insisted upon mixed schools, but failed to carry their contention.

The secret ballot was introduced in place of the ante-bellum method of voting by the human voice.

On the seventeenth day of April in the same room of the same building and sitting in the same seats, seven years after another Convention had adopted the Ordinance of Secession, the Underwood Constitution was adopted (51 pro, 36 contra). A change of eight votes would have defeated the new Constitution. (A change of fifteen votes, seven years before, would have defeated the fatal Ordinance of Secession.)

The Convention fixed June 2, 1868, for an election to accept or reject the document. After the Constitution-makers had adjourned, General Schofield quietly announced that there would be no election June 2. As he was in constant communication with General Grant, now the rising star in the political firmament, and as he was also a friend of Andrew Johnson, the postponement of the election was evidently inspired from Washington.

Despite its origin the Underwood Constitution was on the whole a good constitution. The ignorant constitution-makers had before them the excellent constitution of 1850—Virginia's third. They also had the good constitutions of many other States. After the objectionable features were amended or stricken out, Virginia grew and prospered under the Underwood Constitution until a fifth constitution was proclaimed in 1902.

A learned historian, Frederick Logan Paxson, of Philadelphia, has told the whole story in one line. "Under congressional direction a Negro-Radical Convention made a new Constitution, which was forced upon the people in January, 1870."

CHAPTER XXXI

THE PRESIDENT IMPEACHED

It is but just to say that our intimate acquain-
tance with what he would himself have called the
anfractuosities of his intellect and of his temper
seems only to strenghten our conviction that he was
both a great and a good man.
                    —*Thomas Babbington Macaulay.*[1]

While we have gazed with rapt attention at the
Constitutional Convention, its iniquities and enormities, events potent and ominous were moving to a
culmination at Washington. The hall of the House
of Representatives staged a scene far more wicked
than the hall of the House of Delegates at Richmond.

There is a divine law of retribution. Those who
degrade others are themselves degraded. Those
who persecute others are themselves persecuted.
"With what measure ye mete it shall be measured
unto you again"; an inexorable truth. Tyranny in
the South brought tyranny to the whole nation.

Andrew Johnson was regarded as a Radical leader
—far more Radical than Lincoln. But when the
immense responsibility of the presidency was imposed upon him, he sobered more and more. One
by one he broke with his Radical friends, and one
by one the Radical members of his Cabinet re-

---

[1] Macaulay refers to Samuel Johnson.

signed; but not Edwin M. Stanton, the most vindictive of them all. He remained in office "a spy
upon his chief."

The story of the struggle between Stanton and
Johnson is long; and it shows to what depths of
shame and disgrace the Radicals drove this country.
As a London reporter said, "The United States is
no longer a republic, except in name. Eight million
people are now subjects; but not citizens. Ten
great States are locked out of Congress and the
nation because they failed to secede."

The struggle at Washington between President
Johnson and the rabid Radical conspirators was
intently watched from the right bank of the Potomac.
One historian[2] boldly states that the Radicals of
Wisconsin and Ohio openly asserted that Andrew
Johnson was privy to the assassination of President
Lincoln.

The Virginia Radicals, such as Underwood and
Hunnicutt, hated and berated Johnson, but the
Virginians sympathized with him. They felt that
he suffered for them. Andrew Johnson was never
really popular in Virginia, but he was respected.

After three years of bitter struggle, President
Johnson removed Secretary Stanton (February 21,
1868) and appointed Lorenzo Thomas, Secretary of
War. The Senate immediately passed a resolution
that the President had no such authority. Meanwhile the wily Secretary barricaded himself in his
office after the manner of a Mexican insurgent. To
such disgrace had the United States descended!

---

[2]HOWARD K. BEALE, *Critical Year*, p. 361.

Two years had passed since President Johnson made his sensational speech against the Radicals, naming Stevens, Sumner and Phillips to an angry crowd. Thaddeus Stevens, aged, cadaverous, trembling with malice, rage and suppressed excitement, his eyes agleam with hatred, offered a resolution "That Andrew Johnson, President of the United States, be impeached of high crimes and misdemeanors," which was carried (February 24) by a strictly party vote. All the Democrats and two conservative Republicans voting in the negative. (126 pro, 47 contra.)

One week later (February 29) a committee from the House, Thaddeus Stevens, chairman, presented to the Senate nine articles of impeachment.

Managers were appointed to proceed with the trial, a memorable roll of dishonor: Thaddeus Stevens, Benjamin F. Butler, John A. Bingham, George S. Boutwell, James F. Wilson, Thomas Williams and John A. Logan.

Chief Justice Salmon P. Chase took the bench in the Senate chamber (March 5) and summoned President Andrew Johnson to appear. He appeared by counsel and asked forty days to prepare his defense—ten were granted.

The President's counsel presented an able defense (March 23) and the Senate—which in such cases is the jury—adjourned until March 30. For a month many witnesses were examined, and then arguments for impeachment began (April 22).

The chance of the President to escape the vindictive Radical persecution seemed slight. Secretary Gideon Welles wrote in his diary (March 14, 1868): "It is evident that the Radicals in Congress are in a conspiracy to overthrow not only the President but the Government. . . . I have very little expectation that the President will escape conviction. His deposition is a party necessity, and the Senators have not individually the strength, ability nor honesty to resist the Radical caucus decision, which Stevens, Ben Butler and other chief conspirators sent out."

The case was closed May 6, and the decision rendered twenty days later. The most notorious criminal has the right to be tried by an impartial and disinterested jury . . . not so the President of the United States! He was tried and the verdict rendered by a jury fiercely hostile to him and his policies. Not one Senator who voted for or against the President could have taken oath that his judgment was free from bias and unprejudiced.

Thirty-five Senators, Republicans all, voted to impeach the Republican President, and nineteen voted to acquit. Seven Republican Senators, to their everlasting honor be it said, bolted their party associates and voted to sustain the President.

Fessenden of Maine, Fowler of Tennessee, Henderson of Missouri, Grimes of Iowa, Ross of Kansas, Trumbull of Illinois, and Van Winkle of West Virginia. It is also claimed that two others were prepared to change their vote, if it were necessary to secure an acquittal—Sprague of Rhode Island and Willey of West Virginia.

A change of one vote would have reduced our

country to the verge of anarchy. To such depths of misery had Radical politicians brought this nation! The first vote was taken[3] May 16, the second and third May 26.

II

The trial was, of course, from first to last, political blackmail.[4] And this was the last and the crowning ignominy in the career of Thaddeus Stevens. Since the fall of Lincoln he had swept all before him, and dominated the country. Now, at last, thank God, his bolt was shot. The impeachment of Johnson and the confiscation of the "rebels'" property were the two policies upon which he had set his heart . . . in both he failed. He made one other pathetically feeble attempt. On July 7 he introduced[5] five additional articles of impeachment.

Death grappled with him and won. With his faithful Negro housekeeper, Lydia Smith, standing beside him, he passed from this world August 11,

---

[3] WILLIAM A. DUNNING, *Reconstruction*, p. 106.

[4] WILLIAM HENRY ELSOM, *History of the United States*, p. 776.

When Benjamin Franklin Wade, senator from Cleveland, Ohio, voted against the President, he voted to seat himself in the Executive Chair by political fraud and blackmail. The audacity of such political effrontery sounded his political death. The people never forgave him that iniquity.

Senator Lyman Trumbull of Illinois in a fine and reasonable argument (which may be read *verbatim* in SAMUEL EAGLE FORMAN'S, *Our Republic*, p. 523) declared that President Johnson "had violated no law and it has not been shown that he violated the Constitution."

[5] SAMUEL W. MC CALL, *Life of Stevens*, p. 349.

This biography is a brave but futile effort to present an impossible character. The *New York Herald* (March 14, 1868): "The country is in the hands of Congress. That Congress is the Radical majority, and that Radical majority is old Thad. Stevens. Government by the people has its glories!"

1868. She prepared him for burial and he was laid in a Lancaster cemetery, where Negroes were buried. He declined to lie in the city's cemetery because the rules would not permit Negroes to be there interred.

And there beside the dust of his humble friends we leave him. Posterity has taken the measure of the man, and may God have mercy on his soul. Walter Lippmann, writing as late as 1932, referred to those who had inherited the implacable hatred and evil genius of Thaddeus Stevens, such is his place in history.

On May 26, three years to the day that the last Confederate soldiers furled their flag,[6] Secretary Edwin M. Stanton unbarricaded himself, and stepped down from his office into the mists of political oblivion. His race, too, was run. That he served his country well, no one doubts. That he had an immense capacity for hatred and evidently none for tolerance, forgiveness nor brotherly love, his most ardent and partisan admirers must admit.

President Johnson immediately appointed the Virginia satrap, John McAllister Schofield, Secretary of War. The General left Richmond with the blessings of Virginia upon him. Under the Reconstruction monstrosity, called law, he might have been a tyrant of the worst type; as it was, his tact, sympathy, generosity and saving common sense were a benison Virginia will never forget.

[6]The father of the writer lowered the last Confederate flag on land, at sunset May 26, '65, in Navarro County, Texas, and so far as the records are written this was the last flag that floated to the breeze on land—there was a number still at the mast-heads of ships at sea.

III

Under the Constitution of Virginia, Governor Pierpont's term ended January 1, 1868, as it was supposed to have begun January 1, 1864 . . . but we had no Constitution and there was no Virginia in Reconstruction times. To the Fortieth Congress, Constitutions, National and State, were mere scraps of paper. And so Governor Pierpont continued to be "Governor of Virginia," until summarily removed, April 4, 1868. At that time, the Underwood Convention was still sitting in Richmond, and the impeachment was in progress at Washington. Henry Horatio Wells was appointed Governor by General Schofield (as has always been supposed, but never proved) at the instance of Senator Zachariah Chandler of Michigan, a rabid Radical.

Virginia has had executives for three hundred and fifty years, men of every conceivable character, temperament and ability, or lack of it, but when General Schofield named Wells he gave this Commonwealth the worst Governor in our history, not even excepting Lord Howard of Effingham. But as bad an appointee as Henry Horatio Wells was, he was better than James W. Hunnicutt or John Hawxhurst, both of whom had gubernatorial ambitions. And General Schofield (it is our guess) appointed Horatio to the gubernatorial chair to save the State from James and John. A Radical it must be, so matters might have been worse; and with this enthusiastic endorsement, let Horatio enter.

Meet the new Governor as he takes a seat occupied by mighty men[7] before his day and since.

He was born forty-five years before (September 17, 1823) in Rochester, New York, but moved to the new State of Michigan to practice law. His neighbors in Detroit sent him to the State Legislature for a term (1854-'56). When war began, Horatio became a colonel of the 26th Michigan Infantry; and, after three years of service, a brigadier. His opportunity came when as provost-marshal south of the Potomac, John Wilkes Booth was captured. That, at least, gave him publicity. His military record is not one of glory.

He evidently considered his opportunities better in the poverty-stricken city of Richmond than in the prosperous metropolis of Michigan. So he practiced law in Virginia until appointed, April 4, 1868.

"As soon as Wells entered upon the duties of his office, he declared all the offices of the State vacant; and the State, county and municipal officers, including the judges, were expelled. The vacancies were filled rapidly by carpet-baggers and scalawags."[8]

It was a thrifty beginning for the adventurer from Detroit. Woodrow Wilson[9] once wrote that to secure rich prizes in the South all laws and the Constitution were trampled under foot.

[7]*Land of Decision*, SQUIRES, Chapter IX.
Through Centuries Three, SQUIRES, Chapter CXII.
R. A. BROCK, *Eminent Virginians*, p. 390.
[8]W. C. PENDLETON, *History of Southwestern Virginia*.
[9]WOODROW WILSON, *History of the United States*, Vol. V, p. 53.

If the masters at Washington did not hesitate at large grafting, why should Horatio, a modest servant, hesitate to pluck the poor prizes at Richmond?

IV

The prospect was never darker for Virginia than when the lilacs bloomed in the dooryards three years after the surrender.[10] With such a Governor as Henry Horatio Wells and such a Constitution as the Underwood Convention framed, with the only friend the South seemed to have in Washington defending himself against impeachment[11] by an overwhelming Radical majority, with the other nine States south and southwest in worse case even than Virginia, the patriotic Virginians felt that hope was dead. Yet events were moving to a consummation more rapidly than they guessed.[12] The sun of a brilliant day was still below a dark horizon, but the star dials pointed to dawn.

---

[10]THOS. P. ABERNATHY, *Francis Harrison Pierpont, Dict. Amer. Biog.*
[11]ST. GEORGE L. SIOUSSET, *Andrew Johnson, Dict. Amer. Biog.*
[12]A. HOWARD MENEELEY, *Edwin M. Stanton, Dict. Amer. Biog.*

CHAPTER XXXII

MIDSUMMER MADNESS

Villainy, when detected, never gives up but boldly
adds impudence to imposture.
—*Oliver Goldsmith.*

No one knew when an election might be called in
Virginia to adopt the monstrous Underwood Consti-
tution, elect a governor, congressmen and a legisla-
ture. The people were now slowly gathering into
two political camps—Radicals and Conservatives.
The Conservatives made the first gesture. The
State executive committee on April 17 (the day the
Underwood Convention adjourned, and the seventh
anniversary of the Ordinance of Secession) called a
Convention[1] which met May 10.

Colonel Robert E. Withers, of Wytheville, was
nominated for Governor. General James A. Walker,
of Stonewall Jackson's staff, Lieutenant Governor,
and John L. Marye, Jr., of Fredericksburg, Attorney
General. It was a small convention, only eighty-
four attended. They wisely adopted no platform.

The Radicals met in Richmond, May 6, James H.
Clements, of Portsmouth, presiding, and nominated
the new Governor, Henry Horatio Wells, for Governor to succeed himself. He secured 153 votes;
Hawxhurst 45; Hunnicutt 11, and Pierpont 6. The

---

[1] *Annual Cyclop*, for 1868.

figures are interesting for they show how completely the influence of Hunnicutt had waned . . . and also, as we fancy, the potency of the General's wishes. If General Schofield (in touch with Washington) wishes Wells, then Wells let it be . . . and it was. J. H. Clements was nominated for Lieutenant Governor, and G. W. Booker, Attorney General.

The same day (May 6) General Schofield quietly removed Honorable Joseph Mayo, who for fifteen years had been mayor of Richmond, and appointed George Chahoon. No explanation has ever been made. The appointment was not well received.

Ten days later General Schofield reported to General Grant (May 15), "I have already appointed five hundred officers and would have appointed more, but qualified persons could not be found."

The National Republican Convention met at Chicago while the disgraceful impeachment was dragging its scandal like the coils of a venomous serpent through the Senate chamber. It did not sound well—a Republican President being blackmailed by a Republican House before a Republican Senate. It was a foregone conclusion that General Grant would receive the nomination although he was an ante-bellum Democrat. He was unanimously nominated on the first ballot, May 20, 1868.

General Grant became on the instant the most influential citizen, the leader of a reunited and dominant party. All men turned to greet the "rising sun."

The South was gratified. The great soldier had been courteous, even generous to Lee. He often plead for peace. He sympathized with the South. He (or his wife) had owned slaves. A letter from Grant, written three years before, pleased the Virginians. It read:

"The action of Judge Underwood in Norfolk has already had an injurious effect and I would ask that he be ordered to quash all indictments against paroled prisoners of war and desist from further prosecution of them." (1865.)

In a letter accepting the nomination (May 29) General Grant used the phrase, which he made famous, "Let us have peace." That was the one great desire of all Southern hearts. But Southern hearts trembled when the suave Schuyler Colfax, Speaker of the House, a friend of Thaddeus Stevens (if that misanthrope ever had a friend) and a well known Radical, was nominated as Vice-President.

And Southern hearts sank in despair when the platform was adopted, with a Radical plank declaring for universal suffrage. No one doubted the sweeping success of the Republican ticket. From Negro suffrage there now seemed no way of escape. A Radical minority by close organization and persistence, worthy better men in a better cause, controlled the huge majority in the Republican ranks. It is an interesting sidelight on the inconsistency of human nature, especially political human nature, that the Republican platform[4] contained this line, "Sympathy for the oppressed of all nations." That did not mean they had any sympathy for the out-

---

[4]The platform was "hazy and meaningless." The only emphatic pronouncement it made was that Andrew Johnson was a scoundrel, altho that word was not used.

W. E. WOODWARD, *Meet General Grant*, p. 396.

rageously oppressed people who inhabited one-third
of the territory of the United States and whose
brain, blood and brawn had made America a nation.
But let that pass. No political platform is to be
taken too seriously. A platform is for candidates
to stand on until elected, then let the platform and
its promises go to the Devil, where it probably belongs.

II

With the first day of June General George Stoneman[5] came to Richmond as Virginia's satrap. The
new General never achieved the popularity of his
predecessor. He remained only nine months, but
that was long enough (June 1, 1868-March 5, 1869).

Governor Wells and his close friend, Judge H. C.
Bond, of Richmond, reasoned (and reasoned correctly) that the sooner the election was held, the
easier it would be for the Radicals to get the Underwood Constitution adopted. Congress would soon
adjourn. The nation and the patient Northern
press were becoming ever more disgusted with the
Radical program at Washington and in the South.
In Virginia the Virginians were becoming ever more
alert. The Conservatives were well organized, and
seeking votes. The Ku Klux Klan was riding—
with remarkably quieting effect upon the Union
Leagues.

Taking advantage of General Schofield's departure
and Stoneman's arrival, Governor Wells and Judge

---

[5]OLIVER L. SPAULDING, JR., *Dictionary of American Biography*, Vol. XVIII.
George Stoneman (1822-1894), Democratic Governor of California (1883-1887).
No mention of his Virginia sojourn, which adds nothing to his credit.

Bond visited the Committee of Fifteen and urged an immediate election in Virginia; and they also wanted funds. They did not want any more registration, but the voting should be confined to the books made up in 1867. The Radicals had reason to fear the effect of President Johnson's recent proclamation of General Amnesty, under which he granted full and unconditional pardon, after July 4, 1868, to all who had participated in "the late rebellion," except such as were under indictment or presentation for treason or felony, etc.

Manifestly great multitudes, who could not and would not take the iron-clad oath, might henceforth exercise the rights of citizens unmolested.

The Reconstruction Committee was sympathetic to the Radical appeal and set August 13-15 for the election. But they insisted that new registration be allowed, as just, proper and fair.

III

Governor Wells hastened to Washington to protest the opening of the books, but he overdid his cause. James Burnie Beck, of Kentucky, came to the aid of Virginia at this crisis. This canny Scot was elected from Kentucky to the House in 1865. He made a scathing address which turned even the Radical House against Wells and Bond.

"The real object of those who manipulated this bill is to put all power into the hands of a few ultra-Radical leaders, and to deprive the rights of suffrage to 25,000 white men in Virginia. The present Governor of Virginia, General Wells, wanted a liberal

appropriation to carry on the election. He wanted
no further registration, because, he said, there were
25,000 white men entitled to register and vote; and
if they registered they would carry the State against
the Republican party."[6]

The one hope of the Virginians lay now in the
Democratic party—the "Copperheads," as they
were contemptuously called. Though thoroughly
discredited by the War Between the States, and dis-
organized, the Democrats were a mighty host. The
border States, New Jersey, New York City, with
its teeming population, and such doubtful States as
Indiana, Connecticut and California might be captured. The situation before the Democrats in 1868
was less discouraging than it had been since the
Breckenridge-Douglas split of 1860.

Sober people of second thought were absolutely
disgusted with the spectacle presented at Washington and were ready to rebuke the Radicals. Countless thousands of true Republicans like W. H.
Seward and Horace Greeley were anxious to put an
end to the orgies at the national capital and throughout the South. The Radicals swung too far. Stevens, Sumner and Stanton overdid their part. The
"best government on earth" (1860) had become the
"worst government on earth."

IV

The Democrats had a better chance than they
guessed. Had they selected a strong standard-
bearer, placed him on a platform of honesty, justice

------

[6]Congressional Code, July 24, 1868.

and the Constitution of the United States, and gone to the people with the full truth, they would likely have carried the country in spite of General Grant's popularity.

What the Democrats did was exactly the reverse. The National Democratic Convention met in Tammany Hall, from which a denunciation of extravagance and political iniquity would come with poor grace. They nominated Horatio Seymour, of New York, the weakest candidate ever put before the country. Their campaign was as dilatory, vacillating and inept as their candidate.

Horatio Seymour was rich and aristocratic. As a young man (1833-39), he was military secretary to Governor Marcy. He became mayor of Utica (1842) and pushed the development of the canals which gave New York City such an impetus a century since.

In 1850 the Democrats nominated him Governor, but the Whigs defeated him though by only 262 votes. Two years later he ran against the same Whig, Governor Washington Hunt, and defeated him.

In the trying years preceding the war he was a strict party man supporting Buchanan and Breckenridge. He deplored the war, but was loyal to the Lincoln Government, and was elected Governor in 1862.

He did his utmost to keep the peace during the dreadful draft riots which cost a thousand lives (July 12-17, 1863).

He presided at Tammany Hall, but declared that he was not a candidate, although he allowed himself to be overpersuaded and finally accepted the nomination.

When the votes were counted Seymour carried only eight States (Delaware, Georgia, Kentucky, Louisiana, Maryland, New Jersey, New York and Oregon), which was more than one would have suspected from such a dilatory campaign and such a vacillating candidate. When the popular vote was tabulated the nation was amazed to find that General Grant, with his immense prestige, the huge military vote, the potent organization behind him, and his extravagant campaign chest polled only 3,015,071 votes and that Seymour who lacked all the great General possessed, received 2,709,213 votes. A change of 150,000 votes correctly placed would have brought the Democrats into power! An energetic leader with an organization that functioned even moderately well would have defeated General Grant! Dr. Muzzey points out the extraordinary fact that Grant received 650,000 Negro votes without which Seymour would have been swept into the presidency. The discouraged Democrats were themselves amazed at the result.

In view of such figures one can not understand the statement of Henry Adams:[7] "At least four-fifths of the American people had united in the election of General Grant to the presidency." As a matter of sober fact, the overwhelming majority of Americans (who had white faces) voted against him. He was elected by a slim majority of whites and blacks luckily placed.

---

[7] HENRY ADAMS, *The Education of*, p. 269.

The election of Grant on a Negro suffrage platform meant for Virginia the Fifteenth Amendment. There was no escape. Bitter enders like Henry A. Wise declared for continued military rule. But to what purpose? Military rule under George Stoneman with a puppet governor like Henry Horatio Wells also meant Negro suffrage, as well as white disfranchisement.

There was only one way to save Virginia; and Alexander H. H. Stuart[8] seems to have been the only statesman who had thought the proposition through. Virginia must adopt the XIV and XV Amendments, and the Underwood Constitution; bitter medicine, but necessary since the election of General Grant. Perhaps Congress would permit some changes in the Constitution which would render it less offensive.

Once rid of the Federal General who occupied the "White House of the Confederacy," once readmitted to the Union with two senators and eight congressmen to watch Virginia's interests and speak in her behalf, the people might elect a State government of Caucasians. A series of tactful educational tests "without regard to race or previous condition of servitude" and white supremacy might be secured and ever maintained. Stuart saw the future with the prescience of an Hebrew prophet.

---

[8]THOS. P. ABERNATHY, *Alex. H. H. Stuart, Dict. Amer. Biog.*

Chapter XXXIII

THE END OF A DREADFUL YEAR

And after awhile this trouble went, as nearly all troubles go, with time.
—Richard Doddridge Blackmore.

The hectic year 1868 was drawing to a close. It had been filled with sensations, and every development seemed to portend evil to the prostrate, poverty-stricken, mourning and discouraged South. The impeachment of the President, all but accomplished; the cruel rigors of Reconstruction, the removal of Pierpont and the installation of Wells, the promotion of Schofield and the advent of Stoneman,[1] the Underwood Constitutional Convention and the hybrid product it produced, the complete Radical triumph in the Republican party and the complete disorganization and defeat of the Democrats, every turn of the road presented a prospect more discouraging. No wonder many valuable citizens left this State as an impossible place of residence. The future was dark indeed.

The Fortieth Congress met for its second and final session, December 3. It would adjourn sine die March 4 at the inauguration of General Grant. The Fortieth was the most rabidly radical of all

---

[1] PHILIP ALEX. BRUCE, *Rebirth of the Old Dominion*, Vol. II, pp. 120-123.

Congresses. Its stain upon the page of history is blackest and most shameful. It was elected in the Bloody Shirt Campaign of 1866 and it lived to a consistent if dishonorable end.

To this Congress the Underwood Constitution was reported and from it received official endorsement. No protest was offered when the matter came before the House, December 8.

Alexander H. H. Stuart from his home in Staunton urged the central committee of the recently organized Conservative party to register a vigorous protest against those sections of the Constitution which required test oaths of officeholders, and which disfranchised so many of the best citizens in the State. For some inexplicable reason (never explained by the dilatory statesmen at Richmond) no action was taken.

Perhaps the House of Representatives would have passed the Underwood Constitution, protest or no protest. But the eloquent defense made the preceding summer by Senator James Bernie Beck, of Kentucky, was evidence that the Southern people had some friends in the Capitol and that common honesty and ordinary justice were not completely obsolete in the City of Washington.

In later and happier days Mr. Stuart asked James Brooks of New York (a leader of Conservatives in the House—the same who had protested the omission of the Southern States from the roll-calls in 1865, 1867) why he allowed such an instrument to be passed without protest. He replied, "If the people of Virginia will not attend to their own interests, how can they expect others to do so for them?"

Surely such logic is unanswerable.

Fortunately the crowded agenda of the Senate made consideration of the Underwood Constitution impossible before the Christmas recess. Taking advantage of this opportunity, the "Tribune of Virginia" leaped again to the defense of the State—and he did not wield his sword in vain, as these pages prove.

II

A year had passed since the eight hundred patriots met and organized the Conservative party under the "Tribune's" guiding hand. Many unforeseen changes in State and Nation had taken place. Nothing was now as it had been. But Alexander H. H. Stuart believed that a moderate and reasonable appeal made to the United States Senate against the objectionable features of the Underwood Constitution would be hospitably received . . . he was correct.

He determined to appeal to the people of Virginia through the Richmond press. The compromise he offered was "Universal suffrage and universal amnesty," which when translated into simple English meant—"We will agree to let the freedmen vote, if the Congress will agree to let all the white people vote."

He prepared a letter, really a State document, with great care and deliberation, signing it "Senex," the Old Man. As a friend and neighbor, General John Echols, was going to Richmond, Mr. Stuart entrusted the document to him. At the Exchange

JAMES W. HUNNICUTT

Horace Greeley spoke of "agitators like Mr. Hunnicutt, whose zeal is bitter and abusive."—Pages 225, 251.

"The rebels have forfeited all their rights and we will see that they never get them back."—Page 293.

JUDGE WILLIAM CURTIS UNDERWOOD

"The faithful patriot, whom no flattery could seduce, no bribery corrupt nor fears intimidate."—Radical Resolution, Page 178.

"The greatest curse visited upon Richmond was John C. Underwood."—William A. Christian, Page 306.

"We say without fear of contradiction that if Abraham Lincoln had done nothing else to discredit him, the nomination of such a creature as Underwood and his approval of the act creating West Virginia established his unfitness for his high office.—Geo. L. Christian, Page 308.

Hotel, General Echols met another Old Line Whig, Colonel W. T. Sutherlin, of Danville.

General Echols visited the editor of the Richmond Dispatch and requested the publication of the Senex letter. The editor declined. The General then applied to the editor of the Richmond Whig . . . he also declined. He then appealed to the Enquirer. Here the refusal was so absolute as to be rude.

That evening General Echols recounted his disappointment to Colonel Sutherlin. The Colonel volunteered to go with the General and make a second appeal to Alexander Moseley, editor of the Whig. After long consideration it was decided that the Whig and Dispatch would publish Mr. Stuart's letter on Christmas morning. And it so appeared.

III

The reaction was prompt and unfavorable. Mr. Stuart knew that it would be so. "I knew full well that the simple announcement of the proposed compromise would arouse a storm of fierce indignation throughout the State, and draw a torrent of denunciation and obliquity." He was not deceived. The Richmond Enquirer bitterly opposed the movement, let come what will. A torrent of denunciation came from former Governor Henry A. Wise.

When asked what he thought of Stuart's plan, he cried:

"I think it the basest abandonment of principle in the history of politics. I think it is a living lie! A base hypocrisy! A disgrace to the Confederate living. What would our dead comrades say if they

saw us embracing the Negro as our political equal?
Ah, I hear their reproaches ringing in my ears. I
hear them saying: 'We had the courage to die like
men, but you have not the courage to live like men.'
A little more of endurance, a little more of patient
martyrdom and you would have regained honorable
liberty. You have bartered your birthright for a
mess of Negro-suffrage pottage. You are liars and
hypocrites when you do it. You have out-carpet-
bagged the carpet-baggers. Woe unto a people who
buy peace at the sacrifice of truth and self-respect!
The time will surely come when Virginians will curse
the day they yielded to the unprincipled counsels of
this band of time-servers under the name of Conservatives."

The phillipic makes intensely interesting reading
three generations after date. We suppose that every
close student of history will now agree that wise
Henry A. Wise was not a true prophet when he said
that a little more passive resistance would win Virginia her place in the Union without accepting the
hated XIV and XV Amendments. The National
Republican party demanded it and it was and is the
law to this day (technically, if not really). The
long future has vindicated the strategy of Stuart.
To be sure Stuart was the most influential Old Line
Whig in the State, and Henry A. Wise the most
influential Democrat. They had fought innumerable battles through three generations. It was a
foregone conclusion that Wise would denounce any
suggestion that came from the sage of Staunton.[2]

---

[2] *Through Centuries Three*, SQUIRES, p. 503.

Everyone who read the Senex letters in the Whig and Dispatch recognized Alexander H. H. Stuart. His argument may be succinctly stated as follows:

"Negro suffrage is now inevitable. The Democrats have been completely and hopelessly defeated. General Grant and the Republicans demand and have the power to enforce Negro suffrage, and have decided to do so. We are unanimously opposed to it, as unreasonable and unjust, but it is part of our punishment for the fatal error of secession, war and defeat.

"It is wise to face the facts. The Underwood monstrosity not only gives the vote to Negroes, but it disfranchises practically all the white men of Virginia. This double iniquity is manifestly unjust, unfair and unreasonable.

"An appeal to the better instincts of the North, to the less Radical press and to the more conservative Republicans will likely be heard.

"Many Northern people sympathize with us, and many Republican senators and representatives have never heard our side of this vexed question. Let us agree to enfranchise the freedmen if they will permit the ex-Confederate soldiers and civilians also to vote, 'Universal suffrage and universal amnesty.'

"This proposition must be advanced before the Senate adopts the Underwood Constitution, as the House has already adopted it. It is to remember that the intelligence, wealth and character of any community rule it. If once we secure the control of the State without National interference we can and will take care of future problems as they arise."

IV

Mr. Stuart did not rest with the literary appeal. On Christmas Day a number of public-spirited men met in his office: Thomas J. Mitchie, Judge Hugh W. Sheffey, Nicholas K. Trout, Mayor H. M. Bell, R. H. Catlett and others. They called a conference of leaders from all parts of Virginia to the Exchange Hotel in Richmond December 31.

Twenty-eight political leaders assembled. Mr. Stuart was elected chairman and Christopher C. McRae, of Chesterfield, clerk. A committee was appointed to suggest the wisest method of procedure, namely, George W. Bolling, of Petersburg; Thomas S. Flournoy, of Halifax; John L. Marye, Jr., of Fredericksburg; Daniel C. DeJarnette, of Caroline County; Frank G. Ruffin, of Chesterfield County; B. H. Magruder, of Albemarle County, and James F. Johnston, of Bedford County.

They decided that a committee of nine, Alexander H. H. Stuart, chairman, should visit Washington and in the name of the citizens of Virginia, without reference to party affiliations, enter formal protest against the Underwood Constitution as written. But they were to agree that Virginia would accept the document if certain objectionable articles dealing with disfranchisement and test-oaths were eliminated. They further insisted that, at the very least, in the name of justice, honesty and fair-play, an opportunity should be given the people of the State to express themselves in reference to a matter so vital to them and their civilization. The committee,

famous as "The Committee of Nine," were Alexander
H. H. Stuart, John B. Baldwin, Wyndham Robert-
son, ex-Governor of Virginia; John L. Marye, Jr., of
Fredericksburg; W. T. Sutherlin, of Danville; James
Neeson, of Richmond; James F. Johnston, of Bed-
ford; William L. Owen, of Halifax, and John F.
Slaughter, of Lynchburg.

After the conference adjourned, the members attended a New Year's reception given by General
Stoneman. He received them courteously, expressed
sympathy with their plans, and hoped they would
succeed. Yet of this satrap John B. Baldwin, an
astute and judicious leader, wrote:

"I am afraid of General Stoneman. They say he
has no instructions from Washington, and yet he
goes on to kick and cuff our people as if he were a
very Radical aiming at political objects. Truly we
are fallen on evil times and I fear worse are coming."

There was no time to be lost, so Mr. Stuart called
the nine to Washington, January 8.

These patriots of the "New Movement" came at
their own charges and on their own initiative solely
to serve and save Virginia. Though misunderstood,
maligned and criticized, they pushed their plans to
a splendid conclusion.

They have never received from Virginia the gratitude and appreciation they deserve. All are long
since gone. Passion has subsided. Politics has
become history, but the Patriots of 1869 are still
strangely ignored. Some day perhaps posterity will
acknowledge the debt we owe them, and some
memorial to their courage and superb strategy will

be erected. Theirs was a triumph of peace; for they snatched victory and success from the very jaws of defeat and despair.

When the midnight hour fell, and the chimes rang in a new year, those who heard could not guess that Tennyson's familiar lines were destined to splendid fulfillment in Virginia:

"Ring out the old, ring in the new,
  Ring happy bells across the snow,
  The year is going, let him go,
Ring out the false, ring in the true.

"Ring out false pride in place and blood,
  The civic slander and the spite;
  Ring in the love of truth and right.
Ring in the common love of good.

"Ring in the valiant man and free,
  The larger heart, the kindlier hand;
  Ring out the darkness of the land.
Ring in the Christ that is to be."

CHAPTER XXXIV

TAXED AND TOILING MILLIONS

Of Virginia's first governor, Sir Walter Ralegh,
Robert Cecil, Lord Burleigh, once said: "I know
that he can toil terribly." Like their first Governor
the Virginians learned to "toil terribly."
—*W. H. T. Squires.*

The War Between the States lasted just four
years. The agony of Reconstruction lasted fully
ten years, and the unfortunate reactions which
followed that period of political persecution have
not disappeared after the lapse of seventy years!

The typical Virginian of 1868 was a farmer; who,
after Lee's surrender, lived and labored as a peaceful
citizen. Yet as he watched the affairs of State and
country (and the typical Virginian watched narrowly), he found but little evidence of justice or
of generosity.

Through the long, hot summer days he worked, as
no slave ever toiled, from sun to sun.

A farmer he must be, for the land was all he had,
and farming the only occupation he understood.
Even the land, and his modest home, which he had
inherited from his fathers of colonial days, might
be wrested from him at any time. He knew that
Thaddeus Stevens and thousands of hungry Radicals
were demanding that the land be confiscated, the
"rebels" driven out, and that their hereditary fields

be cut into forty-acre farms and given to the freed-men. Of course, that threat never materialized, but it gave many millions of Southern citizens years of mental anguish, until the death of Honorable Thaddeus Stevens.

Many a Virginian had been wounded. Thousands made their living with one arm, one eye, one leg, or a bullet in their body, and with nerves so shocked that they were never physically normal.

It seemed to them as the years passed slowly that the harder they worked the poorer they got. They were discouraged, wearied in mind and body, taxed to the limit, and humiliated, broken, libelled. On every side they heard it said, and read in countless papers, that the people of the South were ignorant, besotted and lazy;[1] they were naturally rebels and traitors, degenerate sons of a once noble race. In fact, no epithet was too harsh for the Radical orators, statesmen and editors to describe the Southern people. The easiest and cheapest way for the Radicals to gain place and hold power was to fight the rebels over and over again, and sell the slaves countless times on the auction block! Voters North and West must not be allowed to forget what "unrepentant" devils the rebels were. That word "unrepentant" was flung back and forth in Senate and House for twenty years. It was echoed from ocean to ocean by Radical editors.

---

[1]The writer has never understood by what logic the typical Virginian is "lazy." Those who work 40 hours a week will tell you that the Virginian who plows from 6 a. m. until 7 p. m. six days a week is "lazy."

SAND DUNES WHITE AS SNOW

Photo by H. C. Mann

"Every section of Virginia from Cape Henry to Point Pleasant was wrested from the Indians by bloodshed. Upon these sand dunes, as white as the driven snow, the warriors of Powhatan wounded two of the first colonists the first day (April 26, 1607). Not until the surrender of Corn Stalk at Point Pleasant (October 10, 1774) was the land redeemed." —Page 439.

II

In this one item, at least, the Radicals told the truth about the South. We have never heard of a soldier who followed Robert E. Lee being "repentant." One could hardly expect a patriot, who offered his life for constitutional liberty, as he understood it, and for the protection of his home from ruthless invasion to be "repentant."[2] The South has never repented.

All this was in the farmer's mind as he followed the plow through the live-long day. He had no money to buy labor, stock, seed, tools nor fertilizer, so he labored in a few of his fields as best he might and the rest he allowed to grow up in brush and young timber.

It was quite the fashion for twenty years after the war to refer to the Silent South, an unintentional tribute to the superb self-control of our people. Nothing was more useless than to answer the slanders and slanderers. The South had no voice in National affairs, and none even in State or local affairs. The natural leaders of the South were not permitted to vote, much less to hold office. The press of the South had only local patronage. The few voices raised were not heard. The South was silent until Henry Grady, Thomas Nelson Page, Father Ryan, Sidney Lanier, J. Q. C. Lamar and others found a place. Since the eighties the South has produced an ever-increasing number of orators, statesmen, editors, poets, authors and economic and industrial leaders.

---

[2] THOMAS J. WERTENBAKER, *American People*, p. 381.

But in 1868 the South labored and toiled through the silence, which we insist was and is a superb tribute to the self-control of that tortured generation.

The farmer's home was unpainted; the roof probably leaked; the plaster, and maybe the porches, were falling; the fences were down or merely patched; many fertile fields were growing up in briars; the roads were impassable; the live stock scrawny and poor.

The farmer's wife, often reared in luxury, labored now as hard as he. Far into the night she stitched by the light of a tallow dip. There was plenty to eat; and when that is said, all is said.

The children had little chance for education, but mothers, aunts and neighbors taught them. Often twenty or thirty neighbors would unite to hire a tutor and give her a home and board with a salary of perhaps $100 for the year's work.

Once a month there was preaching, and once a year a big revival meeting. The clergy took what they were paid and made no complaint. A cultured Presbyterian divine once said to the writer: "After the war I preached at a church for a year and they paid me $50 and a pair of socks . . . but I was happy in the work."[3]

On court day, the farmer would hitch the mules to a wagon and drive to town. Maybe his wife would go with him, and maybe the children, too, not leaving the baby . . . and there always was a baby. The thrifty woman probably had eggs, chickens and butter, maybe pickles and jellies to sell. The mer-

---

[3]REVEREND ROBERT GRAY, of Abingdon Presbytery, in Virginia.

chant looked over the work of her tired hands and remarked casually that eggs "are worth eight cents a dozen, chickens two-bits apiece, and butter a shilling a pound." He would also probably remark that he had more country truck than he could sell, but he would take it as a favor to her, if she would "take it out" in trade.

The Virginia shilling was 16 2-3 cents, the York shilling (sometimes called the York State shilling) was 12½ cents, which was also the value of the "bit" (the Spanish real, a long-time survival of Spain's vast American Colonial Empire).

Whiskey flowed freely, and the temptation to drown one's troubles in alcoholic stimulants was ever present and often too acute to be successfully resisted.

Miss Ellen Glasgow, the dean of America's literary artists, has, in her exquisite novels, drawn many an accurate picture of Virginia rural life. John Fox, Jr., has done the same for the mountaineers of the extreme southwestern part of the State.

Newspapers were read at the store, and were passed from hand-to-hand at church, or at court. When a month old they were still being read. The speeches of President Johnson, Thaddeus Stevens, Charles Sumner, Ben Wade, General Benjamin Franklin Butler—also the Radical editorials of many Northern papers were widely read and discussed. The conservative papers, especially the New York World, were treasured. Old magazines, especially Harpers', were preserved. Many Southern homes, at this moment, have stacks of old

Harper's put by with meticulous care by hands long since laid to rest.

As the typical farmers labored and thought it all over, his back was literally broken by the taxes he was forced to pay. His farm was taxed, his tobacco was taxed, his head was taxed. Officers, paid salaries by the State, collected fifty cents every time the farmer signed his name—and that iniquity continues to this day, double pay for the same bit of work, if it is work to sign one's name.

III

The Virginian read of brilliant social and political events in Washington and New York, dinners at $150 a cover, women loaded with diamonds and buried in costly furs. Floral pieces at banquets and balls costing $1,000 each, imported champagne flowing like water and other dazzling luxuries that suggested Cleopatra's dinners for Mark Antony.

It did not burnish the patriotism of the plodding farmers to know, and none better, that he, and a million other Southern men like him, were taxed unjustly and outrageously to pay for the flowers, furs, champagne and flashing gems.

He was taxed to support the army and navy, to pay the admirals and generals, to provide food for countless hordes of idle freedmen still eating at Government expense.[4] He was taxed to pay for the soldiers, white and black, who called him to

---

[4]JAMES BRYCE, *American Commonwealth*, Chapter 92.
NELSON M. BLAKE, *Mahone*, Chapter IV.
MARY NEWTON STANARD, *Richmond*, Chapter XXXV.

halt at the street corner, or who insulted his wife when she went to town. He was taxed to pay a neat salary to Henry Horatio Wells, formerly of Detroit, now snugly lodged in the executive mansion at Richmond. He was taxed to pay a handsome salary to General George Stoneman, living in the "Confederate White House" in Richmond, who "kicks and cuffs our people," to quote John B. Baldwin, of Staunton.

Though the farmer paid his taxes he could not vote, nor hold any office, but the Negroes living off the Government might do both! He was taxed to support such a judge as the unspeakable Underwood, and the vast army of Union League teachers, preachers, agitators and propagandists who literally swarmed over Virginia and the South, and who reported to the Radical press how unrepentant, disloyal, ignorant and lazy the rebels were!

All these items and a thousand like them did not foster any great devotion for the "best Government on earth."[5]

IV

Only the Recording Angel in Heaven knows how many millions (if not billions) of dollars the Southern third of the United States has paid in pensions to the vast army of pensioners, now mostly dead, who

[5] *Through Centuries Three*, SQUIRES, p. 7.
RICHARD LEE MORTON, *History of Virginia*, Chapter VIII.
PHILIP ALEXANDER BRUCE, *Virginia*, Vol. II, Chapter III.
ALEXANDER H. H. STUART, *Address*, University of Virginia, June 29, 1866.
JOHN WARWICK DANIEL, *Address*, University of Virginia, June 27, 1877.

killed their sons and brothers, burned their cities, trampled their farms, drove off their cattle, liberated their servants. We do not know of another Christian, civilized and modern land, whose citizens were forced to pension those who despoiled them. If the Germans are paying pensions to those who defeated them in the World War, we have not heard of it. Yet that is what the silent, patient and uncomplaining Southern farmers did for two full generations.

BOOK FIVE

JANUARY 1, 1869—JANUARY 26, 1870

CHAPTER XXXV

THE STRUGGLE IN WASHINGTON

Reconstruction was the work of sentimentalists
controlled by knaves.
—*E. L. Godkin.*

The first day of the last year of Virginia's anguish
brought from Washington a proclamation that the
Fourteenth Amendment was now a part of the Constitution of the United States. As the pronouncement was expected, it did not discourage Mr. Stuart
and his friends of the New Movement.

The familiar adage, "God helps those who help
themselves," may have occurred to the patriotic
Virginians as they faced many and great discourage-
ments in Washington. Two friends rallied to their
support: Horace Greeley, the most influential editor
in America, and the uncrowned king, General
Ulysses S. Grant, President-elect.

Mt. Stuart, who knew Horace Greeley well in the
old Whig days, invited him to meet with the Committee of Nine, advise with them and aid them with
his trenchant pen and enormous political influence.
He replied that he could not come to Washington,
but assured Mr. Stuart that the Tribune would
plead the cause of Virginia. And it did, almost
every day, in no uncertain tones. He thundered
against those Radicals who would enslave the South

for private profit and political expediency. The New York Times, Boston Advertiser, Chicago Tribune and others re-echoed the New York Tribune.

John L. Marye, Jr., of Fredericksburg, wrote Mr. Stuart, as follows:

"There is a gentleman at Norfolk, Mr. Gilbert C. Walker,[1] who could help us in some of our needs. He is a Northern man, largely and influentially concerned in Norfolk's commercial and financial affairs; a man of integrity, intelligence, experience in public affairs and most favorable personal relations, with access to official personages, whose ear we should have. Mr. Walker has been a decided and outspoken foe to the Underwood Constitution, and cordially in favor of our movement. I am convinced it would be well to ask Mr. Bolling to write Mr. Walker at once and request that he, Mr. Walker, would be in Washington and extend his aid to us."

George W. Bolling, of Petersburg, was a close friend of General John M. Schofield, now Secretary of War in Johnson's Cabinet.

II

The Committee of Nine met in the National Hotel, Washington, January 8, and all were present. Mr. Bolling, Colonel Walker, his brother, Jonas Walker, and other prominent Virginians in Washington were asked to cooperate with them. The Committee called promptly at the White House. The President received them cordially, but no effort was made to secure his official sanction as it might

---

[1] *Through Centuries Three*, SQUIRES, pp. 507-517.
LYON G. TYLER, *Cyclop of Virginia Biography*, Vol. III, p. 4.

prove an embarrassment. His term was almost ended. He was so very unpopular with his own party, and it was well known that General Grant cordially hated him.

III

The activity of the Committee of Nine in Washington was widely heralded in Virginia. The Radicals were alert. The Governor of Virginia, by grace of Federal bayonets, hurried to Washington with a delegation, some of whom had white faces and some black,[2] determined to block any effort of the Committee of Nine. With fierce energy, they declared that if the rebels were allowed to vote it would be the end of Radical rule in Virginia. In that statement, at least, "Governor Wells of Virginia" told the truth!

The Committee of Nine met the Reconstruction Committee of Fifteen for an interview, January 8. Fortunately for Virginia the Reconstruction Committee had been reconstructed for the better during the last three years.[3]

The Virginians were politely welcomed by George Sewall Boutwell, of Massachusetts, and shown to seats arranged for them. As Mr. Stuart stated the object of the visit, he was interrupted by the arrival of Governor Henry Horatio Wells and his committee of whites and blacks. Mr. Stuart requested that

---

[2]w. e. h. lecky, describing such politicians as Wells, says that they brought to the South "a grotesque parody" on government. Theirs was an "hideous orgy of anarchy," with corruption, libel, malice, violence and "undisguised insulting robbery."

[3]alexander f. robertson, *Alexander H. H. Stuart*, Chapter XXXII.

John B. Baldwin be heard. Baldwin's appeal was intense and vivid. He evidently made a fine impression.

Governor Wells took the floor and declared that the self-appointed Committee of Nine misrepresented conditions. He quoted at length and with emphasis such extreme Conservatives as former Governors Henry A. Wise,[4] John Letcher and Extra Billy Smith. Should not three Governors know conditions existing in Virginia—and three such able executives? Did they not oppose Stuart, Baldwin and his Committee and criticize their plans even more drastically than the Radicals?

Politics make strange bed-fellows. Who would have dreamed that such a Radical as Wells would quote, and with great approval, such an ultra-Conservative as Henry A. Wise? It is a queer example of the meeting of extremes.

IV

It was exceedingly unfortunate that, at such a critical time, when vital issues trembled in the balance, the Virginians could not present a united front. It was indeed the weak joint in their armor. None knew it better than the Radicals and they made use of it with telling effect.

Fortunately for Virginia there were Republicans, not so radical as Wells and his motley crew. They, too, came to Washington, and were heard by the

[4]For a brief sketch of the three Governors, and their terms, see SQUIRES, *Through Centuries Three*, pp. 463-483.

The three Governors were uncompromising Democrats, and the Committee of Nine were Whigs.

Committee. As Republicans, taxpayers, men of probity, integrity and property, they evidently had the welfare of Virginia at heart. Had it not been for them it is doubtful whether the "New Movement" could have succeeded.

Franklin Stearns,[5] L. H. Chandler,[6] Edgar Allan, chief of the Union League, and Gilbert C. Walker entered a categorical denial of Wells' allegations. Since the defeat of Seymour and the election of Grant, the Virginians recognized that Negro suffrage was inevitable; the will of the majority. If the Confederates were allowed to vote, they would agree to permit Negro suffrage—surely a fair compromise.

They also testified that from long observation the whites treated the Negroes with justice. Every Negro worked with and for a white man. Their relations were just and even cordial. Mr. Stearns argued that the Underwood Constitution was unjust in the suffrage provision. It disfranchised 95 percent of the native white population. A Republican party could be built in Virginia only upon honest and honorable foundations, not upon force, fraud and prejudice.

Gilbert Carleton Walker, of Norfolk, made a decided impression upon the congressional committees. Both he and his brother had many friends in Con-

---

[5]Franklin Stearns was a financial leader in Richmond. He was a director of the First National Bank, organized soon after the surrender (1865), and had served on the Committee to welcome Governor Pierpont to Richmond (1865), and later on a similar Committee to welcome Walker (1869). He died in Richmond, June 11, 1888.

[6]H. W. BURTON, *History of Norfolk*, p. 167.

T. J. WERTENBAKER, *History of Norfolk*, pp. 263-270.

gress. His service brought him full recognition and prompt reward, as we shall see. In less than nine months Walker succeeded Henry Horatio Wells as Governor of Virginia.

The Committee of Nine received encouragement from many Senators, especially William Morris Stewart, of Nevada; Henry Wilson, of Massachusetts (soon after elected Vice-President of the United States); Jacob Merritt Howard, of Michigan, a member of the Reconstruction Committee of Fifteen; John Sherman, of Ohio, whose name is forever associated with the monstrous Sherman-Shellabarger Bill; Edmond Gibson Ross, of Kansas, who offended the Radicals by voting against the President's impeachment; Cornelius Cole, of California; Roscoe Conkling, of New York, notorious for an hectic career; Thomas Andrews Hendricks, of Indiana, in later years elected Vice-President of the United States with Grover Cleveland; Garrett Davis, of Kentucky, and many others, Republicans as well as Democrats, who believed that the South had been punished enough, who desired a reunited country, who were disgusted with the Radical policies and Radical leaders and who, like General Grant, now desired peace of all things.

Four years of fratricidal strife had now been followed by four years of Reconstruction; was there never to be an end to such vindictiveness?

CHAPTER XXXVI

HEAVY SEAS RUNNING

Grant's administration outraged every rule of ordinary decency.
—*Henry Adams.*

Andrew Johnson's day was almost done. The most wretchedly abused President who ever tried to rule an impossible Congress, the most iniquitous and radical Congress ever assembled at Washington, was now about to fade from the national picture.

Grant and Johnson had long been political foes in the shameful maelstrom of party strife. Grant refused to ride to the inauguration with the retiring President; only one conspicuous item in that hostility which was the sensation and gossip of the day. A learned historian[1] has said that General Grant was a pronounced advocate of impeachment.

Such unpardonable rudeness in high places is an occasion for profound regret. Had General Grant controlled his personal antipathy for his former East Tennessee friend and ridden to his inauguration as precedent demanded, his character, as a true gentleman, would loom larger with posterity. It wasn't in the General and he ran true to form.

---

[1] WILLIAM ARCHIBALD DUNNING, *Reconstruction*, p. 127.

Then there was another huge, social sensation. The fair ladies of Washington, the social leaders and belles, flatly refused to attend the inaugural ball if they must recognize, as social equals, the wives, daughters and friends of various colored Senators and representatives the zealous Radicals had elected and sent up from the South.

General Grant declined to attend if President Johnson was there—so the function was dropped.

When the Forty-first Congress convened there were 57 Republicans and 11 Democrats in the Senate; 143 Republicans and 72 Democrats in the House.

The new President, it was announced, had two ideals for his term: First, the country reunited, with the obliteration of sectional lines and partisan hatred. Second, an honest, economical and efficient administration of domestic affairs.

No President ever went into office with larger hopes and finer purposes; and none ever left office more completely discredited. Not willing to trust our judgment (necessarily prejudiced for the ills that befell the South during Grant's foul eight years of mal-administration), let others tell of the gaming and shameless speculation, of bribes for shifty politicians and crooked deals, but the President's personal integrity remained untainted.

The burdens of this foul misgovernment fell heaviest on the South because of the weakness, the lack of proper representation and the moral effects of recent defeat.

II

The shrewdest politician in Virginia was a Confederate Major General residing in Petersburg— William Mahone.[2] "The hero of the Crater" was now president of the Norfolk and Petersburg and the Southside Railways. It is an exceedingly interesting phase of Virginia's history that Alexander H. H. Stuart came forward as the "Tribune of Virginia" in the darkest days the Virginians have known. He was now an aged man, and at Washington was about to complete the crowning achievement of his long and notable career. As Stuart recedes gradually from leadership, Mahone almost imperceptibly takes precedence. Stuart began as a Whig and ended as a Democrat. Mahone began as an intense Democrat and ended as a Republican.

It is he, William Mahone, who came forward with a plan to relieve Virginia once and for all of Henry Horatio Wells[3] and put a worthy successor in the gubernatorial chair. Mahone, R. Bolling Wilcox, Franklin Stearns and George R. Smith asked President Johnson to remove Wells and appoint Stearns Governor. Wells got wind of the scheme and secured an order from President Johnson forbidding his removal.

III

It became increasingly evident that General Grant would call an election so the Virginia Radicals held

[2] *The Land of Decision*, squires, Chapter XI.
[3] *Through Centuries Three*, squires, pp. 497-506.
c. c. pearson, *William Mahone, Dict. Amer. Biog.*
nelson m. blake, *William Mahone.*

another riot of a convention, this time in Petersburg
(March 9-10). This meeting, like the two Radical
conventions held in Richmond during 1867, was a
disgrace to the State and the men who participated
in it.

The vexed question of a gubernatorial nomination
was uppermost. Wells was, of course, a candidate
—and a very active, determined and unscrupulous
candidate—to succeed himself. He had the Negro
element almost wholly under his control. The respectable elements of the Republican party were
anxious to nominate James H. Clements who had
represented Portsmouth in the Underwood Convention the previous year.

The career of Wells had estranged the better
element of his party. The Conservatives always
hated him. The anti-Wells Radicals claimed (and
truly) that "Wells[4] attempted to sell the State's
interest in the Virginia and Tennessee Railroad
(from Lynchburg to Bristol) to the Baltimore and
Ohio. It was believed that Wells had been bribed;
George Rye, the State Treasurer, and General
Stoneman frustrated the nefarious plan."

There were also ugly stories[5] as to the purloining
of letters from the mails and complicity in profits
from the ring which controlled the sale of whiskey.[6]

The first test of strengh came with the election of
a chairman. So violent was the voting and such
confusion broke forth that orderly processes were

---

[4]PHILIP ALEXANDER BRUCE, *Virginia*, Vol. II, p. 127.
[5]HAMILTON JAMES ECKENRODE, *Reconstruction*, p. 120.
[6]PHILIP ALEXANDER BRUCE, *Virginia*, Vol. II, p. 129.

impossible. In the midst of the tempest the Clements faction claimed the chair. This precipitated a riot. The police were called, and Mayor Burgess threatened to ask the aid of Federal troops.

When the riot was somewhat quelled Horatio and his Negro cohorts had a majority and Governor Wells was nominated to succeed Governor Wells as Governor of the proudest State in the Union!

The foes of Governor Wells took quick, cruel but logical revenge. Wells wanted a Confederate physician, Dr. W. W. C. Douglas, of Richmond County, nominated as Lieutenant-Governor. But Lewis Linsey, a colored Radical, nominated Dr. J. D. Harris, a large and very sable statesman from Hampton, for Lieutenant-Governor. General Edgar Allan instantly seconded the nomination in a speech which completely captivated the Negroes. Harris was nominated and Governor Wells was forced to accept the Negro and make the canvass with him.

It was a master stroke of diplomacy which Wells richly deserved. Like all his ilk, he would use the Negroes for personal advantage and toss them over when it suited. Their platform, of course, urged he permanent disfranchisement of all "rebels." They wished Virginia restored to the Union, and the Underwood Constitution adopted without change.

IV

When the convention adjourned and the Radical patriots were returning to their homes, General Mahone had a quiet conference "under the inspiration of the Committee of Nine" at Jarrett's Hotel in

Petersburg. Edgar Allan, C. W. Buttz, J. W. Jenkins, W. H. Samuels, George Rye, David White, John D. Parsons and A. S. Segar, of Norfolk, were present and perhaps others. It was planned to defeat Wells by dividing the vote of the freedmen and by uniting the Conservative vote, Whig and Democrat, behind a Conservative candidate.

Ten days after Wells was nominated at Petersburg, he was arrested (March 22) on a warrant sworn by Edgar Allan and W. H. Samuels charging this Governor-of-Virginia-by-Bayonet-Rule with robbing the United States mails and purloining a letter from Samuels to Allan. When the case was called, the United States Commissioner Chahoon dismissed it.

It was claimed that the warrant was political propaganda to discredit Wells. If so, it was successful.

General Mahone was probably the largest employer of labor in Virginia, and what with his success as a railway executive, and what with his intense Democratic affiliations, he was at that time the most popular and influential man in Virginia except, of course, General Robert E. Lee.

No one was so admirably fitted to make the canvass against Wells as Mahone's personal friend and banker, Gilbert Carleton Walker,[7] of Norfolk, whose services with Stuart and the "New Movement" were so valuable at Washington. He was a "true and well-known Republican."

So intense were the reactions throughout this

[7] *Through Centuries Three*, SQUIRES, p. 507.
The Land of Decision, SQUIRES, pp. 177-179.
R. A. BROCK, *Eminent Virginians*, p. 390.
NELSON M. BLAKE, *William Mahone*.

Commonwealth (a State and people accustomed to be proud of its executives), a State claiming Sir Walter Ralegh as first Governor of the Colony and Patrick Henry as first Governor of the Commonwealth . . . so intense and unfavorable were the criticisms of such a Governor that General George Stoneman (March 27)[8] quietly removed H. H. Wells and himself assumed the executive functions. But Horatio relieved of his duties to a people who cordially hated him took the road to Washington. What wires he pulled we do not know, but the Radical pressure was sufficient, if secretive, and lo! General George Stoneman was removed![9] The Virginians wept no tears, for Stoneman made few if any friends, but he was respected as an upright and honest man and officer. General Webb was placed temporarily in command, as monarch, until General Edward Richard Sprigg Canby arrived.

Webb's first act (April 2) was to reinstate Henry Horatio Wells.[10] That was the "government of the people for the people by the people," as interpreted by the Radical leaders of 1869.[11]

---

[8]General Stoneman had been routed at Ashland in 1863 by General W. H. F. Lee.

WILLIAM ASBURY CHRISTIAN, *History of Richmond.*

H. J. ECKENRODE, *Reconstruction*, p. 121, says that "Stoneman reappointed" Wells.

[9]Fourteenth Annual Report, Library Board of Virginia, p. X.

[10]NELSON M. BLAKE, *William Mahone*, p. 103.

DONALD A. ROBERTS, *Dictionary of American Biography*, Vol. XIX.

[11]Alexander Stuart Webb was born February 15, 1835, of distinguished parentage in New York. He was educated at West Point, did valiant duty through the whole war and in later years he was President of the College of the City of New York. He died in 1911 and New York State erected a handsome statue to him on the battlefield of Antietam. The author does not mention his sojourn in Virginia. It surely added nothing to his fame.

V

One hundred and fifty Republicans, men of wealth, culture and influence, signed a call to the voters of Virginia, appealing to men of all political affiliations to defeat Wells, elect Walker and save the civilization of Virginia. They were ready to cooperate with the Committee of Nine, who sponsored the New Movement. Old Line Whigs, antebellum Democrats and Conservative Republicans must now unite. It was the first hopeful and constructive program for the political salvation of Virginia since the collapse of the Confederacy.

But the Conservatives had a ticket nominated the year before for an election which never took place, Colonel R. E. Withers and General James A. Walker. Manifestly to divide the Conservative vote between Withers and Walker would be to elect Wells. Both General Mahone and the Committee of Nine urged Withers to withdraw in the interest of harmony. The Conservatives (meaning the Democrats and many Old Line Whigs) met at the Exchange Hotel in Richmond six weeks later (April 28). Robert E. Withers withdrew his candidacy for Governor, James A. Walker followed Withers, and John L. Marye, Jr., the candidate for Attorney General, followed the graceful lead of the heads of the ticket.

No nomination was made as Gilbert C. Walker was not a Virginian and not a Democrat, but the Executive Committee urged all Virginians to support the Conservative Republican nominee and defeat Wells—after the convention adjourned.

The Conservative-Republican ticket was greatly strengthened by submitting the name of John Francis Lewis, of Rockingham County, to the people for Lieutenant Governor. He was an unreconstructed Old Line Whig, a forthright and courageous son of a fine old Colonial family. His great-grandfather, John Lewis, was the first pioneer to settle in Augusta County, and the substantial homestead he built on a hilltop is still tenanted near Staunton. The statue of Andrew Lewis, son of John, stands under Washington in Crawford's famous group beside the Capitol of Virginia.

So bitterly did John F. Lewis oppose secession that he promised his neighbors in the Valley that he would under no circumstances vote Virginia out of the Union. And he kept his word. His name was never fixed to the Secession Ordinance. He remained through the war an outspoken Unionist and reiterated his conviction that the Confederacy could never win. This attitude made him extremely unpopular; yet all respected his candor. He has frequently been called, "One of the most upright and courageous Virginians."

The position of Attorney General was given Major James C. Taylor, of Montgomery County, an ardent Democratic leader, a lawyer of ability and an ex-Confederate soldier and popular citizen of colonial and aristocratic lineage. In later years Colonel Taylor became prominent in the Readjuster Movement and did much for its ultimate success.

General Mahone managed the campaign. His shrewdness, diplomacy and determination to put the Walker-Lewis-Taylor ticket over, triumphed over every obstacle, some seemingly insuperable.

We suppose that no stronger ticket could have been nominated to redeem the State from Henry Horatio Wells.

Chapter XXXVII

THE BATTLE BEGINS

Bidding farewell to passive resistance they plunged eagerly into the contest as one who flings away his scabbard, when he draws his sword.
—*W. H. T. Squires.*

While the Virginians were absorbed in the fascinating game of politics, the new satrap (and, thank God, the last of them!) arrived (April 20). He came without a welcome, he remained without friends, and he left without regret.

Edward Richard Sprigg Canby, a native Kentuckian (born 1819) was described as "tall and athletic, in manner courteous, but rather reserved and silent, the ideal of a thoughtful and studious soldier."[1]

This well-seasoned son of battle, now forty-nine, had a good but not glorious record. Reared in Indiana, he graduated from West Point in '39, and saw some infantry service in the raw territories of New Mexico. Canby was an intimate friend of Secretary Edwin M. Stanton, which did not ingratiate him at Richmond. He fought the rioters in New

---

[1] WILLIAM ASBURY CHRISTIAN, *History of Richmond*, pp. 303 and 307.

THOS. MARSHALL SPAULDING, *Dictionary of American Biography*, Vol. III, writes courteously and favorably of General Canby.

York at the time of the draft, and, as the war was closing, received the bloodless surrender of Mobile.

At Richmond "he permitted the paroled cavalry of Lee's Army to reorganize and suppress 'bush-whacking' which was rife in the neighborhood. The measure was entirely successful and no bad results followed."

General Canby was not popular in Virginia as General Schofield had been. We know no reason why he should have been popular—and some very cogent reasons why he should not. He seemed to have learned his lesson from Edwin M. Stanton, late Secretary of War, and to have learned it well. Canby was forever removing civil officers of all grades and appointing army officers in their places. His idea was evidently that his friends from the North and West must have all the places on Virginia's pay-roll, and no Virginians had any right to hold office in Virginia. On one occasion he removed the entire City Council of Richmond and appointed his military friends in their places. That was evidently his idea of a republic; it was certainly his method, whatsoever may have been the General's idea.

On at least two occasions he did his utmost to embarrass Walker's campaign for the governor's place, although Walker was, like himself, a carpet-bagger.

II

General Grant before his inauguration promised the Committee of Nine to recommend the readmission of Virginia.

True to his word, he sent a special message to

Congress (April 7) recommending that Virginia and Mississippi "be restored to their proper relations to the Government." He further suggested that the new constitution of Virginia[2] be submitted to a vote; and that a "separate vote be taken upon such parts as may be thought expedient." The bill passed immediately (April 9)[3] and was signed[4] by President Grant next day, April 10.

The execution of its provisions was left by Congress in the hands of the President. President Grant, accordingly, made proclamation (May 14) fixing July 6 for the election, and he directed that the clauses disfranchising Confederate soldiers and sympathizers, and the test oath for all officials of the State, be voted on separately.

A Governor, Lieutenant-Governor, Attorney General, eight members of the national Congress and a General Assembly were also to be elected.

The campaign was off like a pistol shot. And it was a joyous campaign, with a plethora of sensations, thrills and heated debates. There had not been such an election since 1860, when the Old Line Whigs carried the State for Bell and Everett, turning Virginia's back upon Breckenridge on the one hand and Lincoln on the other. For the first time, intelligent white Virginians felt there was a chance to redeem the State. It was a bitter drop in the cup that both candidates were carpet-baggers. But one

---

[2]ALEXANDER F. ROBERTSON, *A. H. H. Stuart*, p. 148, gives text of Grant's letter to Congress, and synopsis of Bill passed April 10.

[3]April 9, 1869, the fourth anniversary of General Lee's surrender at Appomattox.

[4]JAMES FORD RHODES, *History of the United States*, Vol. VI, p. 244.

was allied with the best, the other with the worst Virginia had to offer.

The Conservatives were meticulously careful not to offend the North. Twenty million people watched this movement in Virginia. Ten thousand Radical politicians and a thousand Radical editors were ready at a moment's notice to raise hue and cry. All the old fanaticism, the well-worn bloody-shirt and intense partisan prejudice would be brought to bear upon President Grant and a huge Radical majority in Congress against the New Movement, against Walker and in favor of Henry Horatio Wells and his valiant colored patriots, if one mistake were made. Only one slip, one unguarded word, and the cause of Virginia would be plunged again into the abyss. At least two of the three Conservative candidates (Walker and Lewis) would bring a sympathetic reaction in the North.

On the other hand, the Radicals determined to hold Virginia in thrall. They would rule or ruin. The peril to Virginia was great and the issue critical. But every obstacle found the Virginians more determined to save the Commonwealth for themselves and their children.

The election of 1869 was by far the most significant ever held in Virginia. The issues at stake were vital to the progress, welfare and perhaps the very existence of the Commonwealth. As these issues were clearly drawn, the wealth, culture and intelligence of the State gravitated more and more to Walker's side, while Wells appealed more and more to the lower classes.[5]

[5]RICHARD LEE MORTON, *History of Virginia*, Vol. III, p. 143.

III

The hatred of the Virginians for a Governor by grace of Federal bayonets was well earned. They remembered Wells' words that the only way to hold Virginia was "to establish a military provisional government, to locate a sufficient military force to preserve peace, command respect and secure order; in other words, to vindicate the supremacy of the law. Then disfranchise those who are not loyal, make loyal acts, and not a paper oath, the test of loyalty. This done, create a perpetual balance of power, which will at all times secure you from a political danger; or more plainly, let the Negro vote."

The reaction to such a program of tyranny may be imagined. Thaddeus Stevens at his worst was not worse than Wells. But fortunately, Thaddeus never set his club foot on the soil of Virginia (so far as we know), but Wells resided in the Executive Mansion. Stevens was dead, but Wells much alive. Stevens had a brilliant intellect; Wells, fortunately for Virginia, was stupid to a degree.

The unexplained expulsion of Governor Wells from his office by General Stoneman, and his reappointment by General Webb, a week later, tended to discredit him as a candidate for reelection.[6]

---

[6]WILLIAM ASBURY CHRISTIAN, *History of Richmond*, p. 303. Wells was arrested March 22, 1869, on a warrant sworn out by Edgar Allan and W. H. Samuels, charging that Wells purloined a letter from Samuels to Allan from the mails. The case was dismissed by Major George Chahoon in Richmond. But Stoneman removed Wells. Wells appealed to Washington, Stoneman was removed and Canby became Virginia's last satrap, and the most radical of them all. Wells was reappointed Governor of Virginia.

The story about the purloined letter, his arrest on a warrant sworn out by two Republicans and non-Virginians, his willingness to sell the railways of Virginia to the Baltimore and Ohio for a fraction of their value, his colored running-mate for the office of Lieutenant-Governor; these and many other ugly items gave the Honorable Henry Horatio Wells a cumbersome and dishonorable load to carry.

IV

Behind the shifting lines of the political battle, the figure of Major-General William Mahone was ever alert. When Wells offended Mahone he made an implacable enemy—and an enemy who, as it proved, was to defeat his ambitions, thrust him from the Governor's chair and actually expel him from the State—all in six months. Only William Mahone[7] could have done it. Mahone did not, at this time, appear often in the limelight. He had chosen Walker, he planned Walker's campaign, he handled the funds and was indefatigable in his efforts for the success of the Conservative ticket. He was convinced that Conservative victory meant the political salvation of Virginia. He was content that the glory of victory should rest upon another.

Colonel Walker's campaign, as managed by Mahone,[8] is altogether interesting and enlightening, even after sixty-five years.

[7] *Land of Decision*, SQUIRES, Chapter XI.

NELSON M. BLAKE, *Mahone*, pp. 106-110

HAMILTON JAMES ECKENRODE, *Reconstruction*, p. 120.

Campaign of 1887, Library of Congress Pamphlet, "New Virginia," p. 27.

[8] NELSON M. BLAKE, *Mahone*, p. 106.

"It is perfectly apparent that General Mahone is the life and soul of the Walker ticket."—*Evening State Journal*, May 5, 1869.

The Colonel began his campaign (May 12) at his home town of Norfolk—his "home town" for the last five years. He then made speeches in Lynchburg, Salem, Marion, Liberty (Bedford), Christiansburg, Wytheville and Abingdon.

"I wish," wrote an influential Conservative, "Walker would canvass the upper portion of the State. If the people could see him they would certainly vote for him."

We do not know what reply General Mahone made to this. Probably he said, "Wait a bit and see."

During June the Colonel's calendar was crowded with important dates. He spoke in Lexington, Woodstock, Harrisonburg, Winchester, Leesburg, Alexandria, Front Royal, Luray, Culpeper, Warrenton, Charlottesville, Louisa and Staunton, in the order named.

Only five days remained in July, yet he managed to cover Mathews, Yorktown, Williamsburg, and Gloucester, in the order named.

In the midst of his journeys, he wrote General Mahone from Alexandria (June 13):

"I have now been through the Southwest and down the Valley, and have heard and learned much, not only of those sections of the State, but also this and others. There are but two serious dangers which threaten us. Both ranges of mountains, the Alleghany and Blue Ridge, extending through the western portions of the State, were the hiding places of deserters, etc. In the Southwest they gradually organized into a society, called by outsiders, the 'Red Strings.' These fellows, for the most part, drifted subsequently into the Union Leagues. Many of them are now for Wells, not because they love Wells, or his Negro associates more than we, but because they have an unconquerable hate to the great body of my supporters, whom they allege were their former persecutors. From these fellows, all through the mountains, Wells will obtain many white votes, from seven to even ten thousand. Again, the second source of danger is the Orange and Alexandria Railway Company. I find the effect of its harmful influence here: first in the general apathy of the people, and second in the positive avowal of the R. R. men that they would support Wells. I fear that we shall lose three thousand votes from this cause. They will not all be cast for Wells, but what are not will be kept from the polls. Wherever else I have been the people are awakening, and we shall get a very fine vote."

Before General Mahone received that letter, a great multitude, five thousand strong, assembled in the Capitol Square, Richmond, to hear Robert Ould,[9] Assistant Secretary of War in Davis' Cabinet, James Neeson and William M. Walker, of Westmoreland County. Ould opposed the Committee of Nine, but Neeson was one of the Nine he had opposed. The occasion evoked immense enthusiasm.

Since his surrender General Lee had withstood every effort (and there were many) to bring him into politics. His interviews and letters were always moderate and conservative. He insisted that true patriots should eschew politics, work hard, and en-

---

[9] One of the most influential Virginians. For an excellent pen-portrait of him see C. G. CHAMBERLAYNE, *Chamberlayne, Virginian*, p. 198.

dure in patience the indignities needlessly and gratuitously heaped upon them.

But now he spoke a word for Colonel Walker.[10] "General Lee has declared for the election of Walker, and the adoption of the Expurgated Constitution; the Baltimore and Ohio Railway is working for Wells."

During the month the Norfolk newspapers published a list of 103 Radicals "known to be dead." It was explained that the Conservatives objected to their "corpses voting"!

---

[10]*Norfolk Journal,* June 5, 1869.

CHAPTER XXXVIII

REDEEMED AT LAST

My heart leaps up, when I behold
A rainbow in the sky.
—*William Wordsworth.*

In the midst of the campaign the colored allies of
Wells and Harris threatened open rebellion; for
the places, honors and emoluments were not fairly
divided. Their complaint was reasonable as Wells'
only hope lay with the Negro vote. Dr. Bayne, of
Norfolk, was one of the influential leaders in this
revolt. While this pen has no inside information,
it is a safe guess that the hand of General Mahone
was moving behind the scenes to torment and
threaten Wells. Mahone was always a master in
manipulating colored voters.

A convention of restless colored citizens in Petersburg, May 24,[1] demanded their share of the spoils,
endorsed the Underwood Constitution as written,
and pledged their support to Wells and Harris; but
in many counties where the Radical and colored
vote was heavy they put colored candidates in the
field against white Radicals. In Norfolk, for instance, there were two candidates for the State
Senate and three for the House of Delegates. In

---

[1] RICHARD LEE MORTON, *History of Virginia*, Vol. III, pp. 153-154.

six of the eight congressional districts, there were
"all Negro tickets" running against the white Radicals and the Conservatives. This was a master
stroke of political strategy, as it divided the Radical
party.

The State Journal of Richmond, supporting Wells,
claimed that Walker did not own a "foot of land in
Virginia."

The Norfolk Journal replied that the Colonel
owned $50,000 worth of stock in the Atlantic Iron
Works Company of Norfolk, an industry employing
150 men and covering several acres of ground.

During the month of June there was but one topic
of conversation—the election.[2] All the picturesque
paraphernalia, laid aside since ante-bellum days,
was now reburnished. There were torch-light pro-
cessions, barbecues, free drinks, fist fights, large
political picnics, free treats, committees of every
conceivable kind, from the State-wide organizations
to the "corporals" who promised to bring five voters
to the polls. Each morning the press blazed with
broadsides against Wells and Harris; against carpet-
baggers, scalawags and colored politicians.

Raleigh T. Daniel urged that great mass meetings,
barbecues and other assemblies be arranged for
Saturday, July 3, to enthuse the voters to the highest
pitch and greater exertions. It was done.

II

All seemed to be going well. Excitement, though
intense, was subdued. Indeed self-control was never

---

[2] J. T. WERTENBAKER, *History of Norfolk*, p. 266.

more insisted upon, nor ever better exhibited, when our new military satrap, General E. R. S. Canby, to the astonishment and consternation of the Conservatives announced (June 26) that every member of the Legislature would have to take the test oath and every officer-elect would have to subscribe to the same. If so, the State would be turned over completely to the Radicals; for practically all the Conservative candidates for the Legislature could not take the oath, and their Radical opponents would be seated, elected or not!

To be sure the iniquity was written into the XIV Amendment of the Constitution and proclaimed January 1, 1869. But on Christmas Day, 1868, Andrew Johnson had proclaimed amnesty for all "rebels." Was a "rebel" pardoned a "rebel" still?

Amidst the intense resentment caused by General Canby's interference Alexander H. H. Stuart came yet once again to the rescue.[3] He appealed directly to President Grant and laid the situation before him. The President was sympathetic and issued a sharp rebuke which in effect told Canby to keep his hands off. Again Stuart, the great Tribune, had saved Virginia.

III

In some districts the Conservatives put forward conservative colored men for the Legislature against white Radicals. At Williamsburg a Dr. F. S. Norton, colored, ran on the Conservative ticket against a bitter Radical from the North named

[3]ALEX F. ROBERTSON, *A. H. H. Stuart*, p. 284, also p. 460.

Richard S. Ayer.[4] His colored neighbor won the seat.

As a huge Negro vote would likely be cast in Richmond, prominent business men encouraged 250 conservative Negroes to have a great barbecue on Mayo's Island, in the James. All the colored population were invited to come, eat, drink and be merry. Incidentally they were to hear some distinguished Conservatives discuss the election. A huge banner depicted a white man and a colored man standing together for Virginia with the well-worn motto, "United we stand, divided we fall." Unfortunately a bridge, crowded to capacity, collapsed, killing several and injuring many (July 1).

Instantly the Radical press blazed forth. High heaven would strike dead those Negroes who deserted their party! We suspect the Richmond barbecue did more harm than good.

Colonel Walker returned to his home in Norfolk, his arduous canvass completed. General Mahone had all things prepared under his capable hands in Petersburg, Governor Wells was ready in the Mansion at Richmond to hear the returns when the votes were counted.

IV

As this day of destiny dawned, violence and even bloodshed were freely predicted. But again to the honor of the Commonwealth be it said the election passed without riot or discord. Everyone was in a good humor. Both parties were confident of victory.

---

[4]Ayer represented four counties on the Northern Neck in the Underwood Convention of 1867-1868.

The saloons were closed, and the voters, for the most part, remained sober. There was but little fighting or quarreling.

At noon an interesting bulletin was received at Norfolk:

"The election in Richmond, as far as it has progressed, is the quietest ever held in Virginia. It is like Sunday. Troops bivouacked in the public parks and ambulances covered with flags are the only unusual sights. A number of blacks have openly voted for Walker, and with no hostile demonstration."

After a long and anxious day the stars came forth, harbingers and symbols of hope. Slowly the news came in by wire, and everywhere it was the same story. In the heavy Radical districts of the east and south the Radical majorities were diminished. In the Conservative strongholds over the Blue Ridge the victory was pronounced. After nightfall the streets of Richmond resounded with cheers for Walker. A huge crowd was addressed by colored and white Conservatives.[5] They claimed the State by 30,000 majority, both branches of Legislature, and the proposed amendments to the Underwood Constitution. The Wells leaders denied all claims, but gave no figures.

In Norfolk, Main street was crowded. About eight o'clock addresses were made by W. H. C. Ellis, J. B. Whitehead, A. S. Segar and others. Enthusiasm ran high. Bonfires were lighted along

[5]One of whom was James W. Hunnicutt. The appointment of Wells was the political end of Hunnicutt. So he became a Conservative, and so disappears from the political picture.

Main street from Granby to Church. A Walker pole was raised in Main at Roanoke.

A band appeared and the cheering crowd moved to the Atlantic Hotel.[6] J. B. Whitehead[7] introduced Gilbert Carleton Walker, of Norfolk, the next Governor of Virginia, who made a graceful speech, congratulating the people that the grand old Commonwealth had at last been redeemed from the harpies and vampires who had so long fattened upon her. He promised the Virginians that they would never have reason to regret their choice. Virginia was again about to take her rightful place in the family of States. He urged generosity to "our opponents" in this hour of victory, and wished our colored citizens especially to rejoice that they were freed from those designing white men who had exploited them.

The band played "Dixie," and the crowd went wild with joy. Colonel Hinton,[8] Colonel Llewellyn[9] and Colonel Lamb[10] made speeches. A. S. Segar[11]

---

[6]Then located on the northwest corner of Main and Atlantic Streets. The street was named for the hotel.

[7]John B. Whitehead, the half-brother of Hugh Blair Grigsby, a scion of one of Norfolk's oldest families, a banker, merchant, churchman and leader in every worthy enterprise.

[8]Colonel J. W. Hinton, of Petersburg, the father of Mrs. Alex. Gordon Milhado of Norfolk.

T. J. WERTENBAKER, *History of Norfolk*, p. 262.

[9]Colonel J. Richard Llewellyn, the first editor of the *Norfolk Public Ledger* (1876), of an old Norfolk family, whose name is retained in one of the streets of the city, a brave Confederate soldier and Democratic leader.

[10]Colonel W. W. Lamb, elected Mayor Norfolk in 1858, again in 1860 and again in 1862. He surrendered the city to General Jno. Ellis Wool, May 10, 1862, but buried the silver Mace in his home, and preserved it until Reconstruction was over.

[11]A. S. Segar, elected to the House of Delegates from Norfolk City and returned in 1870.

announced that Walker's majority would reach 40,000.

When the figures were finally tabulated they showed 270,000 registered (150,000 white and 120,000 colored). About 25,000 whites did not vote, and about 23,000 colored. Walker received 119,535 votes, Wells 101,204.

John F. Lewis polled a better vote than Walker, 120,068, and Dr. Harris fell behind Wells with 99,600.

Three weeks later the following figures were published:[12]

For the Constitution	206,033
Contra	9,189
For the article disfranchising Confederates	84,404
Contra	124,106
Conservatives returned to House of Delegates	42
Of whom 18 were colored.	
Contested: One seat.	
Conservatives returned to the Senate	30
Radicals returned to the Senate	13
Of whom six were colored.	

Charges of fraud and ballot-box "stuffing" were freely made by the Radicals. But if an unprejudiced person studies the figures, he will conclude that the irregularities must have been slight.

At last Virginia found her voice. The people had spoken.

---

[12] *Norfolk Journal*, July 27, 1869.

Chapter XXXIX

GOVERNOR GILBERT CARLETON WALKER

> Dark nights, when hearts are filled with fright,
> Pass on when dawn is near.
> The first faint ray of light brings hope
> And terrors disappear.
> —*Charles Day*.[1]

In the sensational contest between Walker and Wells, the tolerance and honesty of the Virginians to the large number of freedmen voting and for the more part voting against their white neighbors, argued well for Virginia's future.[2]

The civilization of three centuries was at stake, the welfare of future generations hung in the balance. Had Wells been elected, the Confederates disfranchised and kept out of office, many valuable citizens would certainly have left the State, capital would have become discouraged and an enormous debt would likely have been added to an obligation already too large. The cruel experience of South Carolina, Louisiana and Mississippi would have added years of bitterness to Virginia's cup of sorrow. Not that Virginia would in any case have become permanently under African control, which is unthinkable, but our political salvation would certainly have been long delayed.

---

[1] *Lights of Day*, DAY, Vol. III.
[2] *Through Centuries Three*, SQUIRES, pp. 505-506.

The comment of an English statesman[3] long after the event is enlightening:

"In some States the moderate white Republicans united with the Democrats, a union brought about by the disgust of all property holders at the scandals they saw and at the increase of their burdens as taxpayers. These secured legitimately-chosen majorities, and ejected the corrupt officials. In some cases the result was obtained by paying or otherwise inducing the Negroes not to go to the polls, or by driving them away by threats or actual violence.

"Once possessed of a voting majority the whites took care by a variety of devices, legal and extralegal, to keep that majority safe. And in no State has their control of the government been since shaken."

The more the Southern people despaired of getting rid of the Fifteenth Amendment, the more resolved were they to nullify it.

They did not hate the Negro, certainly not half so much as they hated the white leaders by whom they had been robbed. "We must save our civilization," and if it could be saved by suppressing the colored vote, they were ready to suppress it.

A friend wrote a brief but emphatic note of congratulation to General Mahone, little thinking it would be read by thousands long after his hand was dust:

"Didn't we give 'em hell! Wells finds that you will not have to leave the State, but he will. The majority exceeds our most sanguine expectations. I congratulate you on our great victory."[4]

---

[3] SIR JAMES BRYCE, *American Commonwealth*, Chapter 92.
[4] NELSON M. BLAKE, *Mahone*, p. 108.

Another letter to Mahone read:

"Besides sharing in the gratification which all true Virginians feel over our great and hard-earned victory, there is a peculiar joy which pertains to yourself alone. It springs from the proud consciousness that you have done more to effect this splendid deliverance of the grand old Commonwealth than any other of her sons."

Had Mahone done more? Alexander H. H. Stuart probably did more than any other one Virginian to effect the deliverance of Virginia from the chains of Reconstruction; but (except Stuart) Mahone indeed did most.

II

In a republic every election, especially every critical election, brings new men and new policies to the front; and at the same time throws others into the scrap heap of oblivion. The election of July 6 in Virginia was no exception. Gilbert C. Walker was now a name upon every tongue. He was the idol of Virginia, for the nonce, and his astonishing campaign won for him national recognition . . . for a time.

No man ever enjoyed a triumph more than he. After the speeches, bonfires and parades in Norfolk, he journeyed, next day, to Richmond. A great crowd of people met him at the huge shed called "the Petersburg Depot." A committee[5] representing all political factions extended a cordial welcome.

The enthusiastic crowd would not wait upon the

[5]Raleigh T. Daniel, Dr. G. R. Gilmer, A. M. Keiley, Franklin Stearns and H. C. Campbell served on the Reception Committee.

committee, but broke through the lines; and, after the manner of college boys, picked up the Governor-elect and carried him on their shoulders amidst tumultuous applause to a richly-decorated coach. A procession, a mile long, cheering and waving banners, followed him to the Spotswood Hotel while 20,000 spectators looked on.

From the balcony of the hotel Colonel Walker made a very tactful speech, much along the lines of his Norfolk address. He urged generosity for those who differed with us, general amnesty for all political offenders and equal rights for all men before the law. He thanked the people for their votes and for the splendid reception just given him, and promised, as Governor, to do his best for the ancient Commonwealth. He reminded the crowd that these happy days would not have come but for the cordial help, sympathy and cooperation of "our great and good President, General Ulysses S. Grant." At this peroration the crowd again went wild.

The press of the nation reported that General Grant was much gratified with the result of the Virginia election, and especially pleased that such fine self-control was manifest. He hoped it augured an end of race antagonism.

General Canby in an interview with a Republican congressman was gratified that there had been no rioting and no bloodshed, despite the intense excitement. The election, he declared, was as fair as that held in any State.

The Governor-elect did not tarry long in Richmond. He hurried to Washington and talked to President Grant for a full hour and a half at the

White House. He told the reporters that he was a "Conservative Republican," and that he expected to sustain the administration and hoped that Virginia would shortly be readmitted to her place in the Union.

He traveled to New York. Virginia again took the front page in all newspapers and curiosity was a-tiptoe. A metropolitan reporter described Colonel Walker as an uncommonly handsome man, who looks younger than he is. The Virginians, like the Athenians of old, preferred a man of distinguished bearing. The Colonel is tall, healthy, vigorous and athletic. He looks 35.[6] His complexion is dark, his eyes bright and firm, his hair iron-gray. He is a born orator. He can make a telling point and win rounds of applause by his repartee, wit and genial good-humor. He is not a Virginian at all, but was born in Binghamton, New York, and educated at Hamilton College, where he took first prize in public speaking.

To his native town he journeyed to see the good folks there. It was just as well that Gilbert enjoyed his triumph to the limit, for his day of greatness was brief. He was one of those lucky lads who had "greatness thrust upon him," a superb opportunist. If he had been endowed with the intellect of Mahone and the character of Stuart, there was no office to which he might not have aspired. It was not in him, and he soon retreated into the shadows of oblivion, after one term as Governor and two terms in Congress from the Richmond District. He is remembered now only by antiquarians.

[6]He was 37 years of age.

III

After a short week of rejoicing and congratulation, the Virginians were amazed to read an interview given the New York Times by General Canby. If Congress had not so ordered, he would not permit the General Assembly of the Commonwealth, recently elected, to meet in October. As he could not prevent it, he felt it his "duty" to require all the Senators and delegates to take the test oath.

It is exceedingly difficult to understand General Canby's psychology.[7] He was sent to Virginia to maintain a "republican form of government." His idea of government must have been that of Louis XIV.

Throughout the campaign the General did his best (or worse) to defeat Walker and elect Wells. The will of the people was emphatically expressed; now he will set it aside! Canby was an apt pupil of Edwin M. Stanton, long his superior officer, and personal friend; even he who barricaded himself in his office at Washington!

"We have been informed that General Canby has sent circulars to all members of the Legislature, recently elected in Virginia, asking each if he can take the iron-clad oath, namely, whether he has ever given aid or sympathy in any manner, directly or indirectly, to rebellion.

"This oath can not be taken by the great majority, and it will secure to the Radicals the control of the General Assembly. They will send, of course, two Radical Senators to Washington.

---

[7]The *New York Herald*, July 21, 1869.

"We hope that General Grant will interpose his authority to correct so flagrant a wrong. We can see no reason and no justice in overturning the will of the majority of the people so recently and so emphatically expressed."

Horace Greeley,[8] long the most influential Republican editor in the country, came out promptly and emphatically against General Canby's ideas of duty. In speeches made during a tour in Southwestern Virginia two weeks later, Mr. Greeley insisted that such a policy was not "Republican doctrine."

Despite indisputable evidence, James Barron Hope,[9] could not believe that so brave a soldier as General Canby "who now holds the destiny of Virginia in his hands will permit himself to be made the catspaw of a set of designing politicians."

James Barron Hope would not believe it, but that was precisely what Canby proposed to do.

"The Radicals[10] will have no trouble about this matter, for in General Canby they have found a first-rate tool ready to hand."

Behind Canby, of course, one catches the sinister and familiar faces of Henry Horatio Wells and Judge William Curtis Underwood.

The State was torn with many clashing opinions.

"General Grant's policy,[11] ever since his election, has been consistently Radical, especially in regard to Virginia. He reinstated Governor Wells after General Stoneman removed him. He sustained

[8]The *New York Tribune*, June 14, 1869.
[9]*Norfolk Journal*, July 26, 1869.
[10]The *New York Record*, July 27, 1869.
[11]*Alexandria Gazette*, October 24, 1869.

General Canby in all his proceedings, and has consistently removed all those from office who are not Radicals."

That statement is certainly prejudiced, for next day we read:

"General Grant concurs in the removal of Senator Johnston's disabilities." The enemies Grant made are to his credit. Wendell Phillips, abolutionist and ultra-Radical, was abusing General Grant daily by tongue and pen. "Nothing is so foul that he does not shower down" upon President Grant and his administration.

"Great interest is attached to Friday's Cabinet meeting[12] when the test oath in Virginia will be decided.

"In the meantime General Canby has been ordered to take no action" (July 28).

A week of ominous silence, then:

"The action of the Cabinet last week has not been made public, but one member has been heard to remark that the test-oath will not be applied." There was also a persistent rumor that General Canby would be transferred to Mississippi.

Another week: "General Canby is in Washington for an interview with General Grant. It is 'generally understood' that he has been told not to apply the test-oath."

Then a bomb shell in all the metropolitan papers. The Attorney General[13] of the United States has

---

[12]These quotations are gathered from many contemporary newspapers; for endless columns were written on Canby and Virginia.

[13]Ebenezer Richwood Hoar, the less distinguished brother of Senator George Frisbie Hoar, of Massachusetts.

given his opinion that the Virginians must take the test-oath."

Next day brought another sensation:

"The Attorney General denies he has made any such decision, and the rumor was traced to the door of the National Radical headquarters in Washington."

IV

At last the Attorney General spoke. The legislators-elect need not take the iron-bound oath, but any "general legislation by the Assembly would not be lawful until Virginia was fully restored to the Union."

In other words, the General Assembly must obey the behests of Congress. The General Assembly was legal so long as they passed the acts Congress demanded, notably the Fourteenth and Fifteenth Amendments. Anything else they did was illegal. Ah, John Marshall was long since dead![14]

---

[14]CHARLES A. and MARY R. BEARD, *History of the United States*, pp. 370-377.
S. E. FORMAN, *Our Republic*, pp. 506-523.

CHAPTER XL

THE SKIES BRIGHTEN

A light that gleams across the wave
Of darkness, down the rolling years
Piercing the heavy mist of tears
A rainbow shining o'er the wave.
—*Alfred Tennyson.*

From the long and exciting political events of the summer of 1869, it is pleasant to turn to other matters of permanent interest and value to posterity.

The equestrian statue of Washington, which adorns the Capitol Square, certainly one of the most artistic groups of bronze in America, if not the very finest, was designed by Thomas Crawford (1814-57), a native of New York City, who studied in Rome under Thorwaldsen. His model, submitted to the State in 1849, gained the decision over forty-one presented. Crawford's plan included smaller statues of Jefferson, Henry, Marshall, Morgan, Richard Henry Lee, an allegorical "Virginia," Madison and Monroe. George Mason was later substituted for Madison, Nelson for Monroe, and Andrew Lewis for Morgan.[1]

The cornerstone was laid[2] in the presence of President Zachary Taylor and Vice-President Millard

---

[1] MARY NEWTON STANARD, *Richmond*, p. 66.
[2] *Through Centuries Three*, SQUIRES, p. 465.

Fillmore, February 22, 1850; and the statue, as completed, was unveiled February 22, 1858. Only Jefferson and Henry were then in place. George Mason was put upon his pedestal in 1860. After the War Between the States John Marshall was set in place, March 4, 1867.

Of course it was unintentional,[3] but it was certainly an irony that America's great jurist, the illustrious son of Virginia, whose very name is a synonym of legal justice and civic righteousness, should have been unveiled two days after the tyrannical Military Reconstruction Bill of a Radical Congress blotted Virginia from the map of America and substituted "Military District No. 1."

Andrew Lewis was unveiled September 26, 1867, and Thomas Nelson the next day, September 27.

The allegorical and lesser figures were slowly added: "Justice," August 17, 1868; "the Bill of Rights," December 15, 1868; "Finance" and "Independence" were added later during the intense excitement of the Walker-Wells campaign. The cost of the monument completed was $259,913.26, which was reasonable for such an enduring monument to the world's greatest statesmen.

---

[3]MAJOR INNES RANDOLPH commemorated the event by reading an original poem of six stanzas, one of which is given:

> "You come rather late to your pedestal, John;
>   Much sooner you should have been here.
> The book that you hold is no longer *Law*
>   And this is no longer *Virginia*.
> The Justice and Right you expounded of yore
>   Is nothing at all to the purpose.
> The *Martial* law of the new Brigadier
>   Is stronger than Habeas Corpus."

II

Richmond, the State and country, enjoyed a mild sensation when Miss Elizabeth L. Van Lew, daughter of John, was appointed postmistress of that city.

John Van Lew, a prosperous merchant, lived in a great house on Church Hill. He was an intense Unionist, and when Virginia seceded, clung to the Union with a tenacity which made him exceedingly unpopular. He joined the Federal army, while his daughters, remaining in Richmond, are credited with acting as spies and giving the Federal commanders much valuable information. How much of this delicate and questionable "patriotism" is true will probably never be known.

It was interesting to read this comment written long years after by one[4] who claimed to have direct information:

"As soon as Richmond was evacuated, General Grant wanted I should go (sic) to Elizabeth Van Lew's house on Grace St., and see that she had been protected."

Miss Van Lew said to him:

"You probably know I have been in communication with General Grant all the time."

When Colonel Ulric Dahlgren was buried in Richmond, after his daring raid, his father, Admiral John Adolph Dahlgren, sent President Davis one hundred dollars in gold, and requested the return of his son's remains. When the Confederate authorities opened his grave in Oakwood Cemetery, it was

---

[4]DAVID B. PARKER, *A Chautauqua Boy.*

empty! Miss Van Lew and some of her friends had disinterred his body, placed it in a metallic coffin and buried it in a sequestered rural grave.[5]

III

One of the last public executions in Virginia was staged in Richmond, May 29, 1869. A Negro, Albert Taylor, murdered a woman of his own race. It is said that 5,000 spectators viewed the execution.[6]

A dispatch from Washington carried to all parts of the Republic (September 3) the news that General E. R. S. Canby would immediately proclaim the gubernatorial election in Virginia! The citizen who reads that word today will not believe it possible! The military satrap of Virginia had the power to set aside an election, two months after a quarter of a million voters had gone to the polls at the call of the President of the United States, acting under authority of law, passed by both Houses of Congress! This Commonwealth was no more a republic in 1869 than was Poland under the Czar! Surely all who love the Republic and its institutions will blush for shame; and the Virginians will flush with righteous indignation.

Nor was that all. The General called the General Assembly, elected July 6, to meet in Richmond October 5. The test-oath would not be required of the legislators; but they may consider only such

---

[5]MARY NEWTON STANARD, *Richmond*, p. 200.

[6]C. F. WHITFIELD witnessed a public hanging at Jerusalem (Courtland), Virginia, so late as 1882.

items as Congress permits. The Governor-elect will be installed as "Provisional Governor" before the Assembly convenes, but the Lieutenant-Governor-elect will not be installed as Provisional Lieutenant-Governor until the Assembly meets. Then he will be qualified and permitted to preside over the Senate.

The proclamation came from Canby, but it was not of Canby. It was of Grant and Hoar.

The opinion of Attorney General Ebenezer Rockwood Hoar was printed in all the newspapers of the State, September 6, 1869; addressed to General John A. Rawlings, Secretary of War (who died the following day), it was really spoken to E. R. S. Canby.

Mr. Hoar's opinion is far too long to be quoted here, but there is one line that should be preserved:

"Virginia," wrote the Attorney General of the United States, "not being in all respects a State of the Union . . . "

Will the wisest of jurists enlighten posterity as to what "Virginia" was in 1869?

IV

A small, quiet and unostentatious gathering assembled at noon (September 21) in the Governor's Mansion at Richmond. The Governor-elect, Gilbert Carleton Walker,[7] of Norfolk, took the oath, administered by Justice John B. Crenshaw. General E. R. S. Canby graced the occasion by his presence. The retiring Governor, Henry Horatio Wells, was

[7]Fourteenth Annual Report, Library Board of Virginia, p. X.

also present. Besides the oath of office the new
Governor could and did take the iron-clad oath. As
he was a Colonel in the Federal army he might
readily swear that he had not aided nor abetted
"rebellion."

The few who were present shook hands with the
new Provisional Governor and wished him well in
all sincerity and truth.

V

His first official act was to appoint William E.
Cameron as his private secretary. Nothing pleased
the Virginians more. The new secretary came of a
very aristocratic, Colonial family of Petersburg.
As a lad Charles Campbell, the Virginia historian,
was his teacher. He went through the war with
Mahone's brigade and returned to Petersburg as
editor of the Index, one of the boldest of Southern
papers.

The trenchant pen of the dashing young Colonel
got him into trouble with another editor, Robert W
Hughes,[8] who supported the Wells-Harris ticket in
the election; Hughes argued that Wells, being in
touch with the Radical element at Washington,
could serve the State better than Colonel Walker.

Cameron and Hughes decided to shoot it out, but
the Commonwealth stopped them. They repaired

---

[8]Editor of the "State Journal." During the war he edited the "Richmond
Examiner," with John M. Daniel. When Cameron published an editorial in
the "Index-Appeal," which Hughes considered an insult, he sent the Colonel a
challenge. They planned to meet near Chester, but were arrested. The duel
took place "on the tow-path of the Dismal Swamp Canal, just over the North
Carolina Line, June 14, 1869," three months before Cameron was appointed
Secretary.—ROBERT M. HUGHES (private correspondence).

to the Dismal Swamp near the North Carolina line for the duel, and Cameron was badly wounded.

Colonel Cameron was one of General Mahone's closest friends, and most ardent admirers. His appointment came of Mahone. Had not Mahone made the Federal Colonel Governor of Virginia?

If one might have peeped into the Sibylline Books that September morn, he would have read that the day will come (1882-86) when the hands of General Mahone will make William E. Cameron the Governor of Virginia.

Let us meet the new Governor who for the next five years will fill so large and tempestuous a place in the political, financial and economic life of Virginia.

Governor Gilbert Carleton Walker,[9] was born in Binghamton, New York, August 1, 1832. The youth studied law and was something of a Democratic politician in Tioga County, New York. He moved from Oswego to Chicago (1857). His military successes were not important, although he acquired the title of "Colonel." He left the service of a grateful country (while the fighting was still in progress) to embark upon the uncertain seas of finance at Norfolk, as president of the Exchange National Bank.[10]

---

[9] *Through Centuries Three*, SQUIRES, pp. 507-509.

[10] *Norfolk Journal*, January 9, 1867: "The Exchange National Bank, a fine institution, nearly two years old, has declared a dividend of 5% for six months. Gilbert C. Walker, Esqr., is president and has held the position since its organization and has won for himself a high position in this community, through his amiable disposition, affable and graceful manners and undaunted energy. As a citizen of Norfolk he is devoted to her interests, commercial, financial and social. He is one of our best citizens."

He said he located in Norfolk on account of his health (1864); but, as his health seemed to be excellent, the Colonel should have thought of a reason less trite. A ready and fluent speaker (although no Patrick Henry), his gifts made him popular.

After his term he remained in Richmond and was elected, as a Democrat, to the House of Representatives. He was reputed the handsomest man on the floor (1874-78), of the House.

But let others speak of the Governor-elect:

"The true Republican party selected a handsome, dissolute fellow[11] for Governor. He drifted into the State with the Federal army and was now in a bank at Norfolk."[12]

A gifted historian[13] says, "He was a moderate and intelligent man, strongly connected in congressional circles."

"If the Virginia politicians had shown even reasonable astuteness, they would have discovered that their carpet-bagger candidate for Governor did not merit the support of our people."[14]

Walker was selected to make a whirlwind campaign and capture votes. His Northern blood and breeding were immense assets in Washington. For all the criticism directed against him we doubt whether Mahone and Stuart could have found a man better fitted to lead the coalition campaign.

---

[11]It must be confessed that there was much unfavorable gossip touching the Governor's private life and his morals.

[12]JOHN SERGEANT WISE, whose caustic pen is not always gentle when it deals with political and professional rivals.

[13]C. C. PEASON, *History of Readjusters in Virginia.*

[14]WILLIAM C. PENDLETON, *History of Appalachian Virginia.*

His rigid enforcement of law and order won for him the sobriquet, "Political Saviour of Virginia." "When he retired he was the most popular man in Virginia[15] and the one-term principle alone prevented his re-election." His final migration was to New York City where he enjoyed a large practice until his death (May 11, 1885).

[15]LYON G. TYLER, *Virginia Biography*, Vol. III, p. 4.

CHAPTER XLI

THE GENERAL ASSEMBLY CONVENES

And now, as the night was senescent
And star-dials pointed to morn—
As the star-dials hinted of morn—
At the end of our path a liquescent
And nebulous lustre was born,
Out of which a miraculous crescent
Arose with a duplicate horn
Astarte's bediamond crescent
Distinct with its duplicate horn.

—*Edgar Allan Poe.*

Two and a half years had passed since the Old Line Whigs finished their agenda and adjourned. To these familiar halls used by the legislature for three generations and by the Confederate Congress for four bloody years, new representatives gathered October 5, 1869.

They elected Zeph Turner president of the House of Delegates, and J. Bell Bigger, clerk. The roll of the House was read as follows:

Accomac—Edmund R. Bagwell, J. R. Read, Thomas C. Parramore.
Albemarle—J. C. Hill, S. V. Southall, James D. Jones.
Alexandria—G. L. Seaton, R. Johnston.
Alleghany and Craig—B. L. Woodson.
Amelia—John R. Moss.
Amherst—Joseph H. Massie, L. P. Richeson, J. E. Adams.
Appomattox—R. B. Poore.
Augusta—H. M. Bell, Marshall Hanger, A. B. Cochrane.
Bath and Highland—J. R. Popham.
Bedford—B. H. Moulton, J. O. Hensley, J. R. Thurman.
Bland—Addison Davis.

Botetourt—Cary Breckinridge.
Brunswick—John Duggar.
Buchanan and Wise—J. T. Chase.
Buckingham—J. H. Noble, Caesar Perkins.
Campbell—R. A. Murrell, Robert C. Burkholder, John W. Daniel.
Caroline—R. O. Peatross, J. M. Hudgin.
Carroll—F. W. Lindsey.
Charles City—R. G. W. Jones.
Charlotte—G. W. Graham, W. H. Ragsdale.
Chesterfield and Powhatan—S. F. Maddox, Henry Cox, B. T. Edwards.
Clarke—W. W. Arnett.
Culpeper—J. R. Strother.
Cumberland—James Lipscomb.
Dinwiddie—Ellis Wilson.
Elizabeth City and Warwick—William Bartlett, B. D. White.
Essex—W. R. Wentworth.
Fairfax—Job Hawxhurst.
Fauquier—James Keith, F. L. Marshall, A. Glascock.
Floyd—George Young.
Fluvanna—John Henson.
Franklin—B. N. Hatcher, G. H. T. Greer, S. F. Hutcherson.
Frederick—D. J. Miller, John F. Wall.
Giles—F. W. Mahood.
Gloucester—J. N. Stubbs.
Goochland—J. B. Miller, Jr.
Grayson—L. H. Bryant.
Greene—T. M. Sherman.
Greenville—Peter K. Jones.
Halifax—Alexander Owen, W. W. Wood, Isaac Edmundson.
Hanover—W. R. Winn, C. L. Thompson.
Henrico and City of Richmond—A. Bodeker, A. M. Keiley, William
    Lovenstein, L. H. Frayser, J. S. Atlee, Stephen Mason, John H.
    Guy, G. K. Gilmer, J. B. Crenshaw.
Henry—C. Y. Thomas.
Isle of Wight—George R. Atkinson, John W. Lawson.
James City and Williamsburg—F. S. Norton.
King and Queen—J. W. Bulman.
King George—W. A. J. Potts.
King William—B. F. Jones.
Lancaster—Josiah Tatum, John S. Chowning.
Lee—William McDonald.
Loudoun—I. D. Budd, William Mathew.
Louisa—F. M. Perkins, B. McCraken.
Lunenburg—Stith Bolling.
Madison—J. W. Walker, Jr.

Mathews—Henry Bell.

Mecklenburg—S. M. Dodge, John Watson, Ross Hamilton.

Middlesex—L. C. Bristow.

Montgomery—R. A. Miller.

Nansemond—David Thayer.

Nelson—W. L. Williams.

New Kent—W. H. Brisby.

Norfolk City—H. M. Bowden, A. S. Segar.

Norfolk County and Portsmouth—Luther Lee, Jr., C. E. Hodges, A. L. Woodworth, E. B. Holloman.

Northampton—J. C. Toy.

Northumberland—B. G. Haynie.

Nottoway—George H. Southall.

Orange—David Pannill.

Page—John W. Ashby, Henry M. Keyser.

Patrick—W. F. B. Taylor.

Petersburg—Peter G. Morgan, George Fayerman.

Pittsylvania—M. H. Clark, Walter Coles, W. J. Fulton, T. H. Gosney.

Prince Edward—T. P. Jackson.

Prince George—A. N. Fretz.

Prince William—W. A. Bryant.

Princess Anne—John Q. Hodges.

Pulaski—W. J. Wall.

Rappahannock—Zeph Turner.

Richmond County—L. R. Stewart.

Roanoke—J. A. McCaull.

Rockbridge—W. McLaughlin, S. B. Morrison, A. Graham.

Rockingham—Philo Bradley, H. B. Harnsberger.

Russell—J. H. A. Smith.

Scott—E. F. Tiller, J. H. Horton.

Shenandoah—J. L. Campbell.

Smyth—J. A. Kelly, James L. Buchanan.

Southampton—R. U. Burges.

Spottsylvania—J. H. Kelly.

Stafford—J. C. Shelton.

Surry—W. H. Andrews.

Sussex—W. N. Stevens.

Tazewell—Henry Bowen.

Warren—Smith S. Turner.

Washington—George Graham, J. F. Terry.

Westmoreland—Geo. Walker.

Wythe—J. H. Fulton, Joseph J. Graham.

York—Robert Norton.

The Senate was organized with the Provisional Lieutenant-Governor John Francis Lewis,[1] President, and Shelton C. Davis, clerk.

Thomas E. Taylor, Edgar Snowden, Jr.—*Alexandria, Fairfax and Loudoun.*

Thomas N. Latham—*Fauquier, Rappahannock and Prince William.*

Daniel A. Grimsley—*Orange, Culpeper and Madison.*

Charles Herndon—*Louisa, Spottsylvania and Stafford.*

William P. Moseley—*Powhatan, Goochland and Fluvanna.*

Robert S. Beazley—*Albemarle and Greene.*

Frank Moss—*Appomattox and Buckingham.*

Thomas P. Fitzpatrick—*Amherst and Nelson.*

James Patterson—*Henry and Franklin.*

Abner Anderson—*Pittsylvania.*

Robert L. Owen—*Campbell.*

William R. Terry—*Bedford.*

Marcus A. Harris—*Halifax.*

James W. D. Bland and John T. Hamlett—*Charlotte and Prince Edward.*

Albert P. Lathrop, Frank W. Haskell—*Mecklenburg.*

Meriweather Lewis—*Lancaster, King George, Richmond, Westmoreland, Northumberland.*

Edmund W. Massey—*Caroline, Essex, and King William.*

William K. Perrin—*King and Queen, Middlesex, Gloucester, Mathews.*

Charles Campbell, Normand Smith, Alfred R. Courtney—*Richmond City and Henrico.*

Walter Herron Taylor—*Norfolk and Princess Anne.*

George Teamoh—*Portsmouth and Norfolk County.*

Washington L. Riddick—*Isle of Wight, Nansemond, Southampton.*

David G. Carr—*Greenville, Sussex and Dinwiddie.*

Isaiah L. Lyons—*York, Surrey, Elizabeth City and Warwick.*

William A. Austin—*Brunswick and Lunenburg.*

William T. Martin—*Prince George, Chesterfield.*

Franklin Wood, Roscoe G. Greene—*Petersburg.*

Abel T. Johnson—*Accomac and Northampton.*

J. Ambler Smith—*Hanover, New Kent, Charles City, James City.*

John Robinson—*Amelia, Cumberland, Nottoway.*

William D. Smith—*Clark, Shenandoah and Frederick.*

John E. Roller—*Page, Warren, Rockingham.*

Joseph A. Waddell—*Augusta and Highland.*

William A. Anderson—*Bath, Rockbridge, Alleghany.*

Edmund Pendleton—*Botetourt, Roanoke, Craig, Giles.*

---

[1] After John F. Lewis was elected Senior United States Senator for Virginia, the Senate elected John L. Marye, President of the Senate.

John E. Penn—*Patrick, Floyd, Montgomery.*
Alexander M. Davis—*Wythe, Grayson, Carroll.*
James M. French—*Pulaski, Tazewell, Bland and Russell.*
George H. Kendrick—*Lee, Scott, Wise, Buchanan.*
James S. Greever—*Smythe and Washington.*

In his message to the General Assembly,[2] the Provisional Governor recommended that the General Assembly ratify the Fourteenth and Fifteenth Amendments, which must be done before the State could be readmitted to the Union.

Despite his previous experience General E. R. S. Canby sprung a disagreeable surprise.[3] He withheld the election certificates of 27 Conservative members; and required all the members of the General Assembly to take a new variety of oath: That they were now loyal to the United States, and that they would support the Constitution; and that they would never hereafter be guilty of armed rebellion against the nation.

The stubborness, petty tyranny and gratuitous rudeness of General Canby were amazing. That kind of oath was, under the circumstances, an insult to the Assembly and to the million citizens there represented.

But it is to be patient and forgiving! The race of Virginia's last satrap is almost run; and, in a few short years he will lie in his own blood, assassinated by a treacherous band of Modoc Indians (April 11, 1873).

The Radicals, although now a helpless minority, left no stone unturned. They promptly protested

---

[2] R. L. MORTON, "submitted on the third day of its session."
[3] General Canby had the typical Bourbon spirit, which (to quote Voltaire) learns nothing and forgets nothing.

(October 6) that any member, who could not take the test-oath, should be denied a seat in the Assembly. Their protest was quietly laid on the table. No doubt it still reposes there, for it has never been taken up.

This protest was said to have been inspired by Benjamin F. Butler, who, it seems, could not keep itching fingers off the affairs of Virginia.[4] Perhaps he planned to use the protest as ammunition at Washington, if occasion required. Many staunch Republican papers, North and West, were outspoken in disgust at the useless and unsportsmanlike attitude of General Butler and the Virginia Radicals.

A dispatch from Baltimore gave the Virginians pause. General Benjamin F. Butler, the implacable Radical, influential in the House of Representatives, and Senator Charles Sumner, proposed to keep Virginia, Mississippi and Texas out of the Union and under bayonet rule.

The motion to admit any one of them would, according to the Baltimore dispatch, be quietly referred to the Radical Committee on Reconstruction. Its report would be delayed from time to time, debated, amended, re-referred and otherwise delayed until Congress adjourned.

"General Butler[5] is determined to keep the Union asunder as long as it is possible. He will do his utmost to prevent the readmission of Virginia, but he will not succeed."

There is a Divine law, "with what measure ye

[4]It is astonishing how that man enters and reenters the history of this Commonwealth; with a shadow always repugnant and repelling.

[5]*Norfolk Journal*, November 3, 1869.

mete, it shall be measured unto you again." Three
weeks later the same paper carried this news item:
"Mrs. Florence, of New Orleans, has had General
Benjamin F. Butler arrested, charging him with
taking three valuable swords, one the property of
General Twiggs, one belonging to the State of
Georgia, one to Texas; the three estimated to be
worth $35,000. He also took a box of silver belong-
ing to the plaintiff, worth, she said, $2,000. The
General claimed he had deposited the swords with
the Treasury Department; at the Department it
was stated they could not be found. He gave bail
for $15,000."

We suppose no officer in the Federal Army was
more cordially hated by the Southern people than
Benjamin Franklin Butler. His name, especially in
New Orleans and Norfolk, causes a shudder to this
distant day.

It seems that General Butler was not more popular
in the North than in the South. General Grant removed him for incompetency in 1864, and he never
forgave General Grant.

He ran as a Republican for Governor of the very
Republican State of Massachusetts in 1871, and was
defeated.

He ran for Governor as a Democrat in 1878 and
1879 and was twice defeated. General Butler
changed his politics with ease. In 1860 he was a
pronounced and ardent Jeff-Davis-for-President
Democrat.

In 1882 the Democrats elected him Governor of
Massachusetts, but in 1883 he was again defeated.

In 1884 he became the Greenback candidate for President, running on a printing-press-currency platform against Cleveland and Blaine. It need hardly be said that General Butler was defeated, but there were 133,825 men who voted for him. All of which has only remote connection with the thread of this narrative, but it is introduced as Virginia bids General Butler farewell and forever.

II

The two offensive amendments to the Federal Constitution, the Fourteenth and Fifteenth, were adopted with practical unanimity (October 8), by the General Assembly. Not because Virginia desired or approved them; but it was demanded, a punishment for secession and defeat. The Fourteenth Amendment passed the Senate (40 to 2) and the Delegates without opposition.[6] It will be remembered that the Fourteenth Amendment had been adopted by the requisite number of States and that the President proclaimed it on New Year's Day preceding. Nevertheless the Virginians were required to adopt it, a bit of mental and moral subjection and humiliation.

III

It was a moot question as to whether the Legislature might legally elect two senators to be seated when Virginia was readmitted. The Radicals cried

[6] R. L. MORTON: "The XIV Amendment was ratified by the Senate 36 to 4 and in the House of Delegates by a vote of 126 to 6. The XV Amendment was ratified by the Senate 40 to 2, and in the House unanimously."

out against such presumption! So the problem was submitted directly to the Attorney General of the United States, Ebenezer Rockwood Hoar. He decided that they might be elected.

Accordingly, on October 19, John Francis Lewis was elected senior Senator for Virginia by a vote of 116 on joint ballot over the Radical nominee, Alexander Sharpe.

John Francis Lewis was a pronounced Scotch-Irish Unionist, one of those men who never change their minds. He went to the Secession Convention of 1861 from his native heath and fought the Secessionists tooth and nail. When the Ordinance was passed Lewis was as bitterly opposed as ever. Unlike his neighbor and Unionist friend, Alexander H. H. Stuart, he never signed the fatal document. Lewis led the ticket in the Walker-Wells campaign and now the Legislature rewarded the stout old Whig with a seat in the United States Senate. He deserved it.

Judge John Warwick Johnston, of Tazewell County, whose disabilities were removed by a special act of Congress, and who had been appointed to the bench by General Stoneman, was elected by a vote of 110 over L. H. Chandler, of Norfolk, the Radical candidate.

John Warwick Johnston was the brother of Joseph Eggleston Johnston, the great Confederate chieftain. They were grandsons of Peter Johnston, who ran away from school to join Light Horse Harry Lee and fight the battles of the Revolution. After the war he married Mary Wood (Johnston), a niece of Patrick Henry.

The two Senators were well chosen, Confederate and Unionist, Democrat and Whig, each represented an influential element in the population. It was good politics and incidentally each belonged to a fine, old Colonial family. The bottom rail was no longer on top in Virginia! As there was nothing else they could do, the General Assembly adjourned October 20 until February 11, 1870.

IV

A month after the General Assembly left the Capitol, the defeated and discouraged Radicals held a rally at Richmond (November 24) and made their last, a futile appeal. Well they knew that their only hope was in Federal bayonets.

Charles Howell Porter, of Norfolk,[7] was chairman and his was the influential voice. This amateur statesman filled a large place (for a short time) in local circles. A paragraph may be dedicated to his memory.

He was born in Cairo, New York, some thirty-seven years before. He practiced law in Greene County, New York, and joined the First New York Mounted Rifles. After an unimpressive military career, the young lawyer settled in Virginia. He

---

[7]LYON G. TYLER, *Cyclop of Virginia Biography*, Vol. III, p. 125.

H. W. BURTON, *History of Norfolk*, pp. 99, etc.

In 1865 Porter was Commonwealth's Attorney.

In 1867 he secured the arrest of five prominent citizens (W. W. Lamb, A. L. Hill, John E. Doyle, Conway Whittle and S. Marsh) for refusing to admit evidence of some Negroes in a larceny case.

He was a member of the Underwood Constitutional Convention, 1867-1868, sitting for Chesterfield and Powhatan Counties.

He died in Cairo, New York, July 9, 1897.

was a member of Congress for two terms. His political career in Virginia done, he returned to New York; but the good folk there did not avail themselves of his talents.

The Radicals were cheap politicians, stupid to a degree. Instead of acquiescing in the will of the people, they declared that the election of July 6 was a "Confederate triumph," that President Grant made a blunder in allowing some sections of the Constitution to be eliminated by popular vote. The Legislature, just adjourned, had not adopted the XV Amendment . . . in fact, it was an illegal body, hence all its acts were illegal. They asked Congress to set aside the election and that the unexpurgated Underwood Constitution be forced upon the people who had repudiated it.

"The secret of our defeat was in the unfortunate submission to a separate vote, the test-oath and disfranchising clauses of the State Constitution; in direct opposition to the deliberate opinion of the rank and file of the Republican party in Virginia."

The Radicals asked a new referendum and in event of a new election[8] for a military force. "This is perhaps our last stand. If we are defeated, the colored people will again be at the mercy of their former masters, the national debt will be repudiated, and the rebel, Democratic yoke will be placed on the American people in 1872."[9]

It would be difficult to find a paper which combined more truth with more falsehood!

---

[8]"In the event of a new election we would ask for a military force sufficient to protect us in our political and civil rights."

[9]*Through Centuries Three*, squires, p. 508.

Against this Radical folly the native Virginians, those who expected to remain in the State and who were really interested in building a Republican party in Virginia, protested, and finally withdrew from Porter's convention.

The schism in the party was fatal.

It was now increasingly evident that the Virginians were about to regain control of Virginia, that the night was waning and that the light of a new and better day trembled at dawn.[10]

---

[10]SIR EDWARD COKE: "Truth, per adventure, by force, may for a time be trodden down; but never, by any means whatsoever, can it be trodden out."

CHAPTER XLII

VIRGINIA READMITTED TO THE UNION

Our Union is river, lake, ocean and sky;
Man breaks not the medal, when God cuts the die!
Though darkened with sulphur, tho cloven with steel,[1]
The blue arch will brighten, the waters will heal!
                    —*Oliver Wendell Holmes.*

When Congress met at noon, December 6, 1869, the eyes of a million citizens in Virginia and 10,000,-000 in the South turned toward the National Capitol, with alternating hope and fear. This attitude was well expressed:[2] "Congress meets today. For Virginia it will be the most important event since the Revolution. We suppose that our State will be very promptly admitted. Senator Wilson, of Massachusetts, is reported to have said last Friday that Virginia would be in the Union in ten days.

"We see no reason why the State should not be admitted at once, for she has complied in good faith with every demand made upon her by Congress and the President. There may be some effort on the part of Sumner and Butler to prevent her reconstruction, but it will amount to nothing."

President Grant in his first annual message (De-

---

[1]That was Dr. Holmes' idea of the Federal Union in 1861-1865. It was certainly not the idea of Hancock, Adams, Franklin and the founding fathers of New England in 1789.

[2]JAMES BARRON HOPE, *Norfolk Journal*, December 6, 1869.

cember 6, 1869), recommended that Virginia's representatives be seated in Senate and House, and that the Commonwealth "be fully restored to its place in the family of States."

Congress referred this recommendation to the Judiciary Committee: Lyman Trumbull of Illinois, chairman; George Franklin Edmonds of Vermont, Roscoe Conkling of New York, Matthew Hale Carpenter of Wisconsin, and Allen G. Thurman of Indiana.

Some still radically inclined insisted that additional conditions be required, but the Committee finally decided that it was better to pass a simple resolution declaring the "State of Virginia is entitled to representation in Congress," as she has complied with the Reconstruction resolution of March 2, 1867, fully and in good faith. A committee of ten prominent Virginians was in Washington to urge readmission.

Although the Radicals raised every objection possible and insisted upon additional conditions, the resolution was passed by the House (January 13, 1870), 136 pro, 58 contra.

II

But when the resolution reached the Senate, the Radicals were more successful. Charles Sumner had lost none of his hatred for the "accursed section." He cried vehemently, "Virginia is still smoking with rebellion."

Recent elections both in Virginia and Georgia made the Radicals fear that these two States, once freed of bayonet rule, would send Democratic representatives to Washington . . . (exactly what they did).

The Senate then passed the following resolution (47 pro and 10 contra) and sent it to the House for concurrent action. An act to admit the State of Virginia to Representation in the Congress of the United States:

Whereas, the people of Virginia have framed and adopted a Constitution of State government, which is Republican; and

Whereas, the Legislature of Virginia, elected under said Constitution, have ratified the Fourteenth and Fifteenth Amendments of the Constitution of the United States; and,

Whereas, the performance of these several acts in good faith was a condition precedent to the representation of the State in Congress; therefore,

Be it enacted, etc.

That the State of Virginia is entitled to representation in the Congress of the United States:

Provided,

That before any member of the Legislature of said State shall take or resume his seat or any officer of said State shall enter upon the duties of his office, he shall take and subscribe, and file in the office of the Secretary of the State of Virginia for permanent preservation, an oath in the form following:

"I, ———— ————, do solemnly swear that I have never taken an oath as a member of Congress, or as an officer of the United States or as a member of any State Legislature, or as an executive or judicial officer of any State, to support the Constitution of the United States, and afterward engaged in insurrection or rebellion against the same, or given aid or comfort to the enemies thereof, so help me God"; or such person shall in like manner take, subscribe and file the following oath:

"I, ————— —————, do solemnly swear that I have, by act of the Congress of the United States, been relieved from the disabilities imposed upon me by the Fourteenth Amendment of the Constitution of the United States, so help me God," which oaths shall be taken before and certified by any officer lawfully authorized to administer oaths. And any person who shall knowingly swear falsely in taking either of such oaths shall be deemed guilty of perjury, and shall be punished therefor by imprisonment, not less than one year, and not more than ten years, and shall be fined not less than $1,000 and not more than $10,000. And in all trials for any violation of this act the certificate of the taking of either of said oaths, with proof of the signature of the party accused, shall be taken and held as conclusive evidence that such an oath was lawfully and regularly administered by competent authority.

And provided, further, That every such person who shall neglect for the period of thirty days next after the passage of this act to take, subscribe and file such oath as aforesaid, shall be deemed and taken, to all intents and purposes to have vacated his office.

And provided, further, That the State of Virginia is entitled to representation in Congress upon the following fundamental conditions:

That the Constitution of Virginia shall never be amended or changed as to deprive any class of citizens of the United States of the right to vote who are entitled to vote by the Constitution herein recognized, except as a punishment for such crimes as are now felonies at common law, whereof they shall have been duly convicted under laws equally applicable to all the inhabitants of said State:

Provided—

That any alteration of said Constitution, prospective in its effects, may be made in regard to the time and place of residence of voters.

That it shall never be lawful for the said State to deprive any citizen of the United States, on account of his race, color or previous condition of servitude, of the right to hold office under the Constitution and laws of said State, or, upon any such ground to require of him any other qualifications for office than such as are required of all other citizens; that the Constitution of Virginia shall never be so amended or changed as to deprive any citizen or class of citizens, of the United States of the school rights and privileges secured by the Constitution of said State."

III

The debate was graphically described,[3] "The debate in the House today (January 24) on the motion to concur with the Senate upon the amendments to the Virginia bill was sharp, short and decisive. It was probably the most exciting, as it was certainly the most amusing, of the session.

"The whole subject was disposed of in little over an hour, during which time there were six or seven speeches made, all of them compact and full of well-sustained points, from the standpoint of the respective members who took part.

[3] *Norfolk Journal*, Washington Correspondent, January 26, 1870.

"The old quarrel between Butler and Bingham was opened, and each made it apparent that they had not buried the tomahawk, but each was only waiting to take a scalp. General Butler, like the Senator from his State (Sumner, of Massachusetts) has undertaken to read some of the Republicans out of the party and has been severely taken to task for his presumption. General Logan, of Illinois; Mr. Bingham, of Ohio, and General Farnsworth, of Illinois, revolted this afternoon and would have none of it. They severely attacked General Butler and alleged that while he has been vacillating and erratic, they have been consistent politicians and consistent Republicans. Mr. Farnsworth was especially emphatic. It was acknowledged that he made one of the happiest speeches the House has heard this season. Severe, yet, parliamentary, his statements and facts were conclusive; so much so that they were not controverted by General Butler. Throughout the debate with its acrimony, humor and repartee the vast audience was held in deep interest and at times the members gathered around the speakers in crowds, the better to hear and appreciate their words. The vote was taken very quietly, and before the yeas and nays were announced many had left for dinner, it being apparent that the only dissentionists were on the Democratic side of the House and the Senate bill, with the amendments, would pass by a large majority. Virginia was admitted without the slightest manifestation of feeling.

"The burden of Mr. Bingham's speech was that the conditions imposed by the Senate amendments

are void and of no effect in law; that unless they
are based upon the Constitution they can not be enforced after Virginia has been admitted. And this
was substantially the argument of Logan and Farnsworth. The new Constitution of the State was
lauded as the most perfect of any of the States on
this Continent. It was charged that the very men
who are here opposing her admission are from States
whose fundamental laws compare most unfavorably
with those of Virginia. It is claimed that in passing
this Constitution the State has added new lustre to
her name.

"General Butler wanted to know what party Mr.
Bingham belonged to. Bingham replied that the
question was uncalled for and impertinent. Vul-
garity, he said, is not wit. Here the Democrats applauded and Butler, who had run down the aisle to
get off his little query, returned discomfited.

"Butler complained that the House bill was passed
by snap judgment, that advantage was taken of his
absence when he was enjoying a holiday. He had
read that the Virginians intended to give Bingham a
dinner, and he would like to see them feasting with
the man they had so often denounced. Butler
raged and fairly foamed, as though taken with
rabies, as he hissed across the hall. Bingham sat
smiling in derision and quietly took a new chew
of tobacco. Butler expected the House to come
down with laughter, but even his usual claqueurs did
not respond. He agreed that Virginia's Constitution
was the best on the Continent, but reminded the
House that it was written by carpet-baggers and
scalawags. The amendments were intended to give

notice to the world that if Virginia failed to keep her promise she would feel the power of Congress as Georgia now feels it.

"He believed that Governor Walker was a high-minded man, and he doubtless will do all he can to keep the faith. There was no evidence of widespread fraud in the recent election! Butler labored to make an impression and to excite laughter, but he failed.

"Farnsworth replied that he had been a Republican when Butler was chasing fugitive slaves in Massachusetts (laughter and applause). He had been a Republican when Butler[4] was voting to make Jefferson Davis President of the United States, and when he was electioneering for Breckenridge (roars of laughter and rounds of applause). Butler's convictions and his conversion to Republicanism were so sudden that it put St. Paul to shame (laughter). But he really thought that the brave general resembled St. Peter who deserted his Master. The general's conversion was so recent that he must curse and swear to make people believe it genuine (laughter). So the gentleman from Massachusetts must be exceedingly radical (much laughter).

"This bill had been debated four days while General Butler was enjoying his holiday.

"General Farnsworth's speech so completely upset Butler that he sat wiping the perspiration from his forehead, to the rare and evident delight of those whom he had often hectored and bullied.

---

[4] To the other items that blacken the character of B. F. Butler should be added that of plagiarist. In the "Democratic Review," May, 1838, p. 196, he has a sonnet on "La Fayette," copied *verbatim* from the poem written by Dolly Madison. *Fugitive Verse*, ARMISTEAD C. GORDON, p. 197.

"While the conservative Republicans did not concur in the Senate's amendments, they would vote to admit Virginia and so close the matter."

The bill passed the House 136 pro, 58 contra; all the Democrats voting in the negative.

IV

In this long but illuminating quotation from a reporter, who was evidently a witness of the scenes he describes, there are several items that need remark.

Mr. Bingham's contention that the Senate's amendments were void was correct as time has long since proved. Once readmitted, Virginia could and did manage her own affairs and none could molest her under the Constitution.

Virginia's admirable Constitution, probably the "best on the Continent," was the old Constitution of 1850, from which much that the Underwood Constitution-makers added had been pruned away. The complimentary remarks, intended for the carpetbaggers and scalawags, were really an involuntary tribute to the able Constitutional Convention of 1850.[5]

The Radicals always claimed that Walker was elected by fraud. Butler's statement that there was no fraud in that election was certainly intended to be humorous and ironical.

It is true that Ben Butler was an ante-bellum Democrat and he voted at Charleston some 54

---

[5] *Through Centuries Three*, SQUIRES, pp. 455-456.

times to make Jefferson Davis the Democratic nominee, instead of Stephen A. Douglas.[6]

The Democrats voted solidly against the admission of Virginia as a protest against the Senate's Radical amendments. The Democrats labored incessantly for the readmission of all the Southern States, Virginia included. They knew the State would be admitted. Had there been any doubt, enough Democratic votes would have been thrown to the proposition to carry it. Their negative vote was strictly party tactics.

[6]HARRY THRUSTON PECK, *Twenty Years of the Republic*, p. 201.

Chapter XLIII

UNLEASHED

> All the future, in some sense, has its roots in the past. We cannot ignore the past and live wholly in the future. If we were stripped of the ability to remember, we should never be civilized. The power to convert past things to present uses, and present things to future uses measures the civilizing forces of men and nations.
>
> —*Henry Ward Beecher.*

Richmond received the news of the readmission of the Commonwealth to the Union after nightfall, January 24, 1870. The City Council meeting that night hailed it with delight and requested General Canby to fire a salute of one hundred guns in the Capitol Square next day.[1]

At noon, January 25, the salute was fired in the presence of 5,000 people. The National flag was raised over the Capitol and Governor Walker made a brief address, in which he predicted a future for Virginia, greater and more glorious even than her past.

There were also colored orators who took occasion to say that if Virginia did not keep all the Senate's amendments the State would again be reduced to the status of a Territory. It is interesting to note this local echo of General Butler's speech at Washington the day before.

---

[1] WILLIAM ASBURY CHRISTIAN, *History of Richmond*, p. 312.

James Barron Hope[2] made this comment, "To the friends of the New Movement we offer our hearty congratulations; and to its enemies—if there be any left—we propose a general amnesty."

Those words were surely a gracious and well-earned tribute to Alexander Hugh Holmes Stuart and the other Old Line Whigs who had labored through long, hard and discouraging years to save the civilization of Virginia. Next morning, January 26, President Grant affixed his signature, and sent the document to the State Department. "The failure to send it to the House of Representatives today was a blunder," wrote an alert reporter.

With the firing of the salute and the hailing of the national emblem, and the usual flood of oratory, there followed less sensational but significant functions. Colonel Walker took the oath as Governor of Virginia, and again appointed Colonel William E. Cameron, of Petersburg, his secretary. He promptly issued a proclamation to the effect that Virginia was once again an integral part of the nation, which could never have been established without her prowess and generosity. He called a meeting of the General Assembly for February 8, 1870. He appointed John L. Marye, Jr., of Fredericksburg, Lieutenant-Governor of Virginia to serve the term of John Francis Lewis, now seated as the senior Senator from Virginia.

[2]Editor of the *Norfolk Journal* and frequently quoted because of his clear thinking and logical statement, his fine self-control and exalted patriotism.

II

At Washington, as well as at Richmond, events were making history for the Virginians.[3] In the Senate Virginia had been represented and misrepresented for nine years lacking two months. When the Thirty-seventh Congress met March 4, 1861, the day President Lincoln was inaugurated, the senior Senator for Virginia, James Murray Mason, was in his seat. And the junior Senator, R. M. T. Hunter, was also present. Although the Ordinance of Secession was not adopted by Virginia until April 17 following, both Senators resigned March 28, '61, and left Washington.

Senator Mason (1798-1871), of Winchester, entered the United States Senate in 1847 and was regarded as one of the most brilliant and influential leaders on the floor.

Robert Mercer Taliaferro Hunter (1809-'89), of Lloyds, the junior Senator, had also served since 1847. He later became Secretary of State in the Confederate Cabinet.

Four months after the two Senators withdrew, July 11, both were "expelled" by action of the Senate, for it was the theory of the Lincoln administration that Virginia was still in the Union and that the Ordinance of Secession was invalid.

Two days later, July 13, two new Senators were seated from "Virginia"; the new senior Senator was

[3]HARRY WESTBROOK DUNNING. Seven unwholesome years were required to demonstrate that the government which could and did quell the greatest rebellion in history could not maintain the freedmen on the necks of their former masters.

Waitman Thomas Willey (1811-1900), of Morgan-town, still in Virginia. He became the successor of Senator Mason.

John Snyder Carlile (1817-'78), of Wheeling, was seated in Hunter's place, as junior Senator.

In this same troubled year, 1861, Virginia had thirteen representatives in the House. Muscoe Russell Hunter Garnett (1821-'64), of Loretto, serving his second term.

John Singleton Millson (1808-'73), of Norfolk, who had been a member of the House of Representatives since 1849.

Coleman DeJarnette (1822-'81), of Bowling Green, now serving his first term.

Roger Atkinson Pryor (1829-1919), of Petersburg, who was also serving his first term. Mr. Pryor later became a Brigadier in the Confederate Army, and still later a judge in New York City.

Thomas Stanley Bocock (1815-'91), of Appomattox, serving since 1847.

Shelton Farrar Leake (1812-'84), of Charlottesville, seated in the House since 1845, Lieutenant-Governor of Virginia 1851-'54 and again returned to the House in 1859.

William Smith (1797-1887), of Warrenton, the picturesque "Extra Billy," was first seated in 1841. He became Governor of Virginia (1846-'49), and was returned to the House again in 1859. At the age of 65 he entered the Confederate Army, became a Brigadier and was a second time inaugurated Governor (1864-'65).

Alexander Robinson Boteler (1815-'92), of Shepherdstown, now serving his first term.   Later he became a member of Stonewall Jackson's staff.

John Thomas Harris (1823-'99), now serving his first term, and after the readmission of Virginia he served from 1871 to 1881.

Sherrard Clemens (1820-'81), of Wheeling, seated in 1852.   He later served in the Confederate Army.

Albert Gallatin Jenkins (1830-'64), of Green Bottom, seated in 1857.   He became a Brigadier in the Confederate Army and was killed in the Battle of Cloyd's Mountain, Pulaski County, May 9, 1864.

Henry Alonzo Edmondson (1814-'90), of Salem, seated in 1849.

Elbert S. Martin, of Lee County, now serving his first term.

Some of the Unionist members of Congress remained after the Commonwealth seceded.

Jacob B. Blair, of Parkersburg, took the seat John S. Carlile vacated when he was promoted to the Senate.

William G. Brown, of Kingwood, did not retire.

Joseph E. Segar, at Elizabeth City, claimed a seat February 11, 1862, but was at first denied.   He was finally seated May 2, 1862.

Charles H. Upton, of Falls Church, was recognized and seated July 4, 1861, after the election was unsuccessfully disputed by S. Ferguson Beach, of Alexandria.

Lewis McKenzie, of Alexandria, was seated February 16, 1863, and he was returned to the House again in 1870.

Kelliam V. Whaley, of Ceredo, retained his seat.

When the Thirty-eighth Congress assembled,
March 4, 1863, four months before West Virginia
was admitted as a State, John S. Carlile and Lemuel
J. Bowden were seated as the two Senators from Virginia. There were no Representatives recognized
or seated.

The Fortieth Congress assembled March 4, 1867,
as has been described in detail, and the second term
began March 4, '69, four months before the Virginia
election of July 6.

When Virginia was readmitted, January 26, 1870,
John Warfield Johnston was seated as the senior
Senator and John Francis Lewis as junior Senator.

John Warfield Johnston was introduced to the
Senate January 28, by Senator Willey, of West
Virginia, who stated that Senator-elect Johnston
asked to take the oath and be seated as the junior
Senator of Virginia, his disabilities as a Confederate
sympathizer in the late war having been removed by
an act of Congress.

Senator George Franklin Edmunds, of Vermont,
objected. He understood that the disabilities of
another Johnston had been removed. Senator Willey
had the necessary documents and identified the
Senator-elect as the "J. W. Johnston, of Washington
County."

Senator Charles Sumner,[4] of course, had a remark
to make. It was to the effect that no objection
could be raised if the Senator-elect were the party

[4]GEORGE H. HAYNES, *Life of Sumner*, p. 390, admits that Sumner was one
of the most unpopular men in the Senate. He was domineering, nagging,
snobbish, pedantic, supercilious and careless of the views and the feelings of
his colleagues. Yet he had friends and for a time wielded great influence.

named in the act of Congress. The oath was administered and Mr. Johnston took his seat.

Senator John Francis Lewis appeared at the bar of the Senate, January 27, took the oath and was seated.

The first delegation seated in the House were as follows:

Richard S. Ayer, of Warsaw, seated January 31.

James H. Platt, Jr., of Petersburg, seated January 27.

Charles Henry Porter, of Richmond, seated January 27.

George W. Booker, of Martinsville, seated February 1 after a contest with George Tucker.

Robert Ridgeway, of Cool Spring, seated January 27. He died October 16, 1870, and was succeeded by Richard T. W. Duke, of Charlottesville, December 5, 1870.

William Milner, Jr., of Shenandoah Iron Works, seated January 27.

Lewis McKenzie, of Alexandria, seated January 31 after a contest. Charles Whittlesley claimed the seat.

James King Gibson, of Abingdon, was seated January 28.

The election committee of the House postponed indefinitely the seating of Joseph E. Segar,[5] congressman-at-large.

---

[5]JOSEPH E. SEGAR, *Address* (1867): "I am an Old Line Whig of the Henry Clay, Daniel Webster type, or, more properly, a Federalist of the older school. I struggled for the Union in Secession's gloomy hour."

III

Our last satrap, General E. R. S. Canby, who had made few friends in Virginia, issued an order (January 27) which relinquished the administration of State affairs to the civil authorities. The auditor and secretary, who held their positions by virtue of bayonet rule, had the grace to resign.

General Canby[6] returned to Washington, and the newspapers next day told the country that General Sherman would erect a new military department, including Maryland, the two Virginias and North Carolina, over which General Canby would be appointed commander.

The sands of his life were almost run. The tall, silent, cold but just General was sent to the Pacific Coast. A little more than two years after he left Richmond (April 11, 1872) he met "Captain Jack," leader of the treacherous Modoc Indians to discuss a peace treaty. The Indians treacherously assassinated Canby and two officers with him.[7] The murderers fled to the lava beds, but were later captured and executed.

IV

In striking contrast to General Canby, General Grant was ever helpful and sympathetic to the Virginians[8] in their struggle with adversity. Of him

[6] WILLIAM ASBURY CHRISTIAN, *History of Richmond*, p. 337: "General Canby surrendered his authority January 28 and left."

[7] An interesting sketch of Canby, but with slight allusions to his Virginia service in APPLETON's *Cyclop of American Biography*, Vol. I, p. 518.

[8] *Alexandria Gazette* (October 24, 1869) carried this sensational editorial against General Grant: "His policy since his election has been consistently

Alexander H. H. Stuart once said, "He received our representatives with kindness and affability, and extended to them all the courtesy due them as gentlemen. He listened to all complaints with patience and close attention. He met every appeal in behalf of justice to Virginia in a spirit of fairness and generosity.

"I believe in 1869 he was disposed to make every concession in the interest of peace, which he could consistently with his obligations to the party, which had chosen him as its representative. He was head and front of a great party flushed with victory, and still laboring under the excitement of the recent fierce conflict. As such, he was necessarily a 'party man,' but he was more. He was a patriot, and in the language of William Cabell Rives, he ever remembered 'that he had a country to serve as well as a party to obey'."

Radical, especially in regard to Virginia. He reinstated Governor Wells after General Stoneman removed him. He favored the election of Wells over Walker, and the election of all Radical congressmen from Virginia. He sustained General Canby in all his proceedings and has consistently removed all those from office who are not Radicals."

This editor is too prejudiced. The day after the above appeared, President Grant concurred in the removal of Senator Johnson's disabilities. The enemies Grant made are to his credit. Wendell Phillips was abusing him daily by tongue and pen. "Nothing is so foul that Phillips does not shower it down upon the President and his administration."

CHAPTER XLIV

AT LONG LAST

Virginia Invicta
Unconquered despite defeat.
                    —*W. H. T. Squires.*

Very often a battle lost is progress gained, and
less of glory means more of liberty. When the
drummer is silent, reason speaks; it is the game
of one who loses to win. When the sabres have
finished the turn of the thinkers arrives.
                    —*Victor Hugo.*

To the question, "Who won the War Between the
States?" (or the Civil War, as it is also called), the
answer on almost every lip, both North and South,
would be "The Federal States, of course."

In discussing so large a subject it is to remember
that the processes of history are long, intricate and
much involved. Reactions political, economic, racial,
industrial, financial and many another also are to be
considered.

Three-fourths of a century has passed since the
surrender at Appomattox, and the subsequent persecutions of Reconstruction. The names mentioned
in these pages have for the more part only anti-
quarian interest. Like shadows, they move dimly
in the mists of long-dead years. Now, at long last,
a calm appraisal of men and policies may be had.
As one reviews the varied results of war and Recon-

struction, he may, perhaps, conclude that the erst-while Confederate States really won the war.

William the Conqueror gained a complete and compelling victory on the bloody field of Hastings, nine centuries ago. He and his Normans won, not the battle only, but the campaign and the crown. None will deny that King Harold fell; and with him the flower of Saxon chivalry lay dead in hideous heaps. The White Horse was trampled into blood and mire by the victorious Lions of Normandy. The Angles and Saxons were denied[1] all rights of freemen. Justice had no answer to their agonizing cry. Death and desolation laid a frightful pall over all the land. When the fury of Duke William was unleashed, the sky was darkened with smoke, and the carcasses of men and beasts lay side by side in smoking ruins, once happy homes, pleasant villages and prosperous towns. In those dreadful days of the Normans, not a human habitation remained from the Humber to the Tyne.[2]

And yet the Saxons won! By patience and endurance, by passive resistance, by sheer weight of numbers in their political units and by the eternal principles of justice and fair play; and, chiefest of all, by the inherent right of local self-government, the Saxons, not the Normans, won the Norman Conquest.[3] England is not French, but Anglo-Saxon.

---

[1]H. A. TAINE, *English Literature*, p. 30.

[2]CHARLES DICKENS, *History of England*, p. 49.

"In those dreadful days of the Normans there was not, from the River Humber to the River Tyne, one inhabited village nor one cultivated field; nothing but a dismal ruin where human creatures and beasts lay dead together."

[3]JOHN FISKE: "The effect of William's conquest upon English history was incalculably great; the effect upon the English race-constitution was incalculably small."

English language, blood, culture, law, religion, ideals, traditions and civilization have prevailed; and, by reactions through long years, potent, silent, invisible, intangible but invincible; Britannia Invicta.

* * * *

Incidentally, it should be remembered that the Southern States are almost wholly British in blood and culture. There are counties in Virginia more English in blood than Oxford, and towns in North Carolina more Scotch-Irish than Belfast.[4]

America witnesses a similar cycle. Like their Saxon forebears, the English folk of Virginia, the Carolinas and the South, have plucked victory from defeat. The Anglo-Saxon race lost nothing of vigor on this side the Atlantic.[5] The British in America are Britons still. By passive resistance, by sheer weight of numbers, by superb self-control, by the eternal principles of righteousness, justice and fair-play; and, chiefest of all, by the inherent Teutonic right of local self-government, the South has emerged more and more the victor—over defeat and Reconstruction.

It is not denied that a proud and valiant people resisted invasion and protected their homes and farms to the bitter end. The Southland, and especially Virginia, was swept by a besom of destruction. The slaves were set free. The Calhoun doctrine of secession was buried in eternal oblivion. The Constitution of the United States was thrice amended. The United States is not and will never

[4] PHILIP ALEXANDER BRUCE, *Rise of the New South*, Chapter I.
[5] NATHANIEL SOUTHGATE SHALER, *The United States of America*, pp. 69-79.

again become the Federal Union of Washington, Jefferson, Marshall, Clay and Webster. The foundations and the fabrics have been shifted.[6] The Revolution was less a revolution than the civil strife of the Sixties. Those called "rebels" fought to maintain unamended and unimpaired the Constitution of James Madison and the fathers of 1789. But the nation was forced to adopt the amended Constitution of Thaddeus Stevens and the Vindictive Radicals.[7]

The South became a vast grave-yard. Death and mourning rode upon every breeze. One hundred thousand men, fine and noble men, heroes as truly as any who ever drew the gleaming sword, gave their lives to retain their constitutional liberties. They lie in graves, for the most part, nameless and unknown.[8]

The Caucasian majority, incidentally including all the taxpayers, were denied their inherent and hereditary rights as citizens, while the Ethiopian minority and their false leaders became, by grace of Federal bayonets, the masters of their former masters.[9]

---

[6] S. E. MORRISON, *Oxford History of United States*, Vol. II, page 325.

[7] E. BENJAMIN ANDREWS, *The United States of Our Times*, page 18.

Sumner and Stevens and their ilk claimed that the war left Virginia and the South "nothing but men and dirt."

[8] N. G. SHEPHERD, "Roll Call," *Amer. War Ballads*, p. 262.

"'Twas a victory: yes, but it cost us dear,
For that company's roll, when called at night,
Of an hundred men who went into the fight,
Numbered but twenty, who answered 'Here'."

[9] This also was theoretical, not practical. There was never a time that the white master did not dominate the former slave in all matters save politics.

The defeated, disfranchised, often maimed and always poverty-stricken Confederate soldiers returned to find their homes in ashes, their farms in ruins, their servants gone, the stock stolen, their barns empty, their trade destroyed, their money worthless, their savings and their inheritance swept away, their parents dead, their children starving and vituperation and malediction laid like a pall over all the land. All too often the Confederate soldier returned with one eye, one arm, one leg,[10] or one cheek, shell-shocked, stricken with camp fever,[11] or tuberculosis,[12] maimed in body,[13] forspent, discouraged, nerves a wreck, under-nourished and a political out-cast. Without complaint he began at once to lay again the foundation of a new order and a new civilization. There was no law, save the whim of martial tyrants. They labored in constant dread that their farms and cottages would be con-

---

[10]Two brothers, Roberts, returned to their home in Norfolk County, one with one leg, the other with one arm. Yet they made a living on their farm and each reared a family.

[11]Like John Bannister Tabb at Point Lookout prison.

[12]Like Sidney Lanier, *Land of Decision*, SQUIRES, Chapter VI.

[13]Seven Confederate soldiers became governors of Virginia:

KEMPER, who fell in Pickett's Charge and was picked up for dead.

HOLLIDAY, who lost one arm in the battle of Cedar Run.

CAMERON, severely wounded at Second Manassas.

FITZ-HUGH LEE, who had three horses killed under him in the battle of Winchester.

MC KINNEY, severely wounded at Brandy Station.

O'FERRALL. "His regiment held the last line, had the last fight and took the last prisoners on Virginia soil." He was once left for dead on the field of battle.

MANN, who carried a bullet in his back to his grave.

fiscated.[14]   At every turn they were confronted by Negro or alien soldiers and agents, who made them pariahs in the land their fathers carved at incredible cost and years of labor from the tractless wilderness. Their homes and farms often represented the toil, sweat and blood[15] of two hundred years.   This is the man to whom Henry W. Grady referred, when he addressed the New England Society in New York and spoke of "the hero in gray with a heart of gold."   That was no rhetorical exaggeration, but the truth.

The typical Confederate soldier, his sons and now his grandsons, have in point of practical fact won the war, which was lost in 1865 upon desperate fields of battle.[16]   It is not strange that so much of wealth, and those possessions more precious than wealth, were lost from 1861 to 1875.   The marvel of it is that so much survived.[17]   This is a tribute to the unconquerable spirit of the Southern people, and this is why we claim Virginia Invicta.

* * * *

Seven fundamental and revolutionary reactions have enured to the United States and especially to the South as the result of the War Between the States:

[14]General John M. Schofield (March 12, '68) suspended sales of property under deeds of trust in cases of poverty and misery. *Annual Cyclop.*, 1868. The Virginians have always remembered Schofield as a friend and benefactor.

[15]Practically every county in Virginia, from the Chesapeake to the River Ohio was wrested from the Indians by bloodshed. Bacon's Rebellion, the French and Indian War, and innumerable Indian massacres, raids and murders, took a frightful toll of blood from Cape Henry to Point Pleasant.

[16]PHILIP ALEXANDER BRUCE, *Rise of the New South*, Chapter XXXII.

[17]ARMISTEAD C. GORDON, JR., *Virginia Writers*, p. 114.

I

THE EXTINCTION OF SLAVERY

The incubus of slavery[18] shackled the South since
early days colonial (1619).   This wretched system
of labor became more and more Southern because
it was profitable on large plantations raising cotton,
tobacco and rice.   It was not profitable on small
farms, nor in industrial communities.

Slavery was not perpetuated in the South because
the planter who inherited slaves was more cruel or
brutal than his neighbor,[19] kinsman,[20] or friend[21]
who owned none, but because the system paid, although always recognized as economically unsound.[22]

With the curse of slavery the South could never
have achieved its destiny.   The master of the plantation was, by far, the chiefest slave upon it.   His
were the difficulties, the responsibilities, the em-
barrassments and maledictions of the system, as well
as its profits and questionable benefits.

[18]The people of the South always realized this.   During the War Between
the States General Robert E. Lee set the slaves of the Arlington estate free
(1863) under the terms of the will of George Washington Parke Custis, Mrs.
Lee's father (1858).—See w. e. carson, <i>Historic Shrines</i>, p. 7.

[19]In the Confederate armies only one soldier in 33 came of slave-holding
families.

[20]In the family of the author one brother owned two slaves, in Virginia,
his brother in New York City owned none.

[21]In a great block of the Appalachian Southland, Western Virginia, Western
North Carolina, Eastern Kentucky and Eastern Tennessee, Northern Georgia
and Northeastern Alabama, there was little slavery, and in many counties
practically none.   It did not pay.

[22]william byrd of Westover, many Colonial Quakers and the Revolutionary
fathers of Virginia.

morris birkbeck, <i>Journey to America</i>, pp. 17-20.

There was, to be sure, a school[23] (they called themselves the New Democrats) who claimed that slavery was a moral and economic blessing. Their following was neither large nor influential in Virginia.[24]

The Proclamation of Emancipation set every slave-holder free. While one may question President Lincoln's motive and his constitutional right to issue a Proclamation of Emancipation, it must be freely admitted that the Proclamation was at once a master stroke of political diplomacy and a blessing unspeakable to the South. As to diplomacy, by a stroke of his pen, Abraham Lincoln changed an un-constitutional war of invasion, aggression, and co-ercion into a crusade for human liberty! Really the Proclamation won the war.

For the South Abraham Lincoln by the same sig-nature solved the South's greatest problem and re-moved at once and forever the greatest obstacle to Southern progress.

Frightful as was the price, Emancipation was worth all it cost. The prosperity, wealth, industry, genius and abounding civil development everywhere evidenced in the South since Reconstruction, could never have been achieved with the incubus of slavery. Lincoln is not the Emancipator of the

---

[23]BEVERLEY B. MUNFORD, *Virginia's Attitude Toward Slavery and Secession*, p. 49.

JOSEPH D. EGGLESTON, in *Virginia Teacher*, September, 1882.

[24]One of the most enthusiastic leaders of the New Democrats in Virginia was Roger A. Pryor.

So good and noble a man as Rev. George Dodd Armstrong of Norfolk wrote a book to explain the blessings of slavery—and Dr. Armstrong was born in Connecticut!—*Dictionary of American Biography*.

Negro only, he is the Emancipator of the Southern Caucasian as well.

The XIII Amendment was no particular benefit to the North and West.[25] To those sections it was merely a noble ideal. But to the South it was political and economic salvation.

It is altogether significant that no voice has ever been raised to re-introduce slave labor in any form[26] whatsoever, despite the various and sensational changes this nation has experienced.

II

NEGRO CITIZENSHIP

The second major constitutional enactment, a direct result of war and Federal victory, was the adoption of the XIV Amendment. The long, intricate and bungling phraseology of the Amendment[27] from the pen of Thaddeus Stevens conferred full

---

[25]Thomas Jefferson and the Commonwealth of Virginia rescued the Northwest Territory (Ohio, Indiana, Illinois, Michigan and Wisconsin) from slavery. The very day that Virginia deeded that enormous territory to the Federal government (March 1, 1784), Jefferson reported an Ordinance forbidding slavery in all Federal territory west of a line from Lake Erie to the Florida (Spanish) border. Had that law been adopted, slavery would have been excluded after 1800 from Kentucky, Tennessee, Alabama and Mississippi, as well as from the Northwest Territory. Unfortunately only six states voted for the Ordinance—one less than was necessary.

But three years later the famous Ordinance of 1787 was adopted and "No one was more active in bringing it about than William Grayson and Light Horse Harry Lee, both of Virginia." Grayson, afterward a Senator from Virginia, has a great county named for him. So has Lee, later Governor of Virginia and the father of Robert E. Lee.

[26]Those propagandists and even those learned historians who read into the "Vagrancy laws" of 1866 an ill-disguised effort and intent to reintroduce slavery are mistaken. Such legislation was, and still is, on the statute books of practically every state, just and necessary laws.

[27]JAMES WILFORD GARNER and HENRY CABOT LODGE, *History of the United*

citizenship upon the colored population of the entire country. The Negro became a citizen like his late master.

Before the war a slave was counted for federal representation in Congress as 3–5 of a man—an absurd compromise for which there was no logic and no justification. The Negro was a man, or he was not. He paid taxes[28] as a man, directly or indirectly. He was amenable to the law of the Commonwealth. The promulgation of the two war amendments wiped from the statute books of the nation the legal absurdity which had disgraced American jurisprudence for seventy years. Even the bungling politicians of the Fortieth and Forty-first Congresses knew that they must recognize the Negro as a man and count his family as human beings. By this rather simple logic the South gained representation at Washington in the ratio of 2–5 of a man for every freedman.[29]

But the forty additional Representatives in Congress and the forty additional votes in the Electoral College were by no means the most important reaction to the South. The ex-slave was free to travel— and he went.[30] The typical freedman set his face

States, Vol. III, pp. 1378-1380. In a hasty and not very scholarly discussion of the Amendment, the authors admit that the Civil Rights Bill was put into the Constitution lest the Democrats, returning to power, would revoke the Act. It was prostituting the supreme law of the land to partisan politics of the lowest order.

[28]The free Negro directly; the slave in the tax bill of the master.

[29]CHARLES RAMSDELL LINGLEY, *Since the Civil War*, p. 11.

E. BENJAMIN ANDREWS, *The United States of Our Times*, p. 1, calls attention to the fact that one man in seven in America had a black skin.

[30]In numerous instances, especially among the household servants, and more especially in the case of the elderly, female servants, the former slaves

and his feet afar. It was natural and inevitable.
At first they followed the army, a second and sub-
sidiary army of camp-followers and dependents.
They gathered by the thousands about the army
camps, and drifted more and more to the slums of
the cities. The industrial, mining and urban centres
beckoned to the young Negroes of both sexes. There
was great demand for labor, especially crude labor,
and there were high wages, and many comforts and
pleasures unknown in the sequestered, rural centres
of the South.

Every decennial census tells the same tale of migration to the North and Middle Western States.

In 1870 almost 42 per cent of Virginia's population was colored.[31]

In 1880 the colored population was slightly over
41 per cent.[32]

In 1890 the colored population was 41 per cent.

In 1900 it was 35½ per cent.

In 1910 it fell to 32½ per cent.[33]

---

preferred to remain with the family and in the familiar home, even when no
wages could be paid. Loyalty to their white employers has ever been a marked
characteristic of the colored people.

[31] The Freedmen's Bureau reported a marked diminution in the Negro
population of Virginia after the withdrawal of the armies.

The erection of West Virginia in 1863 took a vast Caucasian population
from the State, but left to the old State those counties which had huge Negro
populations.

[32] The explanation of the very slight increase in the white population is
explained by the heavy migration of Virginians to the new states of the West,
especially during the "hard times" that followed 1872 and prevailed for seven
years. Coming upon the heels of war and Reconstruction, this depression
was an agony to Virginia. The migration from the State continued well into
the Eighties, but was not so marked as a reasonable degree of prosperity returned.

[33] The first decade of the Twentieth Century brought great prosperity to
Virginia, the first real and substantial prosperity since 1860; although there
were several good years before the collapse of business in 1893.

In 1920 the colored population was less than 30 per cent.

In 1930 only 26 per cent.

From 1920 to 1930 the Negro population of the State showed an actual decline of 40,000. Virginia had 4,000 fewer colored people each year.[34]

The last census (1930) shows 83,000 more Negroes in Ohio than in Kentucky. Mrs. Harriet Beecher Stowe, in a pathetic passage, describes the escape of "Eliza" over the ice from Kentucky to the Ohio shore. "Eliza" is still crossing the Ohio, but not now on ice-floes. She travels at present by train, boat or automobile, and her children increase prodigiously in Ohio.

The XIV Amendment was forced upon a prostrate and hostile South. It was bitterly resented, coming as drastic punishment, dictated by Thaddeus Stevens. The citizens of 1867 could not be expected to foresee in it an ultimate blessing to the South.[35] It has made and is making Virginia and the South more solidly Anglo-Saxon every passing year. By shifting the surplus of Negro labor from the South, it has solved the race problem once so dreaded. There is a race problem,[36] to be sure, but it is now national not sectional.

The XIV Amendment as a practical factor has materially aided the South in winning the war.

---

[34]It is interesting to note that in the same decade New York State gained 214,000 Negroes, the number increasing 21,000 each year.

[35]MAX FARRAND, *Development of the United States*, p. 242, admits the utter failure of the XIV Amendment, in a rather vague and unsatisfactory discussion of it.

[36]The gentle and kindly disposition of the typical African is proverbial, and has gone far to ameliorate the asperities of race conflict. Only when a false

III

Negro Enfranchisement

The third result of the Civil War was the adoption of the XV Amendment. From that time forth no citizen could be denied the right to vote, if a male, twenty-one years old, and of character not criminal.

It would be impossible to exaggerate the bitterness and animosity this law aroused among all classes of Southern people. It was admitted, on all hands, that the purpose of the XV Amendment was strictly partisan, even more nakedly partisan than the XIV Amendment. The South felt that the law was not passed in the interest of the African, but to place a political embarrassment upon a conquered people.

The Southern States must be controlled permanently by carpet-baggers, scalawags and their Negro allies. This Radical party in the South was to strengthen the Radical faction in the North. The XV Amendment was to serve a three-fold purpose: First, to build a Radical party in the South; Second, to hold the former leaders of Southern life forever in leash; and Third, to secure many precious votes in the Congress, not to overlook the Electoral College. Democrats, Copperheads, and Conservative Republicans must be kept out of power forever!

The iniquitous Amendment was forced upon the Southern States at the point of the bayonet. Threats of confiscation and other drastic punishments might

---

and mistaken leadership has encouraged criminal or immoral instincts, have the freedmen and their children become dangerous or obnoxious. There are "bad men" among them, as there are in every race, but the great majority are law-abiding, patient, loyal and content.

be laid if the legislatures did not agree to the Amendment. The passage of the XIV and XV Amendments was required of Virginia, Mississippi and Texas before they would be admitted to representation.

There were vast numbers of Northern people, Republicans as well as Democrats, who opposed both the law and the spirit which motivated it. That the XV Amendment was unjust, cruel and unconstitutional, we suppose no scholar will now deny.

The Southern leaders dealt with this delicate problem firmly and tactfully. As soon as the Caucasian majority obtained control in Virginia and her sister States, educational and intelligence tests were applied to all voters—black and white. Massachusetts, Connecticut, and other States had similar laws; just and good laws. The effect has been to place a premium on education and a stigma on illiteracy. The educational revival[37] in the South during the last fifty years has no parallel in any land among any people—and that in spite of poverty and other privations.

Illiteracy has not yet been banished but ultimate victory is assured.

The XV Amendment has been no advantage to the States of the North, but it has stimulated the South to phenominal advances in the education of both races.

---

[37]No Southern community has at any time denied the privilege of public education to any colored child. The tax-burden is supported almost wholly by the white people. The aid which has come from Northern people to help educate the colored child in the South has been so small as to be negligible.

The threat of political domination by the colored race has long since disappeared; but the intellectual and cultural revival continues.[38]

It should always be remembered that little or nothing has been done to elevate the former slave population except what has been done by those who were his former masters, and later Confederate soldiers and citizens. It is the Confederate soldier and his sons to the fourth generation who have given the colored man a job. It is they who have furnished him a cottage to live in, police protection, schools, hospitals and churches. It is the taxpayers of the South who provide free clinics, insane asylums, alms houses, medical treatment, and who protect the living and bury the dead. There are colleges, and endowments, placed in the South by Northern philanthropy—and this help is appreciated, but if that had been all the colored population had to depend upon, there would be more millions of ignorant Negroes in the South today than there were in 1865.

The same master who fed, clothed, housed and gave labor to the slaves, feeds, clothes, houses and gives an opportunity to work to the sons of the slave—nor is the help begrudged.[39]

It must not be overlooked that the Southern Negro is the only branch of the African races that has, since the creation of the world, become literate. And, furthermore, the Southern Negro is the only Negro race in the world that is literate[40] at this time.

[38]PAUL LELAND HAWORTH, *The United States in our Times*, p. 9.
[39]PHILIP ALEXANDER BRUCE, *Rise of the New South*, pp. 466-468.
[40]There are small but steadily growing groups of literate Negroes in Africa,

IV

Secession

A sharp, practical and very real distinction should be made between the right of secession for just and reasonable cause, and the wisdom of secession.

William Gordon McCabe once wrote Judge George L. Christian: "Now in my old age I am more and more convinced of the absolute righteousness of our contention and I hold that it is not good that a righteous cause shall perish from the earth." We have no desire to read into that characteristic contention of all the Confederate soldiers anything that is not there. To question the political expediency of secession, war and the rending asunder of the Union of these States is one item, to justify the invasion, coercion, the unjust and unconstitutional war of subjugation, terrorism, arson, robbery, bloodshed and the absolute denial of all civil rights to one-third the people of the country by the stronger two-thirds, is quite another matter.

The Southern people can never agree that the method used to suppress the South was wise, good or necessary. It was cruel and as unnecessary as it was unjust and unconstitutional. It has never been justified, and can never be justified. But if the invasion and the subjugation of the South were justified, the outrages practiced upon the Southern people

the work of missionaries in Uganda, the Congo, South Africa, etc., who deserve all praise and commendation. But these groups are negligible as compared to the ten million literate Negroes in the South, educated almost wholly by the taxes paid since 1865 by the Confederate soldier and his sons.

The corner of City Hall Avenue and Granby Street is now one of the busiest in the South. The picture above shows the corner as it appeared in 1870. The picture below shows the same corner as it appears today.

"Since 1902 the population of Virginia has increased 35 per cent, but the value of property has increased 340 per cent."
—Senator Harry F. Byrd in *Scribner's Magazine* 1928.—Page 460.

for ten years after the surrender can certainly never be justified nor defended.

The wisdom of secession is quite another matter. Secession was contrary to the intense convictions and deliberate judgment of the better element of the South. It was the result of diabolical propaganda which used the press,[41] the prejudices, the passions and the extreme Radical pronouncements of the Abolitionists to stir hatreds and make the worse appear the better reason.[42]

The folly of secession was largely the result of mutual misunderstanding and persistent misinformation.

Had the Confederate States been victorious, their chief tenet must have been a confirmed right of secession, which any disgruntled State might invoke at any time upon any real or fancied grievance, and that by a sheer, even a temporary majority, acquired under pressure or prejudice. When any serious misunderstanding arose between the national majority and (let us say) Texas or Louisiana, Florida or Arkansas, such States or others would certainly have seceded from the Confederacy. Any one who knows human nature and especially political human nature motivated by fluctuating and precarious economic and financial interests, cannot doubt that the success of secession, once established, the South would have become not one, but a series of smaller nations. As George Washington said of the Con-

---

[41]It is interesting to read the editorials of the Norfolk and Richmond papers in 1860-1861. And we presume that the press farther South was even more rabid.

[42]LYON GARDINER TYLER, in *Tyler's Magazine*, April 29, pp. 268-270, takes an opposite view which we respect, but do not endorse.

federation, "We are one today and thirteen to-morrow."

Calhounism[43] as preached by the "Young Democrats" of the Fifties, must have become a political calamity. In the long process of the years, such a Balkanized South would have been far worse than the defeats of Gettysburg, Vicksburg and Appomattox.

The War Between the States should never have been fought. The principles for which the South justly contended should have been demanded and could have been secured under the dome of the Capitol of the United States.[44]

From the calamity of Secession and the ultimate disintegration of a great nation, the decision of 1865 saved us.

V

INDESTRUCTIBLE STATES

One notable result of the War Between the States was a definite decision as to the nature of this Federal Union. Alexander Hamilton and the old Federalists would have preferred an Indestructible Union of destructible states, as England is a unit, conveniently divided into shires, and as France is a unit, the old provinces completely swept away and the area divided into artificial departments.

---

[43]The author has no authority to speak for others, but it is his earnest conviction that the extreme States' right position of John C. Calhoun was *historically* logical, but in 1861 *practically* unjustifiable.

[44]The Radicals in their hour of victory admit at the bar of history that they did not fight for, but against the Constitution of the United States by their frantic and drastic Amendments which changed the character of Constitution and Nation.

John Caldwell Calhoun contended that the Federal Union was a Destructible Union of Indestructible States, as Scandinavia was once united in the Crown, with Norway and Sweden retaining each her sovereignty.

It was the intermediate doctrine of John Marshall and the Old Line Whigs which has prevailed. Salmon P. Chase cast the old Marshall Doctrine[45] into permanent form.[46] It is rather inconsistent that a Republican Chief Justice, who declared himself a Democrat at heart, should have promulgated the Whig doctrine of the Federal Union; an Indestructible Union of Indestructible States.[47]

In this connection one must consider the situation of Virginia, the only State whose integrity has been violated, and that despite the decision of the Supreme Court rendered only three years after the forcible partition of Virginia's territory and the erection of West Virginia.[48]

The South and the Nation are blessed that this vexed question was settled once and for all time. It

---

[45]CHARLES WARREN, *Supreme Court*, gives a delightfully lucid portrait of Chief Justice Chase.

[46]Justice Chase was a New England, anti-slavery Democrat. He said in 1868: "For more than a quarter of a century I have been in my political views and sentiments, a Democrat."

[47]ALBERT BUSHNELL HART, *Chase*, p. 372. He considered the Commonwealths "buttressed" each with impregnable rights.

IBID, p. 378. His words were, "The Constitution in all its provisions looks to an indestructible union of indestructible States."

WENDELL PHILLIPS actually advocated the abolition of the Supreme Court in his fanaticism and wrath.

[48]West Virginia was admitted only under violent protest, strictly as a war measure. President Lincoln so admitted to his Cabinet, which was equally divided on the unconstitutional action.

will probably save America many future troubles, perhaps from other appeals to the sword.

The decision is a compromise in which the Southern doctrine of the Indestructible State divides honor with the Hamiltonian doctrine of an Indestructible Union.[49]

VI

The American Section of America

The intense industrial activity quickened by the war and holding until the financial depression of 1872, attracted a vast horde of alien peoples to America, a polyglot multitude, difficult to amalgamate, and wholly foreign to the colonial stock that made New England mighty, and that laid the foundations of the great commonwealths of the Middle West.

The political influence of the aliens,[50] guaranteed by the XV Amendment, and their solidarity in party lines, their immense political influence in our greater States and powerful cities, has become a grave danger to this nation.

The South has been saved from this alien rush;[51] protected for a generation by the extreme poverty

[49]ANDREW JACKSON seems to have been as much influenced by this doctrine as Lincoln or Hamilton.

[50]Just before the War Between the States the American or No-Nothing Party, a survival of the expiring Whigs, made a valiant but futile effort to stem this tide of barbarians and save America for the children of Americans. The day may yet come when the downfall of American institutions and colonial ideals may be traced to this human inundation.

[51]WILSON GEE and JOHN J. CORSON, III, *Statistical Study of Virginia* (1927), gives complete tables and shows that Virginia had in 1920 only 1.4 per cent of foreign-born in her population.

of the country, and protected for a second generation by the abundant labor supply found among the colored population. Save only during the World War there has never been a scarcity of unskilled labor in the South.

In the meantime the native stock has multiplied and filled the waste places. Large families have been the rule, especially on the farms. Many small farms now take the area of the great ante-bellum plantations. Many cottages have appeared, where in 1850 there was only one, large homestead. In 1850 the farms in Virginia (including West Virginia) had each, on the average, nearly 350 acres. In 1920 the average farm in Virginia (excluding West Virginia) had only 100 acres.

The typical Virginian today is an Anglo-Saxon, with perhaps a dash of German, Scotch or Huguenot blood. There are some of Dutch and Scandinavian descent. North Carolina is the most American State in the Union.

It is interesting to compare the per cent of citizens of foreign blood in Massachusetts,[52] New York,[53] and Minnesota,[54] with those of Virginia,[55] North Carolina,[56] Alabama,[57] and Texas.[58]

It has often been claimed that the decision on the battle-field was won by foreign soldiery. That cannot be successfully denied. The volunteers in the

[52]Massachusetts, 28.3 per cent foreign-born (census of 1920).
[53]New York, 27.2 per cent foreign-born (census of 1920).
[54]Minnesota, 20.4 per cent foreign-born (1920).
[55]Virginia, 1.4 per cent.
[56]North Carlina, 0.3 per cent.
[57]Alabama, 0.8 per cent.
[58]Texas, 7.8 per cent (census 1920).

Union Army, given by States, as "born in Germany," aggregated 176,817.[59] Probably 200,000 Germans marched in the Union armies. To these must be added those "born in Ireland," in Italy, Great Britain, the Scandinavian and other European countries. These figures reach an impressive total.

The South is today the Anglo-Saxon section of America,[60] and among these conservative folk the Ark of the Covenant of American ideals is still cherished. In the preservation of American ideals, culture and civilization, the Southern people have won the War Between the States. "In 1860 the native population of the South was computed as 6,798,698, and the foreign born as 383,470, about 136,000 less than in 1900. But by 1900 the native population had increased to twenty-two million."[61]

I know no better way to close this paragraph than to quote Edwin Anderson Alderman: "He was of the group of young Southern men who knew the contributions of the South to American history, who had no apologies to offer for its part in the great struggle, ennobled by so much valor and self-sacrifice; but who felt that the South must again become whole-heartedly a part of the Federal Union it had done so much to establish."[62]

[59]ALBERT BERNHARDT FAUST, *The German Element in the United States*, Vol. I, p. 523.

[60]FRENCH STROTHER, *World's Work*, December, 1926.

HARRY FLOOD BYRD, *Scribner's Magazine*, June, 1926.

WILLIAM JOSEPH SHOWALTER, *National Geographic Magazine*, April, 1929.

These three articles give fine first-hand evidence of the permanent colonial influence in Virginia.

[61]PHILIP ALEXANDER BRUCE, *Rise of the South*, p. 7.

[62]EDWIN A. ALDERMAN, Address before the two Houses of Congress, December 15, 1924, in memory of Woodrow Wilson, late President of the United States.

VII

The Wealth of the South

It is beyond the ken of the wisest of mortals to estimate, even approximately, the waste and financial loss to the Southern people as the direct result of the folly of secession and the failure of their appeal to arms.

Quite aside from the anguish, sorrow and bitterness aroused by the loss of the South's young manhood, by death, wounds, shock, imprisonment and other destructive agencies, the economic loss to the South of this manhood, the potential leaders, husbands, fathers, and producers of a generation must be set down as the South's chief liability. For this no figures could ever be compiled.

Aside from the destruction of human life, the people of the South invested their savings, the accumulated wealth of two centuries in Confederate money and bonds—an absolute loss.

To the loss of human life and of accumulated wealth one must add the actual destruction effected by invasion. Here again no accurate figures can be adduced, but let General Sherman testify:

"I estimate the damage done the State of Georgia and its military resources at $100,000,000, at least twenty millions of which have inured to our advantage[63] and the remainder is simply waste and destruction."[64]

---

[63] In plain English he means that $20,000,000 was stolen from non-combatants.

[64] In plain English, vandalism.

But be it remembered that Georgia was only once invaded,[65] while Virginia, Kentucky, Tennessee, Alabama, Mississippi, Louisiana and Arkansas were constantly and continually invaded.

"Apart from the frightful destruction[66] of life," wrote W. Gordon McCabe, "we reckon the destruction of material wealth at $180,000,000, or $190,-000,000, which does not include the loss of homes, private business enterprises, nor the destruction directly the result of Reconstruction policy."

Some of the farms of Virginia were so completely devastated that they are still unproductive after seventy years of peace! Perhaps it is not an exaggeration to place the devastation to property at $2,000,000,000.[67]

To the loss of man power, Confederate securities and the actual destruction wrought by the constant invasion, for four years, the commercial value of the

---

[65]From Chattanooga by way of Atlanta and Savannah to the sea.

From May 8, 1864, until the end of hostilities.

ARTHUR CHAS. COLE, *The Irrepressible Conflict*, pp. 328-9, discusses Sherman's methods of making war.

[66]R. A. BROCK, *Virginia and the Virginians*, Vol. II, p. 498, presents this table of battles and engagements:

Virginia had......519 actual conflicts		
Tennessee.........298	Louisiana........118	Alabama......... 78
Missouri..........244	Georgia..........108	South Carolina... 60
Mississippi........186	North Carolina .. 85	Florida.......... 32
Arkansas..........167	West Virginia.... 80	Maryland........ 30
Kentucky.........138		

[67]WOODROW WILSON, *Division and Reunion*, p. 251. The famous author states and truly that the people of the South threw every ounce of strength into the struggle and exhausted every resource. For the first three years her chances for success were as good as the Federal chances. The British philosopher was right who declared that the last shilling wins every war. It won the decision in our fratricidal struggle.

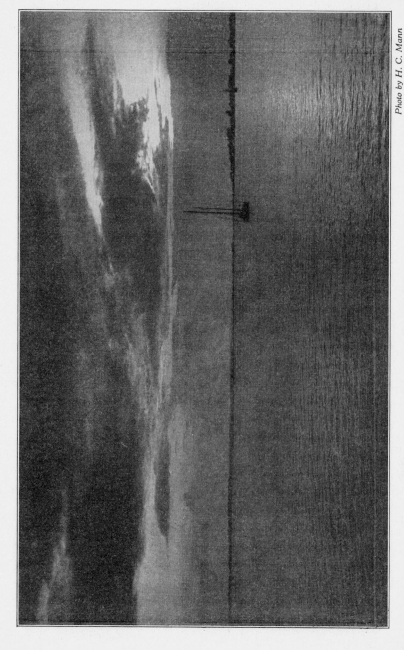

"Nowhere in the wide world does twilight fall so softly and night descend so 'velvet-footed through the air' as on the gentle hills, the pleasant valleys and the murmuring waters of Virginia." —Page 1.

emancipated slaves must be added. This represents another $2,000,000,000.[68]

To this enormous total add, again, the theft, waste, corruption and debts of the Reconstruction regime. Not only the State administrations, but the counties, cities, towns and even the magisterial districts were shamefully plundered. Many of these obligations are not yet fully liquidated. The cost of these shameless exploiters of the South was not less than $1,000,000,000.

When the Southern States were re-admitted to the Union they also paid their share of the National debt,[69] accumulated by the Federal government, which crushed and then exploited them, to which must be added the vast sums paid in pensions to the Union soldiers, sums so huge that they became a national shame and international scandal. The debt January 1, 1866, was $2,682,000,000.

The wisest statistician does not know how much must be added to this sum for pensions, a form of just reward for service really rendered, and for hideous graft besides. Hundreds upon hundreds of

---

[68]EDWARD A. POLLARD, *The Lost Cause*, p. 743: "The war closed upon a spectacle of ruin the greatest in modern times. We may cite the case of South Carolina. The census of 1860 placed the value of her property at 400 million dollars. It is estimated that the injury to her banks, private securities, cities, railways, homes, plantations, stock, amounted to $100 million. The same census valued the 400,000 slaves at $200 million. This leaves $100 million, the chief portion in lands which have shrunken enormously in value.

[69]DAVID SAVILLE MUSSEY, *History of the United States*, Vol. II, page 23, places the national debt at $2,846,000,000, or $74.28 per capita. He declares that the taxes laid were the heaviest ever levied in a civilized country. If heavy for the rich and prosperous North and West, how much heavier for the poverty-stricken South!

millions have gone from the South into the national debt and pensions.[70]

The Southern people by their readmission to the Union had the privilege of paying the men who killed, destroyed, burned and otherwise ruined them, and continued payments to them and their widows so long as they lived; and many pensioners still survive.

Despite these enormous accumulations of ruthless loss and waste, the loss of man-power, the loss of all Confederate securities, the loss of property destroyed by the hand of the invader, the loss of slaves, set free, the loss occasioned by Negro and carpet-bag rule for ten post-bellum years, the loss paid to the national debt, the loss paid in pensions, the South has not rebelled, has not refused to carry on in good faith and in good spirit, even when those who despoiled the South chide this people with indolence,[71] ignorance and fanaticism. There are such classes in Virginia; as, we suppose, there are in every community. It is noteworthy that those most active in despoiling the South were most vehement in their libels.[72] While these aspersions were being heralded,

---

[70]It should be remembered that almost all the pension money was spent in the North and West. Only in the South was there no return for the funds drained away from the pockets of an impoverished people.

CHARLES and MARY BEARD, *History of the United States*, p. 401: "Released from the hampering influence of the Southern planter business enterprise sprang forward." It would be difficult to find a sentence by any reputable historian so inaccurate, unjust and false to the facts as that.

[71]These false accusations are rarely heard today, for business men from the North and West find the business man of Virginia as practical, alert and industrious as any business executive that can be found.

[72]JOSEPH D. EGGLESTON: "Much was set down in malice, and much in ignorance."

millions toiled to rebuild their factories, restore their farms and educate their children, construct their railways, and dot the land with pleasant villages and progressive cities.[73] No argument can be advanced against truth, honor, diligence, enlightenment and progress.[74]

To quote Senator Harry Flood Byrd: "Since 1902 the population of Virginia has increased from 1,854,184 to 2,519,000—and the true value of her property has increased from $1,102,310,000 to $4,-891,570,000. Population has increased 35 per cent, but the value of her property has increased 340 per cent."[75]

[73]THOMAS JEFFERSON WERTENBAKER, *American People*, p. 381: "It was a stupendous task to erect the great prosperous South of today upon the ruins of the ante-bellum South."

WILLIAM JOSEPH SHOWALTER, *National Geographic Magazine*, April, 1929, an excellent review of Virginia at that date.

WM. J. ROBERTSON, *The Changing South*, pp. 273-80 (now out of date).

HOWARD W. ODOM, *Southern Progress* (a huge encyclop on Southern economics), 1936.

T. J. WERTENBAKER, *The American People*, Chapter XXI.

[74]ALBERT J. BEVERIDGE, *Tyler's Quarterly Magazine*, January, 1930, p. 200: "I was brought up in an atmosphere of intense partisanship and hostility to the South. I was carried to meetings where orators indulged in most shameless misrepresentations of men and measures. I believed these things; I even believed them when I was in the Senate, and I continued to believe them until I began to go back to the original sources for this biography of Lincoln."

[75]*Scribner's Magazine*, June, 1928.

The *Louisville Courier-Journal* of recent date (1939) says:

"Roger Babson, whose opinion on such matters should be worth something, says that the South, 'far from being Economic Problem No. 1, is Economic Possibility No. 1 of the United States.' He supports this view by declaring that 'nine of the eighteen states which are rated as excellent business territories on my sales map are in the South. Every one of the chief cities of the United States whose populations have doubled since 1920, is below the Mason and Dixon line. The fastest-growing states in the Union are nearly all

It has always followed that when the dead have long been buried, and the heated passions of men have cooled, impartial time weighs all verdicts and its decisions are irrevocable.

Presidents and captains, congresses and caucasses, partisan propaganda and passionate agenda, must submit to the impartial verdicts of history.

Reason speaks slowly but her voice is infallible and must be heard.   And her dictum is often

The vanquished are victors.

---

in the South. Today Dixie has twenty-five per cent of the manufacturing establishments in the United States . . . and more than half of the new factory development of the entire country in recent years. If I were a young man, I would come down here in the South to seek my fortune'."

THE LAST LEAF

And so here, O Reader, has the time come for us, two, to part. Toilsome was our journeying together, not without offence; but it is done. Ill stands it with me if I have spoken falsely, thine also it was to hear truly. Farewell.

—Thomas Carlyle.

No people in the Western World have suffered as have the Virginians. In the Seventeenth Century (1676), the Eighteenth Century (1776-81) and the Nineteenth Century (1861-65) the soil of Virginia was drenched with blood, her fairest sons slaughtered, her homes and fields laid waste, her cities turned to ashes and her childless widows watered their bitter crust of poverty with bitterer tears. But never, be it written with becoming pride, have the Virginians lost their courage, their morale nor the determination to achieve ultimate conquest. Like the stalwart oaks of her forests, they bent till the storms were overpassed.

Virginia's Virgin on seal and flag stands forth with her foot upon a prostrate tyrant—it is prophetic. The Virginians negotiated four years of slaughter, and five years of political tyranny as their grandfathers negotiated six years of British pillage and arson, and as their colonial ancestors negotiated bitter years of savage warfare and Bacon's Rebellion.

The scars of Secession, War, Defeat and Reconstruction remain, even as they fade—not to the

South alone, but to the whole nation. No people can harry, burn, slaughter, plunder, rob and persecute one-third of their domain without a frightful reaction. Secession was a blunder; war a brutality; defeat, a disaster; and reconstruction worse than all these evils combined. It poisoned the nation. The dullest reader cannot but observe that America since 1861 is a nation totally different from America before that ominous date.

In the maelstrom of the 60's the current of our history was rudely turned, but the wounds of that disgraceful era are slowly healing. After three-quarters of a century the shadows of the past creep forth like horrid spectres in our politics, national, state and local; and in every meeting of the Congress their curse is evident.

True, every injustice and falsehood carries the seeds of its own dissolution. No lie ever survives. Only truth, honor and righteousness are immortal. With the lapse of the years they are

UNLEASHED AT LONG LAST.

II

Our story is now told, with all its tragedies, its unnecessary cruelties, its drab and even shameful details. Our journey through the slime of a foul pocoson is ended. But it ends with the dawn of a brighter day, a day growing ever more brilliant. Like a hunter who struggles forth at last from the quagmires of Dismal Swamp, befouled with the filth of the quaking morass; we, too, have struggled through days that were dark and years that were hideous. These years were the blackest in the story of the Republic. Civilization is a thin veneer, soon worn and tarnished by passion, venom and revenge. Then man stands forth in all his pagan nakedness.

No offence is intended by the recital of unpleasant truths. Most heartily do we wish that much recorded here were false. But wishing well changes no stubborn facts. There is, however, a modicum of compensation, plainly presented in these pages. The moral and inherent manhood and courage of the Virginians, their stubborn endurance, their patience, their keen discernment of true values, their passive resistance and their abiding faith in their destiny never failed; not even in the fiercest storms that swept down upon them. In the cruelest hours of political persecution, in the pinch of direst poverty, in obliquity and legal ostracism, in injustice suffered and humiliation, the Virginians never once lost their prospective and never doubted their ultimate recovery. Their Colonial fathers suffered and conquered, so could they.

Every page of Virginia's history is touched with the finger of glory. After every tyranny the leash has slipped. True in the dreadful days of Nathaniel Bacon, true again in the struggle under Washington, true in the disasters that befell despite the superb leadership of Lee.

This optimism was justified and the Commonwealth came forth

UNLEASHED AT LONG LAST.

INDEX